COMPUTER ARCHITECTURE

INTERNATIONAL COMPUTER SCIENCE SERIES

Consulting editors   **A D McGettrick**   University of Strathclyde

                     J van Leeuwen   University of Utrecht

SELECTED TITLES IN THE SERIES

Local Area Network Architectures   *D Hutchison*

Distributed Systems: Concepts and Design   *G Coulouris and J Dollimore*

C Programming in a UNIX Environment   *J Kay and R Kummerfeld*

Software Engineering (3rd Edn)   *I Sommerville*

High-Level Languages and Their Compilers   *D Watson*

Programming in Ada (3rd Edn)   *J G P Barnes*

Elements of Functional Programming   *C Reade*

Interactive Computer Graphics: Functional, Procedural and Device-Level Methods   *P Burger and D Gillies*

Software Development with Modula-2   *D Budgen*

Common Lisp Programming for Artificial Intelligence   *T Hasemer and J Domingue*

Program Derivation: The Development of Programs from Specifications   *R G Dromey*

Program Design with Modula-2   *S Eisenbach and C Sadler*

Object-Oriented Programming with Simula   *B Kirkerud*

Parallel Processing: Principles and Practice   *E V Krishnamurthy*

Real-Time Systems and Their Programming Languages   *A Burns and A Wellings*

Programming for Artificial Intelligence: Methods, Tools and Applications   *W Kreutzer and B J McKenzie*

FORTRAN 77 Programming: With an Introduction to the Fortran 90 Standard (2nd Edn)   *T M R Ellis*

The Programming Process: An Introduction Using VDM and Pascal   *J T Latham, V J Bush and I D Cottam*

Prolog Programming for Artificial Intelligence (2nd Edn)   *I Bratko*

Principles of Expert Systems   *P Lucas and L van der Gaag*

Logic for Computer Science   *S Reeves and M Clarke*

Introduction to Expert Systems (2nd Edn)   *P Jackson*

COMPUTER ARCHITECTURE

MARIO DE BLASI

University of Bari, Italy

Translated by Charles Foot

ADDISON-WESLEY
PUBLISHING
COMPANY

Wokingham, England · Reading, Massachusetts · Menlo Park, California
New York · Don Mills, Ontario · Amsterdam · Bonn
Sydney · Singapore · Tokyo · Madrid · San Juan

The programs in this book have been included for their instructional value.
They have been tested with care but are not guaranteed for any particular
purpose. The publisher does not offer any warranties or representations,
nor does it accept any liabilities with respect to the programs.

Many of the designations used by manufacturers and sellers to distinguish
their products are claimed as trademarks. Addison-Wesley has made every
attempt to supply trademark information about manufacturers and their
products mentioned in this book. A list of the trademark designations and
their owners appears on p. xiv.

Cover designed by Crayon Design of Henley-on-Thames using the computer
graphic reproduced by permission © Telmat Informatique and
printed by The Riverside Printing Co. (Reading) Ltd.
Typeset by Dataset Marlborough Design Ltd.
Printed in Great Britain by Mackays of Chatham plc, Chatham, Kent.

First printed 1990.

British Library Cataloguing in Publication Data
De Blasi, Mario
    Computer architecture.
    1. Computer systems. Design
    I. Title   II. Sistemi per L'elaborazione dell'
    informazione. *English*

    004.21

    ISBN 0–201–41603–4

Library of Congress Cataloging-in-Publication Data
De Blasi, Mario.
    [Sistemi per l'elaborazione dell'informazione. English]
    Computer architecture / Mario De Blasi ; translated by Charles Foot.
    Foot.
        p.   cm. – (International computer science series)
    Translation of: Sistemi per l'elaborazione dell'informazione.
    Includes bibliographical references.
    ISBN 0–201–41603–4
    1. Computer architecture.   I. Title.   II. Series.
    QA76.9.A73D4   1990
    004.2'2–dc20   90–277
                                                                      CIP

Preface

This book is intended as a reflection on computing systems, and aims to stimulate the reader to think about the motives which underlie certain architectural choices, rather than presenting them as axiomatic. This means that more emphasis is placed on the concept on which a mechanism is based, than on the mechanism itself.

The subject matter is developed in such a way as to be independent of the specific computer architectures discussed, without however ignoring the problems which gave rise to them. Each explanation of principles and underlying problems is accompanied by concrete examples taken from current architectures. The examples introduced in support of the theoretical elements are numerous. In themselves they constitute a possible parallel way of reading the book, as they are to be found almost exclusively in the figures.

Definition and scope of the discipline

Architecture has been defined [1] as the frontier between two levels in the hierarchical view of computer systems. Hence, there are as many architectures as there are levels in a computer system. Computer architecture, in particular, is the boundary between the complex of hardware and firmware and the machine language level. Consequently, for many years computer architecture has been considered as the view of the computer as it appears to the machine language programmer, thus including all the characteristics and details that can be manipulated at this level. It does not include, following this definition, implementation details and structural characteristics such as data paths, microprogramming and VLSI design partitions.

This definition was valid as long as computer organization was not strongly influenced by operating systems and high-level language compilers. Indeed, both of these are other important 'users' of computer architectures and, as such, have to be considered in specifying the boundary with computer hardware and firmware. The nature of the compiler and operating system requirements is different from the kind that emerged from machine or assembly language programmers. However, all of these concur nowadays to build up a definition of computer architecture.

Although implementation is a concept different from architecture, it nevertheless influences its definition. It is unrealistic, and definitely incorrect, to define a computer architecture without considering its implementation possibilities, that is to say, not using current technology to the best advantage. Thus, although architecture does not include implementation details, it is influenced by them, in the same way as it is influenced by HLL compilers and operating systems. Implementation is another 'neighbour' of computer architecture.

If the scope of a discipline has to include the whole body of knowledge needed for its complete definition, then computer architecture should enlarge its boundaries to incorporate all those characteristics of high-level language compilers, operating systems and implementation, which are most directly exposed to hardware and firmware performance.

Outline of contents

Chapter 1 is an introduction to the hierarchical view of computing systems.

Chapters 2, 3, 5, and 6 are about the 'classical' discipline of computer architecture, that is, the computer viewed by the machine language programmer, and includes addressing methods, instruction formats, data types and instructions.

Chapter 4 deals with addressing method support for block-structured high-level languages.

Chapter 7 covers microprogrammed control and structure related concepts.

Chapter 8 is devoted to operating system support.

Chapters 9 and 10 are about concurrency while Chapter 11 introduces parallel architectures.

The 'non-axiomatic' methodology has been applied equally to 'elementary' topics, such as numbering systems, and to 'complex' subjects like microprogramming. In both cases the axiomatic method fails, leading on the one hand to an unnecessarily complicated explanation, and on the other to a trivial treatment.

It did not seem justified, in this context, to consider microprogramming as merely an alternative to the wired control unit, simply because it arrived later. Rather, it is presented as a natural solution in the context of von Neumann architectures, since it is consistent with the procedural approach. Its critical revision in the light of RISC architectures is also discussed.

Topics such as segmentation, paging, management of shared resources and protection rings are dealt with since they are currently managed automatically by the processor. The operating system makes use of the results of such management, as it does with every other processor operation. Nevertheless, the underlying concepts seemed to be highly relevant, precisely because they are incorporated in the machine structure at its lowest level.

In the process of including material imported by operating systems, high-level language compilers and implementation issues, it is important however that we limit ourselves only to those characteristics that are relevant to computer architecture. These are materialized as architecture supports to HLL compilers and operating systems, and as architectural systems that influence the performance of computer architecture. To digress and present more material than this would be misleading because one would stray away from the area in question, determining a breaking up of the unity of the discipline.

Discussing the subject in the ways outlined above has become possible thanks to the good standard reached by today's architectures, not only in terms of performance, which is inevitably the most striking feature, but particularly in terms of the quality of their design and the systematic incorporation of architectural concepts within them.

Target audience and uses of the book

The book can be used in Computer Science or Computer Engineering courses. It requires as prerequisites a knowledge of block-structured programming languages, such as Pascal or C, and introductory concepts of operating systems, Boolean algebra and logic components. No particular mathematical knowledge is required, only elementary notions.

If there is such a background, as there is normally in 2nd year or senior students, the book can be used in its entirety.

Two other uses can be related to (a) an introductory course (1st year or junior students), or (b) a more advanced course (2nd or 3rd year or senior students).

In the first case, the subset of Chapters 1, 2, 3, 5, 6, 7 and 8 can be followed, assuming that a companion course in programming will also be given.

In the second case, a greater emphasis on Chapters 1, 4, 7, 8, 9, 10 and 11 would be appropriate, possibly complemented with more specific papers or manuals.

A full-range coverage of computer architecture in one book is essential both for the unity of the discipline and in order to adopt a coherent language and view.

The book can also be useful for engineers or computer scientists who either have not studied computer architecture in their university curriculum, or desire to update the knowledge they already have.

Indeed, computer architecture is a field that is rapidly evolving and has only recently reached the level of an autonomous and complete discipline.

Integration with the curriculum

As suggested in the ACM Curriculum '89 proposals [2], computer architecture is to be considered as one of the nine subareas of the 'computing discipline'. The term computing discipline was adopted to unify the two areas of Computer Science and Computer Engineering as far as the definition of core curriculum material is concerned.

Among the recommendations given in order to qualify a subarea, the first of which is cited, and in my view is the most important for its curricular implications, is the 'underlying unity of subject matter'. Examining the Curriculum '78 from the ACM [3], it is evident that computer architecture was spread over too many courses, such as: Introduction to Computer Systems (CS 3), Introduction to Computer Organization (CS 4), Operating Systems and Computer Architecture I (CS 6), and Operating Systems and Computer Architecture II (CS 10).

The same situation has been reflected in the curricula of many departments both in the USA and in Europe.

Nowadays the ACM Committee has recognized computer architecture as a unitary body of knowledge. In my view, this also follows from the progress that the discipline has undergone up to the present, and from the extended view of its scope highlighted above.

Acknowledgements

I would like to express my gratitude and appreciation to my colleagues G. Costa, A.M. Fanelli, F. Tangorra and E. Vaccari, for the suggestions they have given me, and above all for the enthusiasm which they have dedicated to this book during its development and testing over a number of courses.

I have also been very favourably impressed by the high professionalism of the Addison-Wesley staff. Particular thanks go to Simon Plumtree, Publishing Partner, for the care and attention which he has given to this work.

I would like to thank all the consulting editors and reviewers who have encouraged me with their valuable suggestions and highly positive judgements to complete this book.

I thank also L. Campanale for his numerous contributions to the book, regarding especially Chapter 4 and the formal descriptions.

My thanks also go to Inmos Limited, a member of the SGS–Thomson Microelectronics Group, for permission to reproduce figures and tables.

Of inestimable value to me has been the enthusiasm and the patience of my first reader: my wife Anna. And I also would like to thank

M.C. Legrottaglie, J. Hannon, C. Foot and M. Abate, who have contributed to the realization of this book.

Finally, I wish to give my affectionate regards to all my students, who have attended my courses year after year and have always shown me their goodwill and respect.

This book is dedicated to all of them.

Mario De Blasi

University of Bari
April 1990

References

1.   Myers G.J. (1982). *Advances in Computer Architecture* 2nd edn. New York: John Wiley
2.   Denning P.J., Comer D.E., Gries D. *et al.* (1989). Computing as a discipline. *Comm. ACM*, **32**(1), 9–23
3.   ACM (1979). Curriculum '78. *Comm. ACM*, **22**(3), 147–65

Contents

Preface   v

1 The Hierarchical Organization of Computing Systems   1

  1.1   The levels of a computing system   2
  1.2   Relations between levels   5
  1.3   Architectures and languages   6
  1.4   Compiling and interpreting   9
  1.5   The von Neumann computer model   12
  1.6   The formal description of computing systems   17
          Further reading   19

2 The Representation of Information   21

  2.1   Devices for information storing and transmission   22
  2.2   The problem of reliability   23
  2.3   Binary codes   24
  2.4   Physical information structures   40
  2.5   Information structures at machine language level   45
          Further reading   53
          Exercises   53

3 The Instruction Format and Methods of Addressing   59

  3.1   The instruction format   60
  3.2   Methods of addressing   68
  3.3   'Mode and register' addressing   86
          Further reading   91
          Exercises   91

4 Addressing Method Support for High-level Languages **95**

4.1 Memory allocation in block-structured languages 96
4.2 Local and non-local scalar data 101
4.3 Variables referenced by address 105
4.4 Data structures 107
     Further reading 114
     Exercises 114

5 Data Types and Instructions **119**

5.1 Data transfer 120
5.2 Shift and rotation 122
5.3 Processing binary integers 124
5.4 Real number processing 134
5.5 Processing decimal integers 140
5.6 Bit manipulation and Boolean vector processing 142
5.7 Address processing 146
5.8 String processing 148
     Further reading 153
     Exercises 154

6 Instructions for Modifying the Flow of Control **161**

6.1 Jump instruction format 163
6.2 Conditional and unconditional jumps 166
6.3 Jumps to subroutines 170
6.4 Procedure calls 175
6.5 Iterations or loops 178
6.6 Co-routine jumps 180
     Further reading 181
     Exercises 182

7 The Microprogramming Level **185**

7.1 Interconnection structures 186
7.2 The bus 189
7.3 The instruction cycle 196
7.4 The general structure of processors 198
7.5 Microprogramming 199
7.6 Microarchitecture 202
7.7 Instruction decoding 207
7.8 The control unit 209
7.9 The arithmetic and logic unit 211
7.10 Hardwired versus microprogrammed control 213
     Further reading 215
     Exercises 215

8   Operating System Support   **219**

8.1   Exception and interrupt processing   219
8.2   Memory management and protection   230
8.3   Access to shared resources   252
       Further reading   257
       Exercises   258

9   Concurrency in Computer Organization   **261**

9.1   Parallelism inherent within the computational   262
       paradigm
9.2   Dynamic properties of programs   264
9.3   The pipelined model of computation   266
9.4   Instruction prefetching   270
9.5   Instruction queues   271
9.6   Cache memory   273
9.7   Techniques for reducing dependency waits in   285
       instruction pipelining
       Further reading   288
       Exercises   289

10   Concurrency Implementation   **293**

10.1   CISC and RISC architectures   294
10.2   Concurrency implementation in CISCs   295
10.3   Concurrency implementation in RISCs   298
10.4   General models for VLSI microprocessors   305
         Further reading   308
         Exercises   309

11   Parallel Architectures   **311**

11.1   Control, data flow and dependency graphs   313
11.2   Serial computation   314
11.3   Instruction and data pipelining   315
11.4   Array processors   320
11.5   Systolic arrays   324
11.6   Multiprocessors   330
11.7   Multicomputers   335
11.8   Interconnection structures   343
11.9   Data flow and demand-driven architectures   351
         Further reading   354
         Exercises   354

Solutions to Selected Problems and Exercises   **359**

Computer Index   **393**

Index   **395**

Trademark notice

Am29000™ is a trademark of Advanced Micro Devices.

IBM 370™, IBM 3084™, IBM 3090™ and IBM 4341™ are trademarks of
International Business Machines Corporation.

Intel 8086™, 80386™ and 80860™ are trademarks of Intel Corporation.

MC68000™, MC68020™, MC68040™ and MC88000™ are trademarks of
Motorola Corporation.

NS32032™ is a trademark of National Semiconductor Corporation.

PDP-8™, PDP-11™, VAX-11™ and VAX-11/780™ are trademarks of Digital
Equipment Corporation.

Rockwell 6502™ is a trademark of Rockwell International Corporation.

Z80™, Z8000™, Z8010™ and Z80000™ are trademarks of Zilog Corporation.

UNIX™ is a trademark of AT & T.

CRAY X-MP™ and CRAY-1™ are trademarks of Cray Research
Incorporated.

BBN Butterfly Parallel Processor™ is a trademark of Bolt Beranek and
Newman Incorporated.

occam™ and transputer™ are trademarks of the INMOS Group of Companies.

Clipper™ is a trademark of Fairchild.

FPS T™ is a trademark of Floating Point Systems.

1 The Hierarchical Organization of Computing Systems

1.1 The levels of a computing system
1.2 Relations between levels
1.3 Architectures and languages
1.4 Compiling and interpreting

1.5 The von Neumann computer model
1.6 The formal description of computing systems
Further reading

A system is a set of components connected together. This is a general definition valid for any type of system. It only takes on a specific meaning when we specify the type of system (biological, planetary, social, and so on) and therefore specify the component units and the type of connections between them.

Every discipline has developed its own methodologies of system analysis and/or design, which only partly coincide with those utilized by other disciplines. This is due to the specific nature of the systems being studied in the various disciplines, a factor that has prevented the adoption of a single general type of approach applicable in all situations. The degree of maturity of a science can be measured precisely in terms of the number of methodological instruments that it has been able to provide itself with in the understanding of its systems. Furthermore, the ability to adopt methods developed in other sciences to the study of systems belonging to one's own discipline, with appropriate modification, may lead to a further leap forward in this discipline. At the same time, this phenomenon gives credence to the idea of universal thought processes at work in studying the differing systems (natural or man-made) that exist in the universe.

Computer science has succeeded in developing sufficiently

well-grounded methodologies of analysis and designing, despite the relative youth of the discipline.

Information processing systems are extremely complex systems by virtue of the large number of interacting parts that go to make them up. According to the way in which one traces the boundaries between these parts, one sets up functional subsystems of various types. Besides, the problem is complicated by the fact that, for the first time in a man-made object, there exists an interplay between physical parts (**hardware**) and conceptual parts (**software**). This is a feature unique to computing systems, with the obvious exception of human beings themselves.

Hence, there exists no tradition of dealing with systems of this type, and it has been necessary to construct an entirely new framework appropriate to their characteristics. Moreover, since we are dealing with systems in constant evolution, new methodologies are being added to the old to take account of new complexities that are arising all the time.

1.1   The levels of a computing system

The terms in which humans think of a problem are not the same as those used by the circuits which make up a computer. Humans think at a high level of abstraction, and to make use of a computer are forced to transform their concepts, their view of the problem, to the point where it corresponds with the computer's way of operating. At the time when the computing system consisted exclusively of the basic circuits (the hardware) the entire ground had to be covered by the human operator (Figure 1.1a).

Subsequently, much of the evolution of computing systems has consisted in attempts to bridge this gap on the side of the computer itself, by means of its **system software** (Figure 1.1b).

By such means it becomes possible to express the problems at a level higher than that of the circuits, nearer to the human way of thinking.

A great deal has been done to close the gap between hardware and problem, and indeed a lot of work still remains to be done by man. Yet very little has been done to try to reduce the gap by designing different computing models; that is, by altering the hardware (Figure 1.1c).

Through the system software, we are no longer presented with the **real machine**, namely the hardware, but rather with a **virtual machine** that seems to operate in a different way, closer to that required by human beings (Figure 1.2).

The operating level of a virtual machine is oriented towards a more

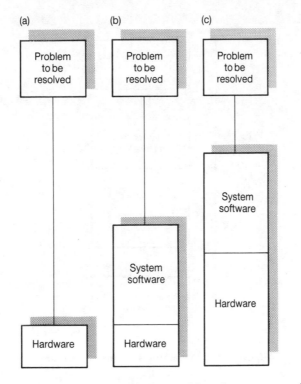

Figure 1.1 Distance between the problem and (a) early computers; (b) present computers; (c) future computers.

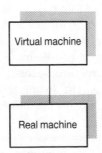

Figure 1.2 Through its software, the computer is presented as a virtual machine.

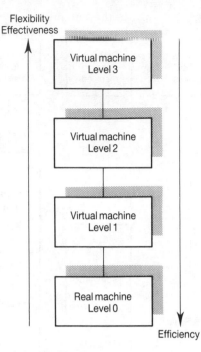

Figure 1.3 Computing systems are hierarchical.

effective representation of the problem, while it is still the real machine that makes it possible to solve it.

At this point it is easy to imagine how to proceed in order to improve the system interface in the direction of the problem, and therefore of the human operator: simply build another level of virtual machine on top of the preceding, then another and so on.

Hence, computing systems are typical examples of **hierarchical systems**; that is to say, systems which are made up of a number of mutually interacting machine levels. In this type of system, a division into components is dictated not only by functional considerations but also the need to establish different levels of efficiency, and at the same time of effectiveness and flexibility in the solving of problems (Figure 1.3).

In fact, every superstructure necessarily implies a loss of efficiency. Thus, in computing systems, the lower the level at which a problem is solved, the more difficult it is to represent it, but the more efficient is the processing.

Each of the levels of machine constitutes a subsystem in itself, to be studied and analysed into its components and the connections that link these components. Each level, however, also exists in relation to the level above and the level below in the hierarchical structure. It provides 'services' to the level above, while it makes use of the one below. It may even be said that each level functions thanks to the one immediately below it, down to the lowest level, that of the real machine, which makes all those above function.

The connections between the various levels of a computing system all have comparatively similar characteristics.

1.2 Relations between levels

The components of each level appear to be **primitive** elements at that level, but **structured** components at the level beneath (Figure 1.4). In the case of computers, the connections that carry out this hierarchical operation are the processes of translation and interpretation.

Translation takes place when each component at level N is substituted by a group of components at level $N-1$.

Interpretation, on the other hand, implies that there are present both the components at level N and those corresponding to them at level $N-1$.

If the connection is a translation relationship, a system is simply represented at level N but not executed, since it is executed at level $N-1$ or those lower down. If on the other hand there is an interpreting relationship, the system at level N is also executed.

Since, as has been said, the lower levels are more efficient, while the higher levels are more effective in representing problems, it therefore seems reasonable generally to adopt translation processes for the higher levels and interpreting processes for the lower ones. It may be said that translation is a way of shifting the problem to a more easily interpretable level. Nevertheless, this schism between the problem description level and the execution level gives rise to a number of problems, including the notable one that any information regarding what is happening within the system while it is functioning is of little interest to the person planning the system.

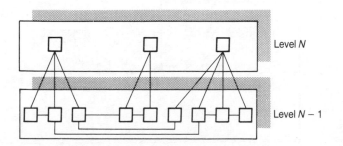

Level N

Level $N-1$

Figure 1.4 The components of each level appear to be primitive at that level but are structured at the level below.

1.3 Architectures and languages

The highest level of a computing system is that which is presented to the outside world. The boundary between the system and the outside world is known as **system architecture**, and may take on three different forms:

(1) applications packages

(2) languages

(3) communication with other systems and with instruments

The first two refer to the man–machine interface, while the third type of interface establishes a direct connection with the physical world. To be precise, even applications packages and instrument communication constitute languages, as in every type of communication.

Both system applications and languages make the system appear to be a machine that operates exclusively for that application or in that language.

Hence, a user who makes use of a personal computer only as a word-processor will tend to consider the system simply as a powerful manipulator of text, even though the user knows the computer is capable of many other things.

In the same way, the applications programmer who is writing a program in a high-level language considers the computer as a machine that operates in that language, though vaguely realizing, without knowing how, that programs in high-level languages are translated into machine code.

Apart from programming languages, type (2) interfaces also include terminal command languages, database description and manipulation languages and job control languages (Figure 1.5).

The interface with other systems usually follows a set of conventions

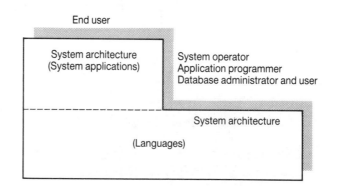

Figure 1.5 The system architecture is the boundary between the computer system and the outside world.

and protocols that more specifically go under the name of **physical input/ output architecture, configuration architecture** and **network architecture**.

These terms reflect a rather different way of considering the boundaries of the system, including in these cases the other systems that are connected to it.

From the point of view of level, the physical I/O architecture is located close to the real machine level.

On the other hand, the network architecture may involve both low-level and application-level aspects, and should be considered as stratified on various levels.

In fact, going back to languages, it may be noted that these are not located on a single level either. System architecture may include not only high-level languages like Pascal, BASIC, FORTRAN and COBOL, but also:

(a)   very high-level languages

(b)   symbolic machine languages or assembly languages

Category (a) is becoming ever more widespread in relation to certain fields of application of great interest, such as artificial vision. This level is generally realized by means of translators or interpreters written in a high-level language (Figure 1.6).

The second category is to be found at a much lower level, similar to machine language. There are, however, two important differences between them: assembly language is a symbolic language whereas machine code is numeric, and the former may incorporate some instructions that do not correspond to machine instructions.

Both high-level and assembly languages are generally translated into machine code. The respective translation programs are called **compilers**, in the first case, and **assemblers**, in the second.

The correspondence established by a compiler between the **source** language and the **object** language is 'one to many'. This means that each high-level language instruction is converted to a sequence of many machine code instructions after translation. On the other hand, the correspondence between assembly language and machine language is 'one to one' or 'one to few'.

All the levels mentioned above make use of resources such as memory and peripherals, not to mention the processing unit itself. These resources must be carefully managed, not only to establish a uniform interface between them and the various languages and applications, but also to reduce the complexity in using them. Furthermore, when there is more than one user involved in the system at the same time (multiprogramming, multiprocessing and timesharing), it becomes necessary to solve any potential conflict in resource use. The system that supervises all these operations is the **operating system**. This level, situated just above that of machine language, provides the series of services described to the levels

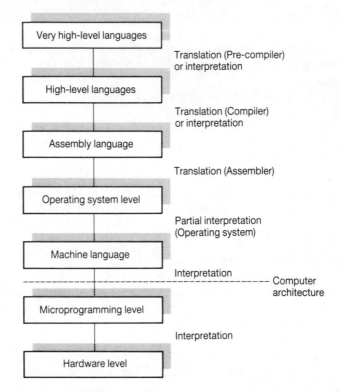

Figure 1.6 The levels of an information processing system.

above. It may be considered as a partial interpreter of the higher levels, in the sense that it analyses all the instructions in the programs being executed, letting most of them pass unaltered down to the levels below, and interpreting those instructions that require use of resources, by means of appropriate programs.

The machine language, since it exists below the level of the operating system, is not under its direct control, even though it may make use of some of the services made available at that level. The machine language is normally the lowest of the levels available to the user, and represents the so-called **computer architecture**. In spite of the hierarchical organization of a computing system, it is generally this level that is the first to be designed and is the one that characterizes the potential of the computer itself. From this moment on, the rest of the work proceeds in two directions. The first of these attempts to bridge the gap between the machine architecture and the higher levels.

The second consists in defining the ways of creating the machine architecture specified, that is, designing the underlying levels. These are the **microprogramming level** and the **hardware level**.

The microprogramming level is a level of language with instructions

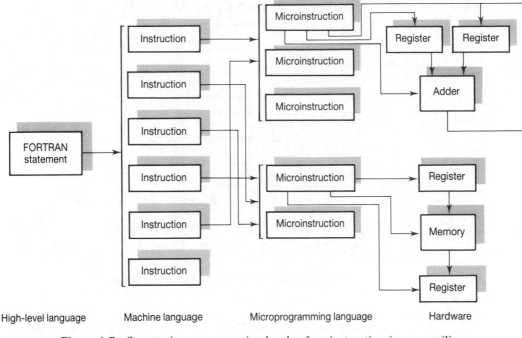

Figure 1.7 Structuring on successive levels of an instruction in a compiling language.

in direct correspondence with the units making up the hardware level. This allows the machine to carry out the interpretation of machine language by means of sequences of these instructions, instead of directly by means of complex circuits. The advantage is a much more systematic and easily extensible design.

Figure 1.7 gives an overall view of the structuring on the successive levels of an instruction in a compiling language such as FORTRAN. As can be seen, the relationship of 'one to many' is respected in the compiling of the high-level language into machine language. Each instruction in machine language is then interpreted by sequences of microinstructions. Finally these activate the adder circuitry, utilize memory and so on.

1.4 Compiling and interpreting

While the relation between the machine level and the microprogramming level is always one of pure interpreting, the relation between a high-level language and machine language may be one of pure compiling or pure interpreting, or even a combination of the two.

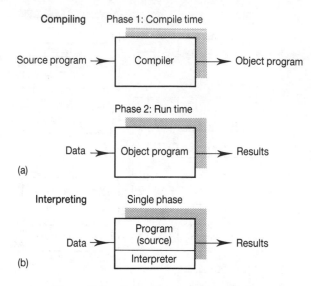

Figure 1.8 Compiling and interpreting.

There is **pure compiling** (Figures 1.8a and 1.9a) when the source language program is substituted at the moment of execution by a functionally equivalent program in a low-level object language. For example, programs written in the language FORTRAN are translated into machine language, thus giving rise to a new program. It is this new program that is executed and not the original versioɪ in FORTRAN.

There is **pure interpreting** (Figures 1.8b and 1.9d) when the program remains in the machine during execution in the original version, and is carried out in this version by interpreting the instructions one by one. Programs written in the language BASIC, for example, are left unaltered in the machine, and each of the instructions is recognized by means of a special machine language program, the BASIC interpreter, which is also resident in the computer during execution. Every time that the computer goes back for an instruction, it is then interpreted again and carried out.

Purely interpreted languages are not only inefficient but have also the disadvantage that syntax errors can only be detected during execution of the program concerned.

In compensation, semantic-type errors can easily be understood, because they always refer to the program written by the programmer and not to a translation of it in a machine code.

Mixed versions tend to be of two types. Both of them are based on the definition of an **intermediate language**, which becomes the object language of the compiling. This intermediate language is then interpreted into machine language. The difference between the two types lies in the level of the intermediate language.

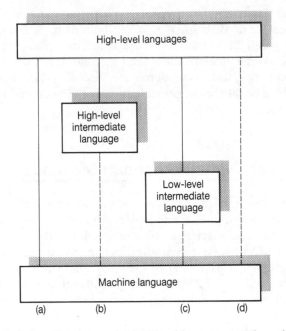

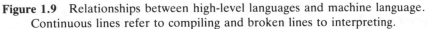

Figure 1.9   Relationships between high-level languages and machine language. Continuous lines refer to compiling and broken lines to interpreting.

If this level is very high, as in APL (Figure 1.9b), it becomes possible for the syntactic errors to be revealed in the compilation phase, while at the same time the semantic errors refer to a level which is practically that of the source language. Owing to the proximity of the intermediate to the source language, compiling is very simple, involving a one-to-one correspondence like that of an assembler, yet the interpretation is somewhat inefficient.

The other possibility is that the intermediate level is very close to that of the machine (Figure 1.9c), so as to permit efficient and simple interpreting. Naturally, the compiling is of the one-to-many type. The advantage of following this technique, which is adopted by Pascal with its P-code intermediate language, is that it allows a reasonable degree of compilers' portability, since it is relatively easy to re-write the interpreter for different machines.

In all cases other than pure interpretation, solving a problem with the computer involves at least two separate phases: the **compile time** and the **run time** (Figure 1.8a). The former is concerned with the **static** properties of the program, while the second regards its **dynamic** properties. That is to say, in the compiling phase the program is considered as it is written, while in the execution phase it is seen as an active entity. Some operations are typically carried out during compiling, others during execution. Bearing in mind that a program is executed many times but only compiled once (or a very small number of times), it is clear that any operation that can be shifted into the compiling phase contributes to increasing the overall efficiency. On the other hand, any operation carried out during run time results in an increase in flexibility. A concise definition of dynamic could be 'at the last possible moment', in contrast to static as 'as early as possible'.

1.5 The von Neumann computer model

The model on which present-day computers are based goes back to a work by John von Neumann, published in 1946, which traced the essential lines on which to base an electronic computer. Since that time, computer architecture has remained essentially unchanged, despite the fact that technological advances have opened the way to enormous progresses both in the direction of the higher levels (high-level languages, operating systems, applications) and at the lower levels (hardware and micro-programming).

The feature that most marks the von Neumann machine model is its **procedurality**.

This refers to the fact that any problem must be described to the computer as a sequence of operations. The machine expects a **program**, a set of instructions, which tells it what to do from one moment to the next.

In recent years, attention has turned towards some interesting alternatives to this way of operating, and the ideas that have emerged are for a complete abandonment of the procedural scheme. These go under the name of **fifth generation** or **non-von Neumann architectures** such as the data flow and the reduction architectures which will be considered at the end of Chapter 11.

According to the von Neumann model, a computer consists of a **memory** and a **processor** (Figure 1.10). The memory contains data and programs. The processor has the job of extracting the program instructions from the memory, interpreting them and executing them one after the other until the problem is solved. The data is transformed during the running of the program through a succession of states, the last of which is the result.

Though there may be a large quantity of instructions and data in

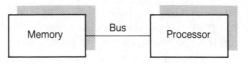

Figure 1.10 Von Neumann model.

memory waiting to be processed, the processor extracts them one at a time and processes them one at a time. Because of this limitation, it clearly becomes necessary to establish in some way the sequence in which the instructions in memory are to be extracted and carried out. This is not to say that it would not still be necessary to observe a certain sequencing even if a number of instructions and data items could be taken from memory at the same time, but in this case it could be made to depend on agents external to the instructions and the processor, such as the availability of the data needed to carry out the instructions, as occurs in the data flow architectures mentioned.

The strict 'one instruction at a time' constraint does not permit the adoption of mechanisms that would be closer to the logic of the problem, like the one mentioned above, and demands that the selection of the next instruction be rigidly fixed either in the processor or in the instruction that is currently being carried out.

1.5.1   The processor

The processor is an **interpreter** of a set of instructions. Incorporated within it are mechanisms for:

- extracting and decoding an instruction (**fetch** phase);
- carrying out the instruction that has been fetched (**execute** phase);
- identifying the next instruction to be fetched and executed.

By this simple sequence of operations, repeated *ad infinitum*, a processor is able to execute programs of any complexity. It is this essential simplicity that makes the von Neumann model so appealing. The interpreting mechanism has always remained as described here, independently of technological advances, though these have obviously influenced the way that the model is implemented.

Returning to the sequence described earlier, it may be observed immediately that the fetch phase is always the same for all instructions, whereas there are as many different execute phases as there are different types of instruction.

Just as the memory has the function of containing the global information relating to a problem (namely the program and data) through the various stages of processing, the processor needs a memory of its own to contain the information relating to the successive **states** it goes through while carrying out each instruction. Moment by moment, the processor needs to know which of the program instructions it is executing, the data it is to operate on and the location of the next instruction to be carried out. Besides, it needs to be able to trace the phase that it is in and have a precise knowledge of all the resources at its disposal. All this information is held in special high-speed memories called **registers**.

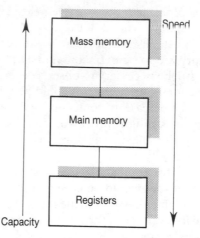

Figure 1.11 The memory hierarchy.

1.5.2 The memory

The memory of a computer is to be found at different levels of a hierarchy which goes from slow large-capacity memories to very fast memories such as the registers of the processor (Figure 1.11).

Usually there are at least three levels to be found in a computer:

- **Mass memories** These contain a quantity of programs and data that are not to be processed *immediately* by the processor.

- **Main memory** This contains programs and data that are *currently being processed* by the processor. This is the so-called on-line level of memory, to indicate that it is from here that the processor gets the instructions and data to work on. If the program is very big or there is a lot of data, only a part will reside in main memory; namely that part which is being processed for a certain period of time. In addition, it is possible to have a number of programs on-line for a given period of time (**multiprogramming**). In this case, only the part of each program that is being processed in that period is to be found in main memory. The rest of each program resides in mass memory and will be loaded into main memory as and when required.

- **Local memory** of the processor This level is the one most closely linked to the processor, and indeed is an integral part of it. It consists of the set of high-speed registers mentioned in the preceding section and represents, as it were, a 'short-term' memory for the instruction being carried out.

There exists a substantial difference between the width of the communication channels linking local memory with the processor and that between all the other memories, as well as between these and the processor. The last type of channel permits access to a single item of information at a time, while the registers are organized in the processor in such a way as to be able to present all the information contained in them at the same time to the units connected.

As has been stated, there is a great difference in capacity as well as speed between one level of memory and the next. Computers are organized in such a way as to regulate the flow of information between the different levels automatically, through operating system software or through hardware. This regulation ensures that information accessed less frequently is maintained in the slower and more capacious memory levels during the successive stages of processing, and the information most frequently needed is brought into the faster levels of memory.

In particular, in the case of main memory, it is essential that the speed at which the processor is able to obtain information should not be very different from the rate at which it is able to process it.

Since speed and memory capacity are parameters in conflict with each other, yet the complexity of the problems to be processed requires large main memories, various techniques have been adopted to try to balance the processor/main-memory system as far as possible. These may be effectively grouped into three categories:

(1)   widening the data bus
(2)   increasing the number of levels in the memory hierarchy
(3)   prefetching

Widening the data bus

The connection between memory and processor (usually termed **bus**) constitutes the so-called bottleneck in a von Neumann-type computer. The image recalls what was said in Section 1.5: that though there is a large quantity of instructions and data waiting in memory to be processed, the processor extracts them and processes them one at a time. This limitation is not technological in nature, but architectural. It is aggravated by the difference in speed between the memory and the processor. This difference has always been present in computers throughout their history and still remains valid, albeit less seriously than in the past. A widening of the data bus, so as to extract several instructions and/or data items at a time, would be an attempt to solve the architectural limitation. Various organizations of memory with wider data buses have been studied. The problem to be solved in all these cases is to make a memory in which the restraint of procedural access has been eliminated (at least partly) compatible with a processor whose way of operating remains essentially procedural. In other words, which instructions and/or data should be allowed a wider access mechanism? Given that the processor will process them in sequence, it is essential that such sequences should be known or at least predictable, if we intend to extract (or write) blocks of information simultaneously.

In any case, the problem would still not be completely solved, since any proposal for organizing memory with widened data buses involves putting together a number of memories with access of the 'one at a time' type, and so each of them will still be subject to the usual bottleneck.

Increasing the number of levels in the memory hierarchy

With this approach, rather than 'widening' the bottleneck, the idea is to improve the flow; that is, to overcome the technological restraint by increasing the speed. This is achieved by inserting a smaller-sized fast memory (**buffer** memory or **cache** memory) between the main memory and the processor. This then becomes the processor's real on-line memory (Figure 1.12).

Initially, the cache memory is empty. When the processor calls for the first instruction of the program, it still extracts it from main memory, but at the same time it begins to fill the buffer with a certain number of instructions and data that are clustered around the first instruction. The

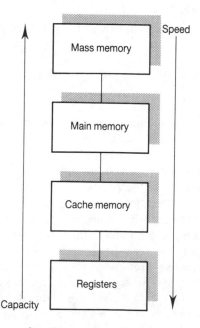

Figure 1.12 Increasing the number of levels in the memory hierarchy.

processor will subsequently find the data and instructions in cache memory and will be able to extract them at its own speed. Of course, after a while it may well happen that another data item or instruction is not to be found in cache memory, and in this case all or part of the cache memory contents will be emptied back into main memory to make way for the new memory area that the processor needs to work on.

Various cache memory handling algorithms have been implemented (see Section 9.6). All have the aim of making the transfers between main memory and cache memory as infrequent as possible. Clearly, even in this case, techniques are based on models of prediction of the sequences of data and instructions to be processed, even if the sequences to be dealt with are much longer than those involved in the data bus widening techniques.

Prefetching

This technique consists of superimposing the processing of the current instruction and the fetching of the following one (or the following ones in sequence). In this way, we introduce parallelism in a time sense, in contrast to the 'spatial' parallelism that is characteristic of the data bus widening technique.

As the sequence may be determined not only by the processor but also by the instruction that is being carried out, prefetching does not always provide the required instruction. In such cases, the processor will simply not utilize the instruction extracted, but will explicitly call for the new instruction that has been referred to.

Among the mechanisms that have been analysed, the most frequently adopted is prefetching, since it produces improvements in performance by exploiting what is, in effect, a redundancy that already exists in computers – the presence of two subsystems, the memory and the processor, that are capable of working in parallel. On the contrary, with both data bus widening and the addition of a buffer memory, the improvements may be greater but are obtained at the expense of additional resources.

1.6   The formal description of computing systems

By the formal description of computing systems, we mean the description of systems or architectural components expressed in a formal language, for example a programming language.

Besides the usual description in natural language it is sometimes useful to adopt a formal description also, since this helps to resolve the inevitable ambiguities that arise in verbal or written communication. Moreover, if this description is carried out in a programming language, this makes it possible to simulate the systems being studied.

At the end of each chapter of this text, apart from the normal exercises, there appear a number of problems of this type, through which the reader is invited to assume an active role in the study of computing systems. Specifically, the reader is asked to practise what has been learned by 'designing' the formal descriptions of the system presented in the text.

It is well known that only by performing and designing does one come face to face with the problems that exist in reality. One comes up against a number of details that escape abstract study, no matter how seriously it is undertaken. Often these details are by no means trivial in their significance, but cast new light on the way to interpret the topics under consideration.

This is particularly true in our subject area, where the functionality may be more important than the structure: the mechanism that makes an architectural system work, rather than a simple specification.

On the basis of this, the natural language description and the formal language description complement each other, and need to be carried out using a similar methodology. In particular, a 'top-down' or 'bottom-up' methodology is needed for the constructive approach. When dealing with computing architectures, it is more useful to adopt a bottom-up approach, since this allows one to equip oneself systematically with the building blocks, and to build up, level by level, the architectural structures that make up the system.

The need to represent various levels of abstraction is linked to the hierarchical nature of computers, in which each machine level may be considered an abstraction of the level below.

The disadvantage of using a programming language for the formal description is that the language chosen suggests, and often imposes, 'implementation details' which may have nothing to do with the definition of the system in question. The very procedural nature of the language may not describe adequately some operations that are normally carried out 'in parallel' in modern computer architectures. However, this defect is really only of secondary importance: it is enough to be aware of it so as to avoid the impression that the system is really implemented in this way.

From the point of view of the simulation, the problem raised above has no relevance for our objectives. The simulation need only arrive at the functionality of the system being described, using the operators and data types available in the language being used.

What counts is that the system behaves 'externally' in the desired way, that is to say, it respects the required relationship between input and output.

The solution to the exercises and simulation problems proposed in this text is suggested in terms of the language Pascal. Since this is a very widely used language, it is most likely to be understood by the majority of readers. It is therefore used as a 'reference' language for describing architectural systems in problems requiring a formal description.

Furthermore, Pascal compilers are commonly available, so that the listings produced may be compiled and used as laboratory instruments to illustrate the dynamic properties of the systems described.

Further reading

A definition of computer architecture, and the levels of architecture within a computing system

Dasgupta S. (1984). *The Design and Description of Computer Architectures*, pp. 1–10. New York: Wiley

De Blasi M. (1989). Methodological aspects and contents for the teaching of computer architecture. *EC Newsletter*, **1**, 47–59

Myers G. J. (1982). *Advances in Computer Architecture* 2nd edn, pp. 3–14. New York: Wiley

Memory hierarchies

Siewiorek D. P., Bell C. G. and Newell A. (1982). *Computer Structures: Principles and Examples*, pp. 227–9. Maidenhead, UK: McGraw-Hill

Stone H. S. (1987). *High Performance Computer Architecture*, pp. 21–9. Reading MA: Addison-Wesley

The formal description of computing systems

Dasgupta S. (1984). *The Design and Description of Computer Architectures*. Chichester, UK: Wiley

2 The Representation of Information

2.1 Devices for information storing and transmission
2.2 The problem of reliability
2.3 Binary codes
2.4 Physical information structures

2.5 Information structures at machine language level
Further reading
Exercises

Information processing systems have many analogies with other systems, such as process control equipment, a car factory or the human body. All of these take raw materials, which are gradually transformed to produce finished products of a higher level, like steel sheets, cars or cells and tissues.

In the same way, raw data enters computers and after a series of transformations emerges as results, which of course are of greater significance for us.

Unlike the materials involved in the other processes, information is abstract. Hence, to be processed, it needs to be represented by means of concrete physical properties that are compatible with the units that make up the computer itself.

Concretized in this way, it needs equipment to maintain it, or memorize it, in the units, and to transmit it from one unit to another in the process of 'working' it in various stages.

Information is a homogeneous substance on which the various units making up the computer operate. It flows from one unit to another through a series of connections known as the **data path**.

2.1 Devices for information storing and transmission

In digital computers, information is represented, transmitted and processed using discrete levels of specific physical properties. If a different symbol is assigned to each level, the result is an **alphabet** through which the information to be processed can be expressed.

Different types of information already make use of their own alphabet: for example, positive integer numbers use the 10 decimal figures, while the words of a text use the 26 letters of the Latin alphabet, plus a certain number of punctuation symbols. The computer could be made to adopt as its alphabet all these symbols put together, thus using this number of levels of a predetermined physical property to represent numbers and words.

A device able to take on n different configurations is called an **n-state device**. If these configurations are obtained by subdividing a continuous physical property (such as a tension, a current or a magnetic flow) in n distinct levels, then it is known as an **elementary n-state device**, since by means of this it becomes possible to construct (non-elementary) devices with any other number of states.

In order to memorize a data item made up of p characters, using an alphabet of n symbols, it is necessary to adopt a set of p elementary memory devices, each with n states. To be able to transmit the same data item between two units, p elementary transmission devices with n states each connecting the two devices are used.

It is clear that information can be codified using any alphabet. The adoption of a particular alphabet is conditioned, among other things, by the instruments that the technology provides us with (for instance, the 10 fingers of our hands). Computers use an alphabet of only two symbols, converting the input data expressed in our alphabet into their alphabet, and reversing the process when they provide the results.

It is interesting to consider the reasons for this choice, bearing in mind the different factors that influenced it.

First of all, the motive of **efficiency** cannot be attributed. Binary calculations are much more rapid than in decimal; but this is important only in scientific processing, in which the calculations to be carried out are very complex. On the other hand, in commercial processing, the calculations are nearly always few in number but the quantity of data to be processed, and therefore in input and output, is generally great. In this case, the conversion time from one base to another becomes the predominant factor, not the true processing time. Despite this, computers always use elementary 2-state devices, providing a support to decimal arithmetic. This means that:

- 10-state memory devices are built up from elementary 2-state devices.

- Arithmetic operations on decimal data are included in the instruction set.

This has the advantages of adopting an n-symbol alphabet, leaving the computer to carry on using its own 2-symbol aphabet.

An important motive is the reduced cost connected to the much greater functional **simplicity** of units working with only two values, compared with any other kind of representation. This cost advantage is maintained even when decimal arithmetic is used, since the elementary components remain binary.

But by far the most important reason regards the need for computer **reliability**. There should be no need to present arguments in favour of this parameter in an era such as ours, in which virtually all activities are connected in some way to the use of computers.

What needs to be understood, rather, is the relevance of the number of memory and transmission device states to the reliability of computers.

2.2 The problem of reliability

As in any other system, the reliability of computing systems depends on that of their individual components, and the greater their number the more important this factor becomes. Computers are complex systems with large numbers of components, with the result that if one of them failed to function during processing, the whole execution would be ruined. An error in a single component is generally due to disturbances from the surrounding environment or noise produced by other components altering its state, bringing it to a value which is close to the next level. Given that noise is of variable amplitude and is always present, it is more appropriate to speak, not of levels, but of **bands** of values around the levels. Their amplitude is given by the interval of separation between the levels (Figure 2.1), and any value within a certain band is attributed to the corresponding level.

The most distinctive feature of computers, compared with other organizations, is that the execution of a program comprises the processing of a very large number of instructions in sequence, each of which exploits all the components of the computer structure. This means that in a given time span every component and every memory and transmission device works on the 'information' medium a very high number of times.

This is in relation to the extreme speed at which the elementary electronic devices, and therefore the whole system, are able to operate.

Hence, to guarantee an acceptable degree of reliability for the computing system, it is necessary that the elementary devices have an extremely high level of reliability. To achieve this objective, it is vital to keep the levels in the physical property, that represents the information, as

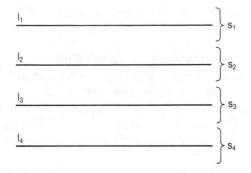

Figure 2.1 Graphic representation of an elementary 4-state device. The continuous physical dimension has been subdivided into four discrete levels: l_1, l_2, l_3 and l_4. The bands of values centred on these levels, with a width of $\triangle l = l_1 - l_2 = l_2 - l_3 = l_3 - l_4$, are attributed to the symbols s_1, s_2, s_3 and s_4 of a base-4 alphabet.

far apart as possible, so that the noise added to any level has a minimal probability of shifting the value into a range belonging to the next level. Once the overall range of usable values has been defined, it is obvious that the optimum choice, the choice that guarantees the maximum separation, is to adopt only two levels, that is, an alphabet of only two symbols. This has been the real reason for the general acceptance of the use of binary code in computers.

Naturally, although this practice guarantees that the probability of error is very small, it is not eliminated entirely. Owing to the very large number of components and data transfers involved in every operation, the probability of a system level error is not infinitesimal. For this reason, special codes have been devised to reveal whether there has been an error in the transmission or memorization of a data item, some of which even discover where the error has occurred and so are able to correct themselves automatically (Sections 2.3.4 and 2.3.5).

2.3 Binary codes

The figure or letter of a 2-symbol alphabet is known as a **bit** (**bi**nary digi**t**). The values that a bit can express are 0 and 1. These symbols derive from the decimal system, but it would equally well have been possible to adopt any symbols, such as the letters A and B, or two words, or even invent two new graphic symbols. The important thing is to adopt two distinct symbols.

Other frequently used symbols are:

- **L** and **H** ('Low' and 'High', referring to levels of voltage).
- **F** and **T** ('False' and 'True', referring to propositional or Boolean algebra).

The information content conveyed by a single bit is highly rudimentary; there exist only two possibilities. However, putting two bits together straight away obtains four different combinations: 00, 01, 10 and 11. If three bits are united, there will be eight combinations. In general, with a **string** of n bits, it becomes possible to represent 2^n different configurations.

With an alphabet of k symbols, a string of n characters can take on k^n distinct configurations. For instance, the number of different 4-letter words that can be formed with a 26-letter alphabet is 26^4, or 456 976. Most of these obviously have no meaning: in this case, we say that human language is **redundant**, that is, it employs strings that are longer than are necessary to convey the same quantity of information. The technique of adopting longer strings, or redundancy codes, is useful in recognizing possible errors, and is also used in computers.

The process of assigning a meaning to different possible configurations of a string defines a **code**. Thus the decimal numbering system, and the binary numbering system, are examples of codes in which a different number is associated with each configuration of a string of figures. The association of meanings to words formed out of the ordinary 26-letter alphabet is another example of codification.

Any information can be coded in binary, that is, by using strings of bits, without passing through the corresponding coding in the 26 letters of the alphabet or in decimal. It is enough to define the correspondences between the binary configurations and the meanings.

In addition to the direct coding of information in binary, however, it is possible to codify the 26 letters of the alphabet (both upper- and lower-case) and the 10 decimal figures. In this way, it is no longer necessary to recodify entire texts or numbers into binary: they can be input directly to the computer, and output in the accustomed format. The information thus undergoes a double coding: at one level in the normally adopted alphabet, and at the other in the binary alphabet of the computer.

2.3.1 The binary numbering system

A numbering system consists of a code plus a set of rules for the fundamental operations. Hence, it must include not only an adequate way of representing numbers but also the fundamental algorithms for operating on them.

Once an alphabet of k symbols has been defined, we know that by stringing together n of the symbols we can generate k^n different configurations. Associating a meaning to each of these configurations is equivalent to defining a code.

In numbering systems, the 'meaning' is the number, and the association is not made directly by writing a table of correspondences, but by:

- explicitly assigning a number only to the base symbols of the alphabet; and
- defining a rule by which other numbers can be assigned to strings of base symbols.

The simplest rule that one can consider adopting is to build up the values of the symbols that appear in a string by addition. To avoid having very long strings to express big numbers, however, two alternative routes have been taken:

(1)   assigning very different numbers to the different base symbols;
(2)   assigning a different weight to the position of the symbols in a string.

The first way was followed by the Egyptian, Etruscan and Roman numbering systems. It should be noted that in such systems the k^n configurations of a string n symbols long do not refer to the numbers $0-k^{n-1}$, but to k^n different numbers taken from a larger range. To represent the missing numbers, it is necessary to adopt strings of greater length. For example:

- I, V, X, L, C, D, M. These are the figures of the Roman numbering system. The base symbols have very different values (1 to 1000). As it is a 7-symbol alphabet, a string n symbols long can assume 7^n configurations, and therefore represent 7^n numbers.
- II, VI, XX, LI. These are some of the 7^2 configurations of a string two figures long. The symbol III is an example of a number, 3, which requires a string of greater length. In fact, strings of two figures permit the representation of $7^2 = 49$ numbers, but distributed in the range 2 to 2000.

Besides, it is well known that to associate numbers to strings of base symbols, the Roman numbering system used not only an addition rule (VII, XI, CXV) but also a subtraction rule (IX, CXIV).

With the **positional** numbering system (introduced by the Arabs and now used universally), a linearly increasing value is assigned to the different symbols of the alphabet, while an increasing weight is assigned to the different figures in a string from right to left. That is to say, the meaning of a figure depends on its position in the string, from which we derive the terms:

- **least significant** figure, for the figure furthest to the right;
- **most significant** figure, for the figure (different from zero) furthest to the left.

The base of a numbering system is defined as the number of elementary symbols that it uses. The base of the decimal system is 10, because that is the number of its base symbols.

The rules of positional numbering systems are the same, independently of the base used. It is sufficient, therefore, to bear in mind the decimal numbering system to understand the general synopsis.

Properties of positional numbering systems

- A number can be represented in a positional numbering system as follows:

$$a_{n-1}a_{n-2}\ldots a_0.a_{-1}a_{-2}\ldots$$

where:

- a **radix point** is used to separate the integer part from the fractional part;
- the a_i are **figures** belonging to the alphabet;
- the indices represent the **position** occupied by each figure in the string.

- A number is defined as **base** b if, when raised to the successive powers i provided by the position, it gives the respective **weights** b^i. The value of a figure a_i in a numeric string depends on the position i that it occupies in the string, according to the formula

$$a_i \cdot b^i$$

- The numeric value associated with a numeric string is obtained by using the polynomial formula:

$$N = a_{n-1}b^{n-1} + a_{n-2}b^{n-2} + \ldots + a_0 b^0 + a_{-1}b^{-1} + a_{-2}b^{-2} + \ldots$$

- The number of figures in a positional numbering system is equal to the base. Associated with these figures are numeric values in linear progression starting from zero. The difference between one figure and the next is known as **unity**.

- To count, one starts from the list of base symbols and arrays them in increasing numerical order.

    To continue further, one adopts a technique known as **carry-over**, introduced by the Indians. The basis of this technique is to write the first figure other than zero and follow it with each of the available figures in increasing order. This operation is repeated for each of the figures, to obtain all the 2-figure numbers. The same method is used to pass to the 3-figure numbers and so on.

- To operate on numbers of any length, it is enough to know the arithmetic tables for addition and multiplication, relating to single-figure numbers. For instance, an addition operation is broken down into a series of additions of figures that occupy the same position in the two numbers, plus the propagation of the carry-over, that is, the addition of any carry-over to the figure in the next highest order or position. The operations of subtraction and division are defined as the inverse of those of addition and multiplication. For subtraction, borrowing is defined as the inverse operation to carry-over: it consists in subtracting one unit from, instead of adding to, the figure in the next highest order.

Properties of the binary numbering system

- The binary numbering system is a positional numbering system of base $b = 2$, and thus its alphabet consists of only two symbols, 0 and 1.

- The weights b^i to be attributed to the succession of positions to the left and right of the binary point are:

$$
\begin{aligned}
&\vdots \qquad \vdots \\
2^4 &= 16 \\
2^3 &= 8 \\
2^2 &= 4 \\
2^1 &= 2 \\
2^0 &= 1 \\
&\quad \cdot \qquad \longleftarrow \text{ binary point} \\
2^{-1} &= 0.5 \\
2^{-2} &= 0.25 \\
2^{-3} &= 0.125 \\
&\vdots \qquad \vdots
\end{aligned}
$$

The value of the number associated with a binary numeric string is obtained using the following polynomial formula:

$$N = a_{n-1}2^{n-1} + a_{n-2}2^{n-2} + \ldots + a_0 2^0 + a_{-1}2^{-1} + a_{-2}2^{-2} + \ldots$$

- Numbering is carried out using the system of carry-over: after writing the available symbols 0 and 1, the same symbols are repeated to the right of the first (and only) symbol other than 0, and so on:

  0, 1, 10, 11, 100, 101, 110, 111, . . .

- The addition table in binary is as follows:

	0	1
0	0	1
1	1	10

  The addition of $1 + 1$ gives the result 0 with a carry-over of 1.

- Multiplication has no need of a 'Pythagorean' table, since only the two figures 0 and 1 exist in binary and therefore partial products turn out either to be 0 or an exact replica of the multiplicand.

Conversion rules for positional numbering systems between a general base b and base 10

- Converting a number from a base b numbering system to the decimal system is performed using the polynomial form:

  $$N = a_{n-1}b^{n-1} + a_{n-2}b^{n-2} + \ldots + a_0 b^0 + a_{-1}b^{-1} + a_{-2}b^{-2} + \ldots$$

- The conversion of a number from the decimal system to a base b numbering system, on the other hand, is not carried out with the base 10 polynomial form, which would require calculations in base b, but with the method of division and multiplication.

  The integer part of the decimal number is repeatedly divided by base b, and the remainders of the division are progressively recorded from right to left, until a quotient equal to zero is obtained.

  Having thus obtained the integer part of the number in base b, one then proceeds to calculate the fractional part by repeatedly multiplying the fractional part of the decimal number by base b and recording the integer part of the successive products from left to right.

  The fractional numbers that have an exact representation in

base b will at some point give a result equal to zero. If this is not the case, the process is stopped when the desired precision is obtained.

The division and multiplication method is the inverse procedure of the polynomial form in base b, that is, of the polynomial form whose coefficients represent the (unknown) figures of the number expressed in the desired base b. Let us examine it at work in the case of integer numbers. The coefficients to be determined are those of the polynomial form:

$$N = a_{n-1}b^{n-1} + a_{n-2}b^{n-2} + \ldots + a_0 b^0$$

where N is the number expressed in decimal notation. Factoring out b results in:

$$N = b(a_{n-1}b^{n-2} + a_{n-2}b^{n-3} + \ldots + a_1 b^0) + a_0$$

and hence the figure a_0 is given by the remainder of the division of N by b. Repeating the procedure on the quotient of this division, a_1 is obtained and so on for all the other coefficients, namely all the figures in increasing order of the number in base b.

Conversion rules for positional numbering systems where one base is a power of the other

● Converting from a numbering system of base b to a numbering system of base b^k is performed by grouping the figures in ks in two directions starting from the radix point and converting each single group.

For example, conversion from binary to octal is obtained by grouping the bits in 3s:

$$
\begin{aligned}
N_8 = \ldots \\
+ a_8 2^8 + a_7 2^7 + a_6 2^6 + \\
+ a_5 2^5 + a_4 2^4 + a_3 2^3 + \\
+ a_2 2^2 + a_1 2^1 + a_0 2^0 + \\
+ a_{-1} 2^{-1} + a_{-2} 2^{-2} + a_{-3} 2^{-3} + \\
+ a_{-4} 2^{-4} + a_{-5} 2^{-5} + a_{-6} 2^{-6} + \ldots = \\
= \ldots \\
+ (a_8 2^2 + a_7 2^1 + a_6 2^0) 2^6 + \\
+ (a_5 2^2 + a_4 2^1 + a_3 2^0) 2^3 + \\
+ a_2 2^2 + a_1 2^1 + a_0 2^0 + \\
+ (a_{-1} 2^2 + a_{-2} 2^1 + a_{-3} 2^0) 2^{-3} + \\
+ (a_{-4} 2^2 + a_{-5} 2^1 + a_{-6} 2^0) 2^{-6} + \ldots =
\end{aligned}
$$

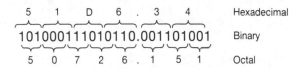

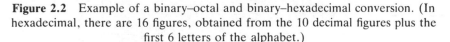

Figure 2.2 Example of a binary–octal and binary–hexadecimal conversion. (In hexadecimal, there are 16 figures, obtained from the 10 decimal figures plus the first 6 letters of the alphabet.)

$$= \ldots$$
$$+ (a_8 2^2 + a_7 2^1 + a_6 2^0)8^2 +$$
$$+ (a_5 2^2 + a_4 2^1 + a_3 2^0)8^1 +$$
$$+ (a_2 2^2 + a_1 2^1 + a_0 2^0)8^0 +$$
$$+ (a_{-1} 2^2 + a_{-2} 2^1 + a_{-3} 2^0)8^{-1} +$$
$$+ (a_{-4} 2^2 + a_{-5} 2^1 + a_{-6} 2^0)8^{-2} + \ldots$$

It is equally simple to pass from base 8 or 16 to base 2, since all that is required is to convert the single octal or hexadecimal figures, and not the entire number.

It may be noted that changing base is straightforward when one base is a power of the other. For instance, the **octal** and **hexadecimal** number systems both have bases that are powers of the binary one. Figure 2.2 shows an example of the use that is frequently made of this property.

The octal and hexadecimal number systems are generally used for a more compact representation of numbers, as in the case of the decimal system. But since their bases are powers of two, the octal and hexadecimal systems continue to use binary arithmetic, with the result that the machine circuits remain unchanged. In the case of the decimal system, however, because the base is not a power of two, it becomes necessary to adopt arithmetic circuits that work in base 10, namely on 10-state devices obtained from elementary 2-state devices (BCD arithmetic, Section 2.3.3).

2.3.2 Character codes

Character codes is the name given to those codes that establish a correspondence between the various configurations of a binary string and the various characters obtained by grouping together the 26 upper- and lower-case letters of the alphabet, the 10 decimal figures, the punctuation symbols and other control characters such as 'space' and 'carriage return'. This set of characters is also known as the **external alphabet**, because this is the set of symbols the computer uses to communicate with the outside world, with man. It is opposed to the **internal alphabet**, made up only of the symbols 0 and 1, with which the computer represents and processes

Table 2.1 EBCDIC (Extended Binary-Coded-Decimal Interchange Code). The numbering of the bits is from left to right.

digit (4 5 6 7) ↓ \ zone (0 1 2 3) →	0000	0001	0010	0011	0100	0101	0110	0111	1000	1001	1010	1011	1100	1101	1110	1111
0000 (0)	NUL	DLE	DS		SP	&	-									0
0001 (1)	SOH	DC1	SOS				/		a	j			A	J		1
0010 (2)	STX	DC2	FS	SYN					b	k	s		B	K	S	2
0011 (3)	ETX	TM							c	l	t		C	L	T	3
0100 (4)	PF	RES	BYP	PN					d	m	u		D	M	U	4
0101 (5)	HT	NL	LF	RS					e	n	v		E	N	V	5
0110 (6)	LC	BS	ETB	UC					f	o	w		F	O	W	6
0111 (7)	DEL	IL	ESC	EOT					g	p	x		G	P	X	7
1000 (8)		CAN							h	q	y		H	Q	Y	8
1001 (9)		EM							i	r	z		I	R	Z	9
1010	SMM	CC	SM		¢	!	|	:								
1011	VT	CU1	CU2	CU3	.	$	,	#								
1100	FF	IFS		DC4	<	*	%	@								
1101	CR	IGS	ENQ	NAK	(	)	_	'								
1110	SO	IRS	ACK		+	;	>	=								
1111	SI	IUS	BEL	SUB	|	¬	?	"								

zone: 0 1 2 3
digit: 4 5 6 7

Table 2.2 ASCII code (American Standard Code for Information Interchange). The numbering of the bits is from right to left.

zone → (bits 7 6 5 4)	0000	0001	0010	0011	0100	0101	0110	0111	1000	1001	1010	1011	1100	1101	1110	1111
digit ↓ (bits 3 2 1 0)																
0000	NUL	DLE	SPACE	0	@	P	`	p								
0001	SOH	DC1	!	1	A	Q	a	q								
0010	STX	DC2	"	2	B	R	b	r								
0011	ETX	DC3	#	3	C	S	c	s								
0100	EOT	DC4	$	4	D	T	d	t								
0101	ENQ	NAK	%	5	E	U	e	u								
0110	ACK	SYN	&	6	F	V	f	v								
0111	BEL	ETB	'	7	G	W	g	w								
1000	BS	CAN	(	8	H	X	h	x								
1001	HT	EM	)	9	I	Y	i	y								
1010	LF	SUB	*	:	J	Z	j	z								
1011	VT	ESC	+	;	K	[	k	{								
1100	FF	FS	,	<	L	\	l	|								
1101	CR	GS	-	=	M	]	m	}								
1110	SO	RS	.	>	N	↑	n	~								
1111	SI	US	/	?	O	–	o	del								

zone				digit			
7	6	5	4	3	2	1	0

information internally.

The number of characters in the external alphabet determines the length of the code: the ones most commonly used in computers are the 6-bit and 8-bit codes.

The 7-bit codes are used mostly for communication purposes, and have not generally been adopted inside computers due to their poor commensurability with the other units of information (which, as will be seen, is an important property of physical information structures (Section 2.4)).

Tables 2.1 and 2.2 show the two character codes most frequently used in computers. ASCII code was initially defined as a standard 7-bit code for the exchange of information between computers. Nowadays it is employed also within computers and therefore has been adapted to 8 bits.

To conserve the order relationship between the 26 letters of the external alphabet, these letters have been placed in a correspondence with the set of natural numbers, instead of adopting a random allocation. In this way, increasing binary configurations correspond to the succession of letters of the alphabet, and so alphabetic sorting operations can be carried out by means of numerical ordering operations. Consequently, computers allow the representation of textual information without having to be equipped with specific operations suitable for this type of data.

Another characteristic of both codes is the subdivision of the 8-bit field into two subfields of 4 bits each, the first called the **zone** and the second the **digit**. By analysing the zone field alone, it is possible to determine if a given character is an upper-case letter, lower-case letter, a decimal figure or a special character. Hence, within the subgroup, the digit represents the particular character (remembering the characters correspond to numbers in ascending order).

2.3.3 BCD codes

In the case of decimal figures, the digit field corresponds in both character codes to the numeric value of the figure represented. Hence, it is possible to carry out not only operations on characters, but also arithmetic operations on strings of numeric figures. The format described for numeric figures is usually referred to as **unpacked BCD**. Arithmetic operations on numbers in this format follow different rules from the pure binary format, and can be formulated in terms of the arithmetic operations on numbers in **packed BCD** (or simply BCD) format.

The BCD (Binary Coded Decimal) code is a binary code for an alphabet in base 10. The 10 decimal figures are coded in strings of 4 bits. In fact:

$$2^3 < 10 < 2^4$$

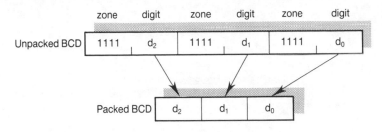

Figure 2.3 Relationship between 'unpacked BCD' and 'packed BCD' formats.

or, if preferred:

$$n = \text{length of the code} = \lceil \log_2 10 \rceil = 4$$

where $\lceil x \rceil$ implies smallest integer $\geq x$.

In BCD format, it is not the entire number that is converted into binary, but each of its decimal figures separately. For example, conversion of:

2	5	5
0010	0101	0101

into pure binary would have given:

1111	1111

or 'FF' in hexadecimal.

Figure 2.3 shows the relationship between the unpacked BCD and packed BCD formats. It can be seen that the second representation is the same as the first without the zone fields, and hence compacted.

Naturally a number will not assume the same configuration in 'pure' binary format and BCD format. Besides, BCD code is redundant, since six of the $2^4 = 16$ configurations that a 4-bit binary string can assume are not used. This means that arithmetic operations on numbers in BCD format cannot coincide with binary arithmetic operations. In fact, if the sum of two figures gives a result greater than 9, denoted by a 'non-BCD' configuration or the generation of a carry, this result must be corrected to obtain the right BCD configuration.

In Figure 2.4 some examples are given showing the method for carrying out what is generally known as the **decimal adjustment** of the result in the case of addition. For the other operations, see the exercises at the end of the chapter.

(a)	(b)	(c)
32 +	62 +	92 +
14	81	81
46	E3 +	113 +
	6	6
	143	173

(d)	(e)
56 +	37 +
25	29
7B +	60 +
6	6
81	66

Figure 2.4 Examples of additions of BCD numbers, using binary adders and 'decimal adjustment'. Every time that a figure in the result is greater than 9 (b and d), or carries over (c and e), 6 is added to the figure.

In conclusion, computers that support decimal data cannot base their operations on binary integer numbers, as happens in the case of character data, but need a set of specific instructions for decimal arithmetic.

2.3.4 Error detection codes

To detect the presence of errors in codified information, use is made of the **redundancy** mechanism.

This consists in deciding to adopt a longer code than that required, so that only some of the new possible configurations have a meaning assigned to them. If a configuration changes into another to which no meaning is attached, it is deduced that there has been an error.

In a binary code, **Hamming distance** is defined as the minimum number of bits that is required to go from one meaningful configuration to another meaningful configuration. The distance of a non-redundant code is 1, since by changing a single bit we move to another configuration that is also meaningful. The distance of a redundant code must be at least 2, signifying that variation in a single bit leads to a non-meaningful configuration.

In the case of distance 2 codes, half of the possible configurations are not meaningful, and can therefore be used for error detection.

Two-state devices, as we have been able to observe, are extremely reliable, since their probability of failing is extremely small.

However, because any computation process, no matter how small, involves an enormous number of transmission operations on such devices, it must be guaranteed that each single error will be detected, even though the probability of such a failure is minimal. The probability that 2 bits

change during a transmission, which is the product of the single proba-
bilities, is so tiny that it gives no cause for concern. This is even more true
of the chance of multiple errors involving 3 bits or more, which is so
remote as to be of no practical interest.

To obtain a distance 2 code, it suffices to increase the length of the
original code by 1 bit: in this way the double set of configurations required
is obtained.

The assigning of meanings to the configurations of this new set (or
rather to half of the new set) is not carried out randomly, but according to
a rule that makes it easy to distinguish between the two subsets: that of the
meaningful configurations and that of the error configurations. This rule
consists of adding together all the 1 bits that appear in each configuration,
and to consider it a meaningful configuration if the sum is even, and an
error configuration if it is odd. Alternatively, the opposite convention can
be adopted. What is important is that all the meaningful configurations
have a definite **parity** (even or odd) and all the wrong ones the opposite
parity. Following this rule, we can be certain of detecting any error in a
single bit, since the inversion of one bit in a string changes its parity, while
two wrong bits in the same string transform it into another that is still
meaningful, that is, with the same parity. It is true that in this way errors in
3, 5 or any other odd number of bits will also be detected, but this is of no
practical relevance, for the reasons of probability already mentioned.

In conclusion, an n-bit code that incorporates a parity check must
have an $(n + 1)$th bit, called a **parity bit**, to turn it into a distance 2 code.

In an odd parity code, for example, this bit will take on the value 0 in
those configurations of n-bit code where the number of 1 bits is odd, and 1
where the number of 1 bits is even, so as always to obtain an odd number of
1 bits in meaningful $n + 1$ bit configurations.

Parity is calculated and set in the parity bit each time a data item is
generated (transmitted or memorized) and each time one is used (received
or read from memory). In this second phase, the parity that has just been
calculated is compared with the parity bit. If the two differ, an error is
signalled. The two bits are compared by means of an exclusive OR, which
gives a logical 1 when two bits are different and a logical 0 when they are
the same.

2.3.5 Error correction codes

The use of the parity bit allows us to have an error detection code, but not
an error correction code. In fact, a parity error simply indicates that one of
the bits in a string is wrong (as it has been inverted), but not which of the
bits is at fault.

On the other hand, a code that was able to determine the position of
the erroneous bit as well as detecting its presence would also be able to
correct it automatically, simply by changing that bit.

Table 2.3 Representation of the equation
$k = \lceil \log_2 (k + n + 1) \rceil$.

n	k	$k + n + 1$
1	2	4
2	3	6
3	3	7
4	3	8
5	4	10
6	4	11
7	4	12
8	4	13
9	4	14
10	4	15
11	4	16
12	5	18
13	5	19

Hamming codes are of this type. Of course, in these codes it is no longer enough to add a single bit because not only the occurrence but also the position of the error needs to be expressed. It is clear that to convey this information, we shall need to add a number of bits to codify the position of the erroneous bit. Yet bearing in mind that the check bits are also subject to error, the position code will also have to represent the position of these extra bits.

In addition, a further configuration must be used to represent the case of 'not an error'.

Generally speaking, a Hamming code for an n-bit code will need to add k bits, with k such that:

$$k = \lceil \log_2 (k + n + 1) \rceil$$

Table 2.3 shows this equation for a number of values of n.

To codify their own position, the check bits are distributed between the bits of the original string so as to occupy positions that correspond to powers of 2 (Figure 2.5). Hence, in the new string, the check bits occupy positions 1,2,4,8, . . ., and the bits of the original string positions 3,5,6,7,9,10,11, . . . (counting from 1 from left to right).

In Hamming codes, check bits are parity bits that check the parity of a particular subset of the bits of the string (Table 2.4).

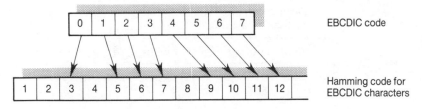

Figure 2.5   In Hamming codes, the check bits occupy positions 1, 2, 4, 8, . . .,
while the original code bits occupy positions 3, 5, 6, 7, 9, 10, 11, 12, ... Note
that the numbering begins from 1 and goes from left to right.

Vice versa, Table 2.5 shows the set of parity bits that check each bit
of the string.

As can be seen, if a bit is erroneous, all the parity bits that check it
will give a parity error, and since in themselves, that is, in their position,
they give the binary code of the integer corresponding to its position, it is
enough to add the position values of these bits to know the position of the
erroneous bit.

For instance, if the bit in position 6 is erroneous, the parity bits in
positions 4 and 2 will give an error. Adding these two numbers gives the
position (6) of the erroneous bit.

As stated in the previous section, parity checking is carried out by
comparing the parity bit with the bit just calculated by means of an
exclusive OR. All the parity bits of a Hamming code are verified through
exclusive ORs. Each will give a logical 1 if there has been an error in one of
the bits checked by that parity bit, otherwise a logical 0. In this way, the
XOR outputs associated with Hamming code control bits provides a direct
'non-error' coding, corresponding to the 'all-zero' configuration, or else
the position of the erroneous bit if the configuration is other than zero.

Table 2.4   Parity bits that check the parity
of a subset of the bits of a string.

Check bits	Bits checked
1	1, 3, 5, 7, 9, 11, . . .
2	2, 3, 6, 7, 10, 11, . . .
4	4, 5, 6, 7, 12, . . .
8	8, 9, 10, 11, 12, . . .

Table 2.5 Parity bits that check each bit of a string.

Bit of the string	Parity bits
1	1
2	2
3	1, 2
4	4
5	1, 4
6	2, 4
7	1, 2, 4
8	8
9	1, 8
10	2, 8
11	1, 2, 8
12	4, 8

2.4 Physical information structures

Information reaches the computer, circulates inside it and is re-presented to the outside world in 'packets' or units of information.

The elementary unit of information, as we have seen, is the bit: all other units of information are structured in terms of this.

Units of information have a hierarchical type of structure, which means that each unit is definable through a set of units of information at a lower level.

Each unit of information is sized in function of the computer components that deal with it, and at the same time in such a way as to have a relation of commensurability with the units of information at the levels immediately above and below.

Otherwise there would be wastes of memory and greater complexity in the processing units, which would have to operate on non-homogeneous sequences of information units.

The structures referred to here are known as **physical information structures** since they are structures on which the computer works directly through its circuits. They are to be considered as something apart from the logical data which makes use of these physical structures. Thus, a physical information unit can equally well hold an integer positive number or a program instruction: the computer will process the two elements differently, with different circuits and microprograms, even though the same physical structure is used for both of them. The definition of logical information structures is the job of the higher levels of the machine. Each level of virtual machine defines its own types of data, and it is these that must be considered the logical data types. The data types defined at any level of the computer make use of data types defined at the level immediately below, as has been stated before. It will be seen in the next section how the data types defined by the computer architecture use the physical data structures directly.

Among the various information units there exists one which is more fundamental than the others: the unit of information transfer between the computer's components. This is usually called the computer **word**. Very often this fundamental information unit happens to coincide with another information unit, like the **byte** in 8-bit microprocessors. However, we shall continue to use the term 'word' to refer to the fundamental unit of information, for the sake of generality.

The attributes of an information unit are its length, the way it is structured in lower-level units and the way higher-level units are structured in it. Since the word is the unit of information that is chosen first in formulating a computer design, it follows that its length conditions most of the other choices to a high degree.

First of all, it influences the width of the transfer bus between the various units, that is to say, the **internal data path** and the **bus** that connects the processor with the memory and the peripherals.

Secondly, the sources and the destinations of such transfers must also be influenced: the registers, the arithmetic and logic unit and the memory. All of these must be one word wide.

Next, even the logical information structures defined by the computer architecture will be influenced indirectly, since these make direct use of the physical information structures, which are in turn conditioned by the choice of word length, for reasons of commensurability.

The hierarchical structure presented by the physical information units (Figure 2.6) is the following:

- **Bit**: the fundamental information unit, in terms of which all other information is structured; logical or Boolean-type information can be expressed in it.

- **Half byte** (4 bits long): this is not found in all computers. Not many instructions act on this data structure; largely the instructions that operate on integer decimal data.

- **Byte** (8 bits): this is normally the smallest information structure present in computers. Sometimes, as in 8-bit microcomputers, it is the fundamental unit of information.

- **Word**: usually composed of a whole number of bytes. Apart from the case of 8-bit microcomputers, this is the fundamental computer unit of information. The communication channel between the

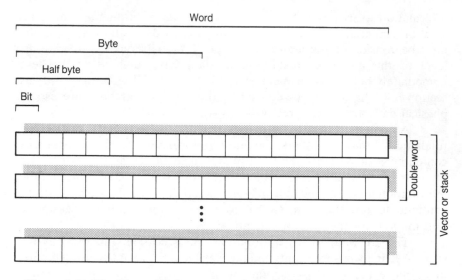

Figure 2.6 The hierarchical structure of physical information units (a 16-bit word is assumed).

processor and the memory is exactly one word wide, the registers are one word long, most of the computer operations are carried out on words and the whole data path is one memory word wide. Not only the data, but also the other information that circulates within the computer, such as instructions and memory addresses, is influenced by the length of the word.

- Multiples of the word, such as the **double-word**, sometimes also called **longword**, the **quadword**, and the **octaword**. Usually they are furnished to support multiple-precision arithmetic.

- **Array** (vector) of bytes or words: a set of consecutive bytes or words on which it is possible to operate *en bloc*, or else on the single elements in any order.

- **Stack** of bytes or words, for which the operations are defined only in the last one or two elements inserted in the data structure, as will be seen in Section 2.5.1.

The registers and the main memory are supports to the physical information structures.

The state of the processor is represented in its **registers**. A register is a memory device that can contain a set of bits. The width of the registers is the same as that of the fundamental unit of information, generally the word or the byte. Thus, a register can be seen as 2^n-state device, if n is the word length, but it may also correspond to a greater number of devices with a smaller number of states. The extreme case is a register made up of

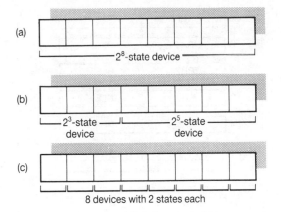

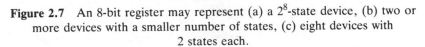

Figure 2.7   An 8-bit register may represent (a) a 2^8-state device, (b) two or more devices with a smaller number of states, (c) eight devices with 2 states each.

n binary devices, representing n independent state bits put together (Figure 2.7).

The registers are conceived in such a way as to provide a representation support for most of the data types that exist in the architecture. Since, as we shall see, some types of data use submultiples and others multiples of words, many architectures provide mechanisms for reconfiguring the available registers in a similar way (Figure 2.8).

Some registers are assigned the capacity of carrying out operations on their own contents, in relation to the type of data represented in them. Every architecture has for example at least one register, called the **accumulator**, on which it is possible to carry out arithmetic operations on integer numbers and logical operations on Boolean vectors. If a register is capable of representing only a data type, but does not have the operators that act on it directly, it is necessary to allow for a transfer of the information into a register in which it is also possible to operate on that data type. In most modern computers there is a tendency to give all the registers the same properties, thus creating a **general register** architecture.

The main memory is a set of p 2^n-state devices, where n is the word length. The number of words, p, is the **capacity** of the memory (Figure 2.9).

The main memory provides only a representation support for the various data types present in the architecture, since all operations are carried out on the internal registers of the processor. Nevertheless, some operations may appear as if they were carried out directly on the data in main memory, though in this case they correspond to internal (transparent to the programmer) sequences of transfers from the memory to the registers, operations on the latter, and transfers back into the memory. This is useful

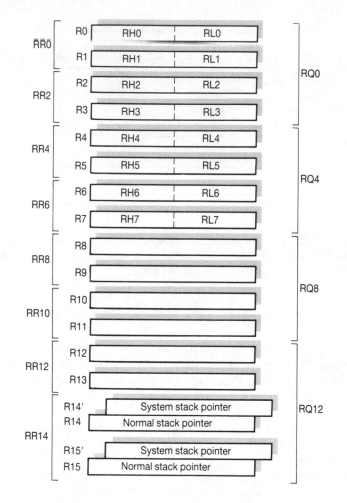

Figure 2.8 General registers of the Z8000 microprocessor. The Z8000 has 16 general 16-bit registers and a set of special system registers (not shown). Flexibility in using the registers is obtained by grouping together or overlapping a number of registers. For operations on byte-type data, the first eight 16-bit registers (R0 . . . R7) are treated as sixteen 8-bit registers (RL0, RH0 . . . RL7, RH7). The sixteen 16-bit registers are grouped in pairs (RR0 . . . RR14) to form long 32-bit word registers. Similarly, the sixteen 16-bit registers can be joined in groups of four (RQ0 . . . RQ12) to form 64-bit registers.

not only in simplifying programming but also in increasing execution efficiency, and furthermore in carrying out operations on types of data that can only be represented in main memory (for example, table look-up). Some architectures have taken this property so far that all instructions refer to data in main memory (**memory–memory** architectures).

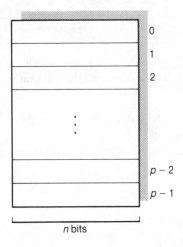

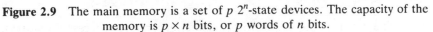

n bits

Figure 2.9   The main memory is a set of p 2^n-state devices. The capacity of the memory is $p \times n$ bits, or p words of n bits.

2.5   Information structures at machine language level

The information that characterizes the machine code level, that is, the data on which the computer operates as it appears through the definition of its architecture, is:

- references to information
- machine instructions
- data relating to programs

Each of these categories of information can assume different forms, which will be analysed when types of addresses (Chapters 3 and 4) and types of data and instructions (Chapters 5 and 6) are discussed. In the following sections, the general features of these three types of information will be investigated.

2.5.1   References to information

The instructions normally contain the name of the operation to be carried out and a reference to the data to be processed (Figure 2.10).

The way in which data is referred to in machine code is by specifying the location in memory. As there exist different memories within the

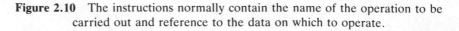

Operation	Reference to the data

Figure 2.10 The instructions normally contain the name of the operation to be carried out and reference to the data on which to operate.

computer, it will also be necessary to specify to which of them the data item in question belongs.

The memories that a machine instruction can refer to are of three types:

- the registers
- the main memory
- the stack

The main memory and the registers are **random access** memories, meaning that an instruction can gain direct access to any location in main memory or any register, without having to pass through other locations or registers.

On the other hand, the stack is a memory to which access is permitted only to the last one or two items of information stored (**top** of the stack). If we want to add an item of data to the stack, we can only put it after the last item inserted. If we wish to take out an item of information that is not the last one to have been inserted, we have to take out all the items necessary until we reach the one desired.

From what has been said, it follows that references to the memory and the registers are generally explicit in nature, while references to data stored in a stack are implicit (Figure 2.11). That is to say, the instructions that make use of memory or registers must specify the memory location or register they intend to refer to. Instructions that use the stack have no need to do this because they will automatically refer to the top of the stack. In this case, the reference is part of the internal state of the processor. It is placed in a special register known as the **stack pointer**.

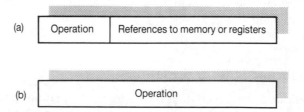

(a)

Operation	References to memory or registers

(b)

Operation

Figure 2.11 Instructions that refer to (a) memory or registers (explicit reference); (b) the stack (implicit reference).

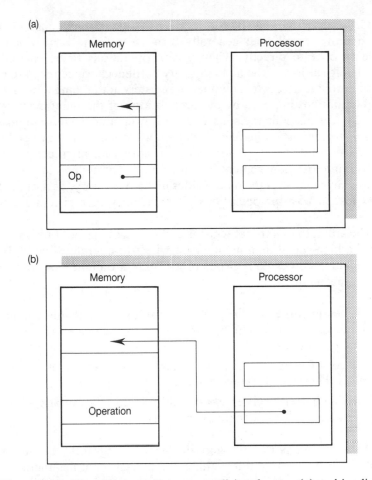

Figure 2.12 The difference between explicit reference (a) and implicit reference (b).

Any explicit reference makes use of the main memory (of one or more instruction fields), while an implicit reference generally utilizes the internal memory of the processor (Figure 2.12). Explicit references are used up in a single instruction, whereas implicit references make use of the state of the processor, and therefore of the processing context transmitted from one instruction to the next.

The registers in a computer may be either dedicated to precise functions, or else of a general type. The former are necessary for the functioning of the computer, while the general registers represent an architectural choice, very common in present-day machines, but not essential to their operation. Dedicated registers can sometimes be accessed through an implicit reference. Besides, some of the general registers can be used as dedicated registers.

General registers can be considered as an extension of main memory (albeit a rather small one: generally 8 or 16 registers), on which it is possible to operate directly. They permit operations to be carried out without being subject to the main memory bottleneck, since they are much faster and provide access to a number of registers at the same time. Hence, the two limitations imposed by the organization of the main memory are eliminated. Yet since the registers are very few in number, it is not possible to keep a very significant number of data items in them, so they need to be managed carefully. The opponents of general register architectures argue that this kind of management is difficult for compilers to carry out efficiently. Since most of the data resides in main memory, part of the time saved is lost in transfer operations from memory to registers and back again.

The strength of general register architectures lies not only in having available a high-speed data memory on which to operate directly, but in having included dedicated registers in it. There are numerous advantages in this arrangement:

- It is possible to equip the general register set with all the operations, at a lower cost than equipping some of the dedicated registers with some operations, and others with others.

- The set of general registers appears as a homogeneous structure, and is therefore easier to manage.

- Each dedicated register is now able to take advantage of all the operations that the computer can perform.

Both the memory cells and the general registers are numbered sequentially from zero, and it is this number that identifies them. In the case of the memory, this number is known as the **address**, while for the registers the most common term is **register number**.

The addresses, both of memory and of registers, are positive binary integers, and so they are structured as such in strings of bits. Naturally, the number of bits necessary to specify a memory location is much greater than that needed to refer to a register.

To refer to a memory containing p locations or registers, we must adopt an address of a length of $\log_2 p$ bits (rounded up to the next integer). For example, a memory of 64K locations ($1K = 2^{10} = 1024$), requires an address length of 16 bits. In fact:

$$64K = 2^6 \times 2^{10} = 2^{16}$$

and

$$\log_2 2^{16} = 16$$

On the other hand, referring to a set of general registers requires a much smaller number of bits; for example, in the case of eight general registers, three bits suffice. Hence, the instructions that make references to memory are not only slower but also longer than those that refer to registers.

A shorter instruction length not only saves memory, but also causes a further time-saving because it occupies the memory–processor channel less. Yet, as observed previously, these savings 'locally' should be balanced against the inevitable losses caused in another point of the program, because of the need to create a register processing environment.

The addresses considered up to now are also called **absolute addresses** to distinguish them from a range of other forms of addressing (Chapter 3), which have been formulated to deal with a variety of data types, as well as to reduce the number of address bits. Naturally, it remains true that an increase in local efficiency must be paid for in efficiency reductions, hopefully of an appreciably lesser order, in some other part of the system.

Many of these other methods of addressing require processing to turn them into absolute addresses. One of the processor's tasks is address calculation. So the processor has to process not only data, but also the addresses.

2.5.2 Machine instructions

Machine instructions tell the processor what it has to do. This is represented in a particular instruction field, called the operation code (or **opcode**). If the operation makes reference to data or other instructions, the opcode field is followed by one or more address fields, to specify these references (Figure 2.13).

The length of the opcode is commensurate with the number of distinct instructions that a given processor can execute.

As regards the length of the memory address field or the register references, what was stated in the previous section remains true. At this point, it suffices to observe that an instruction, with all its fields, must be such that it makes the best possible use of the physical memory structures. This means that it is usual for the instruction length to coincide with a

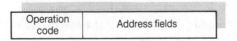

Figure 2.13 Typical structure of an instruction.

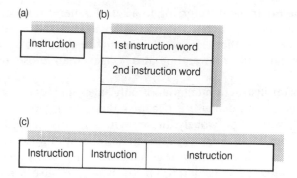

Figure 2.14 Relationship between instruction length and word length: (a) all the instructions are one word long; (b) the instructions occupy a (variable) number of words or bytes; (c) a word can accommodate a number of instructions (possibly a variable number).

whole number of memory words, or else to be a submultiple of them (Figure 2.14).

For this reason, much of the efforts of computer architecture designers are devoted to looking for the best compromise between instruction length, data length and word length.

There is a great deal of variability in instruction formats, depending on whether the instructions may require zero, one, two or three operands, and whether these are to be found in the memory, the registers or the stack. All these factors represent a fairly wide variability in instruction lengths. A not very efficient way to solve the problem would be to adopt a word length commensurate with the longest instructions. Another way would be to subdivide the longer instructions into more words (or bytes), thus permitting the adoption of shorter words.

The processor contains a dedicated register known as the **program counter**, which from moment to moment contains the address of the next instruction to be carried out. Each time an instruction is executed, the content of this register needs to be updated to make it point to the next instruction to extract and execute. Programs are linear sequences of instructions, which means that the instructions are placed in contiguous memory locations, and the processor extracts them and executes them in the same order. This type of organization is the most natural, and the simplest to manage, but it should not be thought that it is the only possible one. For instance, in the earliest computers, which used delay line memories, the instructions 'circulated' in continuation along these lines (Figure 2.15). The head (A) picked up the instructions that passed under it. While the processor was processing an instruction many other instructions were passing under the head, meaning that it was necessary to wait

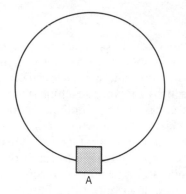

A

Figure 2.15   Scheme of a delay line memory.

almost one complete turn before obtaining the instruction situated immediately after the one just processed in the memory.

To avoid this, the instruction format included an extra field in which
the programmer had to specify the address of the next instruction
explicitly, while the instructions to be carried out in sequence were not
placed consecutively in memory, but suitably 'spaced out' one from
another. This was not an easy task, also because the instructions did not all
have the same length (if they had, the pointer field would have been
unnecessary, as it would have been enough to place them at a fixed
distance and leave the processor to manage them).

The above example is interesting in that it distinguishes between a
kind of implicit reference to the next instruction to be carried out and
a kind of explicit reference.

If the instructions are organized in a program as linear sequences,
the reference is obviously implicit: it will suffice for the processor to
advance the program counter by the number of locations that each
instruction occupies, to obtain the address of the next instruction. Besides,
this advancing is incremental, since every word of an instruction must be
extracted and interpreted in order to execute that instruction. So, when the
processor reaches the last word of the instruction, it will obtain the address
of the next instruction simply by advancing the program counter by
another unit. This is why a counter is used.

Yet it is no secret that programs are not singular linear sequences.
They may more exactly be referred to as sets of linear sequences, each of
which ends with a reference, this time explicit, to the next instruction to be
carried out. The instructions that change sequence are known as **jump**
instructions. In such cases, the value of the program counter no longer
changes linearly, but has a point of discontinuity. The processor, instead of
incrementing the program counter, updates it with the new address
specified in the jump instruction.

2.5.3 The data

The information that a computer deals with at the machine code level coincides only partly with that processed at the higher levels. For example, the 'memory address' information is not usually present in a high-level language, but is essential to every machine code. On the other hand, a 'record' type structure, which can be defined in many high-level languages, does not ordinarily exist on the machine language level.

The existence or not of a data type is decided simply on the basis of whether or not the corresponding architecture provides a set of operations that act on it. Such operations usually correspond to machine instructions, which are used to carry them out. All computers possess instructions to carry out additions and other arithmetic operations on integers, for example, so it is safe to say that the 'integer' data type is present in every machine architecture.

Other mechanisms are provided to deal with some data types. To cite an example, among the various methods of addressing there is one that permits reference to the elements of a vector, simply by providing the address of its first element along with the index of the desired element. In this case, the 'vector' data type exists not because there are machine instructions that operate on it, but because a method of referring to its elements is provided. An operation on a vector can thus be broken down into a sequence of operations on its elements, because there exists a way of referring to them.

In general, we can say that a data item is defined by the following components:

- address
- value
- type

This means that a data item occupies a memory cell located at a particular address. The content of this cell is the value of the data item. This will be interpreted on the basis of type and possibly of other attributes such as 'undefined'.

Despite the fact that the three components refer in a conceptually inseparable way to the same data item, these are used separately in present-day computer architectures. Since the address is used to refer to the data item, this, or rather the information for obtaining it, lies in the instruction which has to process the data item, while the latter, or more precisely its value, may reside in a completely different memory area. Besides, the address is an implicit component of the data item, linked with the type of mechanism by which a main memory functions. It is calculated and utilized by the processor to gain access to the value of the data to be processed. In other words, to process the value of a data item, the processor must first process its address.

The information that the processor works on to obtain the effective address is present partly in some of the instruction fields, partly in other main memory locations and partly in the processor itself.

Similar considerations apply to the attributes of the data item or, in other words, the type. This information, instead of residing with the data value, still forms part of the instruction or instructions used to process it. This may or may not be separated from the other information found in the instruction (opcode, address), but it nevertheless resides in the instruction. For instance, if the data item to be processed is a floating-point number, this will need to be specified in the instruction (through an opcode for floating-point instructions rather than integer instructions), instead of associating such information with the data item itself.

However, having established that the three components, address, value and type, belong to a single entity, the data item, we need to ask ourselves what exactly is being processed by the system at any given moment: the address, the type or the value of the data item?

The values of the data are the primary object of processing of programs, while the addresses and types are processed mainly by the instructions' interpreter resident in the processor.

Further reading

Error-detecting codes and error-correcting codes

Hamming R. W. (1950). Error detecting and error correcting codes. *Bell Syst. Tech. J.*, **29**, 147–60.
McEliece R. (1985). The reliability of computer memories, *Sci. Am.*, (Jan.)

EXERCISES

2.1 Which numbers have the same representation in binary, octal and decimal?

2.2 Without actually converting the following binary integers into their decimal equivalents, decide which are odd and which are even: 101100, 1101, 11001, 1000, 11110, 10001.

2.3 Work out the numbers that represent the string 100 in binary, octal, hexadecimal and decimal numbering.

2.4 With the help of the conversion rules on pages 29–30, write down in base 10 a number whose representation in another base is known, for example the number 213_4.

2.5 State in which bases (X, Y and Z), the following numbers are expressed:

(a) $13_X = 7_{10}$

(b) $70_Y = 56_{10}$

(c) $1A0_Z = 416_{10}$

2.6 Transform the following numbers written in base 10 into the equivalent in the bases specified:

(a) 11, 27 in base 4.

(b) 120, 27, 0.8125, 0.122, 43.75 in base 2.

(c) 39, 27 in base 8.

2.7 Write the tables for the addition and multiplication of the first four natural numbers, in the binary system.

2.8 If X is a natural number other than 0, how is X written in base X?

2.9 What number represents the periodic number 1/3 in base 3? In base 2?

2.10 Convert the decimal number 0.9 into binary.

2.11 Try to work out the decimal adjustment for the operation of subtraction.

2.12 Carry out the following operations in BCD:

(a) $295 + 378$

(b) $24 - 18$

(c) $642 - 354$

2.13 Suppose the following string needs to be transmitted in 7-bit ASCII code:

0 0 0 0 1 0 1

    0 1 2 3 4 5 6

what will be the configuration of the code transmitted, using an odd-parity Hamming code?

    Next, suppose that during transmission and error arises in the position 6 bit, so that '1' becomes '0'. Which will be the control bits that detect this error?

Problem 2.A   Starting from the definition of the bit in an operational language:

> **Type** Bit = 0..1;

define hierarchically the information physical structures (byte, half byte, word, longword, quadword), in such a way that the byte and the word are constituted by a number of bits and the double and quadruple words by a number of words. The word must have a number of bits not defined *a priori*.

2.14   In terms of the language Pascal, a bit can be defined as a data type capable of assuming only the values '0' and '1':

> **Type** Bit = 0..1;

Using the same language, try to define more complex structures, such as the byte and the half byte, on the basis of the definition of bit.

2.15   A computer word has different sizes in different architectures. Define its type in terms of bits or bytes (as defined in Exercise 2.14), in such a way that its length remains undefined.

2.16   Define the type word for a number of processors with different characteristics (Z80, Z8000, Z80000, Rockwell 6502, Intel 8086, VAX–11).

2.17   The physical structures 'longword' and 'quadword' are composed of two and four words respectively. Define them hierarchically on the basis of the definition of the word (Exercise 2.15).

Problem 2.B   Define a representation of the main memory and the read and write operations of an element in it.

The address size in the architecture does not necessarily determine the amount of memory which is present in the computer system, but only the maximum quantity of memory that can be addressed. Hence, in the memory access procedures, we have to take into account the possibility that one might try to access to a non-valid address of memory.

In addition, it is better that the type of memory elements is left undefined, in order to have a description valid for every architecture.

2.18   A computer's memory is a sequence of physical structures (bytes, words and so on). A memory address has values that depend on the number of bits dedicated to the address (a 10-bit address implies that its values are in the range [0..1023]). However, the highest memory address actually implemented depends on the amount of memory effectively present and is less than or equal to the highest value of the address field (in the above example it is not more than 1023).

(a) Define a memory as a sequence of objects of the unspecified type Elem_type:

> **Type**
> Elem_type = . . . ;

using the constants Addr_max_val (maximum value of the address field) and Mem_max_addr (maximum memory address), which are also left undefined:

> **Const**
> Addr_max_val = . . . ;
> Mem_max_addr = . . . ;

(b) Give the values of Element_type, Addr_max_val and Mem_max_addr for a computer based on the 8086 (memory organized in bytes and address field of 20 bits), with 640 kilobytes of main memory.

2.19 Bearing in mind the definition of memory used in Exercise 2.18a, and making use of the type:

> **Type**
> Address = 0 . . Max_addr_val;

develop a procedure in Pascal for writing a data item (of the type Elem_type) into memory at a certain address (of the type Address).

The procedure must also check that the address lies within the limits of effective memory (the range [0..Mem_max_addr]), returning the result of the check on completion.

2.20 As in Exercise 2.19, develop a procedure for reading a data item in memory.

Problem 2.C Describe a possible representation of the general registers of an architecture, leaving undefined the number of registers and the size of each of them.

Describe formally the read and write operations in the registers.

2.21 The set of general registers of an architecture is, like the memory, a sequence of objects (such as bytes, words and longwords) numbered from 0 to a maximum that depends on the number of bits designated to contain the register number (for example, if the architecture provides for a 4-bit field, 16 registers are implemented, numbered from 0 to 15).

Describe the registers without specifying their type and the maximum register number.

2.22 Describe the register access operations for reading and writing a data item in a register (identified by its number).

2.23 The general registers of the Z8000 are represented in Figure 2.8. Leaving out registers R14' and R15', they may be considered as sixteen 16-bit registers,

eight 32-bit registers or four 64-bit registers. Moreover, the first eight 16-bit
registers can be treated as sixteen 8-bit registers.

(a) Define separately the structure of the 8-, 16-, 32- and 64-bit registers using
the definition in Exercise 2.21.

(b) Arrange the various structures (16 × 16-bit registers, 8 × 32-bit, and so on)
so that they coincide or are superimposed (when simulated, they have to
begin at the same memory location). To do this, it may be possible to use
the keyword **absolute** (found in some versions of Pascal, such as Turbo
Pascal), which allows **synonyms** to be defined in the following way:

```
Var
    a : Word; (* 16-bit word *)
    b : array [0 .. 1] of Byte absolute a;
```

Variables a and b coincide (they are synonyms) because they have the same
sizes and because b has a start address that coincides with that of **a**.

2.24 Define the registers of the Z8000, using the following declarations relating to
their range:

```
Type
    Byte_reg_range = (RH0, RL0, . . . , RH7, RL7);
    Word_reg_range = (R0, R1, . . . , R15);
    Dword_reg_range = (RR0, RL2, . . . , RR14);
    Qword_reg_range = (RQ0, RQ4, RQ8, RQ12);
```

How can register RH3 be referred to? And register RQ12?

2.25 Develop procedures to simulate access instruction to the general registers of the
Z8000, bearing in mind the size of the register to be accessed.

Problem 2.D Define the stack of an architecture and the associate stack pointer
by means of the data structures available in a high-level language.
     Leave undefined the stack dimension and the type of its elements.
Specify the 'Push' and 'Pop' operations in such a stack.

3 The Instruction Format and Methods of Addressing

3.1 The instruction format
3.2 Methods of addressing
3.3 'Mode and register' addressing

Further reading
Exercises

In the context of computing systems, as we have seen in Chapter 1, the term 'architecture' refers to the definition of the boundary between two levels of machine. Hence, there are as many different architectures as there are levels of machine.

Among these, the computer architecture plays a special role, defining as it does the boundary between hardware and software. More precisely, it lies between the hardware and microprogramming on one side and the machine language level on the other (see Figure 1.6).

The computer architecture represents the machine as it appears to the machine language programmer, and so does not include the internal structure of the computer. This will be the subject of Chapter 7.

Defining a computer architecture is equivalent to determining:

- what types of data it is possible to treat at a machine code level. A data type must first of all be represented in the machine. Some data types are represented only in memory (for example vectors), others may also be represented inside the processor. Secondly, there must be a suitable access mechanism for that type of data. Finally, it must be possible to operate on that type of data. This may be achieved in two ways: either a set of operations is defined for it, or that data type can be represented by another more fundamental data type, for which the operations are already defined.

- how to refer to the data, that is, what 'name' to call them. We have seen that this reference is commonly made through an address, meaning the place where a certain data item can be found inside the memory. There exist various ways of addressing data, according to the type of memory it occupies (inside or outside the processor), and to the type of data (vector or scalar). Often the location of the data item is already known, by the fact that it is in a particular register or in a stack, or simply in the next memory location, as in the case of vectors or machine instructions themselves. In such cases, it is possible to refer to it implicitly.

- what operations can be carried out on each type of supported data, namely, what the instruction set consists of. This also includes other operations, necessary for the execution of any program, for example the operations to define the **processing sequences**. Instructions are the most important data type that the computer has to deal with. The structure of instructions in a computer may be of various types: this is defined in the **instruction format** (Section 3.1).

- what the register organization is. It is necessary to define the set of registers that memorize the state of the processor, namely, the information that must be passed from one instruction to the next to allow it to be carried out. In some organizations, the internal memory of the processor may also devote itself to maintaining part of the state of the program being executed, with the aim of increasing its speed efficiency.

- what the memory and input/output organization is.

- how the above logical structures and the physical information structures correspond, that is, the connections with the next lower level.

3.1 The instruction format

As has been stated before, an instruction is made up of an opcode followed by an address part. Depending on the type of instruction and the formats accepted by the particular computer, this part may have from zero to a maximum number of addresses. In a computer that uses 3-address instructions, for example, an 'add' instruction will use all three in order to refer to the two addends and the result. But an instruction that inverts the sign of a number only needs one address to specify that number. In this case a

3-address format can still be used, but the bits regarding two of the addresses will not be made use of.

Other instructions are zero address instructions by their very nature. A 'halt' instruction, for instance, stops the execution of the program, and needs no further information in order to do this.

The variability in the instruction formats depends not only on the intrinsic nature of the operations, whether they have zero operands, one operand (**monadic**), two operands (**dyadic**) or more. It also depends to a great extent on architectural choices, by means of which 3-operand operations, for instance, can be 'squeezed' into 2-address instructions. An addition instruction in a 2-address format is interpreted in such a way that the addresses are considered to be those of the addends, and the result is put into either the first or the second address, in place of one of the two addends, according to the architectural design. The 3-address instruction format is:

C ← (A) OP (B)
C ← (A) + (B)

OP	A	B	C

The 2-address instruction format is:

A ← (A) OP (B) or B ← (A) OP (B)
A ← (A) + (B)   B ← (A) + (B)

OP	A	B

The 1-address instruction format is:

AC ← (AC) OP (A)
AC ← (AC) + (A)

OP	A

By convention, the parentheses stand for 'content of', and the arrow indicates 'is placed in'.

In some architectures it is possible to choose the destination. Operation word in the 2-operand format (where the second operand is a register) adopted by the Intel 8086 is as follows:

d = 0 : the destination is the first operand
    1 : the destination is the second operand

w = 0 : the operands are 8-bit
    1 : the operands are 16-bit

Opcode	d	w
6	1	1

The first architectural choice in this respect consists in deciding whether to adopt a fixed length or variable length instruction format. In the former case, each instruction will normally be one word long, and this word will need to be long enough to contain all the formats. The aim is obviously to use formats made up of few addresses. However, the second method is very common today because it permits a certain independence from the length of the fundamental information unit (it is universally adopted in 8-bit microprocessors, as well as in computers with greater word lengths). Moreover, it makes it possible to adopt a large number of different instruction formats without any waste due to unused bits.

Any operation which is not completed within one instruction is based invariably on the creation of an intermediate state, either of the memory or of the processor. The above example of addition using a 2-address format uses an intermediate memory state, since the result is placed in a different location from its final one.

Of course, this could be an intermediate result which does not need to be memorized permanently, but even so it would still not be a single operation completed within a single instruction.

Single-address instructions provide another kind of example. Bearing with our example of addition, the single address would refer to one of the addends, while the other would be found in the accumulator, that is, occupying a state of the processor. The result will also be placed in the accumulator, thus creating an intermediate processor state. In this case, one of the two addends was already supposed to occupy an intermediate state (see p.61, 1-address instruction format).

In general, the more addresses an instruction format contains, the less need there will be to create intermediate states between one instruction and the next, and it will be possible to carry out operations within a single instruction. Once again, variable length instruction formats are well suited to this requirement.

Some architectures have even been designed so as to have **variable length instructions** (and not just formats). This implies that the first instruction word contains, as well as the opcode, the number of addresses that follow (Example 3.1). This variability is not really limitless, since all the addresses have to be represented in the state of the processor during the execution of the instruction. On the other hand, executing the instruction in pieces, that is, considering only some of the addresses at any one time, is the equivalent of carrying out in sequence a number of instructions that transmit an intermediate state to each other. In other words, the advantage of having instructions with a large number of addresses would be lost.

EXAMPLE 3.1 _____

Example of a variable length instruction to be found on the Digital VAX.

The instruction carries out addition and can have two or three operands. In (a) and (b) are given the respective formats, together with the interpretation of the operations carried. In (c) are listed some of the opcodes (symbolic and numeric) for the addition instructions on various data types. One bit defines the number of operands, while the other seven are used for the opcode. In the ADD instruction, the bit that specifies the length is the least significant bit. In other instructions that still form part of the VAX architecture, this bit may be in another position.

(a)   Opcode add, sum
       sum ← sum + add

(b)   Opcode add1, add2, sum
       sum ← add1 + add2

(c)   ADDB2 , ADDB3   80 , 81   Byte
       ADDW2 , ADDW3   A0 , A1   Word
       ADDL2 , ADDL3   C0 , C1   Longword
       ADDF2 , ADDF3   40 , 41   Floating
               .   .   .
               .   .   .
               .   .   .

_____

Instructions with implicit reference to operands make extensive use of the state of the processor, which has the precise task of conserving the data and the information about it from one instruction to the next.

Certain fields, usually called 'mode', which serve to specify the type of addressing used, may also form part of the instruction format. However, an alternative to this method consists in allowing only certain types of addressing with certain types of instruction, and therefore to have as many opcodes for each operation as the number of permitted ways of addressing for that operation. Every time a number of information items are specified in separate fields, as in the case described above, in which one field is used for the opcode and another for the mode, the instruction format is referred to as **orthogonal**.

It is possible to separate the opcode from the data type it is applied to. In this respect, there exists a considerable diversity between computer architectures and high-level languages. In the former, for every possible operation there exist as many opcodes as data types to which they can be applied. For example, there is an adding instruction for 16-bit integers, another for 8-bit integers, another for floating-point numbers, and another for BCD numbers.

The approach of high-level languages is completely different, and nearer to the logic of the problem to be solved. There is a single operator for the addition, and the data type is 'attached' to the data itself. Such considerations have led to the concept of **tagged** architectures, in which every data item has an associated field, called a tag, containing information about its type, its length, whether it has already been defined, and so on. In this way more reliable programs are obtained, since the architecture can carry out consistency checks on the data and even do the required conversions automatically, where this is permitted.

The architecture can even realize if it is trying to operate on data items that have not yet been defined.

Although the idea of tagged architectures has many advantages, the majority of current architectures still tend to associate the kind of information above with the instruction rather than the data. The only type of separation is from the opcode, that is, there is a tendency towards increasing orthogonality. The information that is most often given explicitly concerns the length of the data items.

EXAMPLE 3.2

Two examples of instructions in which the length of the data items is provided orthogonally are:

(a)   2-operand format on the Intel 8086 (see p.61)

Opcode	d	w
6	1	1

(b)   MOVE instruction (data transfer from one location to another) on the MC68000.

OP	Size	Operand	Operand
2	2	6	6

The 'w' parameter in (a) allows the definition of two lengths: byte or 16-bit word. The 'size' parameter in (b) can specify three lengths: byte, word or longword; that is, 8, 16 or 32 bits.

3.1.1 Variable length opcodes

A machine with an instruction format consisting of an n-bit opcode (OP) allows a set of 2^n distinct instructions, which may be monadic, dyadic or with more operands. This means there is a possibility of having an OP with a length that varies according to the type of operation involved. To be more precise, bits from the address field could be used to extend the OP field for those instructions that have a lower number of operands.

An example may serve to clarify the concept. Let us consider a computer with 16 general registers and a 24-bit fixed length instruction format:

OP	R	A
4	4	16

The first four bits are for the opcode, the 4-bit field R for an operand contained in a register and field A for an operand contained in memory.

Under these conditions there are:

16 2-operand instructions

To extend the opcode, one of the 16 combinations could be used to indicate that OP is extending into field R. In this case there would be:

15 2-operand instructions (4-bit OP)

15 1-operand instructions (OP extended to 8 bits)

65 536 0-operand instructions (OP extended to the whole 24-bit word).

Even in the last case, one of the combinations of field R is used to indicate that field A is an OP with zero addresses.

The proposed scheme is presented in Table 3.1.

But clearly this is not the only solution to extending the code. One could have devoted 2 bits to specifying whether the instruction has 2, 1 or 0 addresses, and hence the respective length of the opcode. This would result in an instruction format with variable length opcode as follows:

L = 00 2-bit opcode – 4 2-operand instructions
L = 01 6-bit opcode – 64 1-operand instructions
L = 10 22-bit opcode – 4 194 304 0-operand instructions

L	OP	R	A
2	2	4	16

The above examples were given under the highly restrictive hypothesis of a fixed length instruction format. Yet most computers have a variable length instruction format. This allows greater variability in establishing the length of OP.

It is clear that one of the desirable objectives is to have the average instruction length as short as possible. This can be achieved by acting on the operand field and on its opcode.

Table 3.1 Opcode expansion scheme with: 15 2-operand instructions, 15 1-operand instructions, and 65 536 0-operand instructions.

0000	R	A
0001	R	A
.	.	.
.	.	.
.	.	.
1110	R	A

11110000	A
11110001	A
.	.
.	.
.	.
11111110	A

1111111100000000000000000
1111111100000000000000001
.
.
.
1111111111111111111111110
1111111111111111111111111

The nature of the operand field depends on a variety of situations. Its influence on instruction length will be analysed when we examine addressing techniques.

The OP field may be optimized by fixing variable codes as a function of the frequency of the instructions, that is, assigning shorter codes to instructions used more frequently in programs (static frequencies) or carried out more frequently (dynamic frequencies).

In the first place the aim is to occupy less memory, while in the second the desire is to shorten execution time by reducing the number of bits transmitted from memory to the processor. The most generally followed tendency is to base it on dynamic frequencies, that is, to assign shorter codes to instructions carried out more often. For example, suppose that in a computer we need to encode seven different types of instructions, referred to as A, B, C, D, E, F and G. If we choose an OP with a fixed number of bits, its length will have to be 3 bits. Hence, if a million instructions are carried out in a program, three million OP bits will be transmitted between memory and processor during instruction fetching.

Suppose that the frequency of the instructions is as given in Table 3.2. The objective is to obtain a frequency-dependent code. The Huffman code can be used for this, since it allows a good representation of OP to be generated in this sense.

Table 3.2 Instruction frequencies.

Instruction	p_i
A	0.53
B	0.25
C	0.12
D	0.03
E	0.03
F	0.02
G	0.02

A Huffman code is obtained by constructing a binary tree in the following way:

(1)   The instructions with their corresponding frequencies are written in a line.

(2)   The two smallest frequencies are merged into one, which is the sum of the two.

(3)   Point 2 is repeated using new frequencies and old ones that have not yet been used until a single frequency, with a value of 1.0, is obtained at the root of the tree (see Figure 3.1).

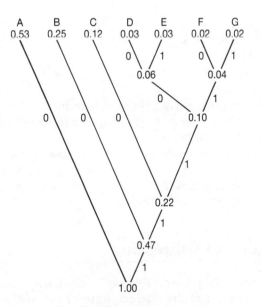

Figure 3.1 Binary tree for the Huffman code relating to the frequencies in Table 3.2.

Table 3.3 Opcodes assigned to the various instructions according to the Huffman code.

Instruction	p_I	OP	Length
A	0.53	0	1
B	0.25	10	2
C	0.12	110	3
D	0.03	11100	5
E	0.03	11101	5
F	0.02	11110	5
G	0.02	11111	5

To describe the code for each instruction, one begins from the root of the tree (1.0) and follows the path to the corresponding leaf node, writing a '0' for each left branch and a '1' for each right branch (or vice versa). In this case the opcodes are those shown in Table 3.3.

It may be noted that the shortest codes are assigned to the most frequent instructions A, B and C, and the longer codes to the less frequent instructions D, E, F and G.

The average length of the opcodes is obtained by adding up the products of the frequency of each instruction by its corresponding length:

$$
\begin{aligned}
l_a &= \sum_i p_i \times l_i \\
&= 0.53 \times 1 + 0.25 \times 2 + 0.12 \times 3 + 0.03 \times 5 + 0.03 \times 5 + 0.02 \times 5 \\
&\quad + 0.02 \times 5 \\
&= 1.89
\end{aligned}
$$

For a program that carries out a million instructions, we now have 1 890 000 opcode bits transmitted instead of the three million bits involved in adopting a fixed length opcode.

One of the disadvantages of variable length codes is that they involve greater decoding cost and hence a longer execution time. This needs to be compared in terms of execution time with the saving of space obtained by their greater compactness.

3.2 Methods of addressing

An addressing method represents the way in which the processor interprets the information present in the instruction to arrive at the operand. This may reside in the instruction itself, in a register or in a memory cell separated from the instruction. In determining the operand, the processor

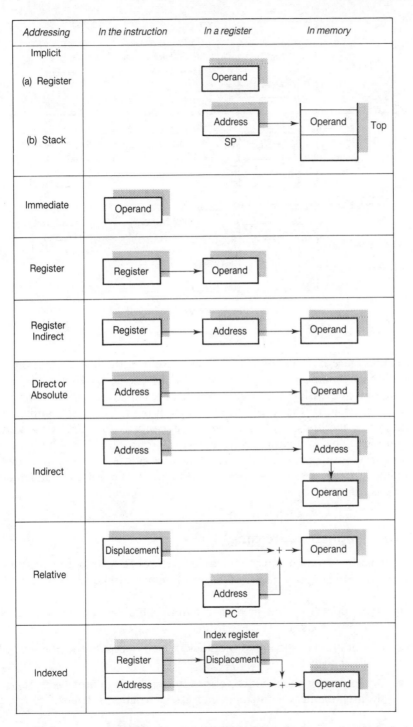

Figure 3.2 Methods of addressing. (*continues*)

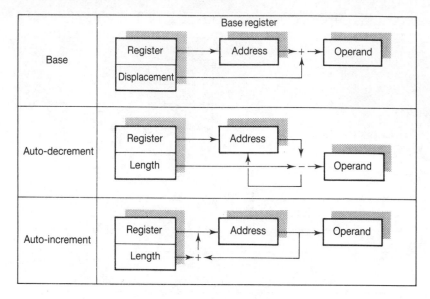

Figure 3.2 (*cont.*)

may make use not only of information present in the instruction, but also of state information in the processor or the memory. Hence, for every method of addressing, it is useful to specify which information items are in the instruction, or the registers, or the main memory. Some fundamental addressing methods, by following these conventions, are presented in Figure 3.2. The computer architectures may refer directly to these, or else may carry out mechanisms through which the addressing methods may be obtained. However, let us begin by doing a survey of the fundamental methods of addressing.

3.2.1 Implicit addressing

Those addresses that have no explicit reference within the instruction belong to this category. Some of these references already encountered are:

- the address of the next instruction, which is always kept in the Program Counter (PC) register;

- the address of the top of the stack, which is kept in the Stack Pointer (SP) register;

- a temporary value which resides in the Accumulator (AC) register, in architectures with single address instruction formats.

Leaving aside the implicit reference to the next instruction, which concerns the way in which the processor extracts and carries out the

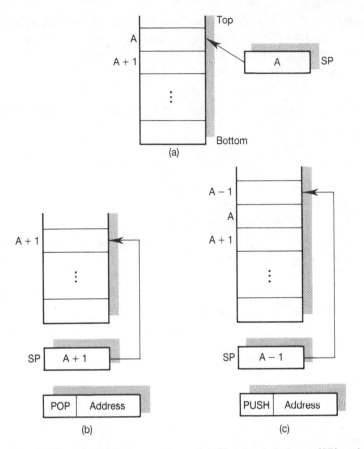

Figure 3.3 POP and PUSH instructions. (a) The Stack Pointer (SP) points to the top of the stack; that is, it contains the address of the memory location corresponding to the top. (b) The instruction POP extracts the data item contained in the top of the stack and transfers it into memory. The SP is then incremented to point to the new top. (c) The instruction PUSH transfers the contents of the addressed memory location at the top of the stack, after the SP has been decremented.

program instructions sequentially, it may be said in general that an instruction's implicit references to its operands may be of two types:

(1)   **register** references, that is, the opcode refers to a particular register;

(2)   **stack** references, that is, with instructions that use the stack pointer to refer to the operand placed on top of the stack.

The stack pointer always contains the address of the top stack. All the instructions that need to extract (**pop**) data from the stack also increase the value of the stack pointer, since the top of the stack after the pop operation is now the next data item (Figure 3.3). Instructions that wish to put (**push**) a data item on to the stack must first decrease the stack pointer, to make it point to the location where the data item is to be put. In both cases, the stack pointer points to the new top of the stack.

More precisely, stack instructions are:

- PUSH M, which is the equivalent to the following operations:
  $$SP \leftarrow (SP) - 1$$
  $$(SP) \leftarrow (M)$$
- POP M, which is equivalent to the sequences:
  $$M \leftarrow ((SP))$$
  $$SP \leftarrow (SP) + 1$$
- OP, which is equivalent to the sequences:

$(SP) \leftarrow OP ((SP))$	(monadic operations)
$(SP) + 1 \leftarrow ((SP)) \, OP \, ((SP) + 1)$	(dyadic operations)
$SP \leftarrow (SP) + 1$	

It has been assumed that the stack 'builds up' towards *decreasing* memory addresses. The contrary case, a stack that expands towards *increasing* addresses, is:

PUSH M:
$$SP \leftarrow (SP) + 1$$
$$(SP) \leftarrow (M)$$

POP M:
$$M \leftarrow ((SP))$$
$$SP \leftarrow (SP) - 1$$

OP:

$(SP) \leftarrow OP ((SP))$	(monadic operations)
$(SP) - 1 \leftarrow ((SP)) \, OP \, ((SP) - 1)$	(dyadic operations)
$SP \leftarrow (SP) - 1$	

The operations described are carried out in the way indicated independently of whether the stack is located in main memory or in a hardware structure. The latter solution may be adopted for reasons of speed efficiency, but does not modify the behavioural norms. It is even possible to have mixed structures, in which only the elements nearest to the top of the stack are to be found in high-speed memory, while the rest is in main memory. In Figure 3.2 it is supposed that the stack is in main memory.

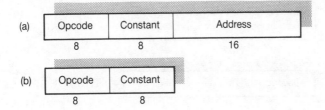

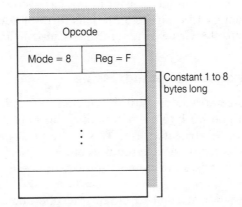

Figure 3.4 Immediate addressing on the IBM 370 (instruction format SI = storage–immediate, in which one operand is a constant and the other operand is in memory), and on the Zilog Z80. In both cases, the constant is only 8 bits long. Other architectures, such as the PDP-11, allow the use of immediate data of greater length (for example, 16 bits).

3.2.2 Immediate addressing

With this method, the operand is in the instruction itself. It is therefore considered to be a constant. This type of addressing has the advantage of not requiring additional cycles of memory, the only limitation being that of the reduced length (Figure 3.4).

In variable length instruction architectures, this limitation does not exist, as it is possible to employ immediate operands of several lengths (Figure 3.5).

The constraint of only being able to express small constants in an immediate way is not very serious, since such constants are by far the most frequent in a program.

Figure 3.5 Immediate addressing in the VAX. This is obtained through a technique known as 'mode and register' (Section 3.3). The length of the immediate item is determined by the particular opcode which may act on bytes, words, longwords and quadwords: that is, on 1, 2, 4 and 8 bytes.

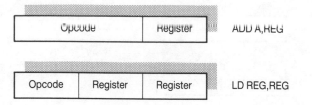

Figure 3.6 Typical instructions with register addressing on the Zilog Z80. The first instruction adds the contents of the register specified to the accumulator. The second instruction carries out a transfer from one register to another.

3.2.3 Register addressing

In general register architectures, reference is often made to these registers. The characteristics of this method of addressing are:

- Access to the registers is very rapid.
- The information needed to access the registers requires a very small number of bits and usually resides in the same word that contains the opcode (Figure 3.6). This makes for a saving both in memory and in execution time. In fact, to carry out an instruction that refers to registers, fewer memory words need to be extracted than with other forms of explicit addressing.

3.2.4 Register indirect addressing

The information present in the register in this case is not the operand but its address in memory (see Figure 3.2). This form of addressing, like the preceding, also has the virtue of requiring few instruction bits.

3.2.5 Direct or absolute addressing

In this case, the memory address of the operand exists in the instruction. The processor has no work to do in obtaining this kind of address, as it is already present in its absolute form. This is the most natural method of addressing, but it is costly, since it requires more memory bits to represent it, and therefore exercises the memory–processor connection to a greater extent.

The information needed to obtain the operand is entirely in the instruction: it is not partly in the instruction and partly in the processor, as occurs with the other methods. This permits a greater independence between the instructions, since there exists a much weaker link between the successive references to operands in the program. Fortunately, there is a fairly high degree of continuity in the references to the operands, which

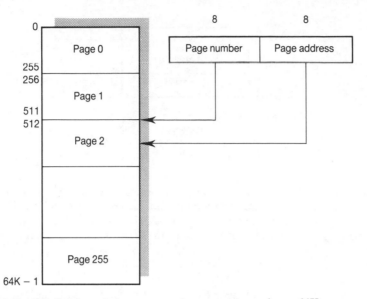
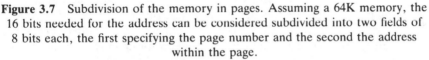

Figure 3.7 Subdivision of the memory in pages. Assuming a 64K memory, the 16 bits needed for the address can be considered subdivided into two fields of 8 bits each, the first specifying the page number and the second the address within the page.

provides ample justification for use of the other addressing methods, that make use of information present in the state of the processor, that is, the processing context that is handed on from one instruction to the next.

The need for a very large field for the representation of absolute addresses derives from the great capacity of the address space. Clearly, the length of such a field must be commensurate with the largest address that can be represented, and this inevitably means a waste of bits when referring to low memory addresses. Hence, some architectures have subdivided the memory into **pages** of much smaller dimensions (Figure 3.7), thus giving the chance of specifying addresses not only for the whole memory, but also for more restricted environments.

In these computers, **page zero** generally holds a privileged position. That is to say, apart from the absolute address, there exists also an absolute address on page zero which requires much fewer bits (Figure 3.8). Consequently, all the most frequently used operands will be placed on page zero, so as to minimize the total number of bits transmitted between the memory and the processor.

It may be interesting to note at this point that the addition of page zero addressing, though it allows the use of shorter instructions in the case of frequently accessed operands, does so at the expense of normal-length absolute addressing, since the information needed to distinguish between the two types of addressing must be added to the instruction. The amount

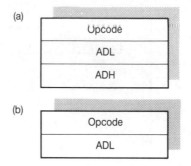

Figure 3.8 (a) Absolute and (b) page zero addressing on the Rockwell 6502. Most of the instructions that operate on data are provided with both forms of addressing. The abbreviations ADL and ADH stand for ADdress Low and ADdress High, respectively, and represent the address in the page and the page number.

of information is one bit, where there is orthogonality with the opcodes. If the configurations for the opcodes are not all exploited, and if the opcode is not required to be orthogonal with the page zero/absolute addressing dimension, some of the possible spare configurations may be exploited to generate opcodes only for some of the instructions, so that these refer to page zero. But even if we assume complete orthogonality, the weighted average of the length of the instructions that make reference to page zero and that of the instructions that use absolute addressing may be much nearer to the former, if the frequency of instructions with operands in page zero is very high.

3.2.6 Indirect addressing

In a program, the set of instructions and the set of data are, theoretically speaking, separated. If the program is correct, the set of values assumed by the program counter will consist of the instruction addresses alone. The instructions, apart from those regarding transfer of control (jumps or jumps to subroutines), make references to data to be operated on, that is, to be transformed. For reasons of symmetry, the set of these references should consist of data references alone.

Yet there is nothing in the von Neumann model that prevents one from considering the instructions themselves as data. Rather, it is one of the distinctive characteristics of this model that data and instructions share the same memory and appear indistinguishable. One consequence of this, that was judged favourably for a long time, was the possibility that a program could modify itself, or rather that it could modify its own instructions. Today, this is considered bad programming practice, since it is practically impossible to determine whether an instruction is subject to modification by the program itself when one examines the program. These programming tricks are obtained at the expense of readability and, therefore, of reliability and ease of maintenance. These considerations are so important that some architectures separate the space for instructions from that for data, at least at the operating system level. The two spaces are protected in different ways, in the sense that the instruction space can only be accessed to execute them, while the data can be modified and not executed.

While modification to the opcode is a classic example of operations that should not be attempted, this is not completely true in the case of the other component of instructions: the address field.

There are situations in which the addresses are also to be considered as data. For instance, the processing of the successive elements of a vector requires the incrementing (or decrementing) of a pointer, in such a way that this takes on the value of the addresses of the elements in the vector one after another. Example 3.3 shows a program transferring a vector from one memory area to another (assuming an architecture with a single-address addressing scheme). It can be seen clearly how the two principal instructions of the loop are modified in each cycle.

EXAMPLE 3.2 ──────────────────────────────────────

Example of a program to transfer a vector from one memory area to another, using direct addressing.

The program has been written in (symbolic) machine code for the PDP–8. This machine has a single-address fixed-length instruction format, so it is equipped with a single accumulator on which all the machine operations are defined. The transfer operations take place using this register.

The first three instructions carry out the transfer of the number of iterations to be executed, namely the number of data items to be transferred, in the loop counter N. This is done by first zeroing the accumulator, then loading the data item to be transferred into it by means of the adding instruction, and finally storing the contents of the accumulator in the destination location. The instruction DCA zeroes the accumulator, as well as transferring into memory. In this way the accumulator is ready for the next data transfer. The next two pairs of instructions serve to initialize the main body of the loop, so that it refers to the first two elements of the source and destination vectors. The main body of the loop carries out the transfer of a single element for each iteration, while the next two instructions modify the main body so as to make it operate on the next elements of the two vectors. The last but one instruction is used to control the loop, by advancing the counter and exiting from the loop, jumping the next instruction, if this counter has reached zero. Otherwise, the last instruction is carried out, jumping back to the body of the loop to begin another iteration. This program is a simplified version which does not take into account a possible carry from the address field towards the operation code. As this example serves only to illustrate the modifiability of programs, in order to introduce addressing techniques oriented towards removing the need for modifiable instructions, it has been thought preferable not to complicate the program with details that are not essential to the main aim.

	CLA	/Clear Accumulator
	TAD NW	/Two's Complement Add the contents of NW /to the Accumulator
	DCA N	/Deposit the Accumulator in N
	TAD LIN	/Add the content of LIN to the Accumulator
	DCA L	/Deposit the Accumulator in L
	TAD SIN	/Add the content of SIN to the Accumulator
	DCA S	/Deposit the Accumulator in S
L	TAD A	/Transfer the content of location A
S	DCA B	/into location B
	ISZ L	/Increment the instruction in location L
	ISZ S	/Increment the instruction in location S
	ISZ N	/Increment the loop index and check if zero: if /so jump the next instruction
	JMP L	/Execute the next iteration
	.	
	.	
	.	
N	0	/Loop index
LIN	TAD A	/Initial values of the instructions
SIN	DCA B	/in the loop
NW	−n	/Two's complement of number of iterations to /be carried out

Modification of the address field can be understood much more easily than modification of the opcode. It answers a programming need, even though the addressing techniques that we shall deal with in this and in the next few sections completely solve this problem.

Furthermore, there exists a very important category of programs, known as **re-entrant programs**, characterized by the fact that they have to be absolutely unmodifiable. These are system programs, such as compilers, which are to be used in a multiprogramming environment. In this kind of environment each program takes control of the processor in turn for a given period of time, after which it has to give way to another program. Later on it will get another turn at using the processor, and so on until it

finishes running. Supposing that two or more programs are being compiled, when one of them loses control of the processor, it must also leave
the compiler. If the latter has been modified even in one location, it can no
longer be used by the second program, and the operating system would
have to load an original copy of the compiler into memory. If the second
program had charge of the processor previously and was already using the
compiler, it would be necessary to load the copy of the compiler in the
state in which it had been left.

The rule followed by re-entrant programs is to make a clear
distinction between the part of the program that can be modified and the
part that cannot. In this way, every time control is handed over from one
program to another, only the modifiable part needs to be saved.

Indirect addressing is a technique employed to take an address that
needs to be treated as data into the data area. If we consider Figure 3.2, it
can be seen that the address located in the instruction points not to the
operand, but to an intermediate state containing the address of the
operand. Hence, it is this intermediate state that occupies the data area;
and it is this state that will be modified, and not the address present in the
instruction. This aspect can be illustrated by reproposing Example 3.3, this
time using the indirect addressing technique.

EXAMPLE 3.4 _____

This shows how to use a program to transfer a vector from one
memory area to another, using indirect addressing. It may be noted
how, in this case, the body of the loop is not modified, but rather the
variables external to the area occupied by the instructions.

	CLA	/Transfer the content of NW into N
	TAD NW	
	DCA N	
	TAD ADDRA	/Transfer the content of ADDRA into INDA
	DCA INDA	
	TAD ADDRB	/Transfer the content of ADDRB into INDB
	DCA INDB	
L	TAD INDA, I	/Transfer the content of the location whose
		/address is in location INDA
	DCA INDB, I	/into the location whose address is in INDB
	ISZ INDA	/Increment the two addresses contained in
		/INDA and INDB
	ISZ INDB	
	ISZ N	/Instructions for controlling the loop
	JMP L	
	.	
	.	
	.	
NW	−n	/Number of data items to be transferred, with
		/sign changed

N	0	/Loop counter
ADDRA	A	/Start addresses of the two memory areas
ADDRB	B	
INDA	0	/Addresses of the *i*th elements of the vectors
INDB	0	

Another important use of indirect addressing is when a program transmits a parameter to a subroutine by means of the address. This technique is much used and contrasts with that of transmission by value, which would not permit vectors or arrays as parameters. This 'transmission by address' consists in the subroutine knowing the memory location containing the address of the data item (which may be a scalar or a vector). Thus, the only way to arrive at the data item is to refer to it using indirect addressing.

In special cases, and in architectures that allow this, it is possible to have multiple-level indirect addressings. For instance, the transmission of a table of memory addresses implies the use of 3-level indirect addressing.

Another reason, completely different from that described above, is the chance to be able to refer to an address space larger than that obtainable by direct addressing on architectures with fixed length instructions (of the same length as the word). In such cases, the direct address occupies part of the word, since the other part is reserved for the opcode, while the address on the second level of indirect addressing can utilize the whole memory word (Figure 3.9).

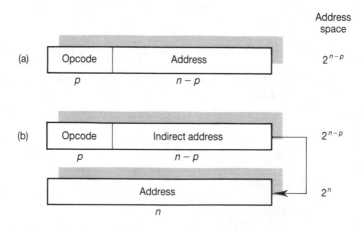

Figure 3.9 By means of indirect addressing, it is possible to widen the address space on certain architectures. This is true of those computers that adopt a fixed-length instruction format one word long.

3.2.7 Relative and base register addressing

In these forms of addressing, use is made of a general property of programs called **locality**: the references to data and instructions in a program, no matter how large it might be, are in some way concentrated in relatively limited areas of memory, for fairly long periods of time. The work area of a program changes rather slowly, which means that the references in memory show a certain continuity.

These considerations lead to the conclusion that the number of bits dedicated to the address field of an instruction need not necessarily be large enough to address the entire memory, but only an area of it of limited dimensions. Naturally, it is necessary to provide a mechanism by means of which we can:

- obtain the absolute address from the reference
- take account of the variations in the location of the area

Both of the above requirements can be fulfilled by using a register to contain the start address of the area and adding to this the reference within this area. This reference is known as **displacement** (see Figure 3.2).

In **base register** addressing, one of the general registers is used to contain the address of the memory area (Figure 3.10). More than one base register may be used, giving the opportunity to address data and instructions in a number of memory areas, wherever they are situated in the main memory (Figure 3.11). A program module may be loaded, even in different stages, in different memory areas: it suffices to adjust the corresponding base register (**dynamic relocation**, see Chapter 8).

Relative addressing implicitly assumes the program counter as base register, and therefore refers to the address of the instruction itself (Figure 3.12). The principal advantage of this method is that, if the program is loaded into a different memory area each time, no register needs to be updated.

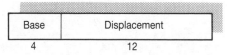

Base	Displacement
4	12

Figure 3.10 In place of absolute addressing, the IBM 370 has introduced the generalized use of base register addressing to limit the number of address bits. To specify the base register 4 bits are used and 12 bits are dedicated to the displacement. In this way, the whole memory space of 2^{24} locations of the IBM 370 can be addressed with only 16 bits, simply by changing the address in the base register. As the registers of the IBM 370 are 32-bits long even greater address spaces could be specified.

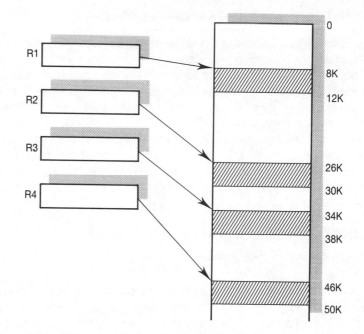

Figure 3.11 Using four base registers and a displacement of 12 bits it is possible to address 16K memory locations that are not contiguous, but resident in four areas of 4K locations each, wherever they may be distributed in memory.

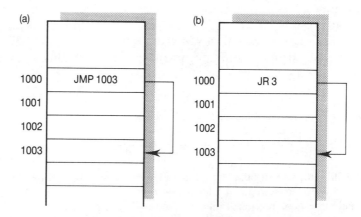

Figure 3.12 Examples of (a) absolute and (b) relative addressing instructions. Relative addressing adds the displacement to the contents of the PC (1000) to obtain the new address. Here, this address is the new value assumed by the PC, as it is a jump instruction.

In fact the program counter will automatically take on the values of that memory area. Programs that utilize this form of addressing are called **position independent**. The memory area that can be reached through relative addressing varies continuously, as it is centred on the addresses of the instructions that are currently being executed.

3.2.8 Index register addressing

This method of addressing was conceived essentially to provide a direct access mechanism to the elements of a vector. An address of this kind needs two components:

- the address of the vector, that is, of its first element
- the index of the element

Besides, one also needs to know the length of each element. This will be the same for all the elements, since we are dealing with a vector.

Vectors were dealt with in Section 3.2.6, first using direct addressing (Example 3.3) and then indirect addressing (Example 3.4). In both cases, there existed no separation between the two components, but rather there was a single location containing the operand address directly. This address was continually updated through increment instructions (or adding instructions if the length of the element was greater than one word). To avoid having programs with modifiable instructions, we were forced to use the technique of indirect addressing. Thus, not only the part responsible for the modification, in other words the information relating to the element index, but also the fixed part, the vector address, were taken out of the instruction zone.

The technique of **index register** addressing keeps the vector address in the instruction, while using a register for the variable part. The absolute address is then calculated by the address calculation unit within the processor, as the sum of these two components. The updating still remains the responsibility of the program, but this time only as regards the variable part, namely the displacement, that resides in the index register. Furthermore, the latter operation is more efficient compared with updating the contents of a memory location, such as that carried out in Example 3.4.

The reference to the index register may be either implicit or explicit. Architectures that adopt implicit reference generally have one or two dedicated index registers that can only be used by certain instructions (Figure 3.13). Very often these instructions only allow incrementing or decrementing, as well as transfers between the index registers and other registers or main memory. Even these transfers may not be allowed with all the other registers (Figure 3.14).

The restrictions involved in using dedicated registers as index

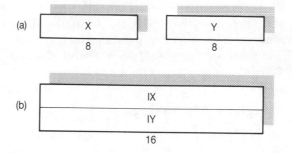

Figure 3.13 (a) Index registers of the Rockwell 6502. These are 8-bit registers, and so allow access to vectors no longer than 256 bytes. There is a certain asymmetry of use between the two registers. For example, register X can be used in connection both with absolute addressing and with page zero addressing, while register Y can only be used for absolute addressing. (b) Index registers of the Zilog Z80. These permit access to vectors of much greater size, being 16-bit registers.

registers have indubitably contributed to the evolution in the direction of general register architectures.

If index registers can be associated with general registers, use can be made of all the operations that the processor can carry out, there is no longer a limit of one or two to the number of usable index registers, and the use of this kind of addressing becomes orthogonal with the opcodes; that is, it is allowed with every instruction with operands. All that is needed is the addition of a few bits for explicit reference to the register.

INX	Increment X
INY	Increment Y
DEX	Decrement X
DEY	Decrement Y
TAX	Transfer A to X
TAY	Transfer A to Y
TSX	Transfer SP to X
TXA	Transfer X to A
TYA	Transfer Y to A
TXS	Transfer X to SP
CPX	Compare with X
CPY	Compare with Y
LDX	Load X
LDY	Load Y
STX	Store X
STY	Store Y

Figure 3.14 Examples of instructions for operating on index registers in the Rockwell 6502. Here is a particularly rich set of instructions which, though it does not exhaust all the possibilities offered by general registers, nevertheless forms a large proportion of the total number of instructions of this processor (16 instructions dedicated to index registers out of a total of 55 instructions).

3.2.9 Auto-increment and auto-decrement addressing

These two forms of addressing (see Figure 3.2) correspond to indirect register addressing, with the addition of an automatic incrementing or decrementing of the register contents, so that this points to the following (or preceding) element of a vector.

Thus vector-type data structures have a mechanism for accessing their elements sequentially. The **length** parameter represents the length of the element in number of words (or bytes) and either may appear explicitly or be incorporated in the opcode (Figure 3.15).

The use of these techniques for addressing vectors has similar characteristics, apart from efficiency, to the method employed in Example 3.4. To conform to sequential access requirements, in the case of auto-incrementing and auto-decrementing the two components 'vector address' and 'element index' are once again united.

As well as permitting efficient sequential access to the elements of a vector, these two techniques can be used for stack addressing. In this case, the register containing the address is the stack pointer, and the decrement operation is carried out *before* accessing the operand (PUSH operation), while the incrementing is done *after* operand accessing (POP operation). This corresponds to a model of stack that expands towards decreasing addresses (Section 3.2.1). In Figure 3.2 this convention has been adopted. Naturally, for stacks expanding towards increasing addresses, the opposite convention would have to be adopted. On the other hand, the order of operations is completely irrelevant (so long as it is known) for the

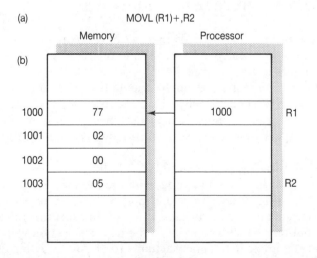

Figure 3.15 Example of auto-increment addressing on the VAX. (a) 'Move Long' instruction with auto-increment; (b) memory and processor states before execution; (*continues*)

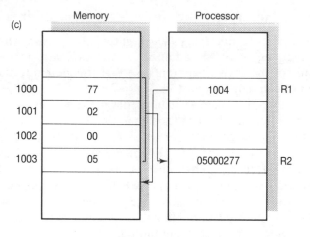

Figure 3.15 (*cont.*) Example of auto-increment addressing on the VAX. (c) states after execution.

addresses of the successive elements of the vector. Vice versa, with architectures that adopt 'mode and register' addressing (next section), we will see that the alternative of adopting the former convention is the only one possible.

3.3 'Mode and register' addressing

Many of the addressing methods that we have analysed make use of an intermediate state located in a processor register. Some use dedicated registers, others general registers.

If the architecture is strongly oriented towards the use of general registers, that is, if general registers are also used for dedicated functions, such as the program counter, it then becomes possible to use a general method for specifying addresses, which always uses information in a register.

Let us turn again to Figure 3.2. If the PC is used as a general register, the auto-increment method, with the PC specified as register, can provide addressing of an immediate kind for architectures that adopt a variable instruction format. In fact, this is reminiscent of the role of the program counter, which is to point to the next instruction word, where in this format the immediate data is actually to be found. After the operand located here has been utilized, the register used for the address is incremented (post-increment) by the length of the operand itself: this is just what the PC needs to point to the next word of instruction.

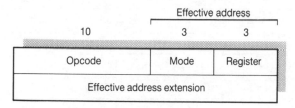

Figure 3.16 In the MC68000, the operand specifier is known as the 'effective address'. It is composed of a 'mode' field of 3 bits and a 'register' field of 3 bits. The MC68000 has 16 registers, with the result that not all the registers are used for every mode. The first word of the instruction may be followed by one or more 'effective address extension' words. The figure illustrates the case of single-address instructions followed by an extension of a single word.

Following this road, it is possible to reduce the number of fundamental addressing methods. Some of these can then be put together and applied also to dedicated registers to obtain the addressing methods desired. The uniting of certain fundamental addressing methods is so frequent that it has given rise to other fundamental addressing modes.

The term used to indicate a fundamental addressing method, in the meaning given in this section, is the **mode** of addressing. Uniting a mode-designating field with a register-designating field is defined as an **operand specifier**. The operand specifier contains the information for locating the operand.

This may, if needed, be followed by an **extension specifier**, consisting of a displacement, an address or an immediate data item (Figure 3.16).

Figure 3.17 shows the addressing modes of the VAX-11/780, together with some addressing methods obtainable by applying them to the general registers (including the PC and the SP).

Modes 5, 6, 7 and 8 have already been analysed in the sections above.

We have seen in this section how the application of mode 8, auto-increment, to the program counter gives rise to an immediate type of addressing. The constant located in the extension of the specifier may be 1 to 8 bytes long.

The introduction of mode 9, indirect auto-increment, among the addressing modes, allows us to refer to the successive elements of a **pointer** vector. It should be noted that in this case the length is no longer a variable parameter, but is fixed at 4 bytes, since the elements of the vector are addresses, and the addresses on the VAX are 32 bits long.

Just as the application of the auto-increment mode to the PC generates immediate addressing, so the use of the indirect auto-increment mode with the PC is the equivalent of absolute addressing. In both cases the program counter points to the extension of the specifier, placed in the

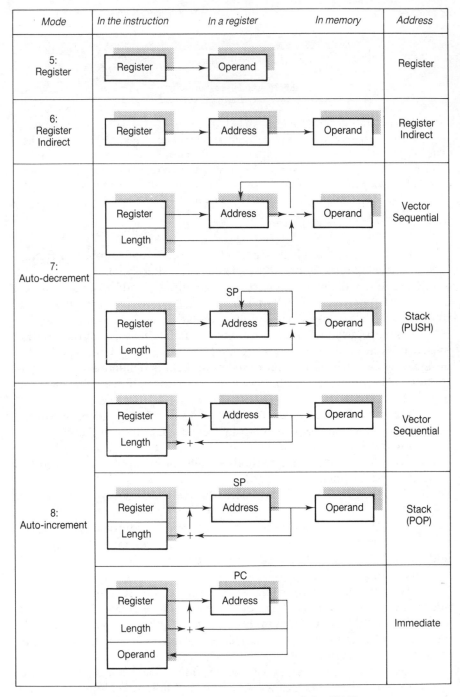

Figure 3.17   Addressing modes of the VAX.

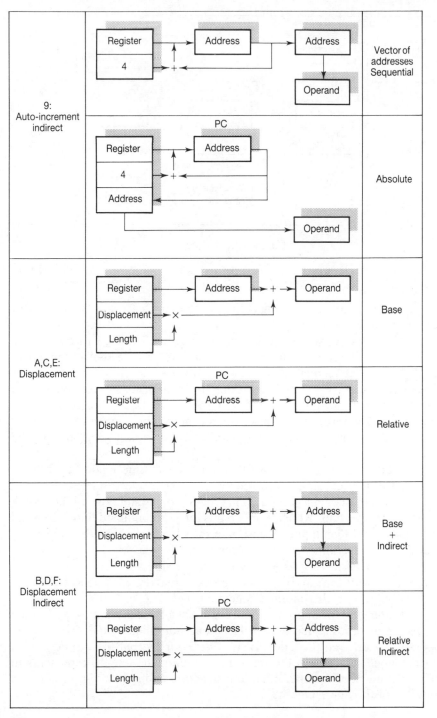

Figure 3.17 (*cont.*)

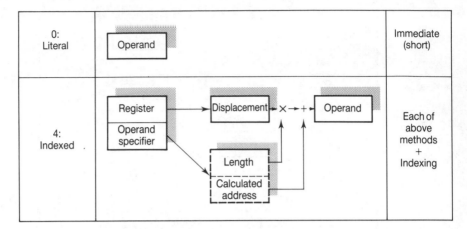

Figure 3.17 (*cont.*)

instruction itself and containing the operand in one case and the address of the operand in the other.

Modes A, C and E, called **displacement**, if applied to any of the registers, are the equivalent of base register addressing, but if applied to the PC, give rise to relative addressing. It is worth noting that there are three displacement modes, according to whether the extension of the specifier represents the displacement in bytes, 16-bit words or 32-bit longwords. The three modes have been brought together in the figure by making the 'length' parameter explicit and multiplying it by the displacement.

Modes B, D and F, **indirect displacement**, simply add the indirect address to the preceding two forms of addressing.

Mode 0, known as **literal**, is in fact an immediate type of addressing in which the constant, which is only 6 bits long, is contained in the operand specifier, rather than in the extension of the specifier. This is the only mode that does not use information in a register.

Finally, mode 4 is **index register** addressing and may be utilized in connection with any of the above modes, that is, it is specified in an orthogonal way to the operand specifier.

Using this specifier, the address is calculated normally, as for the preceding methods. Then the displacement multiplied by the length of the operand is added to this address. It is noteworthy that the displacement, since it does not contain the information about the length, represents in effect the index of the operand in the structure and not its displacement in bytes from the first element.

Further reading

Tagged architectures

Myers G. J. (1982). *Advances in Computer Architecture* 2nd edn, pp. 58–68. Chichester, UK: Wiley

VAX computer architecture

Brink J. and Spillman R. (1987). *Computer Architecture and VAX Assembly Language Programming*. Menlo Park, CA: Benjamin/Cummings

EXERCISES

Problem 3.A   The addressing methods are the techniques by which the references to information are transformed into addresses (where needed) and then into the required information.

The analysis and the formal description of the addressing methods have to be limited to the transformation that they operate in order to produce the addresses, and should not apply to the techniques by which these addresses are utilized for accessing the data.

This depends on the following considerations:

- The address produced may follow different paths inside the machine according to the type of information to which it refers. Indeed, the instruction addresses are put in the program counter and then are used for reading the next instruction to be executed. On the contrary, the data addresses have to be used immediately for accessing the memory.

- Generally, the addressing methods produce *effective addresses*, which are often subject to a transformation process before being sent to the main memory. The access to information in memory is subordinate to the accomplishment of this translation phase, which requires a systematic treatment (logical-to-physical translation, Chapter 8).

- The description of the address calculation modalities tacitly refers to the functionalities of the address calculation unit, which has the task of interpreting the data references in order to transform them into effective addresses.

These considerations suggest that it is possible to have a formal description of the addressing methods, which is also systematic and sufficiently free from the particular implementations of the addressing techniques in the specific architectures.

It is useful to define the effective address and the displacement in terms of one of the physical structures:

Type
Effective_address = . . . ; (*Word, array of Bit, ...*)
Displ_type = Effective_address;

The addresses have to be obtained in a coded form both to simplify the subsequent phase of logical-to-physical translation, and to conform to the practice of connecting the address decoding to the memory access operation rather than to the address calculation phase.

The description of the addressing methods needs a specific procedure to add effective addresses to displacements; its heading can be:

Procedure Address_add (addr: Effective_address,
displ: Displ_type,
Var result_addr: Effective_address)

In addition, in the cases in which a memory access is needed for the determination of the effective address (see indirect addressing), the empty procedure for the logical-to-physical translation can be used:

Procedure Address_translate (in_addr: Effective_address,
Var Physical_addr: Address)

3.1 Develop the procedure Address_add of Problem 3.A.

3.2 Using the procedures for accessing to registers (Exercise 2.22), describe the register indirect addressing method.

3.2 Using the procedure Address_translate, defined in Problem 3.A, and the procedures for access to memory (Exercise 2.20), describe the indirect addressing method.

3.4 Develop the procedures for the relative and the base register addressing.

3.5 Describe the index register addressing, assuming a general register architecture.

3.6 Develop the procedures for the auto-decrement and auto-increment addressing, taking into account the different order of succession of the operations of updating and of transferring in the two cases.

3.7 A linear vector is stored from the 300th location of a memory area whose start address is 1000. Each element of the vector occupies 4 bytes. The aim is to access the third element of the vector by means of the index register addressing method. What information is contained in the instruction and in the index register? If the start address of the memory area containing the vector changes, what needs to be modified?

3.8 Using the vector in the exercise above, the idea is to access the third element using base register and index register addressing together (the base register contains the start address of the data area).

What information is contained in the instruction, in the index register and in the base register respectively? If the start address of the data area is altered, what has to be modified?

What is the advantage with respect to using index register addressing alone, and what are the situations where it is better to use both methods?

4 Addressing Method Support for High-level Languages

4.1 Memory allocation in block-structured languages
4.2 Local and non-local scalar data
4.3 Variables referenced by address

4.4 Data structures
Further reading
Exercises

Nowadays, the computer architecture level is much more frequently 'seen' by a compiler or an interpreter than by an assembly language programmer. Therefore, the way the architecture supports the translators, and the execution efficiency of programs written in high-level languages, are more important than in the past. This is generally true for all the visible and invisible architectural features that have any influence on the translation process or the result.

An example of an invisible feature would be an instruction cache memory, which would speed up loop execution.

A very important visible feature, on the other hand, consists in the addressing method set: composite methods are much appreciated by the translator, so long as they can be used efficiently to address high-level language objects (variables, constants, instructions, procedures and parameters). High-level languages allow us to define and manipulate complex data structures (records, one- or multi-dimensional arrays, dynamic data lists, plus any combination of such structures). In high-level languages, multi-dimensional objects can be built up, and their individual components referred to by name. Yet at the architecture level these structures have to be transformed into a linear set of memory locations, and each object can only be referred to through an address in memory.

Hence, from this point of view, addressing methods are the

technique by which the programmer's references to data can be translated into instructions that access the data representation found in the computer's memory. In the light of this, it is of considerable interest to study which addressing methods are 'adequate' in satisfying the demands of high-level programming languages. Such methods would reduce to a minimum the number of instructions required to access various kinds of information or shorten the time needed to calculate the effective address.

4.1 Memory allocation in block-structured languages

The need to analyse addressing methods 'adequate' to the needs of languages is felt most strongly in the case of block-structured languages, such as C or Pascal. Such languages embody the concept of the **visibility** of program variables.

A program written in C, for instance, can be considered as a collection of subprograms (known as 'functions' in C) on the same level, within a Main program. These can call each other in various ways, even recursively.

The variables defined in a function (which are **local**) are visible (usable) only within that function. There also exist **global** variables (called 'external' in C), which are defined outside the functions, and can be used in any of them.

Lastly, there are local variables which do not lose their value between the various function calls, and therefore behave like externals (being allocated *statically* in memory), even though they are only visible to the function in which they are defined.

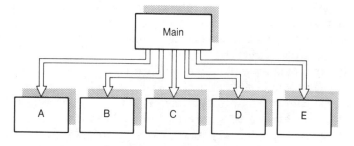

Figure 4.1 The structure of a C program.

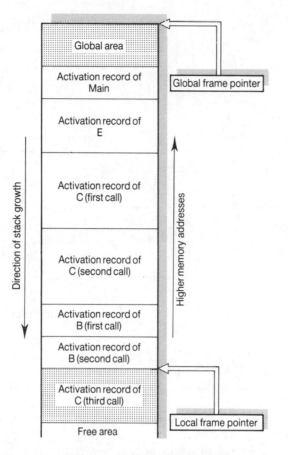

Figure 4.2 The stack after the activation sequence:
Main → E → C → C → B → B → C.

The local variables of a procedure are allocated *dynamically*, every time the procedure is activated, in an area of the stack known as the **frame** or **activation record**.

Given the nature of recursion, multiple copies of the same record may be present in memory at a particular time.

If we suppose the activation sequence: Main → E → C → C → B → B → C, in the program shown in Figure 4.1, the variables that can be accessed during the third activation of function C are those in the shaded areas in Figure 4.2.

It is therefore necessary to store the start address of the area dedicated to the variables local to C (local frame pointer) and the start address of the global area (global frame pointer) in two different registers.

In the language, there also exists the concept of **nested visibility** of

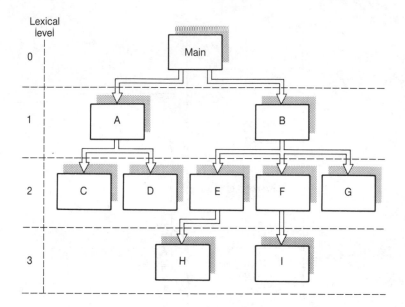

Figure 4.3 The structure of a program in Pascal.

variables, but this is much easier to understand in languages like Pascal or Ada, in which it is connected to the block structuring of the program.

This feature consists in the fact that each data item is visible in the (sub-)program in which it is defined and in any other procedure internal to it.

A typical Pascal program is represented by the tree diagram in Figure 4.3.

The term **static scope** of the program variables is used, since their visibility depends on the lexical structure of the program and not on the way in which the procedures are activated.

In the example in Figure 4.3, every object defined in the Main program is visible throughout the program, every variable defined in A is visible in A, C and D, every variable declared in B is visible in B, E, F, G, H and I and so on.

Procedures can call each other in many different ways. Yet while any particular procedure is being executed, all the procedures higher up in the program tree are also being executed; that is, all the nodes of the tree that have to be passed through to reach the procedure in question (if H is running, so are Main, B and E).

A level number is assigned to each of the nodes, starting with level 0 for the Main and numbering progressively from the root to the leaves of the tree.

It may be observed that during the execution of a level n procedure,

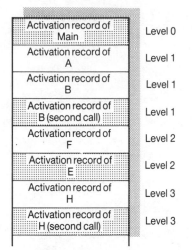

Figure 4.4 The stack after the activation sequence:
Main → A → B → B → F → E → H → H.

the activation records of all the lower level procedures along the route taken down the tree, as far as Main, are present (at least once) in the execution stack.

For example, let the dynamic path be: Main, A, B, B (recursive), F, E, H, H (recursive). The situation in the execution stack is shown in Figure 4.4, where the shaded areas represent the variables accessible during the execution of H.

The references to the variables can be conveniently expressed using two components: the **level number** and the **offset** in the relevant data area.

A data structure organized as shown in Figure 4.5 is used for calculating the addresses. This structure is known as a **display**.

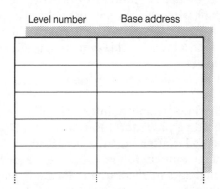

Figure 4.5 Display for calculating variable addresses.

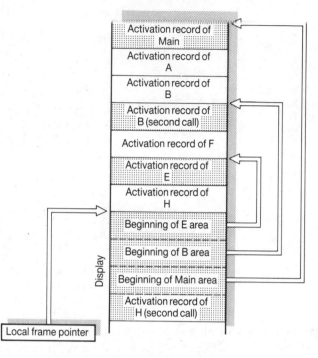

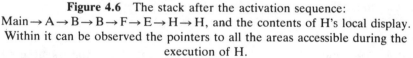

Figure 4.6 The stack after the activation sequence:
Main → A → B → B → F → E → H → H, and the contents of H's local display.
Within it can be observed the pointers to all the areas accessible during the
execution of H.

Note that the size of the display depends exclusively on the level of
static nesting of each procedure.

Consequently, in the activation record of each procedure, a local
display can be kept, containing the start addresses of every data area that
can be accessed during the execution of the procedure.

Figure 4.6 emphasizes the contents of the local display of procedure H.

To obtain the start address of B's data area while H is executing, the
position of the pointer relative to this data area is added to the contents of
the local frame pointer.

This position depends exclusively on the lexical level of B relative to
that of H $(1 - 3 = -2)$.

Note that the local frame pointer contains the address of the last
variable of the preceding procedure. Furthermore, H's local variables are
allocated by the compiler after the area occupied by the display.

From this discussion it follows that, as regards data addressing,
block-structured languages in general, and Pascal in particular, give rise to
greater problems than other high-level languages, by virtue of the concept
of data visibility.

Specifically, the type of addressing needed to gain access to a data item depends not only on its type, but also on the way it is allocated in the stack and whether or not it is local to the procedure that makes use of it.

The following sections analyse the addressing methods that can be used to access each kind of data, based on the requirements of block-structured programming languages.

4.2 Local and non-local scalar data

To begin with, it is worth remembering that activation records are allocated in the stack for each execution of a procedure, with the result that multiple copies of the same record may be present in memory at a given time (in the case of recursive procedures).

It follows that when compiling (or linking) the program, the start address of such a record is not known.

For the compiler, the only static piece of information about a variable is its displacement within the data area it belongs to.

The absolute address cannot be contained in the instruction. Rather, the compiler has to make use of a register, which is updated during execution, containing the start address of the procedure's data area (local frame pointer).

Direct addressing is therefore completely useless for referring to local data.

On the other hand, base register addressing (base + displacement addressing), with a displacement contained in the instruction, appears to be of fundamental importance in accessing **local scalar** objects (see Figure 4.7).

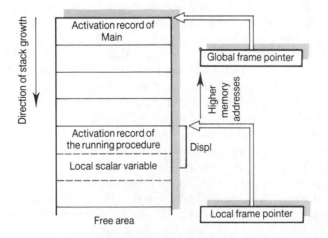

Figure 4.7   Accessing local scalar data (base + displacement addressing):
Address = (Local frame pointer) + Displacement.

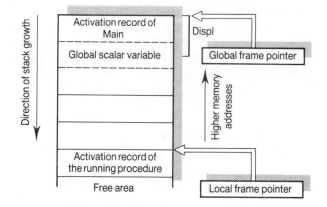

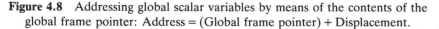

Figure 4.8 Addressing global scalar variables by means of the contents of the global frame pointer: Address = (Global frame pointer) + Displacement.

Bearing in mind that this is the kind of data most frequently used during the execution of a modular program, it comes as no surprise that base register addressing is the most commonly used addressing method. Therefore, the ability to calculate the address by this method in a short time renders program execution more efficient.

Other scalars that can be accessed during program execution are global variables and non-local variables.

Global variables can be catered for in the same way as local ones, using a register (the global frame pointer) to contain the start address of the global data area (see Figure 4.8).

Non-local variables are typical of languages that incorporate nested visibility of program objects and address them by means of the display.

The display defines the accessibility of the objects during the execution of any given procedure.

Observing the program structure shown in Figure 4.9, let the dynamic path through the procedures be: Main, A, A, B, C, D. During the execution of D, the stack is structured as in Figure 4.10.

To access a variable defined in A while executing D, the pointer at the start of A's area must first be extracted from the local display, through the contents of the local frame pointer.

The content of the pointer is then added to the offset of the scalar variable in A's data area, so as to obtain the absolute address.

These operations can be implemented in two instructions: the first extracts the contents of the pointer from the display, by means of the base register addressing method (with the local frame pointer specified as register) and stores it in a register Rx; the second accesses the variable by base register addressing, using Rx as the base register.

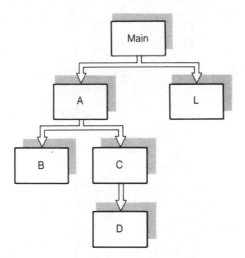

Figure 4.9   Tree structure of a Pascal program.

(1)   Rx ← ((Local frame pointer) + Displ1)

(2)   Ry ← ((Rx) + Displ2)

This is illustrated in Figure 4.11, in which 'Displ1' is the position of the pointer in the display and 'Displ2' is the position of the variable referred to within A's data area.

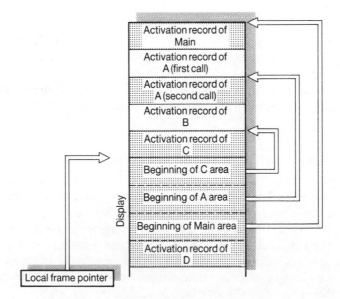

Figure 4.10   The stack after the activation sequence:
Main → A → A → B → C → D.

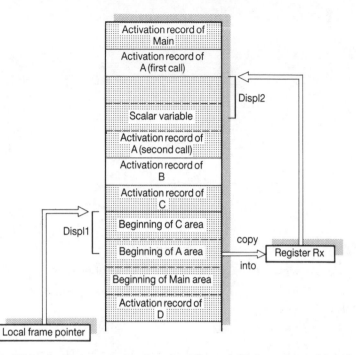

Figure 4.11 Accessing non-local scalars (base + displacement addressing):
1. Rx ← (Local frame pointer) + Displ1); 2. Address = (Rx) + Displ2.

One possible architecture support could be to provide an addressing method that allows the operations described above to be carried out in a single instruction.

The base + displacement indirect + displacement addressing method can therefore be used, resulting in the extraction of the memory word:

$$((\,(R) + Displ1) + Displ2)$$

When R = local frame pointer, the method is used to access the non-local or global scalar variables of a program (Figure 4.12).

While base + displacement addressing is to be found in most computer architectures, base + displacement indirect + displacement addressing is only a feature of some. For example, of the better-known 32-bit microprocessors, it is implemented in the NS32032, but not in the Intel 80386 or the Z80000. Nor is it available on the VAX.

In the Motorola MC68020 it is obtainable by the base + displace-

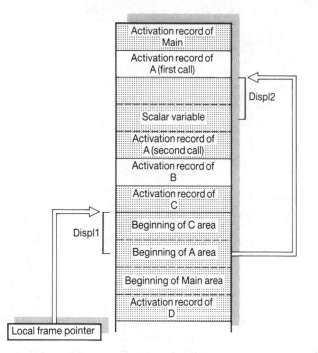

Figure 4.12 Accessing non-local scalars (base + displacement indirect + displacement addressing): Address = ((Local frame pointer) + Displ1) + Displ2.

ment indirect + displacement with index method, which calculates:

$$(((Rx) + Displ1) + Displ2 + (Ry)\ shift\_left\ N)$$

To obtain the above method, it must be ensured that $(Ry) = 0$.

4.3   Variables referenced by address

One data item whose role in programs merits particular attention is the **pointer**, or, more generally, the address of a scalar variable or a structure.

This type of object needs to be used when accessing procedure parameters that are referenced by their address (parameter passing by reference) or in managing dynamic data structures.

Pointers are either local objects (that is to say they belong to the activation record of the procedure, as in the case of parameter addresses)

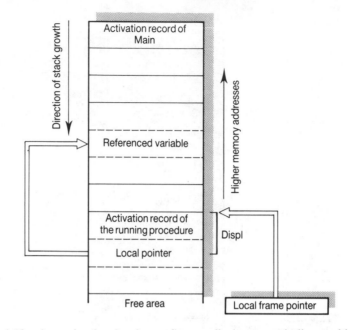

Figure 4.13 Accessing local pointers (base + displacement indirect addressing):
Address = ((Local frame pointer) + Displacement).

or else they are non-local or global. Therefore they can be accessed by means of the two methods discussed above: the base + displacement for local pointers and the base + displacement indirect + displacement for non-local and global ones.

Yet after storing the address in a register, this address must be used to access the referenced variable. Register indirect addressing is used for this purpose.

Hence at least two instructions are needed to access the variable.

A single instruction would suffice, if there were a method that considered the operand extracted by the previous two methods as an address and not just the data item required.

Therefore, the useful addressing methods are:

- base + displacement indirect, which provides (((R) + displacement)) and is usable if 'R' is the 'local frame pointer' and 'displacement' is the position of the pointer in the activation record. It is available on the VAX.

- base + displacement indirect + displacement indirect, which provides ((((R) + Displ1) + Displ2)), is useful for accessing data with a non-local pointer.

Figures 4.13 and 4.14. illustrate how they are used.

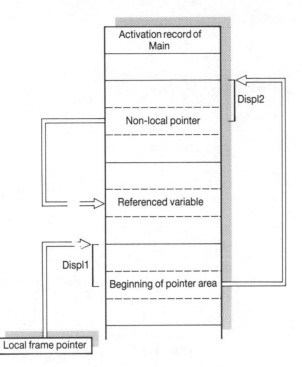

Figure 4.14 Addressing non-local or global pointers (base + displacement indirect + displacement indirect addressing): Address = (((Local frame pointer) + Displ1) + Displ2).

4.4 Data structures

One of the fundamental characteristics of a high-level language is the ability to define and manipulate complex data structures.

Frequently, the complexity of the structure (array of arrays, array of records, and so on) makes the task of calculating the address of the element to be accessed equally complex.

In such circumstances, the compiler produces a sequence of instructions which calculate the effective address in a register. Register indirect addressing is then required to give (R) (the contents of the memory word whose address is in R).

Accessing a less complex structure (a one-dimensional scalar array, or a record), on the other hand, requires a smaller number of operations and so efforts can be made to reduce the number of instructions produced by the compiler, encapsulating all the operations in a suitable addressing technique.

For instance, if the *k*th element in a **local vector** needs to be

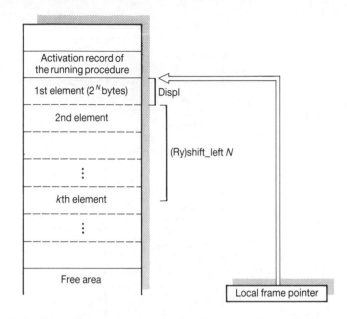

Figure 4.15 Accessing an element of a local vector (base + displacement with index addressing): Address = (Local frame pointer) + Displacement + (Ry) shift_left N.

extracted, and each element of the vector occupies 2^N bytes, the calculation will be:

$$((Rx) + Displ + (Ry) \text{ shift\_left } N)$$

specifying Rx = local frame pointer, Displ = displacement of the vector in the local data area and Ry = array element index.

This is the base + displacement with index addressing method, which is provided by the Intel 386, for instance, with $N = 0, 1, 2$ or 3, but not by the other processors in the Intel 8086 family (see Figure 4.15).

In the case of **non-local vectors**, we need to extract the memory word:

$$(((Rx) + Displ1) + Displ2 + (Ry) \text{ shift\_left } N)$$

and this operation is carried out by base + displacement indirect + displacement with index addressing (available on the MC68020 and the NS32032). This method serves the purpose if Rx = local frame pointer, Displ1 is the relative position of the display element to be extracted, Displ2 is the displacement of the start address of the vector and Ry contains the index (Figure 4.16).

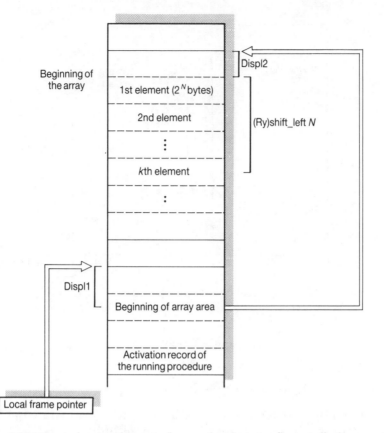

Figure 4.16   Accessing an element of a non-local vector (base + displacement indirect + displacement with index addressing): Address = ((Local frame pointer) + Displ1) + Displ2 + (Ry) shift_left N.

Finally, if a scalar array is pointed to by a variable (for example, if a vector is provided as a parameter to a procedure with **reference** modality), it is better to use base + displacement indirect with index addressing, which performs the operation:

$$(((Rx) + displ) + (Ry) \text{ shift\_left } N)$$

where Rx = local frame pointer, displ = displacement of the pointer and Ry = index.

This technique is supported by the VAX. In the MC68020 and the NS32032 it may be obtained by the previous method (base + displacement indirect + displacement with index) by nullifying the second displacement.

The addressing methods introduced above can also be used in situations other than those in which they were presented.

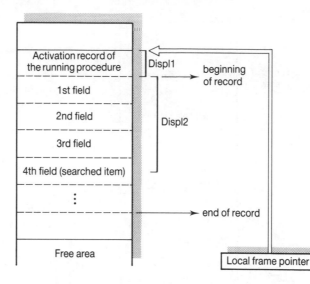

Figure 4.17 Accessing a field of a local record (base + displacement addressing): Address = (Local frame pointer) + Displ, where Displ = Displ1 + Displ2.

For example, accessing a field of a **local record** requires the evaluation of the expression:

((Local frame pointer) + Displ1 + Displ2)

where Displ1 is the relative start address of the record and Displ2 is the position of the field being looked for in the record.

Yet instead of delaying the addition Displ1 + Displ2 until the execution phase of the program, it can already be performed at compile time, since Displ1 and Displ2 are two constants of the compiler.

By substituting Displ1 and Displ2 with their sum Displ = Displ1 + Displ2, the compiler uses the base + displacement method to access the field in the record (Figure 4.17), by calculating:

((Local frame pointer) + Displ)

The same way of addressing can be used to work out more complex structures (such as **records of records**).

Let us consider the following definition in a high-level language:

```
RR: Record
     x : real;
     R : Record;
          y : boolean;
          z : integer;
          . . .
        End
     End;
```

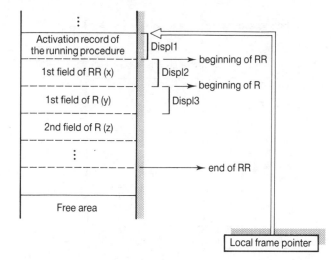

Figure 4.18 Memory allocation for the record defined as:

RR : **Record**
    x : real;
    R : **Record**
        y : boolean;
        z : integer
        . . .
       End
    End

The memory allocation for RR in the activation record is given in Figure 4.18.

Accessing field z is performed by means of:

((Local frame pointer) + Displ1 + Displ2 + Displ3)

where Displ1 represents the beginning of RR in the activation record, Displ2 is the displacement of R in RR and Displ3 is the displacement of z in R.

Here again Displ1, Displ2 and Displ3 are constants known to the compiler, which can replace them with D = Displ1 + Displ2 + Displ3 and so use the base + displacement addressing method.

On the other hand, if we are dealing with a **pointer to a record**, we have to calculate the expression:

(((Local frame pointer) + Displ1) + Displ2)

in which Displ1 is the relative position of the pointer and Displ2 is the relative position of the required field within the record.

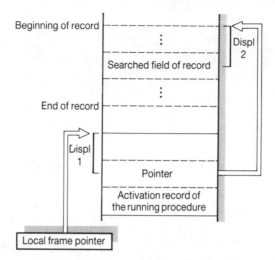

Figure 4.19 Accessing a field in a record referenced by a pointer (base + displacement indirect + displacement addressing): Address = ((Local frame pointer) + Displ1) + Displ2.

Table 4.1 Addressing methods useful to high-level languages.

Object	*Addressing method*	*Fetched operand*
Local and global scalars	Base + displacement	((R) + displacement)
Non-local and global scalars	Base + displacement (2 instructions)	1. $Ry \leftarrow ((Rx) + displ1)$ 2. $EA = (Ry) + displ2$
	Base + displacement indirect + displacement	(((R) + displ1) + displ2)
Scalars with local pointer	Base + displacement indirect	(((R) + displacement))
Scalars with non-local pointer	Base + displacement indirect + displacement indirect	((((R) + displ1) + displ2))
Local arrays	Base + displacement indexed	((Rx) + displacement +(Ry) shl N)
Arrays with local pointer	Base + displacement indirect indexed	(((Rx) + displacement) +(Ry) shl N)
Non-local arrays	Base + displacement indirect + displacement indexed	(((Rx) + displ1) + displ2 + (Ry) shl N)
Local records and records of records	Base + displacement	((R) + displacement)
Records with local pointer	Base + displacement indirect + displacement	(((R) + displ1) + displ2)

Table 4.2 Addressing methods supported by some processors.

Addressing methods			*Processors*		
	VAX-11	*Intel 80386*	*Z80000*	*MC68020*	*NS32032*
Base + displacement	X	X	X	X	X
Base + displacement indirect + displacement					X
Base + displacement indirect	X				
Base + displacement indirect + displacement indirect					
Register indirect	X	X	X	X	obtainable from base + displacement
Base + displacement indexed	X	X	X	X	X
Base + displacement indirect indexed	X				
Base + displacement indirect + displacement indexed				X	X

This operation is carried out by base + displacement indirect + displacement addressing (see Figure 4.19).

It turns out in consequence, that the applicability of the methods described is not restricted to the specific examples shown above, but can be extended to many kinds of situations.

Tables 4.1 and 4.2 sum up the uses of addressing methods as supports to high-level languages, and their availability in a number of well-known 32-bit processors.

The first table associates the most common objects found in high-level languages with the addressing methods that allow them to be manipulated. The second details the availability of the methods in various processors.

Further reading

Addressing methods on 32-bit microprocessors

Ciminiera L. and Valenzano A. (1987). *Advanced Microprocessor Architectures*, pp. 29–57. Wokingham: Addison-Wesley

EXERCISES

4.1 With reference to the contents of the stack in Figure 4.6, which derive from the activation sequence:

$$\text{Main} \rightarrow A \rightarrow B \rightarrow B \rightarrow F \rightarrow E \rightarrow H \rightarrow H$$

and supposing the following conditions:

- the start address of Main's activation record is 1000
- Main's activation record occupies 50 locations
- the activation record of A occupies 50 locations
- the activation record of B occupies 100 locations
- the activation record of F occupies 10 locations
- the activation record of E occupies 10 locations
- the activation record of H occupies 50 locations

calculate the addresses of the elements of the local display of H, together with their contents. Remember that the stack grows towards decreasing memory addresses.

4.2 In the stack in Figure 4.6, under the same conditions as in Exercise 4.1, suppose a scalar variable in the third location after the local display, in the activation record of H.

What is the best addressing method for accessing it? What are the contents of the local frame pointer? What is the displacement of the variable in the activation record?

4.3 During the execution of a Pascal program, the activation record of the Main does not contain a local display. Why?

4.4 In a Pascal program, the Main program is being executed. What are the contents of the local frame pointer? How is the stack structured? What addressing technique is best suited to referring to Main's scalar variables?

4.5 Refer to the organization of the stack shown in Figure 4.10, which derives from the activation sequence:

Main → A → A → B → C → D

Suppose that during the execution of D, we want to copy a variable in A (with a displacement of −100) into a register Rx. Using base + displacement addressing, what type of instructions are generated by the compiler?

4.6 Under the same conditions as Exercise 4.5, what other addressing technique could be used? In what way?

4.7 In the activation record of a procedure being executed, there is a pointer (with a displacement of −100) to a data item. What addressing techniques can be used to access the data item? In what way can they be used?

4.8 A pointer to a data item is passed as a parameter to a procedure with reference modality, that is, the absolute address of the pointer is copied to displacement −20 in the data area of the procedure called (Figure 4.20). Analyse the possible modes of accessing the data item.

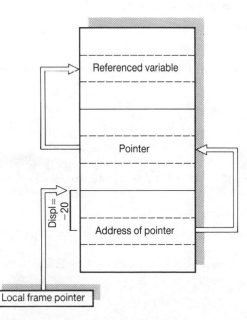

Figure 4.20 A pointer to a data item is passed as a parameter to a procedure with reference modality.

4.9 Consider the following declarations:

> **Var**
> Local_array : **array** [0 . . 99] **of** integer;
> Local scalar : Integer;
> (*the data type Integer occupies one word*)

These are, in this order, the only local variables of a procedure, and they share the data area with a 3-element local display (each of which occupies one word). How does the compiler behave when faced with the instruction:

> Local_array [50] := Local_scalar;

that is, what type of instructions does it generate?

4.10 Suppose that:

> **Var** Nonlocal_array : **array** [0 . . . 99] **of** integer;

is a non-local variable for a procedure under execution. The start address of the data area of this vector is contained in the element of the display that has a displacement of −2, and its displacement in the data area is −7.
Furthermore:

> **Var** Local_array : **array** [0 . . 49] **of** integer;

is a local variable with a displacement of −4.
When:

> Nonlocal_array [10] := Local_array [20];

is encountered, what type of instructions are generated by the compiler?

4.11 The local record:

> **Var** R : **record**
>   a : Integer;   (* 1 word *)
>   b : Real;   (* 2 words*)
>   c : **array** [0 . . . 11] **of** integer; (* 12 words*)
>   d : Char   (* 1 word *)
>   **end**;

is allocated in the activation record of a procedure starting from displacement −25.
What is the displacement of R.b? And that of R.d?
When the instruction:

> R.a. := R.c[10];

is encountered, what addressing methods are used by the compiler and how?

4.12 The vector:

> **Var** V : **array** [0 . . 99] **of**
> **record**
>   a : Integer;
>   b : Real;
>   c : **array** [0 . . .] **of** integer;
>   d : Char
> **end**;

is local to a procedure and has a displacement of −20. Calculate the number of words occupied by each element of the vector. Having noted that this number is a power of 2, state which addressing method is best suited for addressing V[3].d.

How can V[3].c[7] be accessed? (First calculate the address of V[3] in a register . . .).

5 Data Types and Instructions

5.1 Data transfer
5.2 Shift and rotation
5.3 Processing binary integers
5.4 Real number processing
5.5 Processing decimal integers
5.6 Bit manipulation and Boolean vector processing

5.7 Address processing
5.8 String processing
Further reading
Exercises

As has been stated in Chapter 3, a data type is supported by an architecture if the latter provides it with a way of representation, one or more access mechanisms, and a set of instructions capable of operating on it. We will examine the various data types of the computer architecture level, from these three points of view.

The **representation** possibility implies that a data type of the computer architecture level is expressible through the physical information structures of the underlying level, and that there are processor or main memory states suitable to contain it. The representation possibility is the essential condition for the existence of that data type.

The **access** mechanisms are nothing but suitable addressing methods that render possible or easier the access to that data type, or to its components if the data type is structured.

Lastly, the **instructions** defined on a data type represent an operational definition of the latter from the point of view of the computer architecture. They express how the architecture sees that data type, what the executable operations are, and what state transformations are induced from their application.

Hence, data types and instructions are inseparable entities in the definition of the computer architecture: it is for this reason that they are dealt with together in the present chapter.

From this approach there follows a natural classification of the instructions, which is based on the data type concept.

Some instructions modify the state of the system, simply by moving information from one point to another. It is evident that such instructions apply to all the data types, or more exactly to the physical information structures that host the upper-level data. To this category belong **transfer** instructions, **shift** and **rotation** instructions, and **input–output** instructions.

The instructions of **transformation** operate on the other hand on a particular data type, transforming it through subsequent states coherent with that data type.

In this case, the state is modified not only by means of simple transfers, but mainly through processing.

Lastly, a third category of instructions (Chapter 6) is concerned with all those that may modify the processing sequence, that is, **branch** or **control transfer** instructions. These instructions serve to define explicitly what the next instruction to be executed must be, in contraposition to the automatic sequence provided by the incrementing of the PC.

5.1 Data transfer

The simplest operation that can be carried out on a data item is its duplication somewhere else in the system. The corresponding instructions are called transfer instructions:

- MOVE, from one location to another (1), (2)
- LOAD, from a memory location to a register
- STORE, from a register to a memory location
- PUSH, from a location to the stack

Other transfer instructions correspond to actual movement of the data item from a source to a destination, without maintaining a copy of it in the source:

- POP, from the stack to a location

(1) 'Assembly-like' names will be used for instructions, even though we are dealing with computer architecture, which defines a numeric machine language.

(2) The term 'location' refers to both a memory location and a register; otherwise the kind of location will be specified.

● SWAP, or exchange between two locations.

EXAMPLE 5.1 _____

Some examples of data transfer instructions on the Motorola MC68000 where:

s = source
d = destination
EA = effective address
An = address register
Dn = data register

(a) EXG exchanges the contents of two registers:

   EXG $Rx \leftrightarrow Ry$

(b) LEA, Load Effective Address, loads the calculated address into an address register. The MC68000 has sixteen 32-bit registers, eight for addresses and eight for data. The operation codes and addressing modes are not orthogonal with respect to the two sets of registers:

   LEA $EA \to An$

(c) MOVE can act with 8, 16 or 32-bit data items:

   MOVE $(EA)s \leftarrow EAd$

(d) SWAP, in the MC68000, is understood as the exchange between the high and low parts of a data register:

   SWAP $Dn[31:16] \leftrightarrow Dn[15:0]$

_____

These operations are generally carried out on data items as physical information units, independently of the type of data represented.

In some architectures, it is possible to transmit entire blocks of memory with a single instruction.

EXAMPLE 5.2 _____

Instructions for transferring a block of memory (LDIR) and searching for an element in a vector (CPIR) on the Zilog Z80.

   LDIR $((HL)) \leftarrow (DE)$, $BC \to (BC) - 1$, repeat until
      $(BC) = 0$
   CPIR Compare (A) with $((HL))$, $BC \to (BC) - 1$, repeat
      until $(BC) = 0$

Both instructions use implicit addressing. LDIR uses two registers, HL and DE, to point to the source and destination locations of the successive elements.

The CPIR uses HL as the pointer to the elements in the vector and A to hold the data item to look for. A further register, BC, is used in both as a counter. It is automatically decremented with each transfer or comparison, and then compared with zero to determine whether it is the last element or if the processor must pass on to the next.

In other cases, the array of the general registers can be saved in memory using a single instruction. This turns out to be very useful when the processing context changes (multiprogramming, interrupt, subprogram jump) and then the original context is restored after a certain time.

The input–output instructions can even be considered among the transfer instructions:

- IN, for input from a port to a memory location or register. An I/O port contains a buffer register and synchronization circuits for transmission of a fundamental information unit (word or byte) between peripheral units and the computer.
- OUT, output from a location to a port.
- INVECT, input of a series of data items from a port into a contiguous set of memory locations.
- OUTVECT, output of the successive elements of a data vector from memory to a port.

Also the input–output operations are independent of the data type and refer to the information units (bytes or words) or to vectors of such units.

Some architectures, as will be seen in Chapter 7, associate memory locations to the I/O ports, giving rise to what is called 'memory-mapped I/O' technique. In this case, there is no need for input–output instructions any more, because it is possible to use every memory reference instruction that, when applied to one of these locations, effects also an I/O operation.

5.2 Shift and rotation

Another category of instructions that refers to non-typified data is constituted by the shift and rotation instructions. Using these instructions, the bits that make up the data item are moved one or more positions leftwards (Shift Left) or rightwards (Shift Right). In shift instructions, one or more

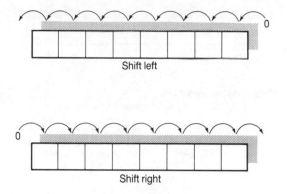

Figure 5.1 Shift instructions.

bits at one of the extremities of the data item will be lost, while some zero bits will 'enter' from the other extremity (Figure 5.1). The rotation instructions make the outgoing bit or bits re-enter from the other end (Figure 5.2).

It should be noted that in carrying out these operations no particular data type is assumed. The shift and rotation instructions can, in a sense, be considered to form part of the transfer instructions. They execute a transfer of each bit of a data item to a neighbouring position in the same data item. Since they occupy the same register or memory location, it clearly makes no sense to talk about duplication, but rather of true transfer.

In general, the transfer of a data item is performed in order to make it available where a utilization unit is present.

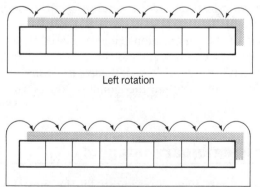

Figure 5.2 Rotation instructions.

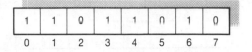

```
/Program to test the k-th bit
        RAL             /Perform k rotations
        .               /   to the left
        RAL             /   of the Accumulator
        SNA             /Jump the following instruction if AC<0
        JMP CLEAR       /Otherwise jump to "CLEAR"
SET     .               /The k-th bit is "1"
        .
        .
        .
CLEAR   .               /The k-th bit is "0"
        .
        .
```

Figure 5.3 Example of a program to bring the *k*th bit into the highest order position, where it can be tested.

Hence, it is to be expected that the transmission of bits that takes place in shift and rotation instructions is in the direction of bit positions connected with utilization units.

One type of utilization is that connected with the leftmost bit position of a word or a byte: every architecture possesses **test** instructions for this bit (Chapter 6). The shift and rotation instructions allow us to bring bits from any position into the leftmost position, and therefore give the opportunity to test all the bits (Figure 5.3).

It may be generally stated that the shift and rotation instructions, together with other instructions such as that testing the leftmost bit, constitute a sequential access mechanism to the bits of a word or byte.

Some architectures allow direct access to the individual bits of a location and provide instructions for operating on these bits (Bit manipulation, Section 5.6).

Other uses of shift instructions can be related to accessing different physical information structures, such as the byte or the half byte. Shift and rotation instructions are essential in all those cases where access is required to information units smaller than the smallest addressable unit.

5.3 Processing binary integers

The binary integer data type is undoubtedly the most fundamental data type supported by the computer architecture. It is represented both in the processor registers and in main memory and may be accessed by all the

Table 5.1 The four arithmetic operations on the Motorola MC68000.

Instruction	Length of operand (in bits)	Operation
ADD	8, 16, 32	$Dn + (EA) \rightarrow Dn$
		$(EA) + Dn \rightarrow EA$
	16, 32	$An + (EA) \rightarrow An$
SUB	8, 16, 32	$Dn - (EA) \rightarrow Dn$
		$(EA) - Dn \rightarrow EA$
	16, 32	$An - (EA) \rightarrow An$
MULS	$16*16 \rightarrow 32$	$Dn*(EA) \rightarrow Dn$ (with sign)
MULU	$16*16 \rightarrow 32$	$Dn*(EA) \rightarrow Dn$ (without sign)
DIVS	$32/16 \rightarrow 16, 16$	$Dn/(EA) \rightarrow Dn$ (with sign)
DIVU	$32/16 \rightarrow 16, 16$	$Dn/(EA) \rightarrow Dn$ (without sign)

- ADD and SUBtract operations are available for integers of byte, word and longword type. They can also operate on addresses. In this case, the lengths are those permitted for the addresses (16 and 32 bits).

- multiplication and division operations are available for integers with or without a sign. The length of the operands is one word (16 bits) in multiplication, and 32 and 16 bits in division. The result in multiplication is 32 bits long, and in division 16 bits for the quotient and 16 bits for the remainder.

Note: for explanation of the symbols see Example 5.1.

addressing methods present in the architecture. A full set of **arithmetic instructions** for processing binary integers is available on every computer.

The length of binary integer data items is the same as the fundamental information unit.

The greater the word length the better the precision of the data that can be expressed. If this length is n, the precision is given by $1/2^n$.

Some architectures allow the representation of integers of differing lengths, simply by stringing together two or four fundamental information units. (In this context see Figure 2.8.) In such cases, instructions are also provided for operating on integers of the different lengths (Table 5.1).

If this is not possible, multiple precision arithmetic may also be carried out by the program. All architectures provide support for a carry-over bit (**carry**), to store any carry-over coming from the highest order figure of the data item. The carry bit is cleared if no carry is generated. This is the only information forming part of the processor state that is oriented towards multiple precision. Multiple precision data items are not represented within the processor; rather, due to the existence of the carry-over bit, it may be said that a mechanism is provided for processing multiple precision data represented in memory as vectors of binary integers of lower precision (Figure 5.4).

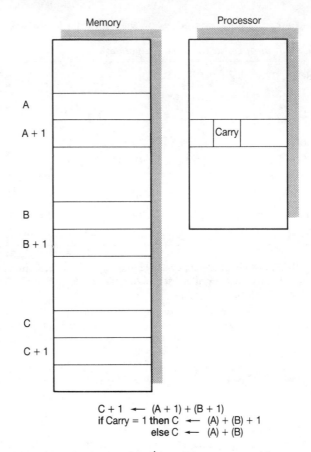

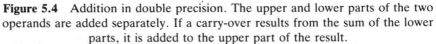

C + 1 ← (A + 1) + (B + 1)
if Carry = 1 then C ← (A) + (B) + 1
else C ← (A) + (B)

Figure 5.4 Addition in double precision. The upper and lower parts of the two operands are added separately. If a carry-over results from the sum of the lower parts, it is added to the upper part of the result.

The problem of precision is very much felt in computing because of the finite word length. In fact, the property of **closure** with respect to the operations of addition, subtraction and multiplication is not valid for integers processed by computers. This property, applied to the set of integers, states that the sum, difference and product of integers are also integers. Closure is not valid for division, as the ratio between two integers may not be an integer in this case.

However, finite-precision numbers do not have the property of closure with respect to any of the four arithmetic operations:

$$800 + 300 = 1100 \quad \text{(too large)}$$
$$040 - 050 = -10 \quad \text{(negative)}$$
$$200 * 010 = 2000 \quad \text{(too large)}$$
$$051 / 002 = 25.5 \quad \text{(not an integer)}$$

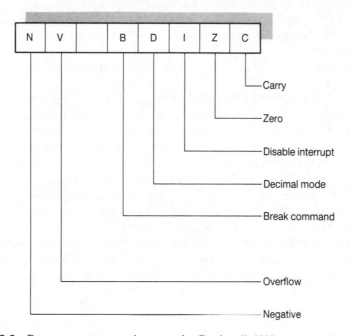

Figure 5.5 Processor status register on the Rockwell 6502. Among the status bits, also called 'flags', we can recognize the sign bit (N), the zero bit (Z), and those for overflow (V) and carry (C).

These may give as a result either a number which is not an integer, as happens with division, or else a number which may be an integer but lies outside the range of values supported by that particular architecture. While the occurrence of such an event is recorded in the carry bit for integers without sign, the processor must be able to note such a condition, and store it in another processor state bit (the **overflow** bit), also in the case of relative numbers (see next section). The instructions that follow an arithmetic instruction can then examine these bits.

Generally the result of an arithmetic operation is not limited to the primary function defined by that operation, but influences also some of the processor state bits (Figure 5.5). Apart from the carry and overflow bits, the **status word** also contains some bits representing the **sign** of the result and whether it is **zero** or not. Using these bits, the processor communicates the processing context from one instruction to the next when it is not possible to complete the required computation in a single instruction.

5.3.1 Relative numbers

The computer architecture provides support for the representation and processing of relative numbering. In terms of the quantity of information, one of the *n* bits of the word must be devoted to the sign (in line with the fact that this can assume only one of two values, + and −), leaving $n-1$ bits for the magnitude of the number.

Of course, the adjunction of the sign does not vary the range of numbers that can be represented, but simply shifts it so as also to include negative numbers.

A more important question regards how the sign should be represented. It can either be considered as an item of information separate from the magnitude, or else be an integral part of the number itself.

The first method, commonly known as **signed magnitude** representation, is undoubtedly useful for the operations of multiplication and division, in which the two kinds of information are treated separately. The sign of the result depends on the signs of the two operands, while the magnitude of the result is obtained by applying the usual multiplication and division algorithms valid for natural numbers.

On the other hand, for operations of algebraic sum and subtraction, the signs taken together with the relative magnitudes of the two operands determine the way in which to carry out the operations.

$$c = a + b \quad \begin{cases} - & |c| = |a| + |b| & \text{if } s(a) = s(b) \\ - & s(c) = s(a) = s(b) \\ - \\ - \\ - & |c| = |a| - |b| & \text{if } s(a) \neq s(b) \;\&\; |a| > |b| \\ - & s(c) = s(a) \\ - \\ - & |c| = |b| - |a| & \text{if } s(a) \neq s(b) \;\&\; |a| < |b| \\ - & s(c) = s(b) \\ - \\ - \\ - & |c| = 0 & \text{if } s(a) \neq s(b) \;\&\; |a| = |b| \\ - & s(c) = 0 \\ - \\ - \end{cases}$$

That is to say, the treatment of the sign and the magnitude cannot be kept separate in algebraic sum and subtraction operations.

To get around these difficulties, a number representation known as **two's complement** is adopted, which allows us to reduce the operations on relative numbers to the corresponding operations on natural numbers without examining the sign. There exists also another representation, called **one's complement**, which is employed by a few architectures and has slight disadvantages with respect to two's complement representation.

- The one's complement of a binary integer is defined as the difference of the number from the highest integer that can be represented:

```
11111111 −
00101001
11010110        one's complement of 00101001
```

- The one's complement is obtained by exchanging the '1' bits for '0' bits and vice versa:

```
00101001
11010110        one's complement
```

- The two's complement of a binary integer is defined as the difference of the number from the power of 2 immediately greater than the highest number that can be represented:

```
100000000 −
 00101001
 11010111        two's complement of 00101001
```

- If n bits is the length of the representation, the two's complement of a number p is given by:

$$2^n - p$$

- The two's complement can be obtained from the one's complement by adding the value '1' to it:

```
00101001
11010110 +      one's complement of 00101001
00000001
11010111        two's complement of 00101001
```

In the three representations of the sign, there is naturally a different utilization of the 2^n configurations existing in a binary string of n bits (Table 5.2). In each of the three cases, the first $2^{(n-1)}$ configurations are dedicated to positive integers. The other $2^{(n-1)}$ configurations are assigned to the corresponding negative numbers, but in the signed magnitude the order is opposed to the complement representations. Furthermore, one's complement and signed-magnitude representations assign one configuration to 'negative zero' and another to 'positive zero', creating an ambiguity that does not exist in relative numbers. Two's complement representation does not suffer from such ambiguity and assigns its $2^{(n-1)}$ configurations to an equal number of negative numbers.

The ranges of values covered are for:

- signed magnitude representation:

$$-(2^{(n-1)} - 1),\ 2^{(n-1)} - 1$$

● two's complement representation:

$$-2^{(n-1)}, 2^{(n-1)} - 1$$

● one's complement representation:

$$-(2^{(n-1)} - 1), 2^{(n-1)} - 1$$

It will be noted that a factor common to all three representations is that the highest order bit represents the sign of the number.

One distinctive characteristic of complement representations is that the sign bit is **propagated** in all the non-significant positions:

00000011	+3 in all representations
10000011	−3 in signed magnitude
11111100	−3 in one's complement
11111101	−3 in two's complement

Up to now we have analysed the codifying of the sign. Let us now examine why a two's complement code makes it possible to transform algebraic sum and subtraction operations on relative numbers into the

Table 5.2 Representation of relative numbers (for 4-bit words).

Decimal number	Signed magnitude	One's complement	Two's complement
+7	0111	0111	0111
+6	0110	0110	0110
+5	0101	0101	0101
+4	0100	0100	0100
+3	0011	0011	0011
+2	0010	0010	0010
+1	0001	0001	0001
0	0000	0000	0000
−0	1000	1111	does not exist
−1	1001	1110	1111
−2	1010	1101	1110
−3	1011	1100	1101
−4	1100	1011	1100
−5	1101	1010	1011
−6	1110	1001	1010
−7	1111	1000	1001
−8	does not exist	does not exist	1000

corresponding operations on natural numbers. It will be easy for the reader to apply similar considerations to one's complement representation.

Consider, for example, subtraction between two positive numbers a and b. This can be written as:

$$a - b = a + (2^n - b) - 2^n$$

assuming as usual a word length of n bits. But $2^n - b$ is the two's complement of b, which we shall call b'. Therefore:

$$a - b = a + (2^n - b) - 2^n = a + b' - 2^n$$

Thus we have transformed the subtraction operation into an addition between positive numbers (the minuend plus the two's complement of the subtrahend), to less than a 2^n term. Now, the result of the sum $a + b'$ may be positive or negative. If it is positive, it will give rise to a carry-over, that is, a 2^n term in addition to the result of the sum, which serves to compensate the 2^n term to be subtracted.

$$
\begin{array}{ll}
00000101 & 5 \\
\underline{11111101} & \underline{-3} \\
100000010 & 2
\end{array}
$$

If, however, it is negative, there will be no carry-over and it will be automatically represented in the two's complement codification adopted for negative numbers.

$$
\begin{array}{ll}
00000011 & 3 \\
\underline{11111001} & \underline{-7} \\
11111100 & -4
\end{array}
$$

In general, an algebraic sum can give rise to four possible outcomes, depending on whether both operands are positive, or only one is, or both are negative:

$$
a + b = \begin{cases}
a + b & a > 0, b > 0 \\
(2^n - |a|) + b - 2^n & a < 0, b > 0 \\
a + (2^n - |b|) - 2^n & a > 0, b < 0 \\
(2^n - |a|) + (2^n - |b|) - 2 \times 2^n & a < 0, b < 0
\end{cases}
$$

The first case will obviously provide a positive result. The second, however, may produce a positive or negative result c:

$$
a + b = (2^n - |a|) + b - 2^n = \begin{cases}
(c + 2^n) - 2^n = c & c > 0 \\
(2^n - |c|) - 2^n & c < 0
\end{cases}
$$

The same is true in the third case. Finally, the fourth case, in which both a and b are negative, can only provide a negative result, with carry-over:

$$
\begin{aligned}
a + b &= (2^n - |a|) + (2^n - |b|) - 2 \times 2^n \\
&= (2^n - |c|) + 2^n - 2 \times 2^n \\
&= (2^n - |c|) - 2^n
\end{aligned}
$$

obtaining the standard two's complement representation for negative numbers.

The use of two's complement arithmetic, together with the finite representation of numbers, leads to automatic processing of the 2^n quantities to be added or subtracted, since these constitute carry-overs or borrowings from the highest order figure.

Overflow can arise only if the relative numbers are of the same sign. In fact, the sum of two positive numbers may generate a carry on to the sign position, and then give a 'negative' result.

Analogously, the sum of two negative numbers may give a 'positive' result if there is not a carry on to the sign position.

On the contrary, the sum of two numbers of opposite signs will be negative or positive according to the relative sizes of the respective modules, but will always be within the range of the relative numbers supported by the architecture, because its absolute value is smaller than at least one of the absolute values of the operands.

From the previous analysis it follows that the overflow bit must be set when the carry bit and the carry on to the sign position ('overflow carry') are different. Indeed, the condition:

$$(\text{Carry} = 0, \ \text{Overflow Carry} = 1)$$

corresponds to the case of overflowing from the sum of two positive numbers towards the region of negative numbers.

The opposite:

$$(\text{Carry} = 1, \ \text{Overflow Carry} = 0)$$

denotes an overflow arising from adding two negative numbers towards the set of positive numbers.

On the other hand, numbers of opposite sign cannot generate different carry and overflow carry bits. In this case, in fact, when there is an overflow carry, there will also be a carry, while, if there is not overflow carry, neither can a carry be produced. Hence the above-mentioned rule is demonstrated to be valid also for numbers of opposite signs.

Apart from the instructions for carrying out the four arithmetic operations, there usually exist increment, decrement, two's complement or

Table 5.3 Arithmetic instructions.

Instruction	Function
ADD	Addition of binary integers
ADDC	Like ADD but utilizing the preceding carry
SUB	Subtraction between binary integers
SUBC	Like SUB but utilizing borrowing
MUL	Multiplication between binary integers
DIV	Division between binary integers
INC	Increment
DEC	Decrement
NEG	Change of sign
EXT	Extension of the sign into the next byte or word
ASL	Left arithmetic shift (multiplication by 2)
ASR	Right arithmetic shift (division by 2)

negation, and sign extension instructions for working in multiple precision (Table 5.3).

There also exist arithmetic shift instructions which, compared with true shifts, take account of the presence of the sign. This means that they propagate the sign for right shift operations, but keep it unchanged (shifting only the $n-1$ bits remaining) for left shift operations (Figure 5.6). These are very efficient when multiplications or divisions to the power of 2 need to be carried out.

Some further observations may be made about Table 5.3. It can be seen that some architectures provide, among the four arithmetic opera-

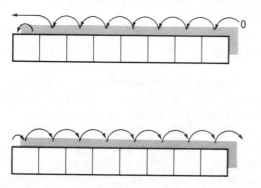

Figure 5.6 Arithmetic shifts, leftwards and rightwards, for numbers adopting two's complement representation.

tions, addition with carry and subtraction with borrowing. Carry and borrow share the same status bit, the carry bit. In the case of a subtraction with borrowing, the carry bit records that a borrowing has taken place. Addition with carry-over and subtraction with borrowing facilitate the programming of multiple precision arithmetic, since no instructions are required to test carry. This is also true of the EXT sign extension instruction.

The instructions MUL and DIV require that the destination and the dividend, respectively, be in double precision, if we wish to guarantee maintenance of the precision normally provided by the architecture.

5.4 Real number processing

Computer architectures generally provide only an optional opportunity of operating on real numbers (also called 'floating point'). Here, additional registers are used with a greater length than the other registers (Figure 5.7). Also the memory representation makes use of two or more words. Of course, this is unless the architecture contains words long enough to contain a real number.

The notation used to represent real numbers is usually known as **normalized exponential notation**:

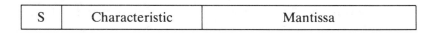

S	Characteristic	Mantissa

where:

- **S** is the sign of the number
- **characteristic** represents the exponent to which an appropriate base is assumed to be raised
- **mantissa** or **fraction** is the numeric magnitude with the radix point generally supposed to be to the left of the most significant figure

The real number is the product of the mantissa by the base raised to the characteristic. The sign refers to the mantissa. The exponent is generally represented with an **excess** given by the semi-interval of values that the characteristic can assume. For instance, if the bits dedicated to the characteristic are 7, the excess becomes 64, meaning that the numbers from 0 to 63 represent the negative exponents from −64 to −1, while the numbers from 64 to 127 represent the exponents from 0 to 63. In general:

characteristic = excess + exponent

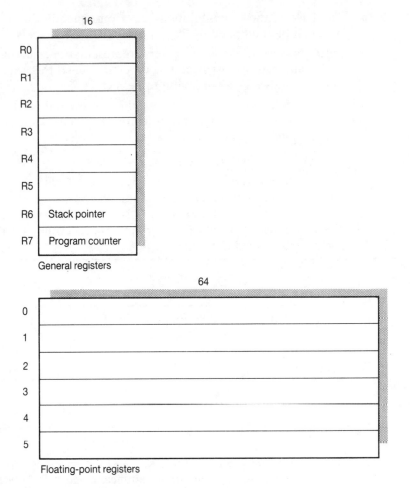

Figure 5.7   Registers on the PDP-11.

Examples 5.3 and 5.4 show two very common formats for floating-point representation.

EXAMPLE 5.3

Floating-point format in single precision established by the IEEE:

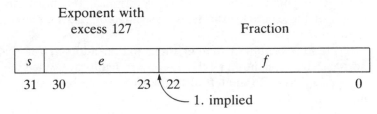

- The base of the representation is 2. Consequently the mantissa will be multiplied by 2^{e-127}, since 127 is the excess.
- Since the mantissa is in binary representation, its most significant figure must necessarily be '1', hence this can be implied, allowing the precision to be increased.
- The binary point is understood, in this representation, to be to the *right* of the first significant figure, such that the value of a floating-point number is given by:

$$(-1)^s \times 2^{e-127} \times 1.f \qquad \text{for } 0 < e < 255$$

- Exponent values equal to 0 and to 255 are reserved in order to represent, for corresponding *f*-values, the value 'zero', 'infinity', or symbolic values known as NAN (= not a number). These are used to convey information concerning invalid results and status information.

EXAMPLE 5.4

Single precision format for floating-point numbers on the VAX:

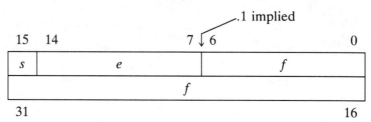

- The base of the representation is 2, and the excess is 128. In the mantissa, the highest order significant figure is implied, with the binary point to its *left*. Consequently, the value of a floating-point number is given by:

$$(-1)^s \times 2^{e-128} \times .1f \qquad \text{for } 0 < e \leqslant 255$$

- If $e = 0$ and $s = 0$, the value is equal to zero. If $e = 0$ and $s = 1$, the value is reserved.

Figure 5.8 provides examples of normalized notation.

The length of the mantissa determines the **precision**, while the length of the characteristic fixes the **range** of real numbers that can be represented.

It may be noted that in the notation adopted for real numbers, normalized exponential, all the figures are significant, since the radix point is supposed to be to the left or to the right of the highest order significant figure.

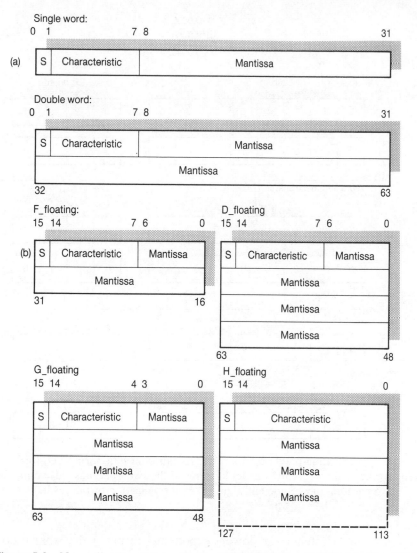

Figure 5.8 Normalized notations for the IBM 370 (a) and VAX (b). The IBM 370 characteristics are to base 16, giving a greater range than the VAX at the expense of precision.

No matter how high the precision may be, the significance of the figures of a number in normalized notation may be fictitious, due to the subsequent loss of accuracy in numerical calculations.

The range of real numbers that can be represented in a computer architecture is usually fairly wide, as can be seen from Figure 5.8. Nevertheless, a situation of **overflow** or **underflow** can arise due to the

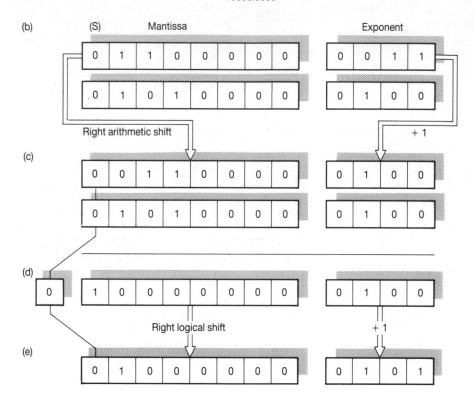

(a)
$$110.0000 +$$
$$1010.0000$$
$$10000.0000$$

Figure 5.9 Floating-point addition. (a) Operation in non-normalized format; (b) normalized representation; (c) aligning of the two operands; (d) addition separating magnitude and sign; (e) renormalization of the result.

presence of a higher or lower exponent, respectively, than those permitted.

For real numbers, it will have been observed, a signed-magnitude representation is used. Arithmetic operations on real numbers must therefore act on three components: sign, mantissa and characteristic.

The addition and subtraction operations involve the usual aligning of the two operands, which consists in right-shifting (arithmetic shift) the operand with the smaller exponent and correspondingly incrementing its exponent until it becomes equal to the exponent of the other operand.

Figure 5.9 shows an example with 7-bit mantissa numbers, with 1 bit for the sign, and 4 bits of exponent in base 2 (without excess). The binary point is supposed to be to the left of the most significant figure. The result

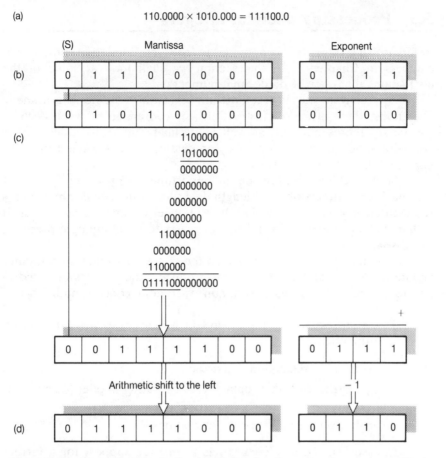

(a)   110.0000 × 1010.000 = 111100.0

Figure 5.10 Multiplication in floating point. (a) Operation in non-normalized format; (b) normalized representation; (c) multiplication separating sign, magnitude and exponent; (d) renormalization of the result. (Note that in (c) it has been necessary to add a non-significant '0' since the result is to contain 14 fractional figures.)

may need to be normalized, as shown in the figure, if a carry is generated. The normalization operation consists in a right shift with a corresponding increment of the exponent.

The case of multiplication is simpler, since there is no need for alignment of the two factors. The sign of the result will obviously depend on the signs of the two operands; the mantissa of the result will be given by the product of the two mantissas, while the exponent will be given by the sum of the exponents. The result may require a further normalization operation (Figure 5.10.)

5.5 Processing decimal integers

Reference has already been made to the representation of decimal numbers in Chapter 2. In this section we shall look at some of the instructions that operate on decimal numbers.

Apart from the instructions for executing the four arithmetic operations, there also exist instructions for **conversion** between decimal and binary representations, as well as **decimal shift** instructions. Other normally supplied instructions are for passing from **packed** format to **unpacked** format and vice versa.

Some architectures provide the opportunity of operating on data of variable length, others on fixed-length data such as the two decimal figures represented in packed format in a byte. Longer decimal strings are dealt with in such architectures by utilizing the carry to effect multiple-precision calculations.

Decimal arithmetic is supported today not only on large computer architectures, but also in cheap mass-produced microprocessors used in pocket calculators. The most common operations concern addition and subtraction.

There are essentially three ways in which an architecture can do decimal arithmetic:

(1) by means of dedicated instructions;
(2) using instructions that define the operating mode (decimal or binary);
(3) through 'decimal adjustment' instructions.

In case (2), the architecture has to provide support for a further status bit, a **decimal flag**, which is set to '1' and left in this state all the time that instructions in decimal are being carried out. The instructions that operate on this bit are:

● SED, Set Decimal
● CLD, Clear Decimal

After a CLD instruction, the arithmetic instructions are once more interpreted as instructions on binary integers.

Case (3) provides for an arithmetic operation in decimal to be effected by two instructions in sequence: the corresponding binary instruction and the decimal adjustment instruction DAA (Decimal Adjust for Add) or DAS (Decimal Adjust for Subtract) and these must be performed for every instruction in decimal.

Figure 5.11 provides an example of addition and subtraction using 'mode', and Figure 5.12 shows an example with the decimal adjustment instruction.

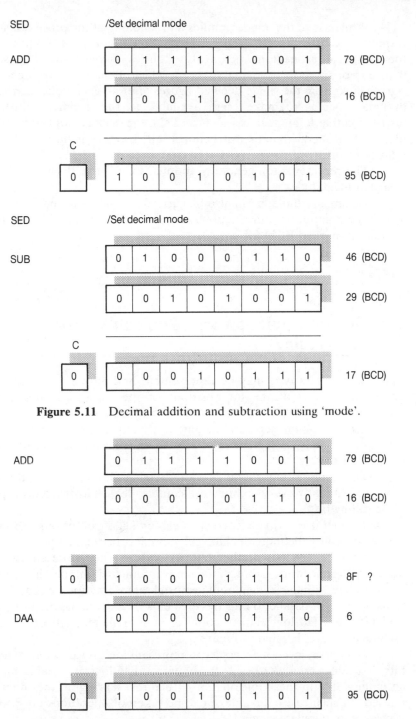

Figure 5.11 Decimal addition and subtraction using 'mode'.

Figure 5.12 Decimal addition using the decimal adjustment instruction.

While use of the 'mode' implies a broadening of the processor status to indicate the range of validity of decimal operations, the method using the decimal adjustment instruction also requires a broadening of the status with one or more bits (auxiliary carry), which memorize any carries (or borrowings) from the single decimal figures after an arithmetic instruction in binary, so as to make them available to the decimal adjustment instruction that follows. In cases (1) and (2), the decimal adjustment takes place within the arithmetic instruction itself, so there is no need for this kind of status.

The representation generally adopted for relative decimal numbers is signed magnitude.

Decimal arithmetic can also be carried out on unpacked BCD data, and decimal adjustment instructions are provided for this, similar to those for data in packed BCD format.

5.6   Bit manipulation and Boolean vector processing

The Boolean data type may be represented, both in memory and in the processor, in any of the bit positions of the respective fundamental information structures (memory locations and registers).

The minimum addressable unit is usually the byte or the word. These units consist of aggregates of bits, so they permit the representation of **Boolean vectors**.

Thus, the normal methods of addressing allow access to this data type, and similarly every architecture contains **logical instructions** capable of operating on it.

Though it is formally correct to call an aggregate of bits a Boolean vector, in reality the individual logical variables that make up its elements are rarely homogeneous. In the majority of cases, they represent the state of very different entities, though they may interact within the same system.

In line with the principles of vectorial representation, logical instructions operate in parallel on all the elements of the vector, or, as is often said 'bit wise'. The logical instructions present in the majority of computer architectures are detailed in Figure 5.13.

Of course, it is not necessary to represent logical variables for all the bits that make up a word or byte. Even a single logical variable may be accommodated in these information structures, leaving all the other bits unused. In such cases, advantage can be taken of operations on Boolean vectors to manipulate single bits.

The AND operation may be usefully employed to isolate single

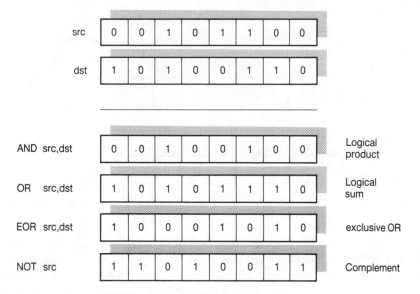

Figure 5.13 Logical instructions.

logical variables (Figure 5.14) or groups of logical variables (Figure 5.15) from a Boolean vector.

An AND is performed between the latter and a Boolean vector containing '1' in the positions that we want to extract and '0' in the others. The operation is often referred to as 'masking' of the undesired bits, and the vector that is used for this purpose is known as a **mask**.

The possibility of isolating single bit positions is generally related to

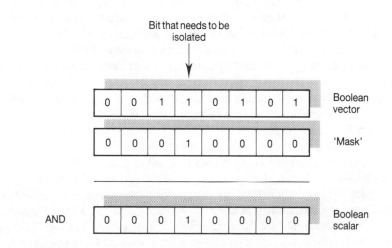

Figure 5.14 Use of the AND instruction to isolate a single bit.

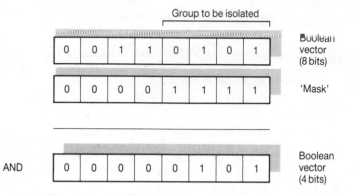

Figure 5.15 Use of the AND instruction to isolate groups of logical variables.

being able to examine them without resorting to shift instructions. In fact, after isolating the desired variable, as in Figure 5.14, it is enough to treat the resulting data item as a binary integer and apply the 'Test if zero' instruction to it (see Section 6.2). The 'masking' operation will give rise to all '0's, or all '0's and a '1' in the bit position to be examined, corresponding, respectively to whether this variable is '0' or '1'.

Hence, this is a demonstration of what was stated in Chapter 3 about the possibilities of reducing a data type to a more fundamental one for which operations have already been defined.

An advantage of carrying out the 'test bit' operation through AND and 'Test if zero' instructions on integers, with respect to the shift and 'test if negative' method outlined in Section 5.2 and in Figure 5.3, is that the former method always requires two instructions, whereas the other depends on the position of the bits to be tested.

Returning to the AND and 'test if zero' sequence, the observation made about using an operation defined for integer data ('test if zero') for a test on a logical variable may be revised if we analyse the 'test if zero' instruction more carefully. A relative number may be positive, negative or null, and there exist a corresponding number of test instructions. But while negativeness or positiveness are prerogatives of relative numbers, this cannot be said of zero. In fact, the 'test if zero' instruction can also be interpreted as 'test if all the bits are zero', that is, as an instruction that operates on Boolean vectors. So, if anything, operations on integer data types can be reduced to operations on Boolean vectors.

Similar considerations may be made in other cases. For instance, the 'test if negative' and 'test if positive' operations are in effect tests on the highest order bit, and therefore operations on single logical variables. In the same way, the previously encountered operations SED (Set Decimal) or CLD (Clear Decimal) are manipulations of single bits, but the function that these operations were conceived for is far removed from this, and it is this that defines them, rather than their real way of operating.

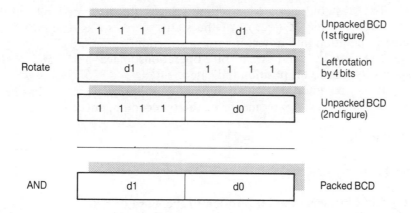

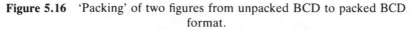

Figure 5.16 'Packing' of two figures from unpacked BCD to packed BCD format.

Another frequently required operation is that of **packing**, namely uniting together a number of fields. Figures 5.16 and 5.17 show two examples of the use of logical instructions for this purpose. Such cases involve other data types that have taken advantage of the existence of operations defined for Boolean vectors.

The requirement of operating directly on single bits has become quite important in many cases. Many modern architectures possess **bit manipulation** instructions. The most common ones are:

Test	bit, dst
Set	bit, dst
Clear	bit, dst
Test and set	dst

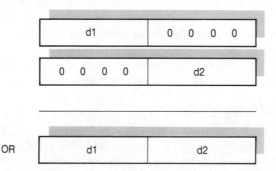

Figure 5.17 Packing of two fields 'd1' and 'd2' by means of the OR operation. In this case the other parts must be zeroed.

The 'test bit' instruction simply places the indicated bit (or its complement) in flag Z ('zero') of the status word, so as to convert the decision operation into a 'test if zero' instruction.

The 'set bit' and 'clear bit' operations place a '1' and a '0', respectively, in the bit position indicated.

It may be noted that, in all three of these instructions, use has been made of 'bit addressing' by means of the two components:

bit, dst

where:

- 'bit' represents the bit position in the word or byte;
- 'dst' represents the address of the destination byte or word.

The 'test and set' instruction is different from the others and is rather special in its application. Its usefulness manifests itself above all in operating systems that have to manage concurrent processes. It brings together the two functions of 'test' and 'set', namely transferring the bit value of a particular position in the word into a status word flag and setting '1' in the original bit. An essential condition in concurrent processing, as we shall see, is the indivisibility of these two operations, and for this reason they have been united in a single machine instruction.

5.7 Address processing

The 'address' data type is normally borrowed by the 'binary integer without sign' data type.

It can be represented either in memory or in the registers. In memory, it may occupy a multiple of fundamental information units. In this case, it will make use of instructions that operate on data in multiple precision. A similar situation may occur with register representation in those architectures that permit the chaining of registers.

In architectures in which chainable registers do not exist, a difference in length between the address data type and the fundamental information unit makes it necessary to have specific address registers available.

These imply the definition of specific instructions. In some cases, the availability of such registers of greater length, with their own instruction set, allows easy processing of integers in multiple precision.

Certain forms of addressing require the presence of address registers (specific or general) such as index registers or the stack pointer. The architecture should provide specific instructions if the registers are specific.

In the above discussion the address has been considered as a particular data type. Actually, as was shown in Section 2.5.3, it is a **component** of a data item.

While the values of the data are the primary object of processing of programs, it is not uncommon for the address to become the object of processing. When this happens, it may:

(1) be treated as a data item, or

(2) maintain its characteristic as a data component.

In case (1), the address component becomes the value of a new data item, with its own address and type. Anything that is processed by the processor can be treated in this way, be it the data type, the instructions, the opcodes, or others, which become the object of processing of programs at a higher level. Machine code interpreters written in machine code themselves, or in high-level languages, behave in this way. Programs of this kind are the simulators of architectures and, for virtual instructions, the operating systems.

Yet the need to process addresses is not restricted to this particular type of program, but may arise in any program.

Furthermore, while the other objects mentioned are mainly concerned with decoding operations, addresses are subject to much more complex processing operations. More precisely, to obtain an effective address from the various address information elements present in the instruction, the processor has to carry out so many operations that it needs its own internal **address calculation unit** (see Chapter 7). All these processing operations would be excessively complex, and therefore inefficient, for them to be realized in machine code (or worse still a high-level language).

Some architectures, particularly those of the 16- and 32-bit microprocessor generation, allow access to the address component of the data.

The address is first calculated according to the procedures described in the operand field and then transferred into the register indicated, or 'pushed' on to the stack, as in the Motorola MC68000.

(a) On the Zilog Z8000:

    LDA R, srg   R ← srg

(b) On the Intel 8086:

    LEA R, srg   R ← srg

(c) On the Motorola MC68000:

    LEA EA, An   An ← EA
    PEA EA   (SP) ← EA

This means that when one of these instructions refers to a data item, it is not its value that is considered but its address; not the content of the memory location referred to but the address itself.

This practice allows us to preserve the conceptual unity of the data item, since some instructions are oriented towards its value, others towards its address. On the other hand, the necessity of creating a new data item whose value is the address of the true data item leads to the separation of the two components, also in conceptual terms.

But the presence of instructions that access the address is important also for the dynamic characteristics linked to this component. Indeed, the calculated value of an address depends on many factors, some of which may not be arrived at directly through the program. For instance, a relative address depends on the value of the program counter, which is not accessible from the program itself. Besides, the relative address depends on where the program is loaded, that is, it is dynamically variable with the position of the program.

5.8   String processing

Because of the way in which the von Neumann architecture has been defined, it should not allow primitive operations on strings of bytes or words to be carried out. In fact, an operation of this kind would have to apply to all the elements of the strings involved at the same time.

It is necessary, however, to distinguish between the way in which the processor carries out the operations and the amount of computation that can be expressed in a single machine instruction. The processor is only able to process one fundamental information unit at a time, so the processing of strings must necessarily involve the sequentialization of the string elements. This may correspond to programming solutions at machine code level of two types:

(1)   The sequence is also present in the machine code instructions.

(2)   The computation required is expressed in a single instruction, but this is transformed into a sequence at the processor level (into microinstructions in the microprogrammed interpreter).

The transformation of an originally parallel task into a sequential one involves the creation of intermediate processor or main memory states to contain:

- One or two **pointers** to the successive elements of the string or strings, which are incremented or decremented with each pass through the sequence;

● a **counter** to count the number of passes through the sequence, which on each pass is compared with the number of elements in the string (the length of the string).

An architecture that is oriented towards dealing with strings must at least possess addressing mechanisms with automatic incrementing or decrementing, so as to express the operation on the individual element in the string and the increment or decrement in its address in a single instruction. It is possible to realize this with general register architectures, which include these addressing techniques, as we have seen in Chapter 3.

In recent years, type (2) architectures have become increasingly widespread. In these it is possible to express some string functions through single instructions. Each of these instructions includes not only operations of incrementing or decrementing of the pointers but also advancing the counter and comparing it with the number of elements.

There exist essentially two ways in which the problem has been faced. One consists in providing the architecture both with instructions for operating on a single element and instructions for the whole string.

EXAMPLE 5.5 _____

Examples of string transfer instructions on the Z8000. 'R' is one of the general registers into which the programmer needs to insert, in advance, the value of the number of elements to be transferred. After the transfer of each element, both instructions update the pointers 'dst', 'srg' and the counter 'R'. Instruction (b) automatically repeats the operation until the counter is zeroed, while instruction (a) carries out the transfer of a single element.

This example, like those which follow, show the instructions that operate on strings of bytes. The Z8000 also permits operations on strings of words.

(a)   LDIB   dst, srg, R   *Load and Increment*
                              dst ← (srg)
                              dst + 1 ; srg + 1
                              R ← (R) − 1

(b)   LDIRB   dst, srg, R   *Load, Increment and Repeat*
                              dst ← (srg)
                              dst + 1 ; srg + 1
                              R ← (R) − 1
                              Repeat until R = 0

Another way, instead, adopts only instructions which operate on a single element, and carries out string processing by preceding these instructions with a **repetition** 'prefix'.

EXAMPLE 5.6 _____

The instruction MOVC, in the Intel 8086, transfers a byte from the memory location whose address is in the register SI to the memory location whose address is in register DI.

SI and DI are then incremented. Hence, SI and DI which are two dedicated index registers ('Source Index' and 'Destination Index') should be pre-loaded with the address values of the two strings involved in the transfer.

The instruction REP, placed before MOVC, decrements the value of the CX register, which in the Intel 8086 is a dedicated counter register, and repeats the MOVC operation until CX equals zero. Also CX is to be set in advance with the value of the number of elements to be transferred. The operation behaves in the same way when the prefix REP is used before the other string processing instructions.

Note a further difference from the Z8000: the use of implicit operands.

```
REP
MOVC        (DI) ← ((SI))
            SI ← (SI) + 1; DI ← (DI) + 1
```

_____

Both solutions (Examples 5.5 and 5.6) are not only simple but also very efficient because they eliminate the repeated execution of a large number of instructions (incrementing registers, executing the required operation, incrementing the counter, comparing with the length and jumping to the beginning of the loop).

More precisely, they eliminate all the **fetch** phases of these instructions. This is an example of the **vertical migration** of functions from the machine code level to the microprogramming or hardware level.

String manipulation instructions are generally of five types:

(1) transfer instructions (Examples 5.5 and 5.6 and Figure 5.18);

(2) instructions for comparing two strings (Examples 5.7 and 5.8) or a scalar value with the elements of a string (Example 5.9);

(3) instructions for filling an area of memory with a given value (Example 5.10); such operations are often integrated with instructions of type (1) or (2) (Figure 5.18);

(4) 'translation' instructions (Figure 5.19);

(5) decimal string manipulation and arithmetic instructions.

MOVC3 len,src,dst
MOVC5 srclen,src,fill,dstlen,dst

MOVC3 transfers *len* characters from *src* to *dst*:

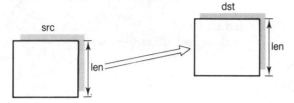

MOVC5 transfers *dstlen* characters if *srclen* ≥ *dstlen*:

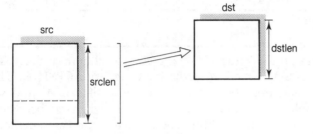

transfers *srclen* charcters and fills the remaining locations of *dst* with *fill* if *srclen* < *dstlen*:

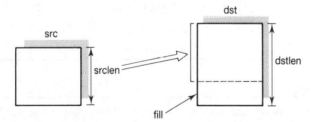

Figure 5.18 String transfer instructions on the VAX.

EXAMPLE 5.7

This example is of a comparison between strings. The VAX possesses two instructions. CMPC3 compares 'len' pairs of bytes of the strings 'src1' and 'src2'. The comparison ends when an inequality is found, or else when all the 'len' bytes have been examined. On the contrary, the CMPC5 instruction allows for the possibility of different lengths. In this case, the shorter string is filled virtually with the value 'fill' and the comparison proceeds on a number of elements equal to that of the longer string.

The Intel 8086 uses the prefix mechanism explained above. It may be noted that two possible prefixes exist: REP repeats the operation up to the first equality, while REPNZ does so up to the first inequality.

VAX

    CMPC3   len,src1,src2
    CMPC5   src1len,src1,fill,src2len,src2

Intel 8086

(a) REP
     CMPC

(b) REPNZ
     CMPC

EXAMPLE 5.8

Strings on the Zilog Z8000 are compared here in decreasing order with CPSDRB and in increasing order with CPSIRB. The way in which the operation takes place is similar to that described in Example 5.5. The comparison is halted when 'cc' becomes false or R = 0. 'cc' is the condition code which is expressed orthogonally in the Z8000. This permits an ample choice of conditions on which to make the comparison. In Example 5.7, on the other hand, the comparison is only made in terms of equality or inequality.

    CPSDRB   dst, srg, R, cc
    CPSIRB   dst, srg, R, cc

EXAMPLE 5.9

Instructions on the Z8000 for comparison of a value contained in register Rx, with the elements of the string 'srg': Ry is the counter, and the comparison continues as long as 'cc' is true or Ry = 0.

    CPDRB   Rx, srg, Ry, cc
    CPIRB   Rx, srg, Ry, cc

EXAMPLE 5.10

Instructions for the memorization of a character in an element of a string on the Intel 8086: if preceded by the prefix REP, the instruction is repeated for all the elements and hence becomes a 'filling' instruction.

    STOC   (DI) ← (AL)
                DI ← (DI) + 1

(a)   MOVTC

srclen,src,fill,tbl,dstlen,dst

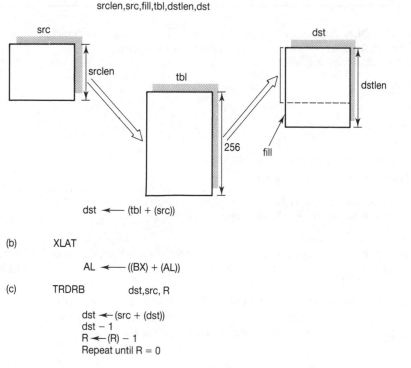

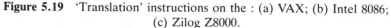
dst ◄─── (tbl + (src))

(b)   XLAT

AL ◄─── ((BX) + (AL))

(c)   TRDRB   dst,src, R

dst ◄─ (src + (dst))
dst − 1
R ◄─ (R) − 1
Repeat until R = 0

Figure 5.19   'Translation' instructions on the : (a) VAX; (b) Intel 8086;
(c) Zilog Z8000.

Further reading

IEEE floating-point standard

IEEE (1985). IEEE Standard for Binary Floating Point Arithmetic, *ANSI/IEEE Std 754–1985*.
New York, USA

Assembly language level

Sebesta R.W. (1984). *VAX 11 Structured Assembly Language Programming*. Menlo Park, CA:
Benjamin/Cummings
Smith B. E. and Johnson M. T. (1987). *Programming the Intel 80386*. Glenview, IL: Scott,
Foresman & Co.
Tanenbaum S. A. (1984). *Structured Computer Organization*, 2nd edn, pp. 350–84. Englewood
Cliffs, NJ: Prentice Hall

EXERCISES

Problem 5.A Develop simulation procedures for the following data transfer instructions, making use of the access procedures to the memory and the registers (see Problems 2.B and 2.C):

- Load
- Store
- Move
- Swap
- Exchange (the contents of two registers)
- Translate (dst ← (src + (dst)))

Develop also simulation procedures for shift and rotation operations, which operate on physical structures (Word, Byte, . . .).

5.1 The memory and the registers represent information structures independently of their logical type. In the same way, transfer instructions operate on non-typified data.

Simulate by means of procedures the behaviour of the 'Store' and 'Load' instructions in an architecture with 16 general registers with the size of one word, and with a memory organized in words (1024 locations).

5.2 The 'Move' instruction transfers data between two locations. Using the following declaration:

Type
    Loc_type = (Memory_location, Register_location);

develop a procedure simulating 'Move'.

Note that it has four input parameters (source location type, source location, destination location type and destination location) and one output parameter (memory address validity check). Write the procedure in such a way that it uses the procedures for reading and writing to memory and registers (Exercises 2.19, 2.20, 2.22).

5.3 Write procedures simulating 'Load' and 'Store', using the 'Move' procedure in Exercise 5.2.

Problem 5.B Define the processor status register as a sequence of bits which have the usual meaning (carry, sign, overflow, . . .), and then develop a procedure that gives a value to such bits according to the result of the operation carried out, by following the indication given in Exercise 5.6.

Define, then, the type binary integer of a size equal to that of the word, and all the usual operations on binary integers:

- increment
- decrement
- addition
- addition with carry
- subtraction
- subtraction with borrowing
- negation
- multiplication
- division
- arithmetic shifts

Ensure that such operations update the processor status register, by directly accessing its bits, or calling the suitable manipulation procedure.

In addition, the carry bit has to be set either when an adding operation produces a carry over or when a subtraction does not use borrow (the first operand is greater than the second).

5.4 The length of the 'binary integer' type, supported by all architectures, coincides with that of the basic information unit: the word. Define its type using Pascal notation.

5.5 Most architectures provide means of operating on integers in multiple precision using the carry bit in the processor status register (processor status word). This register also incorporates the properties of the result of an arithmetic operation, under the form of its sign (sign bit), the overflowing of the result (overflow bit) and the fact of its being null (zero bit). Define the register as a record containing this information.

5.6 The result of an arithmetic operation influences the contents of the 'processor status word' register. Suppose such an operation is carried out by a procedure with the heading:

> **Procedure** Set_flags (result : Binary_integer;
>   carry, ov_carry : Bit);

whose input parameters are:

(1)   result, the result of the operation;
(2)   carry, the output carry-over of the operation;
(3)   ov_carry, the carry-over on the most significant figure of the result.

Develop the procedure, bearing in mind that:

(a)   the carry bit of the status register coincides with the input parameter carry;

(b)   the sign bit is the most significant bit of result;

(c)   the zero bit derives from the check that all the bits of result are null;

(d)   the overflow bit is 1 if carry$\neq$ov_carry, that is, if an output carry-over occurs, but not on the most significant figure or vice versa.

5.7   A procedure with heading:

Procedure Inc (**Var** elem : Binary_integer);

increments a binary integer by one unit.

Develop the execution block of the procedure, using a variable for the carry-over, which (initialized to 1) is added to the least significant bit of the number. The carry-over of the addition (if any) is then added to the bit immediately to the left, and so on. At the end of the procedure, Set_flags (Exercise 5.6) needs to be called.

5.8   How can the two's complement of a relative binary number be calculated? Develop the execution block of the procedure:

Procedure Neg (**Var** elem : Binary_integer);

that would carry out this operation.

5.9   The sum of two integers can be obtained by adding the two operands bit by bit, starting from the least significant, and inserting the carry of the previous pair of bits into the addition. This carry must be previously cleared. The Set_flags procedure must then be called to update the status register.

In the light of this brief description, lay out the executive part of:

Procedure Add (elem1, elem2 : Binary_integer;
                          Var result : Binary_integer);

5.10   Develop a simulation of the addition with carry operation:

Procedure Adc (elem1, elem2 : Binary_integer;
                          Var result : Binary_integer);

like the Add procedure in Exercise 5.9, with the condition that the initial carry is not null, but is equal to the carry in the processor status word register.

5.11   How can the difference between two relative integers be obtained, making use of relevant procedures from the preceding exercises?

Develop:

     Procedure Sub (elem 1, elem2 : Binary_integer;
                Var result : Binary_integer);

proposing a number of different solutions, if needs be.

5.12 It is possible to decrement a relative integer by, for instance, adding the constant '−1' to the number. Complete in this way the procedure:

     Procedure Dec (**Var** elem : Binary_integer);

Are there any other ways of doing it? What are they?

5.13 Write procedures to simulate arithmetic left shift (Asl) and right shift (Asr). The output bit is in the carry of the processor status word.

5.14 If two single precision numbers are multiplied, a result is obtained which occupies two words. That is why the procedure:

     Procedure Mul (elem1, elem2 : Binary_integer;
                Var result_low, result_high:
                Binary_integer);

returns the result in two memory words.
    Using the following algorithm:

```
Clear result_low and result_high:
Repeat 16 times (for 16-bit words):
    Shr (elem2);
    If carry = 1
      then
          Add (result_high, elem1, result_high);
          Store the carry of the sum;
    Shr (result_high);
    Memorize the carry stored in result_high [0];
    Store the carry of Shr;
    Shr (result_low);
    Memorize the carry stored in result_low [0];
    (* result_high and result_low are considered as a single sequence of bits to be
    shifted right *)
```

develop the execution block of Mul.
    Verify that it gives a correct result for the pair (3,5), carrying out the procedure either by hand or on a computer.

Problem 5.C Specify the supports furnished by an architecture to real number processing in the IEEE standard floating-point format.
    After having defined the physical structure suitable for the representation of real numbers, develop description procedures of the main operations for real numbers that an architecture renders available.

It is useful to define extraction operations of the sign, the exponent, and the mantissa of the number from its representation, and the inverse operation, of insertion of such entities in the representation.

One may then develop the alignment operation of floating-point numbers, which is preliminary to the sum, then the addition and subtraction, and lastly the multiplication.

5.15 An architecture has a word length of 16 bits and supports the facility of processing real numbers in single precision in IEEE standard floating-point format (see Example 5.3).

What physical structure is suitable for representing a single real number?

Explain how the bits of the physical structure used for representing the Floating_point type are distributed between the sign, the characteristic and the mantissa. Specify also the relationship between the value of the number and its representation.

5.16 To carry out the addition of two reals, the first step should be to extract the sign, the exponent and the mantissa from the representation. Next, the numbers need to be aligned: the mantissa of the smaller operand has to be shifted right (divided by 2) and at the same time its exponent has to be incremented, repeating the whole operation until the two operands have the same exponent. Describe this preparatory phase of adding two reals in a procedural way.

5.17 After aligning the two floating-point operands (Exercise 5.16), their sum is calculated by evaluating the sign and the mantissa of the numbers separately. A distinction needs to be made between the case in which the sign is the same and when it differs. Finally, the result may have to be re-normalized. Describe these stages in adding two floating-point numbers, using Pascal.

5.18 Using the procedure for simulating the addition of two reals, develop:

> **Procedure** Float_sub (elem1, elem2 : Floating_point;
> **Var** result : Floating_point);

which simulates the subtraction of two floating-point numbers.

5.19 The product of two numbers in floating-point notation is carried out by adding together their exponents and multiplying their mantissas.

Supposing the mantissas of the two numbers are contained in:

> el1_high : Byte;   (* most significant part *)
> elem 1   : Word;   (* least significant part *)

for the first number, and in:

> el2_high : Byte; (* most significant part *)
> elem2   : Word; (* least significant part *)

for the second, describe the multiplication of the mantissas operationally (using Pascal). Note that each mantissa occupies 24 bits, hence the result will require 48 bits (3 words). Make use of the following procedures.

> **Procedure** Mul (elem 1, elem2 : Binary_integer;
> **Var** result_low, result_high :
> Binary_integer);

> **Procedure** Mul_byte (elem1, elem 2 : Byte;
> **Var** result   : Word);
> (* product of two bytes *)

> **Procedure** Add (elem1, elem2 : Binary_integer;
> **Var** result   : Binary_integer);

> **Procedure** Adc (elem1, elem2 : Binary_integer;
> **Var** result   : Binary_integer);

Problem 5.D Define the supports furnished by an architecture to packed BCD processing.

One starts with the formal definition of the BCD figure and the BCD number, and then defines some arithmetic operations on such data types, as:

- addition with carry
- addition
- subtraction

5.20 In representing an integer in packed BCD format, each decimal figure occupies 4 bits (a half byte), while the number in single precision occupies one word (for example, in a 16-bit word the number consists of four figures).
Define the types 'BCD figure' and 'BCD number'.

5.21 Develop:

> **Procedure** Pack_BCD_adc (elem1, elem 2 : Packed_number;
> **Var** result   : Packed_number);

which will carry out addition with carry of two decimal numbers according to the following algorithm:

> Extract the four decimal figures from each of the two addends starting from the least significant.
> For each pair of figures:
>   Perform their addition with carry
>   If the addition gives a carry or if the result is
>   greater than 9
>   then
>   Add 6 to the result;
>   Set the carry (carry for the next figures);
>   Store the resulting figure in 'result'.

5.22   The subtraction of two decimal numbers can be performed by calculating the ten's complement of the second operand (obtained by adding 1 to its nine's complement) and adding it to the first operand.
Develop in this way:

> **Procedure** Pack_BCD_sub (elem1, elem2 : Packed_number;
>   **Var** result   : Packed_number);

(Note that the 9's complement needs to be calculated for each figure of the second operand as '9-figure').

Problem 5.E   Develop procedures which simulate the following bit manipulation instructions, by resorting to the memory access operations (Problem 2.B):

- Set bit
- Clear bit
- Test bit
- Test and set

The instructions of 'Test' and 'Test and set' store the bit into the 'Zero' flag of the processor status word.

5.23   Suppose you have a memory organized in words, and have assigned the type:

> **Type** Bit_range = 0 . . word_max_bit;

Develop a simulation procedure of the instruction:

> Set_bit bit_number, memory_address

which sets a bit in a memory word.
Use the programs of memory access (Exercise to 2.19 and 2.20).

6 Instructions for Modifying the Flow of Control

6.1 Jump instruction format
6.2 Conditional and unconditional jumps
6.3 Jumps to subroutines
6.4 Procedure calls

6.5 Iterations or loops
6.6 Co-routine jumps
Further reading
Exercises

The processing flow of instructions is fixed, as is well known, by the advancing of the processor status variable called the program counter (PC). This operation does not appear explicitly in the data-processing instructions, but is carried out by the processor in such a way as to be transparent to them.

The execution of a data-processing instruction, besides producing the results required by the opcode, modifies the processor status in its two variables:

(1)   the status word, containing the bits N, V, Z, C
       (Negative, Overflow, Zero, and Carry flags)

(2)   the program counter

Other processor status variables such as the accumulator or the contents of the general registers may be influenced by the execution of the particular instruction, but these are the direct result of the operation expressed by means of the opcode.

The updating of the status word or the program counter, on the other hand, is an activity of the processor which takes place as a

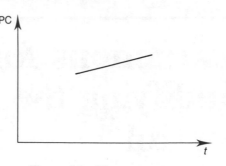

Figure 6.1 Linear sequence.

side-effect as each instruction is carried out. These two status variables represent the most important way in which the processing context is transferred from one instruction to the next.

The address of the next instruction to be carried out, which is contained in the program counter, is usually modified by the processor in a linear way, and is incremented with each instruction by an amount equal to the length, in bytes or words, of the instruction itself. Although not all instructions are the same length, the behaviour of the program counter variable may be considered practically a linear function of time in this case (Figure 6.1).

Each program segment to which a law of program counter variation of the type described above applies constitutes a **linear sequence** of instructions. This may be interpreted as a single act of computation carried out over a number of instructions, rather than finishing in a single instruction. All these instructions will share the same processing context, which allows them to carry out the required computation in a sequence of elementary independent steps.

Points of 'discontinuity' in the program counter function (Figure 6.2) represent a departure from the automatic advancing

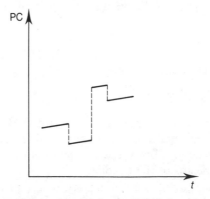

Figure 6.2 Points of discontinuity in the PC(t) function represent 'jumps'.

mechanism performed by the processor. The updating of the PC cannot be carried out at such points in a 'transparent' way, since it cannot be predicted by the processor. It needs to be explicitly requested in appropriate instructions generally called 'control transfer', 'jump' or 'branch' instructions.

An exception to this rule is the interrupt, which, even though it is not predictable, generates an automatic jump to specific procedures (Chapter 8).

6.1   Jump instruction format

Jump instruction format includes not only the opcode but also the address of the location to jump to (the new value of the PC), and perhaps a field specifying a condition on the basis of which it is decided whether to make the jump or continue in the sequence (Figure 6.3).

The majority of addressing methods can generally be used in jump instructions. Among them, however, relative addressing takes on a particular significance, and may even, in some architectures, cause a separation between the two names for this kind of instruction:

- **branch** instruction, if the destination address is relative;
- **jump** instruction, for other methods of addressing.

It should be remembered how important relative addressing is for obtaining **position-independent code** (Section 3.2.7).

In some cases, the address of the instruction to jump to may be implicit. For instance, we will see that in the **return from subprogram** instruction an appropriate status variable is used to update the value of the program counter.

In conditional jump instructions, the 'condition code' field specifies the condition to be tested before activating the jump. These conditions are represented in, or can be derived from, a certain number of bits (**flags**) of the status word, an example of which we have seen in Section 5.3. Table 6.1 lists the most common flags, together with the names used in some architectures.

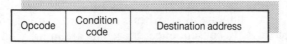

Figure 6.3   Jump instruction format.

Table 6.1 Status word condition flags on some architectures. Note how, on the Zilog Z8000, overflow and parity share the same bit.

Flag	VAX	Zilog Z8000	Intel 8086	MC68000	Rockwell 6502
Sign (negative)	N	S	SF	N	N
Zero	Z	Z	ZF	Z	Z
Overflow	V	P/V	OF	V	V
Carry	C	C	CF	C	C
Parity		P/V	PF		

Nearly every data-processing instruction influences the bits of the status word. Some of them can be controlled directly by the programmer; others depend on the processor.

The status word flags make a convenient way of transferring the processing context between data-processing instructions and jump instructions. In other words, it is possible to separate the instructions that bring about certain conditions from those that test such conditions, thanks to the memorization of these conditions in the bits of the status word.

For example, an ADD instruction may influence the bits of 'sign', 'zero', 'carry', and 'overflow'. The computation 'add two numbers and continue normally through the sequence if the result is positive or null, otherwise jump to another program area' is divided into two consecutive instructions, one for addition and the other for testing the sign bit and jumping if this bit is '1'.

Often the condition to be tested is inherent in the data itself, not a result of processing. Testing a relationship between two data items, such as seeing if one number is greater than another, does not presuppose a data-processing operation that has altered the bits of the status word. In such cases, there generally exist two different methods adopted by the various architectures:

(1)   The comparison and the jump if the condition is verified are contained in the same instruction.

(2)   The operation is divided into two consecutive instructions, similar to what happens for jumps conditional on the result of data processing.

Solution (2) is more frequently adopted, because it requires less lengthy instructions.

Comparison instructions are instructions that test the condition required and set certain status word bits to '1' or '0' on the basis of the result (Example 6.1). In consequence, these bits are influenced not only by data-processing instructions, but also by comparison instructions. The latter, however, cause no transformation of the data: their job is simply to translate the initial conditions into status word bit terms. In this way it becomes possible to use the same conditional jump instructions that are employed with data-processing instructions.

EXAMPLE 6.1

Examples are given here of comparison instructions:

- **VAX**. The instruction CMP compares two scalar quantities (there also exist string comparison instructions: Examples 5.7 and 5.8). The comparison is made by subtraction, without storing the result: the only action is to alter the condition codes. The instruction TST compares a scalar with zero.

    CMP src1,src2   src1-src2
    TST src   src-0

- **Intel 8086**. While the CMP instruction is similar to that on the VAX, the instruction TEST sets the value of the flags according to the result of a logical AND operation.

    CMP dst,src   dst-src
    TEST dst,src   dst AND src

Other comparison instructions exist, as in bit or string manipulation. However, the result still consists in obtaining values for the condition code flags.

Another possibility is the one adopted by the microprocessor Am29000, in which comparison instructions do not alter the status register but store the result in a general register. The instruction:

    Compare_greater_than Ra, Rb, Rc

has the effect:

    If (Ra) > (Rb)
       then Rc := True
       else Rc := False

There exist several comparison instructions (for example >, <, ≤) which operate on data of the different types (integers with and without sign, floating-point numbers with single and double precision, and so on). However, there are sufficient three branch instructions:

- unconditional branch
- branch if false
- branch if true

The main advantage of this technique is that the condition evaluation instruction and the jump instruction do not need to be consecutive.

In the case that the condition for the branch is a Boolean variable, with this technique it is possible to eliminate the first instruction, while with the traditional technique two instructions must nevertheless be used, one of comparison and another of branch.

Jump instructions may be of a variety of types:

- conditional and unconditional jumps
- subprogram jumps
- procedure calls
- iterations or loops
- co-routine jumps

6.2 Conditional and unconditional jumps

As has been said, many architectures distinguish between relative jumps (branches) and jumps with other addressing methods (jumps). It can be seen in Example 6.2 that for some architectures there exists complete symmetry between the two types. In others, branches are preferred, since:

- they are shorter, having only a displacement to specify;
- they allow position-independent code to be obtained.

EXAMPLE 6.2

Examples are given of conditional and unconditional jump instructions for certain processors. Note that the Zilog Z8000 allows complete symmetry between JP and JR with respect to the condition codes, whereas the VAX and the Motorola MC68000 favour branches, using jumps only for unconditional cases.

Zilog Z8000

JP	cc,dst	if cc is true: PC ← dst
JR	cc,displ	if cc is true: PC ← (PC) + displ

VAX

Bcc	displ	if cc is true: PC ← (PC) + displ
BR	displ	PC ← (PC) + displ
JMP	dst	PC ← dst

MC68000

Bcc	displ	if cc is true: PC ← (PC) + displ
BRA	displ	PC ← (PC) + displ
JMP	EA	PC ← EA

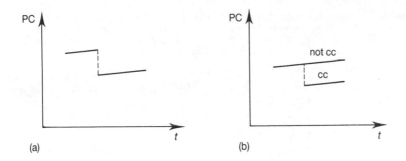

Figure 6.4   PC diagrams corresponding to: (a) an unconditional jump; (b) a conditional jump.

The PC time graphs corresponding to a jump instruction assume the appearance shown in Figure 6.4.

An unconditional jump may be considered a particular case of conditional jump instruction: one in which 'cc' is always true. Some architectures make use of this property by not having any explicit unconditional jump instructions, but only conditional jump instructions in which one particular 'cc' configuration is assumed to represent the Boolean constant 'True'.

Conditional jump instructions are based on the values of the condition flags of the status word (see Table 6.1), or on one of their logical functions, in order to decide whether or not to make the jump. Table 6.2 expresses the conditions that are normally examined, with their respective names used in certain architectures. The names are the condition codes to be substituted for 'cc' in Example 6.2.

A description of the respective conditions is also shown in Table 6.2, although each computer utilizes different expressions for the same condition codes. Table 6.2 can be used as a correspondence table for the names of the condition codes on different computers.

The conditions have been classified into four categories:

(1)   *Simple flag conditions*:   conditions that refer directly to testing the status of status word flags.

(2)   *Arithmetic relations between numbers with sign*:   conditional jumps that use condition codes belonging to this category follow comparison or data-processing instructions, in which the operands are integers with sign, floating-point numbers or decimal strings.

(3)   *Arithmetic relations between numbers without sign*:   in this case the conditional jump instructions follow instructions that act on integers without sign, addresses or strings of characters.

(4)   *Boolean constants*:   these are fictitious conditions, as they are always true or always false. As stated above, they are used to force unconditional jumps.

Table 6.2 Condition codes for conditional jumps.

Flag	Intel 8086	Zilog Z8000	MC68000
(a) Simple flag conditions			
Z = 1	E/Z Equal/Zero	EQ/Z	EQ
Z = 0	NE/NZ Not equal/ Not zero	NE/NZ	NE
S = 1	S Sign	MI Minus	MI
S = 0	NS Not sign	PL Plus	PL
P = 1	P/PE Parity/Parity even	PE	
P = 0	NP/PO Not parity/ Parity odd	PO	
V = 1	0 Overflow	OV	VS Overflow set
V = 0	NO Not overflow	NOV	VC Overflow clear
C = 1	C Carry	C Carry	CS Carry set
C = 0	NC Not carry	NC Not carry	CC Carry clear
(b) Arithmetic relations between numbers with sign			
SxorV = 1	L/NGE Less/ Not greater or equal	LT Less than	LT
SxorV = 0	GE/NL Greater or equal/ Not less	GE	GE
Zor(SxorV) = 1	LE/NG Less or equal/ Not greater	LE	LE
Zor(SxorV) = 0	G/NLE Greater/ Not less or equal	GT	GT

Table 6.2 (*cont.*)

Flag	Intel 8086	Zilog Z8000	MC68000
(c) Arithmetic relations between numbers without sign			
C = 1	B/NAE Below/Not above or equal	ULT Unsigned less than	
C = 0	AE/NB Above or equal/ Not below	UGE Unsigned greater or equal	
CorZ = 1	BE/NA Below or equal/ Not above	ULE Unsigned less or equal	LS Low or same
CorZ = 0	A/NBE Above/Not below or equal	UGT Unsigned greater than	HI High
(d) Boolean constants			
1		–	T True
0		–	F False

Jump instructions, as represented by the more general branch instruction (see Example 6.2), correspond to the instruction:

if cc **then** PC := PC + displ **else** PC := PC + 1

The two alternative sequences are placed: immediately after the branch instruction (conventionally indicated by PC := PC + 1), the one selected by 'else', and at a distance 'displ' one selected by 'then'. It should also be noted that the sequence selected by 'else' makes use of the automatic program counter advancing that takes place with every instruction, and therefore does not appear explicitly in the corresponding machine instructions.

There does not exist in machine code anything equivalent to the **selection instruction** found in high-level languages. This may be obtained as in Figure 6.5. To comply with the condition of 'single exit', a further unconditional jump instruction is generally required, placed at the end of the sequence selected by 'else', whose destination is the exit of the selection instruction, that is, the instruction immediately following the sequence selected by 'then'.

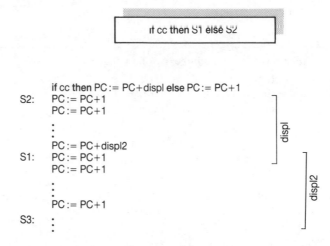

Figure 6.5 A selection instruction. Its realization on the machine code level requires not only a conditional jump placed at the beginning, but also an unconditional jump placed at the end of the alternative sequence (selected by 'else').

6.3 Jumps to subroutines

Subroutines may be considered extensions of the instruction set, realized using the same level of machine code defined by the computer architecture. That is to say, they can be seen as complex instructions that do not exist in the standard instruction set, and which the programmer has created for a particular application.

A subroutine will alter the contents of the memory, the registers and the condition codes in just the same way as a machine instruction.

Of course, any portion of a program could be considered as a complex instruction that modifies the status of the memory, the registers and the condition flags. The difference lies in the fact that subroutines:

- have an explicit well-defined interface with the rest of the program;
- define computations of a general kind, at least in terms of the program in which they are used;
- correspond to a single instruction (a subroutine call or jump) in the program they form part of. It is this instruction that can be considered as a new machine instruction.

A subroutine jump instruction usually limits itself to specifying the address of the subroutine involved, and does not make any mention, either implicitly or explicitly, of possible parameters. If such parameters exist, there will be a convention between the main program and the subroutine as to where the operands and results are to be found.

Examples of subroutine jump instructions are:

Zilog Z8000
  CALL   dst
  CALR   displ

VAX
  JSB   dst
  BSB   displ

MC68000
  JSR   dst
  BSR   displ

It may be noted that both relative (branch to subroutine) and non-relative jumps (jump to subroutine) are to be found in all three architectures. In each case, the generic subroutine jump opcode together with the destination address or the displacement specify a unique binary configuration associated with the subroutine in question, and hence all this taken together can be assumed as the opcode of a new instruction.

The way in which an instruction of this kind behaves must be analogous to a data-processing instruction, not only because of its data-transforming function, but also the mechanism for automatic program counter advancing. This means that the next instruction to be carried out after executing the subroutine must be the one immediately after the call. For this to happen, the processor has to save the current content of the program counter in a status variable, so that, at the end of the subroutine execution, a specific instruction to jump to the address specified in this variable makes the program counter resume the original flow (Figure 6.6).

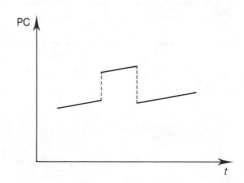

Figure 6.6   PC time diagram for subroutines.

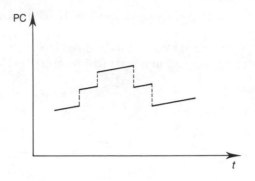

Figure 6.7 PC time diagram for nested subroutines.

The value stored in the program counter is not the jump instruction address but the one that follows it, since the incrementing of the PC takes place before the instruction is carried out, whatever the type of instruction.

The status variable destined to contain the PC value may be:

(a)   a register
(b)   a memory location
(c)   the stack

Solution (a) does not allow 'nested' subroutines (Figure 6.7), unless this register is software-saved in a different memory location for each distinct subroutine. In any case, it does not allow the use of 'recursive' subroutines, that is, subroutines that call themselves (Table 6.3).

Solution (b) has the same limitations as solution (a) if a single memory location is used.

Table 6.3 Comparing the different possible ways of locating the status variable used to save the program counter in subroutine calls.

Status variable used to save PC	Simple call	Nesting	Recursion
Register	yes	no	no
Single memory location	yes	no	no
Memory location associated with subroutine (1st location of the subroutine)	yes	yes	no
Memory location associated with call (stack)	yes	yes	yes

On the other hand, if associated with each subroutine there is a memory location used to save the PC, the nesting problem is solved, but not the recursion problem. Some architectures use the first location of the subroutine to communicate the value of the PC and jump to the second subroutine location. At the end of the subroutine, the programmer will insert an indirect jump instruction to the first location. Thus, saving the program counter in the first location of the subroutine involves:

JSR	dst	dst ← (PC)
		PC ← dst + 1
dst:	.	(PC save location)
	.	(Start of subroutine)
	.	
	.	
	.	
JMP I	dst	PC ← (dst)

Solution (c) allows both nested and recursive subroutines, since it saves the contents of the program counter in a different memory location for each call, rather than for each distinct subroutine.

The sequence of operations carried out by the processor in interpreting subroutine call instructions with method (c), that is saving the program counter in the stack, is:

SP ← (SP) − 1
(SP) ← (PC)
PC ← dst or (PC) + displ

The architectures referred to earlier (examples of subroutine jump instructions, p. 171) like the majority of present-day architectures, follow a scheme of this type.

Apart from the case of using memory locations associated with subroutines already examined, the return to the calling program takes place using an implicit address. If a stack is used, the return instruction corresponds to the sequence:

PC ← ((SP))
SP ← (SP) + 1

The use of the stack is consistent with the type of access required by nested and recursive subroutines. In both cases, the value of the PC to be restored must be the last one to be saved. This means that a LIFO (Last In First Out) type structure is required, of which the stack is a classic example.

EXAMPLE 6.3

Examples of subroutine return instructions.

VAX

     RSB   Return from SuBroutine

Zilog Z8000

     RET cc   if cc is true $PC \leftarrow ((SP))$
                                     $SP \leftarrow (SP) + 1$

MC68000

     RTS   ReTurn from subroutine
     RTR   ReTurn and Restore condition codes

Intel 8086

     RET $PC \leftarrow ((SP))$
                         $SP \leftarrow (SP) + 1$
     RET displ $PC \leftarrow ((SP))$
                         $SP \leftarrow (SP) + displ$

Note that in all the cases illustrated the return address is implicit, since the stack is utilized.

Although return instructions all perform the same principal function, some differences exist (Example 6.3):

- in some architectures the return may be conditional;
- in others the condition codes belonging to the calling program may even be restored, if the program has made provision for them to be saved previously in the system stack;
- in others it is possible to specify a constant to be added to the stack pointer, in place of the usual increment of 1. This proves useful when the stack is also used to pass on parameters (performed by the calling program by means of a PUSHes sequence). To avoid an equivalent number of POPs after the return, some of which will be superfluous because they refer to input parameters to the subroutine, the return instruction may include an operand to indicate the number of parameters to be discarded. If 'by reference' parameter passing is adopted, all references will be discarded.

The processing context of the calling program is also available to the subroutine. However, the status of the processor needs to be saved with respect to the subroutine. Since the number of processor registers is limited, they will be used by the subroutine to maintain its own processing context. Hence, it is necessary to save the processor status, or at least that part of it that will be modified, by means of sequences of memory transfer instructions or PUSHes on to the stack. Operations in the opposite direction will have to be performed to restore the contents of the registers as soon as the return to the calling program takes place.

In some architectures (Example 6.4) there exist very powerful instructions used for 'multiple' saving and restoring of the processor registers. These, together with instructions for saving the status word, are extremely useful not only in subroutine jumps but also in service routines for interrupts and traps, that is, in all cases where the old processing context is substituted by a new temporary context.

EXAMPLE 6.4 ————————————————————————

The instruction used by the Motorola MC68000 to save multiple registers is as follows. The contents of the registers specified are transferred into 'dst' and the locations following:

MOVEM   <register list>,dst

The same instruction may be used to restore the contents of the registers (for example on returning from a subroutine):

MOVEM   src, <register list>

The instruction for saving condition codes (the status register) in the system stack (whose pointer is the index register A7), on the MC68000:

MOVE   SR,−(A7)

Its interpretation is:

$A7 \leftarrow (A7) - 1$
$(A7) \leftarrow (SR)$

Instructions for the 'multiple' saving and restoring of consecutive registers on the Z8000.

LDM   dst,R,n
LDM   R,srg,n

While saving registers is generally the job of the program, saving the PC is the responsibility of the processor. The former has to be explicitly formulated, but the latter is implicitly carried out by the processor with the execution of the two instructions subroutine call and return, which come to share the status variable used for saving the PC.

6.4 Procedure calls

Although the two terms 'procedure' and 'subroutine' are very often used interchangeably, in some architectures the concept of procedure reflects the similar model that exists in the more evolute high-level languages.

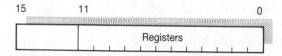

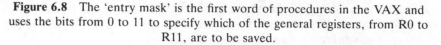

Figure 6.8 The 'entry mask' is the first word of procedures in the VAX and uses the bits from 0 to 11 to specify which of the general registers, from R0 to R11, are to be saved.

Thus, the processor tends to provide greater and more systematic support to 'procedures' than to 'subroutines'. It is only for the sake of convenience that we too shall use the separate terms procedure and subroutine with the distinct interpretations mentioned above.

Many of the more recent processors are oriented towards providing support for high-level languages, and therefore incorporate concepts belonging to such languages. This not only favours greater computing power, but also introduces more systematic concepts into the computer architecture. One of the most widespread examples is the support given to the use of procedures.

In this section, we shall follow the terminology employed in the VAX, since it is fairly general, and also the procedure support provided by this processor is quite rich.

In connection with the use of procedures, we find, as well as the stack pointer, another two registers:

- the **frame pointer** (FP), which contains the base address of a structure in the stack in which the system status at the moment of the procedure call is saved. This structure is known as the **stack frame**;
- the **argument pointer** (AP), which contains the base address of the list of arguments, placed in memory or in the stack.

Besides, the first location of the procedure is used to contain a word, called the **entry mask**, which specifies among other things the registers that are used in the procedure, and which must therefore be saved by the processor (Figure 6.8).

On the VAX, two procedure call instructions exist (Figure 6.9):

(1) procedure call with a list of 'general' arguments, in which the arguments are located in memory;

(2) procedure call with a list of the arguments in the stack.

In both cases, the stack frame appears as in Figure 6.10. It is built up by examining the 'entry mask' of the procedure and inserting the contents of the general registers selected by the '1' bits of the mask, through a series of PUSHes. Then the current values of the PC, FP and AP are saved. Finally the PSW, with the condition codes N, Z, V and C zeroed, the entry

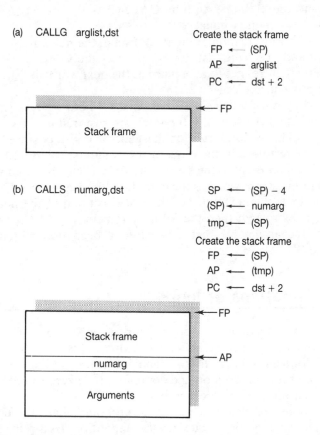

Figure 6.9 Procedure call instructions on the VAX: (a) with list of general arguments; (b) with arguments placed in the stack.

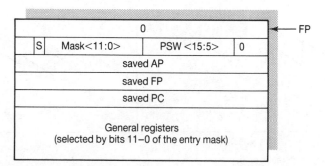

Figure 6.10 Stack frame after a procedure call on the VAX.

mask and the 'S' bit set to 0 by CALLG, or 1 by CALLS, are inserted, followed by an entry equal to 0.

After the creation of the stack frame, the new values are assigned to FP, AP and PC. Note that the PC assumes the values 'dst' + 2, since the transfer of control has to take place at the next word after the 'entry mask' of the procedure.

The return instruction is the same for both types of call. The values of PC, FP and AP stored in the stack are restored into the corresponding registers. The same is true for the general registers stored in the stack, which are restored on the basis of the contents of bits 11:0 of the mask, which is also present in the stack. The PSW is also restored with the value stored in the stack, whereas the condition bits are zeroed. Finally, if bit 'S' is equal to 1, the next entry of the stack, containing the number of arguments, is extracted; then the SP is incremented by $4 \times$ numarg so as to discard the arguments that have already been transmitted through the stack.

6.5   Iterations or loops

The PC time diagram for loops appears as in Figure 6.11.

Each loop must be associated with a status variable, which takes on the role of **loop counter**. This variable is incremented or decremented with each pass through the loop and compared with zero to decide whether to repeat the body of the loop or exit from it.

Loops are clearly the parts of programs that take up most of the program running time, due to the repetition factor in executing the instructions contained within them. These include not only the instructions that have to carry out the processing required, but also the loop control instructions. These consist in advancing the counter, comparing with zero

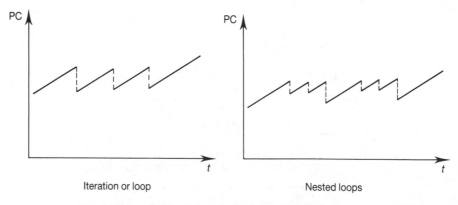

Iteration or loop   Nested loops

Figure 6.11   PC time diagrams for loops.

and jumping to the beginning if different. These instructions too are subject to the repetition factor. If the loop is made up of a small number of instructions, the part dedicated to control may take up a considerable proportion of the running time.

Nearly all architectures possess instructions for controlling loops, which include all the required operations.

EXAMPLE 6.5

Examples of loop control instructions:

Zilog Z8000

DJNZ   R,displ

$R \leftarrow (R) - 1$
if $R \neq 0$: $PC \leftarrow (PC + 1) - displ$

Intel 8086

LOOP   displ

$CX \leftarrow (CX) - 1$
if $CX \neq 0$: $PC \leftarrow (PC) + displ$

LOOPZ,LOOPE   displ

$CX \leftarrow (CX) - 1$
if $ZF = 1$ and $CX \neq 0$:
$PC \leftarrow (PC) + displ$

LOOPNZ,LOOPNE   displ

$CX \leftarrow (CX) - 1$
if $ZF = 0$ and $CX \neq 0$:
$PC \leftarrow (PC) + displ$

MC68000

DBcc   Dn,displ

if cc is true: $Dn \leftarrow (Dn) - 1$
if $Dn \neq 1$:
$Pc \leftarrow (PC) + displ$

In general, loop control instructions correspond to one of the following patterns:

(a)   count := count − 1
      if count <>0 **then** PC := PC + displ **else** PC := PC + 1

(b)   count := count − 1
      if Zflag **and** count <>0 **then** PC := PC + displ
      else PC := PC + 1

(c)   **if** cc **then** Dn := Dn − 1
      next if Dn<>1 **then** PC := PC + displ
      else PC := PC + 1

Type (b) and (c) instructions are interesting in that they combine loop control with a test on the condition codes produced in the loop itself, with the aim of deciding whether to repeat the iteration or exit from the loop.

Returning to Example 6.5, it may be observed that the Intel 8086 uses an implicit reference to the counter, which has to be loaded into the CX register. This renders the LOOP instruction unusable for nested loops, unless this register is continually saved, when passing from an external loop to one further in, and restored for the inverse operation.

6.6 Co-routine jumps

Co-routines are programs that transmit control to each other alternately, according to the model illustrated in Figure 6.12.

The first time co-routine A calls co-routine B as if it were a subroutine; that is, the value of the PC is stored and a jump is made to the beginning of co-routine B. At a certain point, co-routine B returns to co-routine A: it transfers the value of the saved return address into the PC, but also stores its own PC value. A will perform the same operation when it wants to pass control back to B, namely, it will 'return' to B, in turn storing the return address, and so on.

Note how every time one of the co-routines hands over control to the other, there is in Figure 6.12 a return to the preceding level (restoring the old program counter value).

A co-routine jump instruction consists in an exchange between the PC and the top of the stack, assuming that the top of the stack has been initialized with the start address of the first co-routine to be called (Figure 6.13).

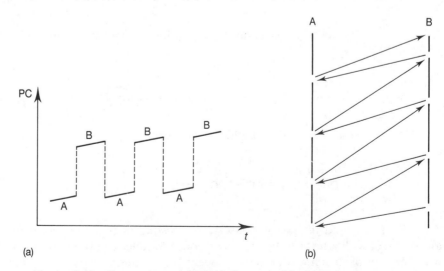

(a)

(b)

Figure 6.12 Co-routines. (a) PC(t) diagram; (b) control transfer model.

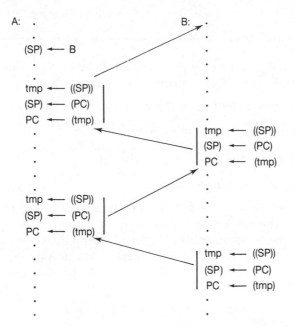

Figure 6.13 The co-routine jump consists in the exchange between the PC and the contents of the top of the stack.

The co-routine jump can be realized with a subroutine jump instruction that has the contents of the top of the stack as its destination address, provided the evaluation of the destination operand, namely the POP of the old PC value, takes place before saving the current PC on the stack. This is what happens on the VAX:

JSB	((SP))+	tmp ← ((SP))	Operand evaluation
		SP ← (SP)+4	
		SP ← (SP)−4	Execution of JSB
		(SP)← (PC)	
		PC ← (tmp)	

Further reading

High-level program structures

van de Goor A. J. (1989). *Computer Architecture and Design*, pp. 195–229. Wokingham: Addison-Wesley

EXERCISES

6.1 Using the conditional and unconditional jump instructions provided by a common architecture, transform the control construct:

> **repeat** <instruction> **until** <condition>

into an equivalent segment of assembly code.

6.2 A compiler can translate the construct:

> **while** <condition> **do** <instruction>

in two different ways, so that the loop termination control is either carried out at the beginning or the end of the cycle. Have a go at constructing both of these translations, then calculate the number of instructions generated by the compiler and the number of instructions executed at run time in both cases.

6.3 How can a for loop with the syntax:

> **for** <variable> := <expr1> **to** <expr2> **step** <step>
> **do** <instruction>

be translated into assembly language?

6.4 Some languages, including Pascal, support a multiple selection construct, with syntax of the type:

> **case** <variable> **of** {<constant> : <instruction>;}
> [**else** <instruction>]
> **end**.

Translate this control structure, using a table of the type:

CONST. 1	ADDRESS 1
CONST. 2	ADDRESS 2
CONST. 3	ADDRESS 3
.	.
.	.
.	.
CONST. n	ADDRESS n
————	ADDRESS $n+1$

in which a loop is executed to look for the relevant constant, to extract the start address of the sequence of instructions to be carried out. The last entry in the table corresponds to the 'else' branch of the construct, and may be absent.

6.5 In translating the 'case' construct in Exercise 6.4, using a look-up table, it is possible to avoid the search loop for the constant in the table, provided the architecture provides the relevant instructions. What kind of instructions are necessary, and what is the alternative translation of the 'case' construct?

Problem 6.A   Develop the formal descriptions of some usual comparison instructions, which fetch their operands from memory (organized with 16-bit words):

- Test src
- Cmp src1, src2

where 'src', 'src1', and 'src2', are physical addresses of memory. Comparisons are to be carried out in such a way as to influence the processor status word, but without 'dirtying' the data.

6.6   The instruction with syntax:

Test src

compares the contents of the memory word at the address 'src' with zero, recording the result in the status register. Its simulation can be implemented by reading the memory word at the address 'src', and carrying out a subtraction of the constant zero from value read, in such a way that the difference is not stored.

Problem 6.B   Describe some jump instructions, making use of a high-level language.

For example, the following relative branch instructions:

- Branch_if_carry displacement
- Branch_if_overflow displacement
- Branch_if_greater displacement

may be described by re-using the simulation procedures of the relative addressing (Example 3.4) in order to modify the program counter.

The following instructions:

- Call displacement
- Return

may be described. 'Call' saves the PC contents into the stack and adds to it a displacement (relative addressing).

'Return' restores from the stack the PC contents. Both, then, resort to stack access procedures (Problem 2.D).

6.7   The instruction with syntax:

Branch_if_carry displacement

carries out a relative jump when the carry bit is set. How can we express its operation by means of a Pascal procedure? Make use of simulations proposed for the relative addressing (Exercise 3.4).

6.8   Describe the operation of the instructions of subroutine jump (call displ) and return from subroutine (Return), by using the definition of stack and its access procedures (Problem 2.D).

7 The Microprogramming Level

7.1 Interconnection structures
7.2 The bus
7.3 The instruction cycle
7.4 The general structure of
     processors
7.5 Microprogramming
7.6 Microarchitecture

7.7 Instruction decoding
7.8 The control unit
7.9 The arithmetic and logic unit
7.10 Hardwired versus
     microprogrammed control
     Further reading
     Exercises

In order to carry out the instructions at a machine language level, an underlying-level **interpreter** is needed to generate the *sequences* of state changes required to pass from the initial states to the final states defined for each instruction. The situation resembles that on the higher levels, where a program specifies, by means of the instructions it is made up of, a sequence of state changes that lead from an initial state to the final results in the solution of a problem. From this point of view, it may be said that the problem solved by the high-level program is replaced at this level by the machine instruction, which is 'solved' by a microprogram. This is made up of 'microinstructions', which specify the required sequence of state changes on to the physical structure of the computer.

The term 'microprogramming' was coined early in the history of computing: the prefix 'micro-' refers to the fact that it takes place at a lower level in the hierarchy.

For a long period, the term microprogramming simply referred to this: a way of describing the behaviour of instructions by means of sequences of more elementary operations, in direct correspondence with the functions of the physical components of the computer. That is to say, in the past there was no reference to a concept of a stored microprogram. The analogy existed merely on the conceptual and descriptive level, but not in terms of implementation, since there were no memories available fast enough to contain the microprograms corresponding to the entire instruction set. Yet, as often happens, current technology has made it possible to extend the analogy up to the implementation, opening up the potential of programming in terms of flexibility and systematicity.

The microprogramming level 'sees' the computer at a level of greater detail than the computer architecture. It needs to be able to specify state changes in components of the physical structure, which are of no interest to the higher levels. For this reason, the discussion in this chapter will first concentrate on the way a computer is structured, before going on to consider how state changes in this structure are brought about.

7.1 Interconnection structures

The structure of the von Neumann computer (Figure 7.1) consists of:

- a processor
- a memory
- a communication channel

To communicate with the outside world, the system needs to be equipped witn a further channel of communication (Figure 7.2).

For its simplicity, this was the technique generally employed by early generation computers and is still used today on some mainframes ranging from small to medium sizes (for example the IBM 4341).

Every communication channel used to transfer vectors of bits, such as instructions or integer and fractional data, which is shared between several sources and destinations, is known as a **bus**. Hence, various buses may exist in a computer: internal and external, local and system buses.

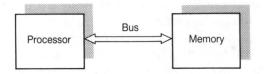

Figure 7.1 The processor–memory combination.

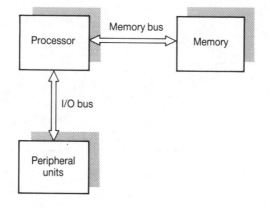

Figure 7.2 To communicate with the outside world, the von Neumann model needs to be equipped with a further channel of communication: the input/output bus.

'Local' and 'system' refer to different levels of the computer hardware hierarchy. A system bus connects major computer components at the highest level: these may be the various processors, shared memories and I/O in a multiprocessor system, or simply the processor, memory and I/O in a uniprocessor system. Correspondingly, local buses connect lower-level components, such as local memory, I/O and processor for each node in a multiprocessor system.

The communication with peripherals may involve both the processor and the memory. If it concerns the memory, the transfer of data and programs can still be made using the processor. If it is preferable not to occupy the resources of the latter in an operation which is after all simply transmission, the system may be equipped with a direct memory–peripherals communication channel (Figure 7.3) (DMA – Direct Memory Access).

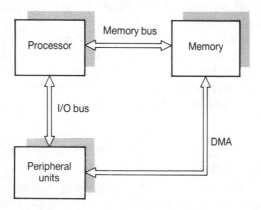

Figure 7.3 Structure with direct memory–peripherals communication channel.

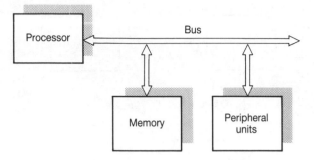

Figure 7.4 Single bus structure.

A different approach consists of connecting I/O only to the memory. In this case, communications between processor and peripheral units have to occur through the memory. In addition, the memory has to be equipped with an arbitration circuitry to resolve conflicts between the processor(s) and the peripheral units.

A more flexible solution, adopted by large mainframes (such as the IBM 3084), is to connect all the components, such as processors, memories and I/Os, to a central switch, which controls and arbitrates all communications. This structure retains the advantages of freeing the processor from controlling transmissions between I/O and memory and it establishes a path between the processor and I/O which does not involve the memory. Furthermore, it is possible to add more modules to the structure without having to change it.

A much more simple structure, which conserves the characteristics of generality and flexibility of the central switch, with the limitation of allowing only one communication at a time, is the single bus structure (Figure 7.4). In this structure, very common today especially with mini-computers and microcomputers, each unit is connected to a bus through which it communicates with the other units.

A function that underlies the functioning of every unit and communication is provided by **control**. So, within each individual unit and in each communication bus, there is a number of control lines, which, as it were, evoke the operation of the various system components.

The **internal structure** of the processor must:

● provide the functions required by the architecture, namely the processing of data, addresses and instructions, as defined in the preceding chapters;

● establish communication with the other system components, that is, the main memory, the peripherals and other processors, if there are any.

As regards the means of communication, the processor sees the external components in a way that is substantially uniform. In fact, in every case it is involved in:

- selecting the external unit
- sending or receiving information
- exchanging synchronization signals with the external units involved in the communication

On the basis of this, it is evident that a further signal is all that is required to discriminate between the types of unit, memory or input/output, or else one of the selection lines may be used.

These considerations, which will be discussed further in the sections that follow, are behind the above-mentioned single bus computer structure.

7.2   The bus

Figure 7.4 illustrates a bus structure that is shared by all the units in the system.

The features of this type of structure are:

- Communication can take place between any two units, not only with the processor.
- Only one communication act can take place at a time, since there is only one resource for this.
- Only one unit can transmit at a time, in order to avoid not only logical interferences but also damage to the components, whereas more than one unit can receive at the same time.
- The bus must be equipped with a sufficiently general set of control lines, taking account of the different characteristics of the units making up the system.

The unit that maintains control of the bus is known as the **master**, and all the others as **slaves**.

For most of the time the processor is the master, but occasionally other units may request, and receive, control of the bus. To do this, the processor has to 'disconnect itself' from the bus, that is, it has to set its bus lines in a state that corresponds neither to logical '0' nor to logical '1', but to a state of high impedance, in such a way that they are virtually interrupted. There are specific components that provide for this, and their outputs are defined as **three-state**.

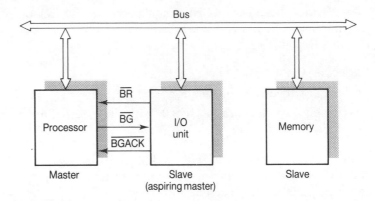

Figure 7.5 Synchronization signals required for passing control of the bus from the MC68000 processor to another unit in the system. Like the majority of control signals, the signals are in 'negative logic', that is logical '0' is associated with the higher tension level (for example 5 volts) and logical '1' with the lower level (0 volts). The bus request ($\overline{\text{BR}}$) is sent by the aspiring master, changing this signal from high level to low level. The processor replies, after setting its bus lines to high impedance, asserting (setting to low level) the 'bus grant' line $\overline{\text{BG}}$. When the unit receives this signal it can become master, and at the same time sends a $\overline{\text{BGACK}}$ acknowledgement signal that it has been granted the bus.

On completing its operation, it will return the $\overline{\text{BGACK}}$ signal to high level (negate it). This passage from low to high of $\overline{\text{BGACK}}$ is used by the processor as the signal that it can resume control of the bus.

Only after the processor has set its bus lines in a state of high impedance, can it communicate to the other unit that control is being handed over.

It should be pointed out that the entire operation requires the emission of two synchronization signals, the request for the bus by one of the units, and the acceptance by the other. A third signal will then be emitted by the requesting unit as soon as it has finished using the bus, to restore control to the processor (Figure 7.5). Obviously this unit will already have set its lines to a high impedance state.

Not all the lines need to be set in a state of high impedance, but only those that are used for output by new masters. For instance, the line the processor uses to grant control of the bus not only is not an output line used by masters other than the processor, but is in fact essential in letting the processor communicate with the would-be master, after the processor is disconnected from the bus.

Figure 7.5 shows an example in which only one unit in the system, typically a DMA controller, can request and receive control of the bus. In this case, the connections for the synchronization signals exist only between the processor and this unit.

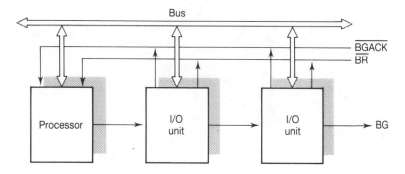

Figure 7.6 Bus arbitration by means of a daisy-chain.

A more general case is where a number of units are able to request control of the bus. Apart from the DMA controller, such units may be other processors in a multiprocessor system. Obviously, the synchronization lines can now no longer be direct, but have to be common to all units. Moreover, to cater for simultaneous requests, a decision-making system is needed to resolve the conflict. Figure 7.6 shows a simple evolution of the situation presented in Figure 7.5, to deal with the presence of several potential masters in the system. As can be seen, the $\overline{\text{BR}}$ and $\overline{\text{BGACK}}$ lines are common to all units, while the $\overline{\text{BG}}$ line is used in **daisy-chain** mode. This can also be considered a common line, but one which passes through the various units in order to resolve conflicts according to a priority based on the physical position of the units themselves. In fact, if a unit receives a bus grant signal, and has made a bus request itself, it uses it to take control of the bus. If, on the other hand, it has not made a bus request, it merely passes on the bus grant signal. Clearly, this arrangement favours the units situated nearest to the CPU, since they are the first to receive the bus grant signal.

The arbitration mechanisms may be much more complex than the one described above, as when non-fixed priorities need to be taken into account. They may even be centralized, that is, incorporated into the CPU or an external unit dedicated to the purpose, or else distributed among the various units that make up the system.

Let us now examine the internal structure of the bus. We have already seen in the previous section that it has to provide support for three different types of function: selection, data transfer and control.

Correspondingly, we can identify the following three components within the bus (Figure 7.7):

● The **address bus** is used to select the unit to be communicated with. This bus is unidirectional, in that it is produced as output by the address calculation unit inside the processor, or any other unit that

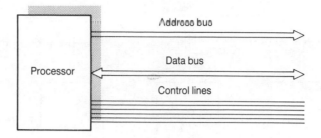

Figure 7.7 The components of a bus.

can become a master. The address bus inputs to the slave units so as to select them. Associated with, or inside, each slave unit there exists an address decoding logic, which is used by the unit to recognize whether it is the unit selected by the master (Figure 7.8). The width of the address bus determines the dimension of the address space, that is, the maximum number of main memory cells and of the registers pertaining to the I/O units.

- The **data bus** is bidirectional and used for transmitting and receiving information between the master and the addressed slave. Its width determines the physical 'bottleneck' inherent in von Neumann computers, and usually lies between 8 and 32 bits.

- The **control lines**; some of these are input to and others output from the processor. The input lines refer to the signals by means of which the other units in the system communicate to the processor that certain conditions or events have come about. Future processing must be synchronized on these lines. The output lines correspond to signals or commands sent by the processor to call up operations from the other units.

We have already encountered some control lines, such as $\overline{\text{BR}}$, $\overline{\text{BG}}$ and $\overline{\text{BGACK}}$. Let us now consider the control lines used to read or write data on an I/O unit or in memory. To this end, many processors use the signals $\overline{\text{RD}}$ (ReaD) and $\overline{\text{WR}}$ (WRite), accompanied by another two signals: $\overline{\text{MREQ}}$ (Memory REQuest) if the operation is in main memory, and $\overline{\text{IORQ}}$ (Input Output REQuest) if the operation is with a peripheral (Figure 7.9). The signal $\overline{\text{MREQ}}$ is used to select memory as a whole, but memory is usually implemented as a set of modules or banks. Figure 7.10 shows how to use some of the address lines to select one of these banks.

Alternatively, the I/O units and the memory may subdivide and share the address space fixed by the address bus, in such a way that, for example, the 'high' address values refer to the I/O units, and the 'low' ones

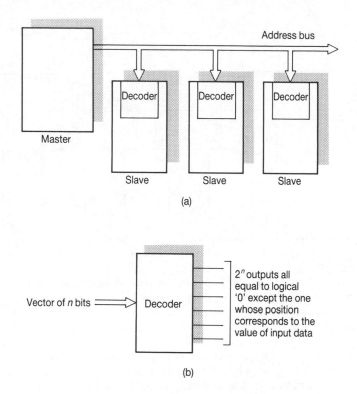

(a)

(b)

Figure 7.8   There is an address decoding logic associated with each slave unit. The functional scheme of a decoder is illustrated in (b).

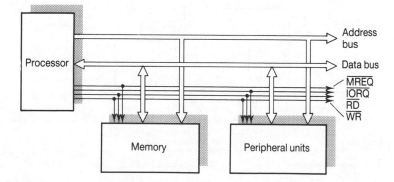

Figure 7.9   Bus lines for reading from and writing to memory and peripherals.

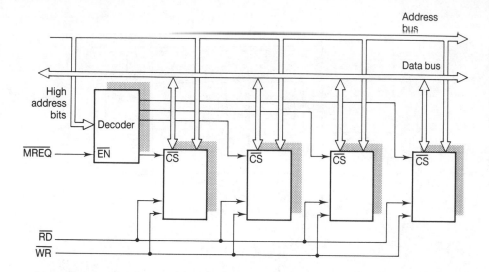

Figure 7.10 The signal $\overline{\text{MREQ}}$ is used to select memory as a whole. This takes place by enabling a decoder ('enable' input $\overline{\text{EN}}$). The high-order bits of the address bus are sent to this decoder, to select one of the banks of memory. If for instance there are four banks, as in the figure, two highest order lines of the bus are sent to the decoder, while the remaining $n-2$ are sent to all the modules. The four decoder outputs go singly to the $\overline{\text{CS}}$ (Chip Select) inputs of the four modules, so as to select only one of them. The $n-2$ lines sent to all the modules will in turn be decoded by a decoding logic which forms an integral part of each memory module.

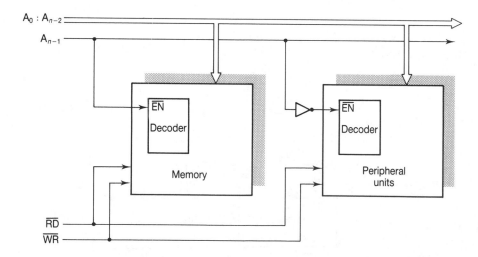

Figure 7.11 Memory-mapped I/O. The address space has been subdivided in two equal parts: the upper half ($A_{n-1} = 1$) is assigned to the peripherals, and the lower half ($A_{n-1} = 0$) to main memory.

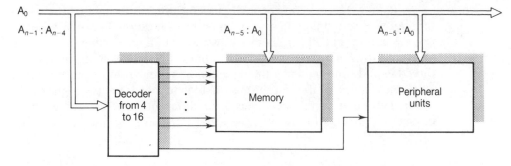

Figure 7.12 Memory-mapped I/O in which the four highest order lines of the address bus are sent to a 4-to-16 decoder. Thus 16 areas of the address space are selected, each 2^{n-4} locations wide. Of these, 15 can be assigned to main memory and the 16th to I/O. The first 15 outputs of the decoder can be sent directly to the $\overline{CS}$ inputs of the different memory modules, provided they have an addressing capacity of 2^{n-4} locations, otherwise they will serve to enable further decoders.

to main memory locations. In this case there is no need for further lines, such as $\overline{MREQ}$ and $\overline{IORQ}$, because the address itself will be employed to determine whether it is to be an input/output or a memory operation. This technique is referred to as **memory-mapped I/O**.

Figure 7.11 gives a simple example of memory-mapping I/O, in which the highest order address line is used to select either I/O or memory.

The registers belonging to the peripherals are much fewer in number than the main memory locations. For this reason slightly more complex decoding is generally adopted, with the aim of reducing the portion of the address space dedicated to the I/O. One solution, which devotes 1/16 of the total address space to I/O, is presented in Figure 7.12.

One advantage of memory-mapped I/O is that the data arriving from a peripheral is treated exactly as if it were in a memory location. It can be operated on in exactly the same way, since the whole instruction set is available. For this reason, computers that make use of this technique do not have specific input/output instructions. For example, if it is desired to obtain a data item from a peripheral and add it to another data item contained in a memory cell, it suffices to carry out a simple adding operation on the two operands, one in a main memory address and the other in an address corresponding to the I/O location of the peripheral.

The control lines needed for a reading or writing operation must substantially bring together three kinds of information:

(1) information about the transmission *direction* (Read or Write);

(2) *timing* information, to indicate when the addressed location or peripheral has to put its data on the bus or take it from the bus;

(3) information about the *type of unit* involved: memory or I/O.

Point (3) has already been discussed: suffice it to say that the control line can be essentially seen as an address line (additional or otherwise). As regards points (1) and (2), there are two ways of approaching the problem. One consists in adopting two separate lines, $\overline{RD}$ and $\overline{WR}$, to indicate the direction and time in which the data can be taken from or put on the bus (the time is given by the transition from high to low of the two signals). The other method uses the two lines in a different way, one to carry the directional information ($R/\overline{W}$), the other (**strobe**) for timing information.

7.3 The instruction cycle

As was stated in Section 7.1, the internal structure of the processor must:

- provide the functions required by the architecture;
- establish communications with the other components of the system.

We have already seen the way in which requests for communication with the outside are made.

Taking as our starting point the discussion in the preceding chapters, let us now try to specify a set of functions required to implement a general computer architecture.

The fundamental task of the level that underlies the computer architecture is interpreting the sequence of instructions of a running program. This consists of the following phases:

(1) extracting the instruction from memory;
(2) calculating the address of the next instruction, by advancing the PC;
(3) decoding the opcode;
(4) calculating the address of the operand, if any;
(5) extracting the operand from memory;
(6) execution;
(7) calculating the address of the result;
(8) storing the result in memory.

Some of these phases correspond to operations in memory, others to processor operations. Figure 7.13 shows the state diagram of the interpretation of a machine instruction, with the states controlled by the processor on the left side and those controlled by the memory on the right side. If there are no logical sequentiality restraints, phases of different type may overlap in time.

Some of the phases may be absent in certain instructions. Typically,

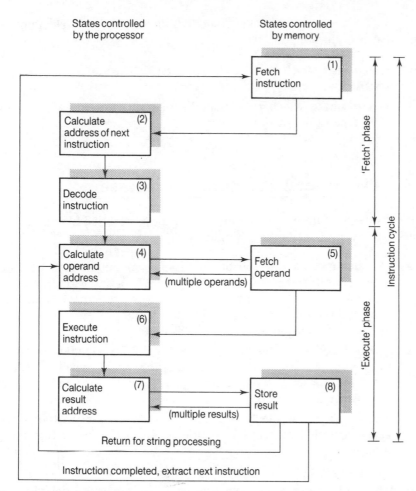

Figure 7.13   State diagram of the interpretation of a machine instruction. Some states may be null.

phases (4) and (5) do not apply to instructions without operands. On the other hand, in instructions that use multiple operands the (4), (5) pair will be executed repeatedly. The same applies to the result.

Phases (5), (7) and (8) are absent in jump instructions. In comparison instructions, the result is not stored and only the condition bits are updated, so phases (7) and (8) are absent.

The sequence (1) : (8) is repeatedly executed for all the instructions of a program: this is known as the **instruction cycle**.

Occasionally there is a return within the cycle. For example, in string processing, after (8) there is a return to (4) which is repeated until the string processing is completed.

It is customary to make a subdivision within the cycle into the following two phases:

(a) **fetch** phase, which includes (1), (2) and (3). This is the same for each instruction;

(b) **execute** phase, which includes all the other phases. This is specific for each type of instruction.

7.4 The general structure of processors

We are now able to abstract, from the functions described, some of the units that make up a processor (Figure 7.14):

- The **bus unit** has the job of establishing communication with the external units (memory, I/O and other processors). More precisely, it is through this unit that the address bus, the data bus and the control lines are formed. The units inside the processor communicate with the outside by means of this unit.

- The **instruction unit** fetches and decodes the subsequent instructions of the program being run. The result of the decoding will be used to select the particular execute phase corresponding to the opcode of the instruction fetched.

- The **arithmetic and logic unit** carries out the data-processing operations specified during the execute phase of the instruction being interpreted.

- The **address unit** carries out the calculation of the address.

- The **control unit** receives inputs from the instruction decoder and generates the set of controls and timings necessary for the corresponding execute phase. The commands generated by the control unit go in part on to the control lines of the external bus, and in part to activate execution by the units inside the processor. The control unit has also the job of generating the timing for the fetch phase and the management of exceptions (Chapter 8).

The functioning of the whole structure is made possible by the existence of an **internal data bus**, which is a replica of the external one, as well as a set of control lines generated by the control unit and connected to the individual units.

The **internal address bus** is generated by the address unit (this is its job, in fact) and is transmitted to the outside by the bus unit, to select the memory location or I/O unit concerned.

Each unit is provided with its own set of registers, which represent

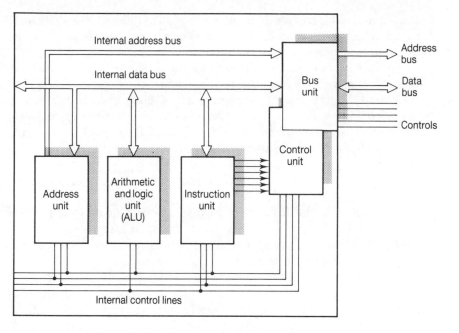

Figure 7.14   The general structure of a processor.

its own internal status, and processing sections which generate the corresponding functions. If necessary, some units can share a section: for example, the address calculation unit and the arithmetic and logic unit can share adding circuits and those performing other arithmetic operations.

7.5   Microprogramming

Every instruction cycle begins by sending the address of the instruction to be fetched on to the address bus. This address is contained in the PC, which, like the SP and the index registers, is one of the address registers that form part of the address unit.

The address set by the PC on the internal address bus is 'latched' on to an address register often called MAR (Memory Address Register), situated in the bus unit. In this way, it can remain set on the external address bus for the entire time required by the reading operation, while it is possible to change the contents of the PC.

In fact, an operation on the external bus requires that the address on the address bus be set for a fairly long time, to allow the external units connected to the bus to decode it and so recognize the address. Only after this time interval has passed can the external unit selected send the information to, or take it from the data bus.

In the case in question, the information is the instruction that the processor requests (RD) from the memory unit.

During the time that the memory unit is sending the instruction to the processor, the latter may be involved in other operations (parallelism between processor and memory). Of course, this parallelism is made possible by the existence, as mentioned above, of a buffer register such as MAR.

A typical operation that can be brought forward is the advancing of the PC.

Depending on the instruction format, this advancing may be by a single word (all instructions are one word long), or else more than one fundamental information unit (bytes or words), the number varying according to the type of instruction.

In the former case, the advancing is very simple and consists in incrementing the PC (advancing it by '1'). The only potential objection to performing this in advance is that it could turn out to be useless if the instruction that is arriving is a jump instruction (conditional or otherwise). Yet though it is a useless step, it is not in conflict with the jump, and since it does not waste resources, it may well be a good idea to do it anyway, so as to exploit the waiting time and not prolong the time taken to interpret the instruction by putting it at the end of the cycle.

However, the situation is different when the instructions are not all of the same length, but consist of a variable number of addressable units, each of which has a precise meaning during the interpretation (for example 1st operand address, 2nd operand address, and so on). In these cases it is not possible to advance the PC before the instruction arrives. Besides, it may be more convenient not to advance the PC all in one go, but to increment it by one unit at a time, so as to use it as a pointer to the different items of information requested successively during the interpretation of the instruction. At the end, when the last instruction byte has been taken up, the PC will find itself ready to point automatically to the next instruction (or rather, to its first byte).

Whatever the instruction format, at the end of the fetch phase either the whole instruction or its first byte (or word) is present on the data bus. In both cases, the information we are interested in, the opcode, is ready, so we might as well capture it and keep it in the instruction unit using its IR (Instruction Register). In this way, the internal data bus is freed for the bus cycles that follow.

The external data bus was already freed by the bus unit, by storing the information present there in its data buffer register, generally called the MBR (Memory Buffer Register).

```
0:      MAR: =PC;RD
1:      PC: =PC+1;RD
2:      IR: =MBR
```

Figure 7.15 Fetch phase.

With these two registers, MAR and MBR, the bus unit renders the processor independent from the rest of the system, allowing them both to operate in parallel.

Note also that the terms used for these two registers recall the way they were utilized for many years in the past, on architectures of the type shown in Figures 7.2 and 7.3. Today, with single bus structures they perform general bus buffer functions, and so are used both for memory unit operations and I/O operations.

Once the opcode is in the IR, the next phase to carry out is decoding. This operation is essential if we want to select the 'execute' phase corresponding to the particular kind of instruction that has been fetched.

Before going on to examine how the decoding is carried out, it is worth noting the procedural character of what has been described. This means that if we had a suitable language we could express the sequence of elementary steps required to carry out the fetch phase, using a program written in this language. Figure 7.15 gives an example of how such a program could appear.

Note the use of the separators. The ';' has been used to indicate commands that have to be issued at the same time. The 'carriage return', on the other hand, is used for commands in sequence.

If we suppose that a command is sent for a time equal to that of the instruction in such a language, and finishes when the instruction finishes, we can understand the reason for repeating the command RD (Read) in instructions to the address 0 and 1: this happens to make the read command last twice as long as the other commands.

If the bus operations had required a longer time, this would have been obtained using further instructions with RD commands.

We are also reminded of what was said previously about exploiting waiting times, when we note the advancing of the PC set in the instruction located in address 1.

Apart from expressing everything that has been said in this section in an elegant and synthetic way, a program such as the one presented in Figure 7.15 exhibits an even stronger characteristic: if a machine existed able to interpret it, the two together would automatically provide us with a control unit for the computer architecture. Just like the fetch phase, we could also write execute phases corresponding to the different instructions of the instruction set, as sequences of instructions at a lower level, and all these could be interpreted by a machine of this kind.

Yet a machine built in this way is none other than the von Neumann model applied to another architecture, simply at a lower level.

7.6 Microarchitecture

The architecture that underlies the computer architecture is called the **microarchitecture**. The corresponding language is called the microprogramming language, and the instructions in this language are known as **microinstructions**. The memory that holds the microprograms is called the **control memory** or microprogram memory.

The microprograms that carry out the fetch and execute phases make up the **interpreter** of the instruction set of the level above. The interpreter is composed of a set of relatively short microprograms. Apart from the microprograms corresponding to the fetch phase and execute phases for the different opcodes, there also exist microsubroutines for calculating addresses and other such operations.

The computer architecture is often known by the name of **target** machine, and the microarchitecture as the **host** machine.

The host machine has a greater visibility of hardware resources than the target machine. Specifically, the former has access to a greater number of registers, including those accessed by the computer architecture.

For this reason, and also in order to control more resources in parallel, the **microinstruction format** is completely different from that used for instructions.

7.6.1 Microinstruction format

Unlike machine instructions, microinstructions contain a large number of fields, each controlling a different unit.

Some of these fields relate to **commands**. For example, the RD and WR fields are 1-bit wide; if they are set to '1', they send a Read or Write command on the respective control lines.

Other fields are **function codes**, such as the ALU field, which represents which of the operations is required from the arithmetic and logic unit.

Other fields may represent **addresses**. For instance, one field may be the register number which is to be operated on in a file of general registers.

Given that the microinstruction may have a great length, there is a tendency to encode into a single field information expressed in a number of

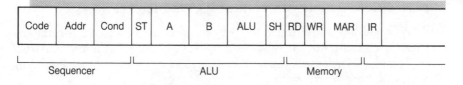

Figure 7.16 Microinstruction fields.

fields. If the result of an operation can be stored in eight different registers, for instance, eight fields of 1 bit each can be used, or alternatively one 3-bit field. With the first method, the result can in principle be memorized in all eight registers at the same time; while with the second it can be memorized in only one of them. It is fairly rare that one wishes to store a result in two or more registers.

Coding a field is also a very useful method when two or more fields turn out to have mutually incompatible configurations. For example, the enabling of a data item on the data bus by three different sources cannot be allowed at the same time, as has been stated before. A very simple way of avoiding microprogramming errors in this case is to use a coded field of two bits, which with its four distinct configurations, allows us to select one of the three sources exclusively, or none of them.

Another difference with respect to machine code instructions lies in the fact that the advancing or updating of the MPC (Micro Program Counter) is generally included explicitly in the microinstruction. This means that a section of the microinstruction is dedicated to the so-called **sequencer**, whose task is to determine precisely the address of the next microinstruction to be carried out. This field is made up of three subfields (Figure 7.16):

- a **code** subfield, which contains the opcode of a conditional microjump;
- a **cond** subfield, which represents the condition to be tested;
- an **addr** subfield, which expresses the control memory address to jump to if the condition is verified.

A microinstruction with encoded fields is often called **vertical**, while one with decoded fields is known as **horizontal**. The former procures a notable saving in control memory, but at the cost of reduced speed due to the need to decode the various fields. Furthermore, it does not allow us to exploit the parallelism in the hardware to best advantage.

The most usual practice is mixed format, with some fields encoded and others decoded, so as to obtain the advantages of both solutions by choosing the more convenient for each field.

7.6.2 Microinstruction coding techniques

The two situations presented in the previous section, horizontal format and vertical format, are not the only possible ways of encoding a microinstruction. Figure 7.17 presents, apart from these two, another three encoding schemes that are worth noting.

Figure 7.17a refers to the horizontal format, in which each bit directly controls an input to a computer unit.

Figure 7.17b illustrates the well-known solution of encoded fields: the control signals are encoded, calling for a second level consisting of a set of decoders, so as to get direct controls to the various units.

As has been pointed out already, the encoded fields scheme restricts the number of possible distinct microinstructions that can be represented to those for which a single control signal at a time for each encoded field can be activated.

Reducing the length of the microinstruction obviously diminishes the number of distinct microinstructions that can be represented. However the microinstruction is encoded, if we go from a length of n bits to a length of p bits, with $p < n$, the maximum multiplicity of distinct microinstructions will change correspondingly from 2^n to 2^p. The point is to identify encoding schemes that will lead to selection of certain microinstructions among the possible ones that exist in the direct control format.

The encoded field schema has the property of being orthogonal, which allows it to obtain any combination of control signals coming from distinct fields. This condition leads one to consider the microinstruction as a set of codes (operative or otherwise), in contrast to the machine instruction on the next level up, which consists of a single opcode and one or few operand fields.

Microinstructions with orthogonal encoded fields turn out to be very readable, since each field, with its subfields, refers to a different unit of the computer. In this way, there is a direct correspondence between the microinstruction format and the structure of the host machine.

Often, however, many of the combinations obtainable with an orthogonal format are not used in practice. In this case, apart from the clarity mentioned above, this would be a poor use of the control memory bits. It is therefore better to make use of more efficient encoding schemas, which take account of the configurations of control signals required by a particular interpreter or a class of interpreters. In this way it is possible to define microinstruction formats of shorter length and include configurations free of the restriction of only one signal per encoded field.

If the idea of distinct encoded fields is abandoned, it would be conceivable to encode the entire microinstruction, in a similar way to what happens on a higher level, in a single field. The number of bits of such a field would be commensurate, in the usual logarithmic relation, to the desired number of distinct microinstructions. It is clear that here too a level

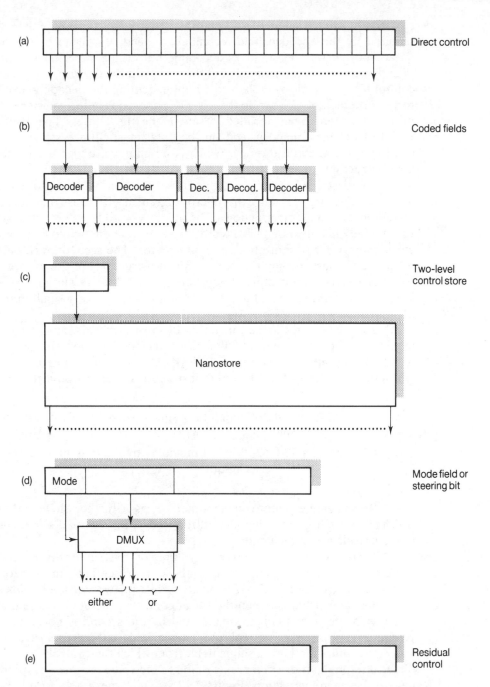

Figure 7.17 Microinstruction coding schemes. (a) Direct control; (b) coded fields; (c) two-level control store; (d) mode field or steering bit; (e) residual control.

of decoding will be needed, and one that will be more complex than that required by the encoded field technique. Indeed, it will no longer be a question of performing a binary decoding, but rather a specific 'mapping' of each microinstruction encoded in this way with the corresponding set of control bits. This may be achieved by implementing the decoding level by means of a memory known in this case as **nanomemory** or **nanostore**. The microinstruction to be decoded is sent along the address lines (Figure 7.17c) of the nanomemory, and on the data lines will appear the set of controls (in horizontal format), which is now known under the name of **nanoinstruction**.

The described technique is therefore based on two levels of control memory. The first contains the microprogram itself, consisting of completely encoded microinstructions. The memory word length at this level is very small, while the number of words must be great enough to contain the entire interpreter or more than one interpreter. The second level, on the other hand, contains only the distinct microinstructions of the interpreter (or interpreters) in a completely decoded form. Thus, it will have a very long word length, typical of a horizontal format, but a very small number of words.

The advantages gained in terms of the overall amount of control memory occupied are considerable when the nanomemory technique is used. For example, an interpreter of 4K × 128-bit microinstructions in which only 64 types of distinct microinstructions appear would require:

- $4K \times 128 = 2^{19}$ bits of memory, using a single level in horizontal format
- $4K \times 6 + 64 \times 128 < 2^{15}$ bits of memory, by the nanomemory technique

One negative feature of nanomemory is a further slowing-down, which is generally greater than that introduced by the simple decoders used in the encoded field technique.

There exists another possibility: that of 'systematically' selecting subsets of microinstructions among those representable in horizontal format or in encoded fields. If two sets of bits or two encoded fields are used alternately (that is, when the set of controls generated by the first is being used, the set of controls generated by the second is not, and vice versa), it is not necessary to replicate the two fields in the microinstruction. Indeed, it suffices to have a single field, from which the control signals are directed to one unit or another according to the value assumed by another field of the microinstruction (Figure 7.17d). This other field, if it refers to the situation described, in which there are only two alternatives, is often known as the **steering bit**, otherwise it is known by the more general term **mode field**.

Finally, a technique that can be employed together with any of the schemas described above, is based on the possibility that a field remains constant over a number of microinstructions executed in sequence. In this case, no information is added by repeating such a field in each of the microinstructions, but rather control memory is wasted. The schema able to exploit such properties is called **residual control** (Figure 7.17e), and consists in lengthening the microinstruction obtained from the control memory with an additional register containing the constant field. At the beginning of the sequence, a microinstruction loads this field with the required configuration, and the microinstructions that follow contain the remaining control fields, which may vary from microinstruction to microinstruction.

Note that, in this case too, an encoding schema has been devised with the aim of restricting the set of microinstructions that can be represented to those that demonstrate a particular feature: that of having a field that remains constant over a number of instructions. The advantage in terms of saving memory is greater the longer the sequence over which the field stays constant, and should be compensated by the microinstruction bits that need to be used each time the field has to be preloaded and by the time taken to do this, unless it can be done in parallel with other operations.

7.7   Instruction decoding

The decoding phase consists in making each instruction opcode correspond to the start address of a different microprogram in control memory, each one connected to a separate execute phase. This effectively means constructing a 'case' operation.

There exist various ways of creating this correspondence.

One method consists in examining the bits of the opcode so as to trace a **decoding tree** (Figure 7.18). The corresponding microprogram has to make as many comparisons as the number of opcode bits.

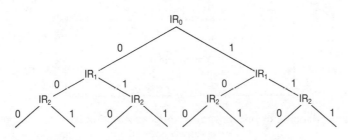

Figure 7.18   Decoding tree for a 3-bit opcode.

```
DECODE:     ADDR := JTAB+IR
            JMP ADDR

JTAB:       JMP OPCODE1
            JMP OPCODE2
              ⋮
```

Figure 7.19 Decoding by means of a jump table.

An alternative method consists in the adoption of a **jump table** (Figure 7.19). In this case, only three microinstructions need to be executed, one adding the opcode to the address of the start of the table, another to jump to the address obtained, and finally the jump instruction located in the entry selected in the table.

This method is not always applicable, as it requires the use of an indirect reference to contain the calculated address, and the micro-programming architecture may not provide support of this kind. There is not even an architectural support that allows us to add the opcode to the jump instruction directly, since the microprograms often have to be loaded in read only memory.

Another possibility would be to send the opcode directly on the highest order control memory address lines, and send '0' on the other lines (Figure 7.20). This type of decoding is rather rigid, since it always gives access to the same addresses and so is intolerant of microprogram memory shifts. Besides, it forces us to arrange the microprograms so that they begin from equidistant memory locations, causing serious wastes of memory space.

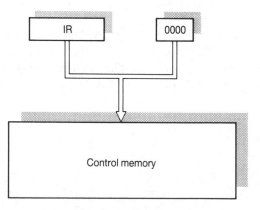

Figure 7.20 Mapping of opcodes to fixed-distance addresses (16 locations in the case shown above).

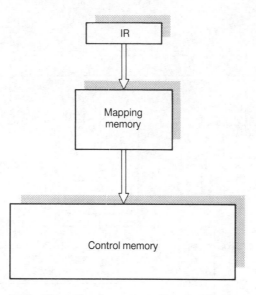

Figure 7.21   Decoding by means of a mapping memory.

The most flexible method is to employ a **mapping memory**. The opcode is sent along the address lines of this memory in order to select a location which contains the micromemory start address of the microprogram (Figure 7.21). If we wish to move the microprogram into another area of control memory, it suffices to change the contents of the corresponding memory mapping location with the new address.

7.8   The control unit

As stated above, the control unit is a mechanism that interprets microinstructions, together with a microprogram located in a control memory. This microprogram is in turn an interpreter of instructions at the machine code level.

Like any other interpreting mechanism, it must be equipped with a microprogram counter, MPC, and a microinstruction register, MIR. It must also have an MPC sequencing logic.

A control unit block diagram is given in Figure 7.22. It receives the start address of the microprogram to be executed from the mapping memory. After the fetch and decoding phases, the first microinstruction of the microprogram constituting the specific execute phase is extracted.

The address of the next microinstruction may be provided by the

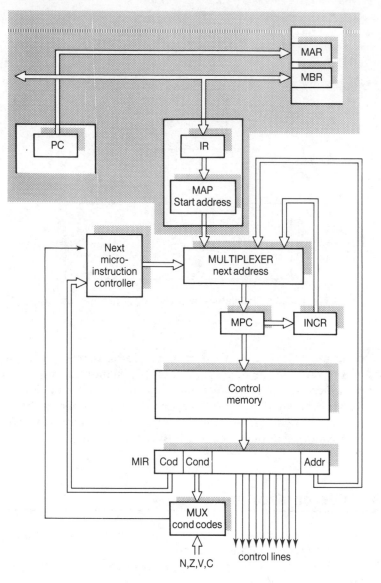

Figure 7.22 Control unit.

mapping memory or alternatively by the automatic advancing of the MPC, or indeed may be the result of a microjump. Which of the three will be used is decided by the 'next microinstruction controller' on the basis of the 'code' and 'cond' fields of the microinstruction. The 'cond' field selects one of the condition codes N, Z, V or C, produced by the arithmetic and logic unit, as the bit to be tested. Finally, the output of the controller selects the source for the next address to be loaded into the MPC.

The microinstruction located in the control memory location pointed to by the MPC is fetched and loaded into the MIR. From here the control lines divide out to the other units, both inside and outside the processor.

7.9   The arithmetic and logic unit

The arithmetic and logic unit is essentially made up of three components (Figure 7.23):

(1)   a set of general registers;

(2)   an ALU (Arithmetic and Logic Unit) proper, capable of carrying out some or all of the four arithmetic operations, perhaps on more than one base (binary and decimal), and the more important logic operations;

(3)   a shift unit, situated at the exit of the ALU.

The general registers are usually connected to both of the ALU inputs. Because of this, two registers can be selected at the same time in the microinstruction, by means of two address fields marked A and B in Figure 7.23 (bottom left). Through the single-bit field ST, it may be decided to store the result in the register selected by field B.

The decoding logic of the addresses A and B is usually constructed within what is known as a **two-port RAM**. Every RAM (Random Access Memory) has within it its own address decoding logic, but this is for a single address, so only one location at a time can be selected.

The data in the ALU may come from a variety of sources. For example, if an internal data bus exists as in Figure 7.23, it is enough to connect this to one of the two inputs of the ALU in multiplexing with one of the outputs of the general registers.

The two **latches** A and B are used to present stable data to the ALU every time that the same registers are used as the input and the output of the operation.

The ALU field of the microinstruction specifies the type of function required from the ALU, while the SH field serves to indicate whether it is desired to carry out a shift on the result, and if so what type of shift.

Among the ALU operations, there exists also a simple **pass** of one of the two operands. This is useful, for example, in transferring a data item from the data bus into one of the general registers, or else in performing shift operations without processing on the part of the ALU.

A collateral result of the ALU is given by the condition bits N, Z, V and C; that is the sign, zero, overflow and carry bits. Every ALU operation influences some or all of these bits, the value of which can be interrogated

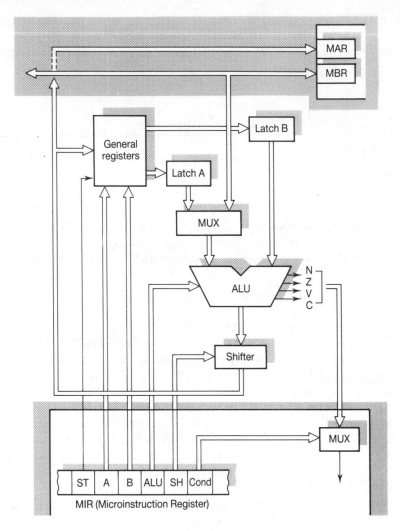

Figure 7.23 Arithmetic and logic unit.

both by the computer architecture instructions and by the microinstructions. As was stated in the previous section, the latter utilize the fields of the sequencer, and in particular the 'cond' field, to determine the next microinstruction to be carried out.

The arithmetic and logic unit may also perform services for the other units, such as the address unit. Indeed, this unit may be equipped with its own ALU, if it is intended to attain a high degree of parallelism; but much more often it uses that of the arithmetic and logic unit.

The operation becomes relatively simple if data and addresses are of the same length. In this case, the address registers can be put on to the data bus and utilized as one of the two operands of the ALU.

If the data bus is narrower than the one used for the addresses, and hence the width of the ALU is less, it becomes necessary to sequentialize the operations on the addresses, using multiple precision arithmetic.

In this case, it is more efficient to adopt a separate, suitably dimensioned ALU for addresses.

The general registers may even emulate address registers. That is to say, some of the general registers may be dedicated as address registers, as happens in many architectures. In this case, there will no longer be any distinction between the arithmetic and logic unit and the address unit, apart from the different microprograms that utilize the same resources.

7.10   Hardwired versus microprogrammed control

As was stated in the introduction to this chapter, the first generations of computers had no microprogramming level. The machine-level instructions were directly interpreted in the hardware by quite complex circuits which had the task of generating the complete timing that corresponded to the execution of each instruction. Correspondingly, the control unit used to be described as **hardwired**, that is, composed of combinatorial networks and sequential circuits. The complexity and the cost of these circuits was such that efforts were made as far as possible to identify the parts common to different circuits, so as not to replicate them. The result ended up even more complex than if separate circuits had been made, with the consequence that designing computers became extremely time-consuming and expensive. Moreover, once the project had been finished, it was very difficult to modify it with updates in the light of new requirements. The result was that once a project was completed, it was considered virtually untouchable.

Designing with these characteristics was in sharp contrast with a rapidly evolving technology. The risk was that a project, born with a certain type of component in mind, lasted so long that in the meantime new components had come out with much better architectural features at a much lower cost.

Furthermore, very high design costs are unacceptable if the technology provides production processes that are capable of cutting the cost of components drastically.

Last of all, designing control units becomes much more systematic and orderly if microprogramming techniques are employed. Hence, as soon as the memory technology was capable of meeting the demands of microprogramming, the technique was almost universally adopted.

The sole exceptions were in cases where very high speeds were required, an area in which hardwired control is unbeatable.

The reason why designing control units is simpler using microprogramming techniques lies in the fact that the problem of timing each instruction is broken down into more elementary timing subproblems. The microinstruction cycle itself is a way of introducing timing in a simple and systematic way. In each cycle, different micro-operations or micro-orders (those permitted by the microinstruction format and the encoding technique adopted) can be executed in parallel. If this simple mechanism does not prove to be sufficient, one may resort to performing an **internal timing** on the microinstruction cycle. This consists in subdividing the microinstruction cycle into two or more identical subcycles and enabling certain micro-orders to be executed only in the first subcycle, others only in the second subcycle, and so on. If only one undivided cycle exists, it is known as **monophase control**, otherwise the term **polyphase control** is used.

As may be observed, the polyphase control technique also introduces a timing of a general sort, allowing micro-orders belonging to different groups to be sequenced. For example, storing the result of an ALU operation can only be performed after selecting its input operands. In a biphase organization, in which the microinstruction cycle is subdivided into two subcycles, the selection of the two operands (from the file of general registers, or from the internal bus, for example) will be enabled in the first subcycle, while the storing of the result, together with any shifts, will be enabled in the second subcycle.

A hardware timing of the same operation, though more efficient, since it can be cut 'to measure', would nevertheless require *ad hoc* analysis and design.

The evolution of computer architecture has always moved in the direction of greater functional complexity, made possible by technological advances. Microprogramming has aided this process by virtue of its inherent capacity for 'programming the timing'.

Nevertheless, with the passing of time, more and more people have become convinced that increasing architectural complexity without taking account of the implementation does not maximize the opportunities offered by the technology. For instance, introducing into the instruction set a new complex instruction, which replaces a lot of machine instructions, is only interesting if that instruction is used frequently. If not, it ends up taking away resources (such as area of silicon) from other more frequently used functions, such as a fast buffer memory or other architectural systems capable of introducing concurrency into the processing.

This is the principle that lies behind RISC (Reduced Instruction Set Computers) architectures, which have practically eliminated the microprogramming level, or, if one prefers, the machine language level. In other words, in these machines the computer architecture has been reformulated in such a way as to have simple, regular machine instructions, with few addressing methods, and making use as far as possible of a large set of registers. Under these conditions, interpreting instructions becomes very simple and efficient, and may be compared to interpreting microinstructions. Architectures of this kind will be discussed in Chapter 10.

Further reading

Interconnection structures

Stallings W. (1987). *Computer Organization and Architecture*, pp. 62–81. New York: Macmillan

The microprogramming level

Dasgupta S. (1984). *The Design and Description of Computer Architectures*. New York: Wiley
De Blasi M., Gentile A., Lopez G. and Sozzo M. (1988). The teaching of microprogramming design. *Proc. IEE on The Teaching of Electronic Engineering in Degree Courses–Shaping for the Future*, 7.1–7.9. Hull
Tanenbaum A. S. (1984). *Structured Computer Organization*, 2nd edn, pp. 117–80. Englewood Cliffs, NJ: Prentice Hall

Bus arbitration

van de Goor A. J. (1989). *Computer Architecture and Design*, pp. 375–83. Wokingham: Addison-Wesley

Direct memory access

Stallings W. (1987). *Computer Organization and Architecture*, pp. 143–9. New York: Macmillan

EXERCISES

7.1 A very simple machine has only the following opcodes:

LOAD	0000
STORE	0010
ADD	0100
ADC	0101
DEC	0111
SUB	1000
JMP_ZERO	1010
JMP_POS	1011
JMP	1100
INC	1111

(a) Using a binary decoding tree, define an optimized decoding path, based on the entropic algorithm of recognition. This consists in beginning the decoding from the bit position which transports the maximum quantity of information, in other words, that whose values are more equally distributed. Then operate repeatedly in the same manner on the subsets of codes obtained.

(b) Dynamic measures show the following relative frequencies:

LOAD	0.125

STORE 0.125
ADD 0.127
ADC 0.126
DEC 0.0605
SUB 0.126
JMP_ZERO 0.0615
JMP_POS 0.0605
JMP 0.0615
INC 0.127

Using the Huffman coding, define a code with variable length, in such a way that the recognition process by means of a decoding tree is the shortest possible.

7.2 The **interleaved** memory is characterized by the fact that memory words at consecutive addresses are on different modules.

How may this memory organization be obtained by using two memory chips? And by using four chips?

7.3 A microarchitecture uses a mapping memory for the instruction decoding. After the fetch phase, formalized in Figure 7.15, the decoding is carried out by the microinstruction:

MPC := Mapping_store[Opcode(IR)]

The execute phase of the instruction:

Load Target_addr, Reg_number

can be carried out by the microinstruction sequence:

```
Load: MAR := Target_addr (IR); RD
      RD
      Register_set[Reg_number(IR)] := MBR; GOTO Fetch
```

Using the same language, describe the execute phase of the instructions:

Store Reg_number, Target_addr
Jmp_if_zero Target_addr

7.4 Describe a possible implementation of the mechanism of the daisy chain (Figure 7.6), without considering the signal $\overline{\text{BGACK}}$.

7.5 A processor has four input lines for the bus request by I/O devices (this is called centralized control of the bus). The lines have a decreasing priority from the first to the last. In the case of simultaneous requests, the processor assigns the bus control to the device connected to the line with greater priority.

How can this priority scheme be realized? Is it possible to connect more than four devices, and how?

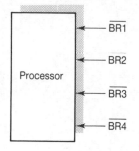

7.6 (a) In a microarchitecture the microinstructions are 50-bits long. The 'sequencer' field alone occupies 10-bits. Evaluate the possible benefits of using the microinstruction coding technique named 'residual control', applied to the sequencer field. Calculate:

   (i) the smallest mean number of contiguous microinstructions that do not effect jumps, which would make the use of the technique beneficial;

   (ii) the mean number of such instructions necessary to reduce by 1/10 the microprogram memory occupation.

(b) Compare the preceding technique with the use of separate jump microinstructions.

7.7 A microarchitecture has microinstructions 100-bits long. The stored microprograms require 1800 control memory locations. The aim is to reduce the quantity of control memory by using one of three coding techniques:

- onc is to code some microinstruction fields making it possible to obtain a length of 60 bits;

- another possibility is that of using residual control, thus obtaining microinstructions 55 bits long, with a mean number of 9 microinstructions in sequence between two register loadings;

- the last technique is that of using a nanomemory, taking into account that there are 300 distinct microinstructions.

   Which of the three techniques is the best for minimizing the capacity of control memory?

⑧ Operating System Support

8.1 Exception and interrupt
    processing
8.2 Memory management and
    protection

8.3 Access to shared resources
    Further reading
    Exercises

8.1 Exception and interrupt processing

The processor is an interpreter of instructions, that is, it receives and carries out commands from the instructions and then prepares for the next instruction to be executed. In each instruction there exists a data processing component and a control variation component (implicitly or explicitly). All this is what is meant by the term **normal** processing state, and is represented by the state diagram of the instruction cycle shown in Figure 7.13.

However, the processor may receive and so have to deal with other types of signal. These may be:

- signals due to events connected with the execution of the current instruction: the so-called **exceptions**;
- signals caused by events generated in any part of the system, which are therefore independent of the current instruction, called **interrupts**.

In both cases, the processor must know how to recognize the nature

219

of the event that has produced the signal and how to interpret it, by carrying out a specific procedure for that type of event. This procedure is known as a **service routine**.

To carry out the service routine, the processor has to interrupt the normal instruction cycle. In this sense, instruction interpreting is normal, while exception and interrupt interpreting is exceptional.

The processing of exceptions is essentially identical to that of interrupts, and both are reminiscent of procedure calls. All three cases, in fact, involve a change of context, though under different conditions.

There is a tendency to group exceptions and interrupts under a single name, together with any other event that may give rise to processing of an exceptional kind. We shall therefore also recognize this practice by using the term 'exceptions' in future to include all these types of event.

8.1.1 Processing states

In accordance with what was said in the previous section, when the processor interprets an exception it carries out a sequence of operations, which tend to save the current processing status and carry itself over to the new status required by the service of the specific exception in question.

This implies the realization of four processing states:

(a) *normal* instruction interpreting
(b) *saving* the processor status
(c) interpreting the *exception*
(d) *restoring* the previous processor status

The state diagram for exception processing is given in Figure 8.1.

The processor is normally in machine instruction interpreting state (a) and returns to this after every interpretation ('normal sequence' in Figure 8.1).

When an exception arises, the processor, after recognizing the agent that has caused it, passes into current status saving state (b).

It then enters into state (c) to interpret the service procedure for the exception in question. This is also a 'normal' instruction interpreting cycle, since in this state a procedure is carried out. This cycle too may be interrupted by the occurrence of a further exception (broken lines in Figure 8.1), which would make the processor return to state (b) in order to save the status acquired during the execution of the service procedure.

This may occur a number of times, and therefore at a certain point a number of different statuses may be saved in memory. These will then be restored one after the other in reverse order with respect to the order in which they were saved. Once again we have a requirement for a stack, which has a characteristic LIFO (Last In First Out) type of access.

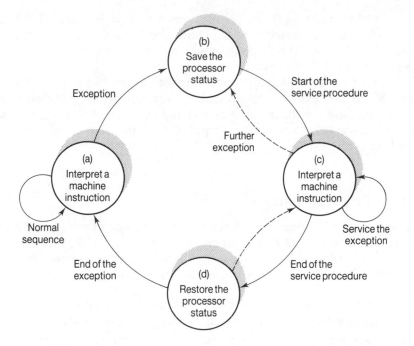

Figure 8.1 State diagram for exception processing.

So, when the processor has finished executing the service procedure, it enters state (d) to restore the previous status. This may concern the normal sequence or else a previous exception state.

Generally the signal that calls the exception treatment must be stored in an internal processor state, so as to allow the processor to complete the interpreting of the current instruction or the phase being executed. The moment when the processor will begin to take notice of the event in arrival may depend:

(1)   *on the type of event*. For instance, a bus error is immediately acted on, without waiting for the end of the instruction.

(2)   *on the type of instruction*. Most instructions allow for the processing of an exception due to an event occurring during their execution to be put off till the end of execution. On the other hand, other instructions have execution times that are too long to permit this. String processing, for example, is usually interrupted in order to deal with an exception arising during execution.

(3)   *on the instruction sequence that the processor is dealing with*. In this case, the event in arrival may need to be more or less urgently dealt with compared with the current processing.

While for cases (1) and (2) the moment when the event should be dealt with can be perfectly well determined by the type of event or instruction, in case (3) this moment may be delayed by the program. An instruction sequence can ask not to be interrupted and so to begin dealing with the outstanding interrupts and exceptions at the end of the sequence itself. Moreover, this moment depends on a certain **priority** relation being established between the event in arrival and the current state of processing. In Section 8.1.3, the different types of exception are analysed and we also look at their priorities.

8.1.2 Privilege states

Another kind of distinction is generally made between states, in terms of the resources exploited by the processor. Indeed, it is the processor that has the job of adequately protecting the resources, and this may be accomplished by creating different modes of access by means of:

- *Instruction execution privileges*, that is, which instructions the processor will be able to carry out in a given access mode.
- *Memory access privileges*, that is, which memory locations the current instructions can accede to.

This becomes necessary when different programs are being executed within the same system (multiprogramming and multiprocessing), so as to protect the memory, processor and input/output resources of each from the other.

Also in the case where a single program occupies the resources of the entire system, there is always the operating system, which needs to be safeguarded from erroneous operations on the part of the user program.

Several modes of access may be found in a processor, but at least two are needed to guarantee protection of resources: the **user** state and the **supervisor** or **system** state.

Most programs can be run in the user state. Their accesses are controlled and the effects they can have on other parts of the system are limited. This is obtained by privileging (rendering available only to programs in system state) certain instructions, such as program execution stop instructions, external device resets and those which modify specific parts of the status register.

All the input/output instructions are also privileged for those processors in which they are 'explicit', that is, those processors equipped with separate memory and I/O address spaces.

The only means that a processor equipped with only two modes of access has of passing from the user state to the supervisor state is through processing an exception.

All exception processing is carried out in the supervisor state. Therefore, the moment the processor prepares to process an exception, it also saves the privilege state in which it is operating and carries into the supervisor state. On its return from the exception, it will also return to the previous privilege state, be it user or supervisor.

Control over memory accesses may be exercised by means of suitable **memory management** and **protection** techniques (Section 8.2).

Both the attempt to use privileged instructions in the user state and the attempt to access non-permitted memory locations generate **violation exceptions**.

8.1.3 Types of exception

Interrupts from I/O devices

These types of interrupt are signals through which an I/O device communicates to the processor the occurrence of an event, such as having terminated an I/O operation and hence being ready for the next operation.

Alternative to the interrupt is making the program interrogate an I/O device status flag.

Since each device has its own flag, the program has to interrogate all of them, or rather all that it intends to communicate with. This technique is usually known as **polling**, since the processor goes through the I/O devices one after another (Figure 8.2).

Interrogating a flag or flags is a technique that wastes a lot of the processor's time: it is forced to spend much of its time in what is called a form of 'busy waiting', in an interrogation loop (Figure 8.3).

Of course the processor can avoid continually asking about the status of flags. It can carry out its normal processing and interrogate the resource flag concerned only at the end of an instruction sequence. If it is ready, all well and good, otherwise it returns to processing and makes the request again at the end of another sequence, and so on.

This way of proceeding, however, involves the risk of missing events if more than one follow on between one flag interrogation and the next and also keeps the processor busy.

An interrupt is the notification of an event that takes place in a way that is **asynchronous** with the activity of the program. It has no correlation with the execution of the program because it originates from outside the program. It may occur at any time during the execution of instructions, but it is temporarily **latched** inside the processor, to be taken account of when the instruction active when it was found finishes executing.

Interrupts are usually divided in two categories: **maskable** and **non-maskable**. Maskable interrupts can be inhibited altogether by means of a

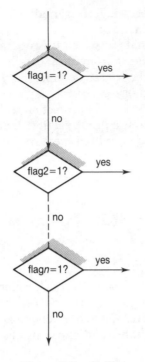

Figure 8.2. Polling.

disable interrupt instruction, which clears the interrupt flag in the status register. Non-maskable interrupts refer to interrupts that must be served in any case.

Selective inhibition can be reached by means of several bits of a mask field in the status register, each one corresponding to one type or class of interrupt. However, a more common and efficient system is based on restricting selection to a hierarchical organization by means of the so-called priority mechanism. This consists in assigning to each interrupt type a

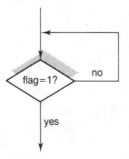

Figure 8.3 Busy waiting loop (for a single I/O device).

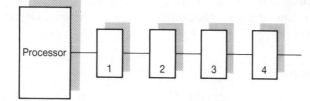

Figure 8.4 Daisy chain.

different integer, called priority level, in a manner such that an interrupt is served if its **priority** is higher than the one the processor finds itself in, otherwise it is suspended and remains waiting until the processor's priority drops below its own.

When the processor enters into an interrupt service procedure, it takes on the priority of the latter. In this way, lower priority interrupts will not be able to interrupt the service procedure. Vice versa, higher priority interrupts break into the service procedure of the preceding interrupt and the processor goes on to serve the new higher priority interrupt.

On returning from an interrupt service procedure, the processor assumes the priority that it had previously.

The priority held by the processor is stored in a field of the status register. The levels of priority may go from 1 to a given highest number (such as 7).

Not only interrupts from I/O devices but also all the other exceptions are subject to the priority mechanism, with the result that the number of levels provided may turn out to be insufficient, especially if the system is equipped with a large number of I/O devices.

The problem is usually solved by using, together with the priority levels, a technique known as **daisy chaining** (Figure 8.4). With this technique, a chain of I/O devices connected each to the next as in the figure is associated with every priority level. The connection line, both in input and in output from each device, has to be on the logical level '1' if it is desired for that device to be able to interrupt the processor. When this happens, the device will set its output line to logical '0', as will all the other I/O devices to its right, when they see a logical '0' arriving in input along the same line.

At this point, while the processor is serving the device that has interrupted it, all the devices that find themselves to its left have both their daisy chain connections set to '1' and can therefore interrupt.

On the contrary, all the other devices, that is, the one being serviced and all those to its right, do not have their daisy chain set to '1' and so cannot interrupt.

Hence this simple-to-realize daisy chain mechanism assigns priority on the basis of the position that the various devices occupy in the chain.

If the priority levels are used in conjunction with this, a number of daisy chains can be used, set at different priority levels and following their rules as a block.

Traps and faults

Traps are interruptions generated by the execution of specific instructions. Thus, unlike interrupts, they are correlated with the program being run, and are synchronous with the activity of the processor.

Examples of traps are exceptions caused by an overflow and by a division by zero. These are events that would be repeated at the same instruction, if the same program were to be run again with the same data. On the other hand, an interrupt, since it is generated by an external device, could never be repeated at the same instant during a subsequent re-run of the program.

It is useful to distinguish traps from faults.

Traps are exceptions generated at the end of the instruction, after the transformation of state caused by the instruction execution has taken place. The PC, after a trap, points to the next instruction.

Faults, on the contrary, refer to exceptions raised during an instruction, with a state transformation which is recoverable, so the PC continues to point to the same instruction. For example, 'divide by zero' is detectable before executing the division and then can be managed as a fault, while an overflow cannot. **Aborts** are also exception conditions occurring during an instruction, but without any possibility of recovery. In these cases the program must be terminated.

Other types of trap may be generated, not by anomalous conditions of the type illustrated, but by instructions for performing a **system call**. In this case, the instruction calls up a trap explicitly, and the processor will proceed to execute a specific service procedure selected by the value of the operand in the instruction. This is the way in which a user program can request services from the supervisor and hence gain access in a controlled way to resources that it cannot make use of directly.

Like interrupts, traps are served at the end of execution of the instruction in which the trap condition was verified.

Among the faults, there are those that refer to notification that the instruction cannot be executed. There can be three types of non-executable instructions:

- *Privileged instructions*: instructions that cannot be executed in the access mode in which the processor finds itself.
- *Illegal instructions*: bit configurations that do not correspond to instructions, which the processor is attempting to interpret as instructions. Typically, this kind of situation can arise if control is erroneously transferred to a data area.

● *Planned, but not yet realized instructions.* These too generate an exception, but one which is interpreted differently from an error. In this case, the service procedure constitutes an efficient mechanism for simulating new instructions. The term 'simulation' is applied to software interpretation, while the term 'emulation' is used for microprogram interpretation of new instructions or instructions from other architectures.

Other faults are generated by the memory management unit (Section 8.2) and are mentioned later under bus errors.

Tracing

It is possible to introduce a new processing state, the **trace** state, in which every instruction generates an exception immediately after being executed. In this way, a program, or some parts of it, can be monitored while being executed without modifying them in any way.

Bus errors

Bus errors are generated by one of two possible causes:

(1)   a bus synchronization signal that the processor is expecting from an I/O device and which is late in arriving, with the risk of blocking the processor indefinitely in a bus cycle. A special logic outside the processor can detect this event and generate the appropriate exception.

(2)   a memory protection violation is detected by the memory management unit (see Section 8.2).

In both cases, the current bus cycle is aborted and the exception is processed immediately.

It should be noted that the saving of the processing context is more detailed in these cases than for trap and interrupt processing. For instance, it is necessary to save also the address set during the aborted bus cycle and to indicate whether it was a reading or writing operation.

Reset

An exception arising from a catastrophic event provokes a system crash. In these circumstances only a reset input from the outside can make the system start up again. This input is also used to launch the system at the start.

A reset input in turn generates an exception of a particular kind. As the reset is sent following a (re)start from the beginning, there is no status saving. In any case, any information relating to status that may have been saved after a catstrophic event would be totally unreliable.

Multiple exceptions

This term is intended to refer to a case where a number of exceptions may arise in the course of the same instruction. The processor needs to have a policy to follow in this kind of situation.

First of all, a priority is assigned to different classes of exceptions, so that reset and bus errors exceptions, for example, always provoke an immediate interruption and ensure that the current bus cycle is aborted, independently of the presence or otherwise of other exceptions.

Apart from this, there are policies that depend on the type of relationship between the exceptions that are present at the same time. To give an example, if an interrupt arrives during an instruction being executed in the trace state, the latter has precedence and is served before the interrupt. Besides, if the instruction in question is a trap instruction, the trap exception will be processed first, then the trace and finally the interrupt.

8.1.4 Exception vectors

Exception vectors are the starting addresses of the service routines and are stored in a table in main memory.

To serve an exception, it is necessary to obtain its vector. This is done by means of a **vector number**, which is an index to the above table that exclusively indentifies the exception. It is generated internally or externally according to the type of exception.

If generated externally, the vector number will be read on the data bus in an interrupt recognition bus cycle. Thus, the peripheral that has generated the interrupt has to make provision to place its vector number on the data bus.

Starting from the vector number 'i', all that is then needed is a transformation of the type:

$$addr = a + b \times i$$

to obtain the address 'addr' of the corresponding entry in the table. The two constants 'a' and 'b' are the start address of the table and the length of each vector measured in minimal addressable units (typically bytes or words) respectively.

These operations are carried out automatically by the processor each time an exception occurs, with the purpose of obtaining the address of the service procedure that control is to be transferred to.

There also exists a less efficient software-based method for solving the problem of recognizing the source of the interrupt. After receiving the interrupt request this method begins a recognition procedure of the type shown in Figure 8.2 (polling routine).

Although it is not as inefficient as the method based exclusively on flag interrogation (the polling routine for recognition is executed only on receiving an interrupt request), this method remains slow and, above all, it has to suspend the processing to identify the exception even if this one is of a lower priority.

8.1.5 Exception processing sequence

The set of operations carried out by the processor before entering the service procedure is relatively independent of the type of exception. It is generally referred to as the exception processing sequence and may appear as represented in Figure 8.5.

First of all, the processor makes a copy of the status register, since it will subsequently need to save it.

Next it updates the status register to indicate that it is entering the supervisor state. It also deactivates the trace status bit, as tracing is not practicable in a service procedure.

The next step involves the processor taking on the priority level of the exception being dealt with (which will necessarily be higher than the current one). This level may also be stored in the status register.

If the exception is an interrupt, the vector number is read; otherwise it is already known by the processor. The address of the exception vector is then calculated.

At this point the processor status may be saved; that is, the copy of the status register together with the program counter. This step is not

1.	Make a copy of the status register
2.	Go into supervisor state
3.	Disable trace if any
4.	Update the processor priority level to that of the exception
5.	Obtain the vector number
6.	Calculate the address of the exception vector
7.	Save the processor state
8.	Extract the new program counter value from the exception vector
9.	Recommence the normal instruction interpretation cycle

Figure 8.5 Exception processing sequence on the MC68000.

carried out in certain types of exception, such as *reset*; while in others, additional information is also saved.

Finally, the new value of the program counter is loaded, derived from the service procedure address table, using the address of the vector as a pointer. In this way the processor is able to return to the normal instruction cycle and so can go on to interpret the exception service procedure.

8.2   Memory management and protection

We have already seen in Chapter 3 that there exists a variety of addressing methods which the processor must be able to operate to obtain what has been called the effective or absolute address. For this purpose, the processor is equipped with an address calculation section, looked at in the preceding chapter.

The address obtained by the unit refers to a linear space of undifferentiated, contiguous locations. And indeed the main memory presents itself in this way: a collection of contiguous, undifferentiated locations. For this reason the following equality relationship appears entirely natural:

logical address space = physical address space

where 'logical' refers to the program and 'physical' to the machine.

Having established the effective difference between the logical address and the physical address, the numerical coincidence between the two may be considered as simply a particular case of a more general relationship.

By means of this relationship, the processor can exercise control over the use of the memory.

Problems of memory management arise for three sorts of reason:

(1)   a need on the part of the user program to utilize a logical address space that is larger than the physical one available;

(2)   the assigning and subdivision of the physical address space to a number of different user programs;

(3)   the protection of the physical address area assigned to a user from possible interference by other user programs. Besides this, the memory areas used by the supervisor need to be protected from user programs.

Point (1) is resolved by the concept of **virtual memory**. This is based on the existence of a secondary direct-access memory (magnetic discs), which make it possible to obtain logical address spaces of enormous capacities, and also on the locality principle. Logical addresses, employed in considerable intervals of time by a program being executed, are generally grouped into a few areas of contiguous addresses, which may vary from one time-span to the next, but whose total size is substantially smaller than the total number of logical addresses used by the program throughout its run.

The virtual memory management mechanism must therefore provide for an efficient arrangement of the logical address areas, used at any given moment, in main memory.

Point (2) requires an easy mechanism for **dynamic relocation**. This hinges on the system's facility for shifting logical address areas between different physical address areas at any time after their first loading. The reason for these shifts is the need to reduce the consequences of the so-called **checkerboard** effect.

This phenomenon arises from the destruction and creation of physical address areas needed to accommodate new logical address areas, which after some time can lead to the creation of a mass of small free areas of physical addresses. These areas, though their total dimensions are considerable, are individually too small to accommodate meaningful blocks of logical addresses (external fragmentation).

The third point, relating to protection, may be satisfied if each area of physical addresses is provided with **access attributes**, which define whether the locations of the area in question can be accessed by the particular subject which is requiring it and, in that case, if these locations can be both read from and written to, or only read from, or even only be executed.

8.2.1 Mapping

One factor in common among the different memory management techniques is the creation of mapping between areas of contiguous logical addresses and areas of contiguous physical addresses. In other words, the law of translation of the addresses and the protection attributes are assigned not to each distinct address but rather to entire areas.

It would not be possible to provide distinct mapping and access methods for each individual address, nor would it be very useful to do so.

The simplest mapping method considers the program as a single area of contiguous logical addresses to which a single area of contiguous physical addresses is made to correspond. In such a case, the **map**, that is the information about where the program is placed in memory, is composed of only two items: the **base** address, starting from which the program is (re)loaded, and its **size**. The **mapping function** $m = f(l, \text{map})$, which makes a logical address l correspond to a physical memory address m, is a simple adding operation:

$$m = \text{base} + l$$

A **protection** can be realized by rendering non-valid the physical addresses obtained from logical addresses which are greater than the size defined in a map.

From an architectural point of view, what is required is an adder to realize the mapping function, a comparator for the protection, and two registers in order to store the program map.

Although this method makes it possible to move the programs after they have started to run, and carries out the mapping efficiently, it does not eliminate what can be considered a major inefficiency: the need to resort to frequent **compacting** in order to reduce the fragmentation, when the need arises to create space for new programs or for programs already resident.

As an alternative to the model of a single contiguous address space, which corresponds to a static vision of the program, the **dynamic** model sees a program in execution as composed of a number of separate address areas, inside each of which the contiguity constraint is observed.

This model is interesting not only because it maintains in main memory only those parts of the program that are 'active' at each moment, but also because it makes it possible to diminish or eliminate the need to effect shifts of main memory areas for compactions.

Passing from the single area model to that of multiple areas, the map becomes more complex, because it must describe the location of the various logical areas in different physical areas not adjacent. The form which the map now assumes is that of a **descriptor table**, in which each entry is the map of a logical area. The mapping function is the same for all the areas and may consist, as we will see, of a sum or of a concatenation.

To render this mechanism possible, it is necessary to pass from a single-component address to a two-component address. The first component specifies the address area, while the second represents the address within the area (the **offset**).

There are essentially two methods of subdividing the logical address space into address areas (Figure 8.6):

- **segmentation**, in which the result of the address calculation that the processor carries out beginning from the 'operand' field of the instruction, is taken as the offset;
- **paging**, in which the calculated address represents the whole logical address with both its components.

In the first case, the number of the segment is predetermined, with the result that the memory management operations may be begun immediately and conducted in parallel with the address calculation.

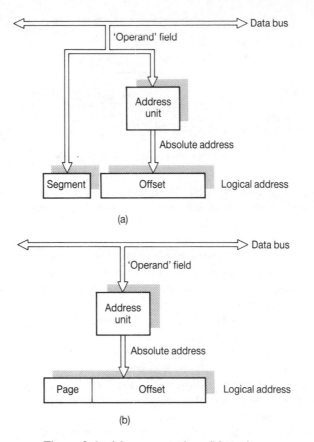

Figure 8.6 (a) segmentation; (b) paging.

In the second case, the management unit has to wait for the address to be calculated before beginning to operate. In fact, the 'page number' is not fixed by the program but, as stated previously, results from the calculation carried out by the address unit.

In either case, the segment number or the page number are input to the memory management unit (Figure 8.7), so that the latter can ascertain the access rights of the current instruction for that segment or page. If access is confirmed, the logical address will be translated into a physical address, using both components of the logical address.

Otherwise, an exception request will be sent to the processor, which will suspend the current bus cycle and proceed to carry out an appropriate service procedure.

Another important consequence of knowing the segment number *a priori* is that the segment can be provided not only with access protection attributes, but also with lengths that differ from one to another. This

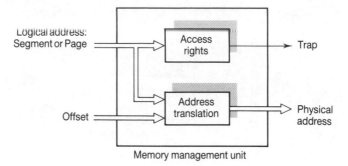

Figure 8.7   The memory management unit verifies access rights and translates the logical addresses into physical addresses.

length will be in relation to the processing 'object' to be memorized in each segment, be it a procedure, an array or a stack. Apart from controlling rights of access, it will also be ensured that the offset is not greater than the length of the segment.

On the other hand, with paged memory, the pages are all of a constant length, since no relation exists between the memory page and the processing object that occupies it. The entire paging process is made completely transparent to the programmer.

Whereas one processing object (and only one) normally fits into each segment, with paging the object may occupy a number of pages, or alternatively a part of a page together with other objects.

Both segmentation and paging have problems of fragmentation.

In the case of segmentation, we have **external fragmentation**, arising from the several segments succeeding each other in the same memory area.

In paging, on the other hand, the phenomenon of **internal fragment-ation** is present. It derives from the fact that the pages can be occupied for a fraction alone. The bigger the page size, the greater the problem. The adoption of small pages requires descriptor tables of great dimensions. So, a compromise is usually reached.

Alternatively, some architectures adopt two or more page sizes, an approach more like the segmentation of using logical areas of any length.

The support provided by the processor to memory management is given through the agency of a specific unit known as the MMU (Memory Management Unit). This support unit includes:

- the table of descriptors or some subset of it, made up from a register set;
- a unit for access type verification and, in the case of segmentation, for comparison with the segment length;
- an address translation unit.

31	16	8	0
Base address 0	L0	A0	
Base address 1	L1	A1	
⋮	⋮	⋮	
Base address 63	L63	A63	

Figure 8.8 Segment descriptor table in the MMU Z8010 memory management unit for the Zilog Z8000 processor. It is made up of 64 32-bit registers, each representing the descriptor of a segment. Each descriptor is divided into three fields representing the base address, the length and the attributes of the segment it describes. Both the base address and the length are in units of 256 bytes.

8.2.2 Segmentation

Figure 8.8 shows an example of a segment descriptor table. The segment number constitutes the index to the table.

Every descriptor is made up of three fields:

- **base address** of the segment, often (but not necessarily) expressed by means of an appropriate scale factor '2^n', that is, with the n lowest order bits equal to zero, and therefore implied. This is done to save bits. Consequently each segment can begin at an address that is a multiple of 2^n (alignment of 2^n);
- **length** of the segment, also expressed with the same or another scale factor;
- **attributes** of the segment.

The segment descriptor is extracted from the table through the segment number. At this point both the verification and the address translation operations begin.

The **verification** consists of:

- comparing the upper part of the offset, that is, the offset stripped of the lowest order bits, with the length of the segment (Figure 8.9);
- checking the access rights for that segment. These are conveyed in the attributes field of the descriptor (Figure 8.10).

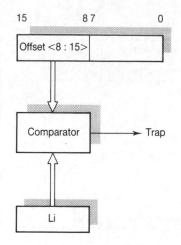

Figure 8.9 Comparison of the upper part of the offset with the length of the segment.

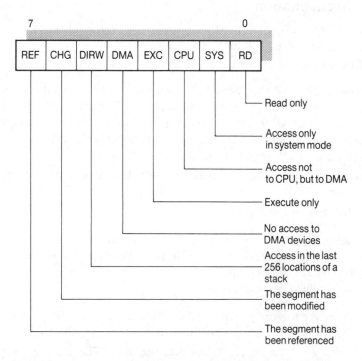

Figure 8.10 The segment descriptor attributes field for the Z8010.

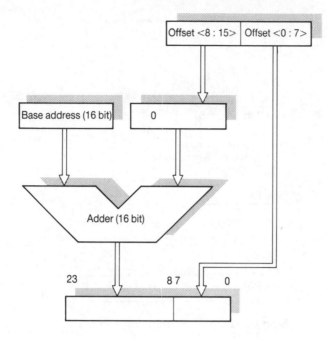

Figure 8.11 Address translation on the Z8010.

A violation of access rights, as well as an 'off-limits' of the segment addresses, generate an exception and at the same time suppress the bus cycle to prevent access to memory.

Only in the case which corresponds to access to the last 2^n locations of a stack is there an exception generated but no suppression of the bus cycle. This situation is not a violation exception, but simply a warning to the operating system to allocate further memory to the stack in question.

The **address translation** makes use of an adding device in which the base address and the offset are added.

The representation of the base address in 2^n units makes it possible to adopt not only shorter descriptor fields, but also an adder with n fewer stages. The adder (Figure 8.11) can avoid adding the n lowest order bits of the offset, which would otherwise be added to the n zero bits of the base address, and can instead be simply concatenated to the result obtained from the adding device.

8.2.3 Paging

In paging, as was stated before, all the pages are of the same size, so there is no need for a field to specify the length in a page descriptor.

Furthermore, for the same reason, it is not necessary to provide a

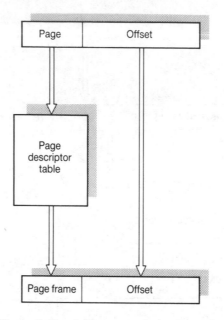

Figure 8.12 Address translation in paging.

start address for each page (the 'base' address in Figure 8.8). In fact, it is enough to provide a physical page number (**page frame**) corresponding to each logical page represented by the descriptors. The address translation mechanism is therefore simpler than the one used in segmentation (Figure 8.12), consisting of just a concatenation.

8.2.4 Virtual memory

Paging is often accompanied by virtual memory management techniques. These correspond to the case in which the pages are more numerous than the page frames.

Since there may be a very large number of pages of virtual memory, the descriptor table requires a main memory support, while the support provided by the processor generally consists of a table containing the descriptors of the pages used most recently and hence most likely to be used again.

The page number cannot constitute an index to the table of the descriptors of the most recently used pages within the processor, since the position of the descriptor in the table no longer corresponds to the page number. This information must now appear explicitly in the descriptor, and a search must be made using this key field.

If a descriptor is found with a key field that corresponds to the page number, the other information will be extracted so as to obtain the physical

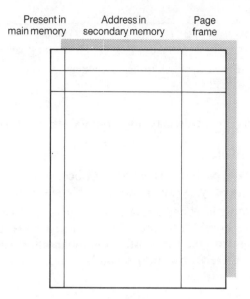

Present in main memory	Address in secondary memory	Page frame

Figure 8.13   Example of a descriptor table in main memory.

address. If this is not the case, we will have to resort to the descriptor table in main memory. This time the page number will be used as an index to the table and the corresponding descriptor can thus be extracted and utilized. At the same time, provision will have to be made for the least recently used descriptor to be replaced by the current descriptor in the processor table.

Figure 8.13 shows an example of a page descriptor table in main memory. In each descriptor there are at least three fields:

- 1 bit of presence which, if set to '1', serves to indicate that the corresponding page exists in main memory;
- the address of the page in secondary memory;
- the page frame in which the page has been loaded, if present in main memory.

If memory access is requested to a page whose presence bit is set to '0', a **page fault** is generated; that is, an exception which suppresses the current bus cycle and loads into a free page frame the page from the secondary memory address indicated in the second field.

If no page frame is free, one of the page frames already occupied must be chosen and liberated by dumping its contents into secondary memory (again using the address located in the second field). Then the required page is loaded in its place.

At this point the system automatically regenerates the bus cycle that had been suppressed.

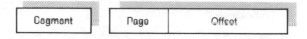

Figure 8.14 A three-component address.

The descriptor fields may also contain other information, such as:

- access attributes;
- how long the page described has not been used, in order to choose the least recently used page for possible substitution;
- whether there has been access for the purpose of writing to the page referred to by the descriptor. This information is useful because, if this page is selected for substitution by another page, it will not be necessary to rewrite it into secondary memory if it has not been modified.

A further support provided by the processor is to use an **associative memory** to contain its own descriptor table. In this type of memory, access is gained through the contents of the key field and not through an address. The page number is compared with the key fields of all the descriptors at the same time, and if it corresponds to one of them, the rest of the information contained in the descriptor is provided. This kind of memory permits a search through a table in a single cycle, and is thus much faster than any kind of procedural method.

Associative memories are only practicable at reasonable cost if they are small-sized: the application described above is eminently suitable from this point of view because the descriptor table resident in the processor holds only a small subset of the descriptor table which is in main memory.

The concepts of segmentation, paging and virtual memory can be used together to create powerful memory management systems. In this case, the address will be made up of three components (Figure 8.14).

It is interesting to examine how logical addresses are converted into physical addresses in the case of MULTICS (Figure 8.15).

As always, the segment number points to a segment descriptor table. Each descriptor has the usual fields (*base address, length,* and *access attributes* to the segment), except that the base address is not that of the segment but of the table of pages of which that is made up. Hence, the segment descriptor table is really a directory of page tables.

Once the page descriptor table corresponding to the segment in question has been selected, the physical address is obtained by the usual paging method, concatenating the offset with the page frame extracted from the descriptor that the page number points to.

The system described here is also adopted by the IBM 370. It is

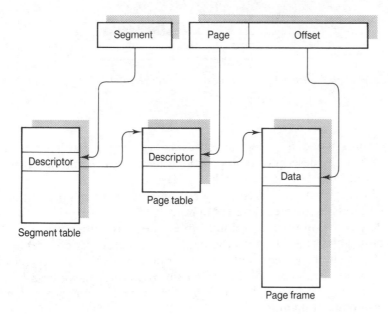

Figure 8.15   Segmentation-paging on the MULTICS and the IBM 370.

extremely powerful, since it is the equivalent of handling as many virtual spaces as there are segments. Both systems make use of an associative memory to contain the descriptors of the last pages referred to. The search is carried out using two **key** fields: the segment number and the page number.

8.2.5   Multilevel paging and segmentation

The scheme introduced at the end of the previous section is an example of hierarchical mapping of logical addresses on to physical addresses. The possibility of subdividing the translation and verification process into two or more passes offers interesting architectural perspectives, which will be examined in this section.

First of all, the various passes may refer to different mapping schemes, as in the example quoted of combined segmentation-paging, or they may involve a single mapping system, that is, segmentation alone or paging alone.

Secondly, the various passes may be independent from each other, in the sense that each may be activated alone without the others necessarily being present. Alternatively, there may exist a hierarchy which involves all the passes. As will become apparent, the hierarchy offers distinct advantages in terms of memory occupied by the descriptor tables.

In general, it may be stated that a system with n levels of mapping

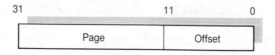

Figure 8.16   Linear address on the Intel 80386.

requires provision of $n + 1$ logical address components, of which n function as indexes to the descriptor tables of the different levels, and the $(n + 1)$th is the offset in the block selected by the last level.

If the system is hierarchical, such components are all present in the logical address in different and contiguous fields.

Moreover, of the n descriptor tables, $n - 1$ are 'directories' of other descriptor tables and the nth is the page or segment descriptor table.

A 'negated' presence bit in a descriptor of one of the directories excludes from the system all the directories (and the pages) described by that descriptor. This is the reason why hierarchical systems prove significantly economic of memory.

For example, in the paging subsystem of the Intel 80386, the address to be translated, known as the **linear address**, is 32 bits long (Figure 8.16), of which 12 constitute the offset in the page.

Thus, the system has to handle more than a million pages (2^{20}) of 4 kilobytes each. A scheme with a single level of mapping would require a table of a million descriptors. The solution adopted was to subdivide the 20 bits representing the page number into two fields of 10 bits each. The first field points to a directory of 1024 descriptors, each of which 'describes' a descriptor table of 1024 pages. The second field extracts the page descriptor from the table selected by the first field (Figure 8.17). In this way, due to the locality principle, the space occupied by descriptor tables in main memory is reduced to a few thousand descriptors.

The price that has to be paid in hierarchical systems is the addition of indirection levels, implying further accesses in main memory, which are known to be extremely slow. However, this problem already existed in the case of single-level mapping and, as was revealed in the previous section, computer architectures solve it by making available associative memories which 'capture' the descriptors of the last references. In the case of the Intel 80386, this memory, known as TLB (Translation Lookaside Buffer), stores the last 32 references. Such systems incorporate a high reference probability (a high 'hit ratio', see Chapter 10). Because of this, the inefficiency introduced by one or more further mapping levels has a minimal effect.

In non-hierarchical systems, the n address components which point to the n descriptor tables do not all necessarily have to be present initially as disjoined fields in the logical address. Some of the components may be

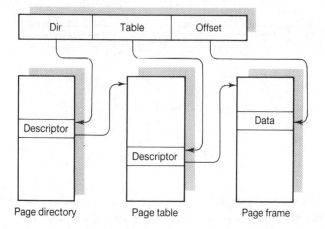
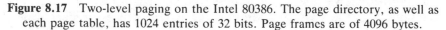

Dir	Table	Offset

Descriptor

Data

Descriptor

Page directory   Page table   Page frame

Figure 8.17   Two-level paging on the Intel 80386. The page directory, as well as each page table, has 1024 entries of 32 bits. Page frames are of 4096 bytes.

functions of others, and the logical address undergoes a series of transformations while passing through the various mapping subsystems.

Figure 8.18 illustrates a high-level scheme of the mapping system used by the Intel 80386. This is composed of two subsystems, one for

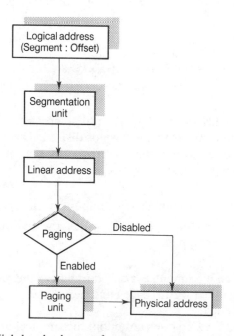

Figure 8.18   High-level scheme of memory management in the Intel 80386.

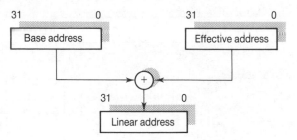

Figure 8.19 The linear address.

segmentation and the other for paging, which are individually activatable, the former implicitly and the latter explicitly. As can be seen, there exists an intermediate version of the address, the **linear address**. This should be considered as the physical address if the paging process is deactivated, whereas it constitutes the logical address for the latter if we choose to operate with a single segment of 4 gigabytes (that is, non-activated segmentation).

The linear address is obtained by adding a 32-bit base address, extracted from a segment descriptor table, to the effective address (also 32 bits), produced by the address calculation unit (Figure 8.19).

There are no restrictions on the possible values assumed by a segment base address nor on the limit values of the effective address: all 32 bits can be used by both. It is possible to state that for this architecture:

$$\text{Dir} = \text{f(segment, effective address)}$$
$$\text{Table} = \text{g(segment, effective address)}$$
$$\text{Offset} = \text{h(segment, effective address)}$$

that is, all three fields of the linear address are also functions of the segment number, in contrast to the case of disjoined components.

Another way of presenting the two different interpretations in mixed segmentation-paging systems is that we can have:

(1)   a large number of virtual spaces, one for each segment;
(2)   a single linear virtual space, on which the various segments are 'distributed' or mapped.

In case (1), an alignment is also adopted for the segments, corresponding to the alignment of the pages and hence their size. In the second case, this is not needed.

While the Intel 80386 does not adopt hierarchical mapping globally, it is adopted in its two subsystems. In fact, even in the segmentation subsystem, a hierarchical organization is adopted for certain segments.

To understand this system, it must be realized that a hierarchical organization generally makes best use of its advantages when:

- not all the descriptors need to be held in memory, but only a restricted number; and
- there exists or it is possible to create a relationship of the pointer–structure type for the descriptors.

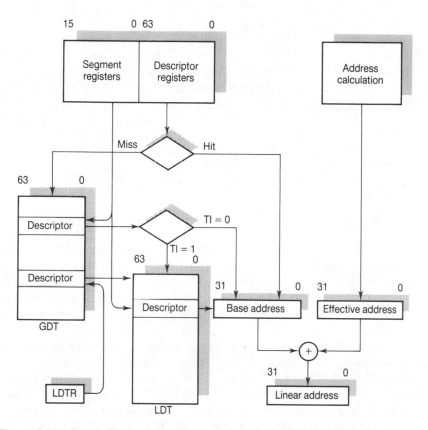

Figure 8.20 Segmentation on the Intel 80386. The descriptor registers, together with the segment registers, constitute a small cache. In the case of a 'hit', they furnish the base address and the other attributes directly. Otherwise, it is necessary to access descriptor tables in main memory. The Table Index (TI) bit, in the selector put in the segment register in use, establishes if the segment is global or local. In the first case, bits 3 . . . 15 of the selector are used as an index to the Global Descriptor Table (GDT) in order to extract the descriptor and then the base address of the segment. In the second case, these bits are an index to the Local Descriptor Table (LDT), whose base address is in a descriptor pointed by the Local Descriptor Table Register (LDTR), which is loaded at context changes.

This has been the case with the examples analysed up to now, and the way segmentation in the Intel 80386 is organized is also based on this. In fact, for each process (or task) it is possible to define two types of segment: **global** and **local**. The global segments are shared, subject to protection rules, between all the processes. The local segments belong to a single process and contribute to an increase in security, by isolating the individual processes.

There exist two corresponding descriptor tables: a Global Descriptor Table (GDT) and a Local Descriptor Table (LDT).

However, there effectively exists a single GDT and there may be as many LDTs as there are processes.

Nevertheless, since a single process at a time occupies the processor, only two tables at a time will need to be maintained in memory: the GDT, which is always the same, and the LDT for that process. At each change of context (each time a different process takes charge of the processor) there will be a change of LDT, if the new process requires it.

All this can be performed by means of a pointer–structure relationship, provided the pointers of the GDT can point not only to segments but also to local descriptor tables (Figure 8.20). Thus, for access to a global segment, there exists a single level of descriptor table, while for access to a local segment, two levels of mapping will be needed.

8.2.6 Protection

The problem of protection has been touched on several times. This is faced and *partially* solved in all architectures that support segmentation or paging. Generally speaking, greater support for protection is provided in segmented systems, since the mechanism can be controlled by the programmer, who places in each segment an object that is personally meaningful.

Nevertheless, the whole subject of protection has been studied in a more complete and systematic way than appears from the individual implementations. Obviously, approaches of a robust kind have been applied in the past in large-sized systems (MULTICS springs to mind), and these have been the ancestors of present-day architectures, in many other ways as well. The concepts that will be discussed here derive from such systems, but have become, so to speak, 'classical', as they are to be found in some popular architectures, such as the VAX and the Intel 80386, which use them in their segmentation and paging systems.

A general protections system works in terms of protection 'subjects' and protection 'objects'. Subjects are processes that operate in a certain **domain**, that is, they enjoy certain **privileges** or **capabilities**, by which they can accede to specific objects, such as files, segments or peripherals. Naturally, a subject may also be an object.

Thus, one of the natural concepts in this field is the **access matrix**,

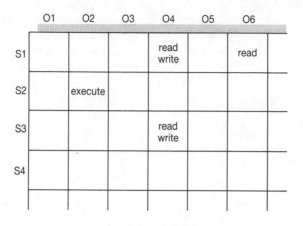

Figure 8.21 Access matrix.

which refers to the capabilities of the various subjects for each object in the system (Figure 8.21).

From this, we may observe that access rights depend not only on the units to be accessed but also on the units making the access.

Therefore, the implementation of protection provided by segmentation and paging schemes, examined in the previous sections, does not appear to be sufficient, as it is only linked to the objects. At the other end of the scale, there are the 'privileged' instructions, which can only be executed in *system* status and so establish privileges that only depend on the subjects. Privileges that are linked only to subjects may be considered reading rights alone that have certain procedures on data segments, or else hierarchical accesses that depend only on the status of the processor, and are therefore different depending on whether the procedure is being executed in one state or another. These two protection schemes are the equivalent of reducing the access matrix to two vectors, of one row and one column respectively (Figure 8.22).

Since the architectures cannot implement the entire access matrix, due to the large number of protection subjects and objects, they support protection systems which may be perceived as 'restrictions' on the general system described by the matrix itself. Two obvious restrictions are the above-mentioned one-row or one-column matrix.

Another very interesting type of restriction consists in limiting oneself to handling **hierarchical domains**, that is, protection systems in which it is possible to establish sets of capabilities that are subsets of each other in an ordered scale of **privilege levels**. That is to say, extending what is done for privileged instructions, with their supervisor and user modes, different states are defined, each with a different privilege level.

These are known as Kernel, Executive, Supervisor and User on the

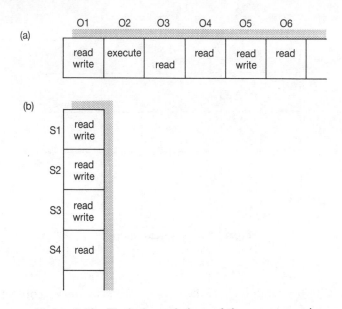

(a)

(b)

Figure 8.22 Typical restrictions of the access matrix.

VAX or simply as PL0, PL1, PL2 and PL3 as on the Intel 80386, and are represented as concentric **rings** (Figure 8.23) with the innermost ring being the most privileged. To access a specific object, a subject must have a privilege level greater than or equal to that specified in the descriptor of that object. Only when the subject has the privilege level needed to access that object is the access type checked with respect to the traditional access attributes of that object. Thus access to more internal rings is forbidden, while access to the ring in which execution is taking place or to more external rings is regulated by the access attributes.

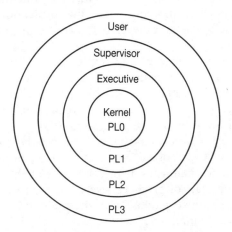

Figure 8.23 Hierarchical domains (rings) in the VAX and in the Intel 80386.

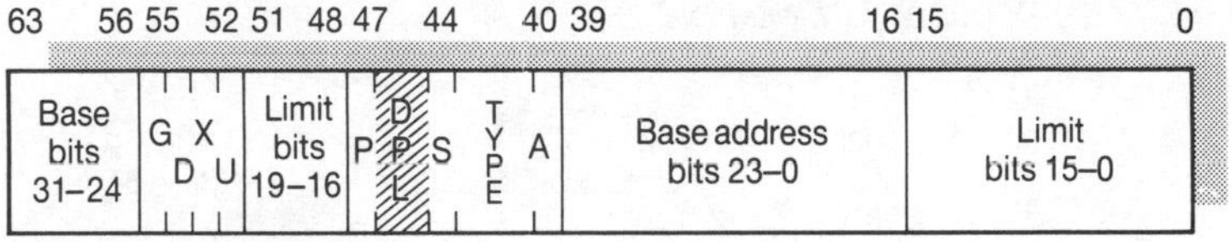

Segment types
000   Data, read only
001   Data, read/write
010   Stack, read only
011   Stack, read/write
100   Code, execute only
101   Code, execute/read
110   Code, execute only, conforming
111   Code, execute/read, conforming

Figure 8.24   Segment descriptor format in the Intel 80386.

In systems where both objects and subjects are segments (or pages, as on the VAX), implementing these concepts is relatively straightforward. Since each segment is described by a descriptor, it is easy to imagine adding another descriptor field that describes the privilege level needed to access that segment. An Intel 80386 segment descriptor is shown in Figure 8.24.

The instruction being executed clearly belongs to a segment of code, and thus the latter has its own privilege level provided by the DPL field of the corresponding descriptor. The instruction currently being executed therefore has a privilege level known as CPL (Current Privilege Level). Now, if this instruction attempts to access a data segment, the CPL will be compared with the DPL of the data segment and access will be granted only if the CPL $\leq$ DPL, otherwise a protection fault will be generated.

The use of hierarchical domains is interesting because it eliminates the need to define explicitly a capability for each subject–object pair. The set of capabilities that a given process possesses is implicit in the number of the ring in which execution is taking place.

In the VAX, the minimum access privilege and the access attributes, instead of being in distinct fields, are coded in a single field, making room for a greater number of possibilities (see Figure 8.25). In fact, a protection code may specify, for instance, that only access from supervisor level processes or higher is permitted, yet the supervisor level may access the page to read only, and so too the executive level, whereas the kernel may access both to read and to write ('SRKW').

While the hierarchical approach is ideal for controlling data access, the same cannot be said of access to segments of code. Data access does not imply changes in the privilege level, so it suffices to check it at the time it is requested, without worrying about future consequences. On the other hand, accessing a segment of code belonging to a domain different from that requesting it involves entering a new domain and so acquiring new

	CODE	MNEMONIC					
DECIMAL	BINARY		K	E	S	U	COMMENT
0	0000	NA	–	–	–	–	NO ACCESS
1	0001		UNPREDICTABLE				RESERVED
2	0010	KW	RW	–	–	–	
3	0011	KR	R	–	–	–	
4	0100	UW	RW	RW	RW	RW	ALL ACCESS
5	0101	EW	RW	RW	–	–	
6	0110	ERKW	RW	R	–	–	
7	0111	ER	R	R	–	–	
8	1000	SW	RW	RW	RW	–	
9	1001	SREW	RW	RW	R	–	
10	1010	SRKW	RW	R	R	–	
11	1011	SR	R	R	R	–	
12	1100	URSW	RW	RW	RW	R	
13	1101	UREW	RW	RW	R	R	
14	1110	URKW	RW	R	R	R	
15	1111	UR	R	R	R	R	

Figure 8.25 Protection codes on the VAX.

capabilities. This would create no problem in a general protection system, since exactly those capabilities needed in that situation would be granted; yet in a hierarchical system, a change of domain always involves an extension or reduction in capabilities.

In protection, there exists a security principle represented by the so-called *minimum necessary privilege*, which states that any program should only be able to access what it needs to know. This is exactly the opposite of hierarchical rings, where a process, when it changes level, acquires not only the capabilities it needs but also many others that give it potentially harmful rights over other processes.

The way in which the Intel 80386 manages transitions of level is through **call gates**. These are special descriptors which specify, not a segment, but an **entry point** to a segment. Hence, a process that wants to utilize a procedure whose code segment is located in a ring further in, can do so by means of an 'intersegment' CALL to a logical address whose segment number (or 'selector') specifies a gate, that is, a descriptor of the type described above. The offset of the CALL's target address is not used, as the address of the entry point, namely the segment code selector and offset, is provided by the gate (Figure 8.26).

Gates are also equipped with a DPL, which must be greater than or equal to the CPL of the CALL, and which therefore serves to specify which processes can use any given gate. On the other hand, the segment specified in the gate will have to have a DPL less than or equal to the DPL of the gate. The overall relationship is therefore:

$$\text{Target DPL} \leq \text{CPL} \leq \text{Gate DPL}$$

with the various possibilities illustrated in Figure 8.27.

63	47	40	36	31	15	0
Destination offset 31–16	D P P 01100 L	000	WC	Destination selector	Destination offset 15–0	

Selector	Destination code segment
Offset	Offset within destination code segment
WC	Word count, 0–31
DPL	Descriptor privilege level
P	Descriptor present flag

Figure 8.26 Call gate descriptor in the Intel 80386.

The idea of carrying out transitions of level by introducing a level of indirection is without doubt valid because it protects the higher privilege-level code from that in the outer rings, letting the latter's code access only precise and well-guarded entry points into the former. The integrity of the higher privilege-level code could be prejudiced if entry were possible at any point (think what would happen if a process entered halfway through a procedure or even in the middle of an instruction), or if it were 'visible' in other ways, other than the uses foreseen by the call gates.

As an alternative to call gates, it is possible to use code segments at a higher privilege level, if these are defined as being of the 'conforming'

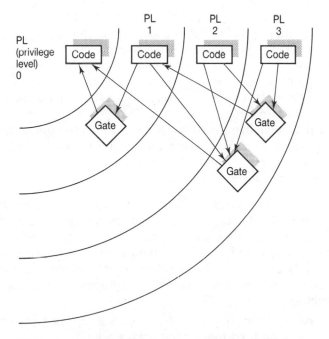

Figure 8.27 Call gate privilege on the Intel 80386.

type, that is, capable of assuming the current privilege level of the requester. To be able to use them, they must have a DPL less than the CPL, but they then assume the value of the CPL for the duration of their use. This type of code can be useful for routines shared by programs at different privilege levels, such as library routines.

It should nevertheless be noted that conforming code does not bring about changes in privilege and therefore does not involve the risk of uncontrolled widening of the domain.

8.3 Access to shared resources

In a processing system, more than one program being run at the same time will have to share the resources of the system. The term 'resources' usually refers to input/output units, mass memory devices, main memory variables and the processor (or processors if there are more than one).

For example, if a **process** (a program being run) has to wait for some data from an input unit, without which it cannot continue processing, it will be temporarily placed in a *wait* state so as not to keep the processor occupied to no purpose. The latter is then occupied (*run*) by another process which is *ready* to enter execution. In this way there are two processes that occupy the resources of the system, one the input unit and the other the processor.

A process state diagram is given in Figure 8.28.

Two or more processes may cooperate in the solving of a problem, or else may compete for the use of a resource.

A classic example of cooperation is provided by the **producer–consumer** problem. One process produces data that the other process utilizes; for example, one process calculates values and these are printed out by the other process.

On the other hand, two processes enter into competition if both need the same resource. For instance, while one process is printing out, the other process requests the use of the printer.

Multiple processes may either:

- *share the same processor*. This is referred to as **multiprogramming**, and the 'simultaneity' is obtained by assigning brief periods of processor time (**time slices**) in turn to the various processes. Each process will finish its work in a number of time slices assigned to it at intervals determined by the number of processes present in the system. Thus we can speak of 'broad-scale' rather than effective simultaneity; or

- *run on a number of processors*. This is a case of true simultaneity, and the term used for it is **multiprocessing**.

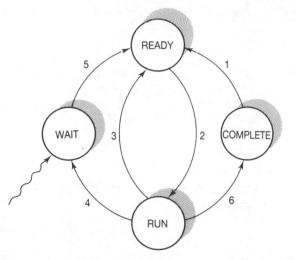

Figure 8.28 Process state diagram. The life cycle of a process may be represented as a series of transitions between four states. COMPLETE = state of completion or non-existence: the process has not yet been created or else has finished running. It no longer has an identity within the operating system. READY = state of readiness: the process is ready for execution, but since the processor is at present occupied with another process, it has to wait its turn according to a fixed scheduling algorithm. RUN = execution state: the processor has been assigned to the process and its program is currently running. WAIT = wait state: the processor cannot continue processing because it needs to wait for an event of some sort.

From the point of view of process management, the situation is presented in exactly the same way to the operating system, independently of whether the processes run on a single processor or on more than one.

More precisely, two or more processes can operate in parallel so long as they do not make use of the same resources. In the period of time that a process occupies a resource, every other process that wants to use the same resource has to be sequentialized; it cannot proceed until the first process has freed that resource (Figure 8.29).

It is clear that this consideration is independent of whether a processor is working in 'time slice' for a process, or is completely dedicated to it.

The busy status of a resource is reflected in the value of a corresponding variable in main memory: in this way we arrive at a homogeneous way of treating shared resources.

When a process occupies a resource, it sets the corresponding variable to '1' to indicate to the other processes that the resource is engaged.

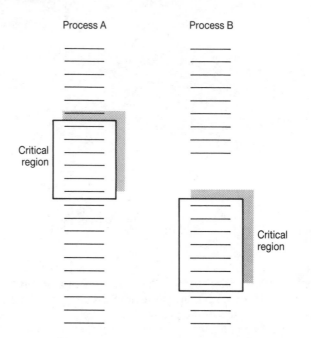

Figure 8.29 Mutual exclusion. Two or more parallel processes need to be sequentialized when they wish to access shared resources. A section of program which uses shared resources is defined as a 'critical region'.

Thus every process that wishes to enter a program area that makes use of a shared resource (**critical region**, as defined in Figure 8.29), must first ask if the corresponding variable is '1' or '0'. If the variable is '1', the process has to stop and wait until it becomes '0'. If it is '0', it can enter the critical region, setting the variable to '1' (Figure 8.30).

The support generally provided by the computer architecture for managing shared resources is an instruction called **test and set**, which tests a variable to see if it is '0' or '1', and sets it in any case to '1'. The result of the test modifies, as always, a status word bit (usually a bit dedicated to other test functions, such as the sign bit or the zero bit, is used, rather than introducing another specific flag) (Figure 8.31).

Setting the variable to '1' in any case is consistent with occupying the corresponding resource. If it is already occupied, the variable is already '1' and it makes no difference to overwrite it with another '1'.

The reason for joining the two operations of testing and setting in a single instruction does not depend on achieving a greater efficiency, but on the necessity not to separate them.

A careful look at the test and set instruction shows why it must be made indivisible. Suppose that process A is competing with process B for the use of a resource and is about to enter a critical region. Process A

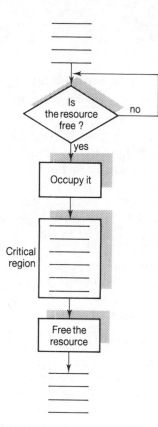

Figure 8.30 Before entering a critical region, a process must ensure that the resource is free.

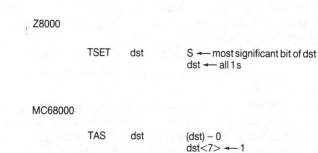

Z8000

TSET   dst   S ◀─ most significant bit of dst
                   dst ◀─ all 1 s

MC68000

TAS   dst   (dst) − 0
                  dst<7> ◀─ 1

Figure 8.31 'Test and set' instruction on the Zilog Z8000 and Motorola MC68000 microprocessors. It may be noted that these behave in a similar way, apart from details: the former influences the sign bit, the latter the zero bit; the former sets all the variable bits to '1' to indicate 'busy', the latter sets only the highest order bit to '1'.

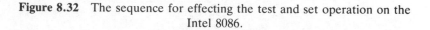

```
            MOV     AL,1
   LOCK     XCHG    dst,AL        AL ←— (dst); dst ←— 1
            TEST    AL, AL        AL and AL
```

Figure 8.32 The sequence for effecting the test and set operation on the Intel 8086.

examines the status of the resource by carrying out a test on the corresponding variable and, let us say, it finds it free. It can now enter its critical region, after indicating occupation by setting the resource's status variable to '1'. But imagine that process B is also doing the same thing, and immediately after A has carried out the test but before it performs the set, B inserts itself and tests the status variable. It also finds the resource free and therefore believes itself able to enter its critical region, setting the status variable to 'engaged'.

Thus both processes have found the resource free and both have occupied it by entering their respective critical regions.

While indivisibility can also be reached by disabling interrupts in systems with only one processor, this is not the case in multiprocessor systems.

More precisely, the test and set instruction is the only instruction during which the bus cannot be released by the processor to be assigned to another bus master. It should be remembered that a 'bus request' on the part of another unit is honoured by the processor at the end of the current bus cycle, not at the end of the instruction.

Thus, once a test and set instruction begins running, every other process is prevented from interrupting it by gaining access to the bus.

The denial of access to the bus is commonly referred to as a bus **lock**. The Z8000 automatically performs a bus lock when it encounters a test and set instruction.

The Intel 8086, on the other hand, expects an explicit request to lock the bus. To do this, an instruction prefix is used to indicate that the instruction is indivisible, that is, it has the bus 'locked'. Every instruction can take advantage of this possibility on this processor. However, there is no specific test and set instruction on the Intel 8086, though it can be realized with the sequence shown in Figure 8.32.

Note that the Intel 8086 manages to guarantee indivisibility not to the test and set sequence, but to the sequence of access (with saving) and set: these are the operations that involve the bus. Once the resource has been occupied, the test on the (previous) status can be made by abandoning the indivisibility condition, since any other process that accessed the same status variable would now find it occupied.

On other processors (for example MC68000 and IBM 370), instead of locking the bus when a test and set instruction occurs, a special bus cycle known as the 'read–modify–write' cycle is carried out. In this cycle, the

Zilog Z8000

```
CHECK: TSET  FLAG
       JR    MI, CHECK
```

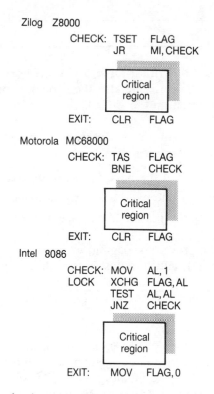

```
EXIT:  CLR   FLAG
```

Motorola MC68000

```
CHECK: TAS   FLAG
       BNE   CHECK
```

```
       Critical
       region
EXIT:  CLR   FLAG
```

Intel 8086

```
CHECK: MOV   AL, 1
LOCK   XCHG  FLAG, AL
       TEST  AL, AL
       JNZ   CHECK
```

```
       Critical
       region
EXIT:  MOV   FLAG, 0
```

Figure 8.33 Entry and exit sequences to critical regions. FLAG is the name of the resource's status variable.

address of the status variable on the address bus is kept unchanged throughout the instruction. It refers to the same variable both in reading and writing.

Since it is added as a new bus cycle to the normal reading and writing cycles, it shares the same characteristics of indivisibility. This means that a bus request can continue to be honoured at the end of the current bus cycle, even in the presence of a test and set instruction.

Figure 8.33 shows the entry and exit sequences to critical regions for the processors under examination.

Further reading

Memory segmentation, paging, and protection on the Intel 80386
Turley J. L. (1988). *Advanced 80386 Programming Techniques*, pp. 45–168. Berkeley, CA: Osborne/McGraw-Hill

EXERCISES

8.1 Define formally the segment descriptor table of the memory management unit MMU Z8010 (see Figure 8.8). Describe also the processes of address translation and limit verification on the Z8010.

8.2 Describe formally the structure of a page descriptor table in main memory (see Figure 8.13), adding some control fields:

- *accessed* (1 bit), denoting if the page has been utilized or not;
- *dirty* (1 bit), indicating if the page has been modified;
- *age* (*n* bits), indicating the period of non-use of the page.

8.3 Write the algorithm for the process of paging, which makes use of a descriptor table in the processor (cache), and of a descriptor table in main memory.

8.4 What kinds of descriptor tables are necessary for the management of mixed-system segmentation-paging?

8.5 Calculate the loss in performance of a memory management system, due to an *n*-level hierarchical translation technique, compared with a non-hierarchical technique, both when using a cache memory with a 'hit-ratio' of 98%, and when not using it. Suppose that the ratio of the access times of the cache and of the main memory is 1/10.

8.6 Write a procedure which implements the paging of the Intel 80386, by using the structure of two-level tables (see Figure 8.17). The fields of interest in each directory entry (PDE) are:

- *page-table address* (20 bits): base address of a page descriptor table;
- *present* (1 bit): it indicates if the descriptor table pointed to in this entry is present or not in main memory.

In a page descriptor table entry (PTE), one has to consider the following fields:

- *page-frame address* (20 bits): base address of a page frame of 4 kbytes;
- *present* (1 bit): it indicates if the page is present in main memory.

8.7 Describe by means of a procedure in Pascal the address translation process by using the descriptor tables in the VAX. Let us suppose we have the appropriate entry in the descriptor table (PTE), in which the following fields have to be considered:

- *valid* (1 bit): it controls the validity of the page_frame_number field;
- *protection* (4 bits): it defines the accesses allowed at each protection level, such as specified in Figure 8.25;
- *page-frame number* (21 bits): it contains the 21 most significant bits of the physical address of the page.

Suppose that the virtual address is defined as:

```
Var virtual_address: record
                virtual_page:
                    array [0 . . 22] of Bit;
                offset:
                    array [0 . . 8] of Bit;
            end
```

and the privilege level of the running process is in the status register:

```
Var processor_status_word: record
                    . . .
                current mode:
                    array [0 . . 1] of Bit;
                    . . .
            end;
```

The access type required by the process can be 'read' or 'write', and this information must be an input parameter of the procedure. The latter must check firstly the protection bits (issuing, if necessary, a 'protection fault'), then the validity bit (issuing, if necessary, a 'page fault'); lastly the address logical-to-physical translation can be carried out.

Concurrency in Computer Organization

9.1 Parallelism inherent within the computational paradigm
9.2 Dynamic properties of programs
9.3 The pipelined model of computation
9.4 Instruction prefetching
9.5 Instruction queues

9.6 Cache memory
9.7 Techniques for reducing dependency waits in instruction pipelining
Further reading
Exercises

Advances in technology have provided support to the large number of architectural features found in present-day computing systems. These have allowed the kinds of problems that can be handled to grow enormously, both in scale and type. The scale of the available resources has grown to the same degree: one only has to think of the quantity of main memory addressable by microprocessors, for example, which has grown from the few tens or hundreds of kilobytes of a few years ago to the gigabytes of today.

More powerful resources have meant opportunities to solve more complex problems, yet the problems in turn have called for even greater computing power. The increase in scale both of resources to be managed and programs to be executed has created new problems of execution time, and these have only partly been solved by the technological advances.

The activities that information is subjected to within computing systems are essentially those of communication and processing. Both can be manipulated to obtain improvements in performance. For instance, a technology that increases the density of integration acts on the communication factor, in that the information has shorter distances to

261

travel within a single chip, rather than having to move from one chip to another.

When one acts on the processing factor to obtain greater speeds, the aim is still to reduce the need for communication, and that can be reached in two different ways:

- representing the information in a more compact way;
- making the processor keep and exploit as much as possible the information read from memory.

Addressing methods are a good example of requests for communication traded off against processing capacity. Another example is the adoption of frequency-dependent opcode length.

It may generally be stated that nowadays, unlike many years ago, processing is a less costly and more easily utilizable resource than communication. Though it is relatively easy to increase processing power by employing systems with a large number of processors, the problems of communicating remain or even increase, as will become clear during the discussion of parallel architectures (Chapter 11).

Even in single-processor systems, the means of achieving high efficiency in terms of speed diverge from the von Neumann paradigm in its fundamental tenet: the principle of sequentiality. Yet while parallel architectures seek to exploit the parallelism inherent in the problems, these systems attempt to extract the parallelism to be found in the very mechanism on which the computing paradigm is based.

9.1 Parallelism inherent within the computational paradigm

It may be said that current systems continue to respect the sequential von Neumann model, but try to take all the possible opportunities for parallelism to be found within its computing paradigm.

In analysing the sequential computing model, with the aim of looking for operations that might lend themselves to parallel execution, it may be as well to begin with an important general observation. Forcing problems that naturally manifest a certain degree of parallelism to be represented in sequential structures that will be executed sequentially has contributed to leaving a wide margin for devices to improve system performance. As soon as the technology has made it possible, solutions have sprung up to overcome the inherent inefficiencies of the sequential model.

The von Neumann computing paradigm relies on a high degree of **determinism**, namely the possibility of predicting at any moment the next instructions to be carried out and the next data to be processed. This has made it possible to implement various forms of:

- anticipating the extraction of instructions and data from memory;
- storing data and instructions that will predictably be re-used in the processor;
- processing a quantity of instructions or data in advance.

The predictions are based on one or more of the following factors:

(1)   *a priori knowledge*, such as knowing that in the von Neumann mechanism the next instruction to be carried out is nearly always the one located in the next memory address;

(2)   *heuristic evaluations* carried out in real time by the system, for example to identify the most frequently used instructions and data;

(3)   *knowledge supplied* by the programmer or by the (optimizing) compiler on which data can be assumed to be used most frequently.

To take full advantage of determinism, one must know how to handle non-determinism, that is, those situations in which it is no longer possible to predict, for instance, which instruction will be carried out next, as normally happens after a conditional branch instruction.

The interaction of one instruction on another may reveal itself not only from a control point of view, as in branch instructions, but also in its data aspect. This means that between two instructions there may exist:

- **control dependence**, that is, whether or not the second instruction is executed is determined by the result of the execution of the first; and
- **data dependence**, where the second instruction uses the results of the first as operands.

In both cases, the execution sequence of the instructions may not be altered, as would happen if some of them were processed in advance, since the sequence forms part of the problem and has been intended by the programmer.

On the other hand, as in the absence of data or control dependences sequentiality is merely a requirement of the computing mechanism, instructions can be executed in parallel, or even in a different order, if the mechanism is changed. In other words, concurrency can be introduced into computing systems on the basis that, in the absence of dependences, the result of a computation does not vary with respect to changes in the execution order of the instructions.

9.2 Dynamic properties of programs

Although computers, and the programs they execute, are systems designed by man, they are among the most unpredictable of objects by virtue of their most important characteristics: the characteristics they manifest while operating, in other words, their dynamic characteristics.

The **dynamic** properties of programs refer to their behaviour when interpreted by a computer, and they therefore depend on the computer model in terms of which the programs are developed.

Determining the dynamic properties of programs that respect the von Neumann paradigm is the equivalent of defining the dynamic properties of the von Neumann architecture.

In contrast to the concept of dynamic properties, we have that of static properties. The **static** properties of programs are those that can be deduced from the written text. These are introduced by the programmer during the writing of the program, with the aim of obtaining certain specific behaviours from the program as it executes, or, to put it another way, suitable dynamic properties. In a sense, the programmer 'imagines' its future behaviour, mentally substituting himself or herself for the machine interpreter which will execute the program being written.

In the same way, an optimizing compiler, which tries to allocate general registers to the most frequently used variables, is making static predictions about the real dynamic situation. It too has only the written text of the program and not the evolution of its behaviour when subject to interpretation by a processor.

Static predictions have in many cases turned out to be completely different from the results of dynamic measurements carried out by various researchers. Systems have often been designed on the basis of such static predictions, and only afterwards has it been realized that they needed to be modified to handle the true dynamic behaviour.

Bearing this in mind, architectural systems for introducing concurrency into current processing systems are based on the exploitation of well-understood dynamic properties and the results of measuring them.

Predictions (1) and (2) of the previous section, that is, knowledge relating to dynamic properties, and real-time heuristic evaluations, are both used in developing architectural systems for concurrency. Only when it is not possible to make the machine 'aware' of such properties is it reasonable to fall back on static knowledge inserted by the programmer or the optimizing compiler.

The dynamic variables that characterize program behaviour are:

(a) *references to operands* on the part of instructions executed in succession by the processor;

(b) *addresses* of the instructions executed;

(c) *operations* of the instructions executed.

Serial correlations between the successive values of such variables are at the origin of the dynamic properties of programs.

The serial correlation in the cases of (a) and (b) can be broken down into two distinct types of property: **linearity** and **locality**.

Linearity of references is displayed by instructions and array elements.

The execution model of the series of instructions in a program is linear or, more precisely, disjointedly linear (or nearly sequential) due to the frequent branches to be found in the programs. During the periods of linear behaviour, an architectural system that is aware of such a property can predict which will be the next instructions to extract and execute.

As regards arrays, their elements, or groups of a few contiguous elements, are generally visited sequentially, or at least at constant intervals (typically of a column or a row).

The locality of references in memory can be of the **spatial** or the **temporal** kind.

Spatial locality refers to successive references in memory tending to be maintained within restricted areas of memory for consistent intervals of time. This property allows architectural systems to be created with small-scale high-speed memories, capable of containing the 'active' reference area or areas.

This principle of locality is exploited, as we have already seen, also in virtual memory and addressing methods.

Temporal locality is the property that certain memory locations have of being referenced frequently. Typically, many scalar variables exhibit this characteristic. They are generally counters, indexes or pointers, temporary variables, or table base addresses. For each access to an array element, it is necessary to access one or more scalar variables to determine its address.

The most often used scalar variables are, however, the variables local to procedures. Bearing in mind that dynamic procedure nesting also reveals a high degree of locality, and that there is a very limited number of local variables in each procedure, it can be deduced that most of the local variables of a few nested procedures have a high temporal locality. This is a case where *a priori* knowledge, of the type discussed under (1) in the previous section, can be inserted into an architectural system, so that the system stores *all* local variables of one or more 'active' procedures.

Loops manifest both spatial and temporal locality at the same time, making them ideal for handling by architectural systems equipped with one or more areas of fast memory.

Serial correlations do not only have positive effects like those described above. Control and data dependences, as we have seen, are among the type of serial correlations that cause most trouble to architectural systems based on the linearity of references to independent instructions.

In conclusion, the general characteristics required of an architectural system that attempts to introduce concurrency into a processing system with the aim of improving performance are:

(1) reflecting a well-defined dynamic property, in the form of *a priori* knowledge or self-adaptive capabilities;

(2) eliminating 'bottlenecks' in the architecture;

(3) being able to handle non-determinism at a reasonable cost, being careful not to re-create bottlenecks in other parts of the architecture;

(4) being competitive with other architectural systems which introduce, or can introduce, concurrency on to the same architecture, as regards the use of resources made available by the technology being used.

9.3   The pipelined model of computation

To introduce concurrency into computing systems, the various phases within the instruction cycle – fetching, decoding, calculating addresses, execution, storing results – need to correspond to distinct, loosely connected operating units.

Figure 9.1 illustrates the difference between a tightly connected system, in which there are frequent interactions between the hardware components units, and a loosely connected system in which the mutual dependences between the component units are greatly reduced, very often consisting merely of a sequential link between one stage and the next.

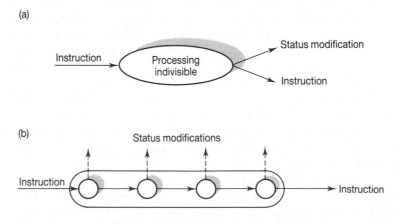

Figure 9.1   Models of serial computation: (a) strongly connected units;
(b) pipelining of loosely connected units.

In Figure 9.1a, only one instruction at a time may occupy the system, using all its resources at the same time. In keeping with the von Neumann model, processing produces state changes, which may be associated with outputting the instruction from the system, given its indivisibility.

Contrastingly, in Figure 9.1b there are a number of independent operating units and so a number of instructions may coexist in the system, each utilizing a different operating unit. The state changes can no longer be grouped together at the point the instructions exit from the system, but need to be locally associated with the operating units that produce them.

Apart from this, there are also considerable differences in the restrictions on enabling an instruction to enter the system. In case (a), instruction $i + 1$ cannot enter the processing system before instruction i exits. In case (b), on the other hand, instructions $i + 1, i + 2, i + 3$ can enter the system in sequence before instruction i (and correspondingly instructions $i + 1$ and $i + 2$) have exited. The only restriction to be respected is to keep the order, namely that instruction $i + 1$ cannot enter the system before instruction i, nor 'overtake' it once inside, for instance by skipping one of the stages.

Assuming the various component units can really be kept independent, as many instructions as the stages in the system can be made to enter in advance. They can then be left to pass through the successive stages at the same time until they are output. The system is fed continuously by a stream of instructions to be executed and provides a similar stream as output.

This computation model is known as **pipeline**, since its properties resemble those of a continuous fluid transport system. In reality, the model is more like a production line consisting of a series of distinct work units.

If the pipeline is made up of n stages, all of the same length, it is capable, once it is filled up, of executing instructions at a speed n times faster than a system without pipelining.

If, on the other hand, the stages do not all last the same time, the pipeline cycle is given by the length of the slowest stage, and the *speed-up* is less than n.

The execution time of each instruction (**latency**) is equal to (if not greater than) the one obtainable without pipelining, and is given by the sum of the lengths of all the stages. What increases is the **throughput** (or **bandwith**) of the system, which is capable of processing more instructions in a given time.

The pipelined computation model remains a **serial** model, since the timing relation between instructions, and between the various phases within each instruction, is maintained; but it operates in **parallel** on a number of instructions to be found at different stages of processing.

The problem of data and control dependences, which has been touched on several times in this chapter, departs from the simple scheme

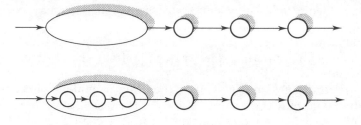

Figure 9.2 Internal pipelining of a slow stage.

discussed here, in which communication only exists between one stage and the next. The pipelined model needs to be elaborated in order to incorporate restrictions governing communication between any of the stages. Such connections are not direct, but come about because of state changes in the processor and in the memory, through which one instruction communicates with those that follow.

The restriction that needs to be introduced into the pipeline to take account of these connections is that any instruction in the pipeline must not be able to make use of a state before it is modified, if it is modified, by any predecessor still in the pipeline. This restriction includes every type of data and control dependency, since they all manifest themselves in terms of a state change.

The concept of pipeline emphasizes that, since there is continuity of flow between the different stages, each stage should be carefully designed to facilitate the flow of instructions along to the following stages. The goal is that each stage can be fed with instructions from the previous stage at a rate that exploits its operating capacities to the full. Thus, the design of each architectural system is closely linked to the performance character-istics of the other architectural systems present in the pipeline.

This casts new light on the concept of eliminating bottlenecks, which arise from the slowest stages in the pipeline. In particular, it is a good idea to investigate the possibility of introducing pipelining within such stages (Figure 9.2). In this case, the number of stages increases, but the pipeline cycle is reduced. Wherever possible, stages should be of the same length.

Increasing the number of stages helps to reduce the cycle, but only up to a certain point. Each stage involves an overhead, independent of its length and connected with managing tasks, which must be added to the execution time of the function it performs. Moreover, the problems of interaction and respecting restrictions become more complex.

Apart from this, conflicts may arise from using the same architec-tural system in numerous phases during the instruction cycle. For example, the 'memory' system is on average used several times during the execution

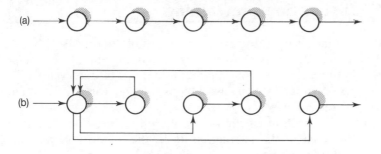

Figure 9.3 (a) Usual representation of a pipeline; (b) multiple re-crossing of a unit in the pipeline.

of an instruction: for fetching the instruction and one or two operands and for storing the result. While an instruction pipeline is generally represented by diagrams such as that in Figure 9.3a, the true route through the pipeline units may well be more like Figure 9.3b, with an instruction passing through the same unit several times before it exits from the pipeline. Obviously, this gives rise to a new bottleneck, which can only be eliminated by partly or wholly replicating the functional unit in question.

During their evolution, architectural systems have tended to adopt replication only of those parts of functional units that are most often used in the stage that needs them, specializing them and so making them more efficient towards the new function. Figure 9.4 represents the insertion of such units into the model. It may be noted that more often than not the system now behaves like a linear pipeline, though it is equipped with mechanisms for resorting to 'principal' functional units (broken lines) in those rare cases where the required operation cannot be carried out on the specialized functional unit.

The following sections deal with the techniques and architectural systems used to introduce concurrency according to pipelining principles into the serial computational model.

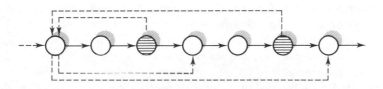

Figure 9.4 Elimination of the bottleneck of Figure 9.3 by inserting new functional units in the pipeline.

9.4 Instruction prefetching

In the pipelined model, the execution speed of the processor has an upper limit: one instruction per pipeline cycle. The pipeline can only emit one instruction at a time, and at minimum intervals of one cycle.

The memory system should possibly be capable of feeding the processor continuously even when the latter is working at maximum speed. Given that for each instruction cycle there is at least one memory access due to the fetch of the instruction itself, the memory system should be provided with an architectural system capable of providing the processor with an instruction per pipeline cycle. Bearing in mind that the pipeline is often emptied by the effect of branch instructions, the feed rate should be slightly greater.

During the execution of most instructions, however, the number of accesses to the memory system is greater than one, since reference is often made to one or two operands and the result is stored in memory. Hence it is necessary to resort to further independent memory systems to access data and store results. In this way, conflicts are avoided of the type discussed in the previous section, regarding access to the same functional unit. Moreover, architectural systems for data access can be made specialized in a different way from those that access instructions, if each type is conceived in such a way as to conform to their respective dynamic properties.

One architectural system capable of providing instructions, while adapting itself to variations in processor speed, is an **instruction buffer**. Different types of buffer are used for this purpose (queues, cache memories, interleaved memory registers); but all are justified by the property of instruction linearity, which suggests that a certain sequence of instructions should be moved in advance from the slow main memory to a fast buffer memory, since it can be assumed that these will be the next instructions to be executed.

The size of an instruction buffer is determined by the fluctuations in the pipeline rate, but also by the most frequent length of 'linear' segments of instructions, and sometimes by the length of the most critical loops.

An **instruction queue** long enough to hold straightline segments of instructions, that is, sequences of instructions between two branches, is an architectural system that is extremely 'compatible' with the pipeline that follows. Oversizing it to allow for loops is an interesting evolution of the idea, based on the high degree of temporal locality to be found in loops. The only disadvantage is that loops are also linear in intervals, so an expensive resource is wasted on containing instructions that will not be carried out. Furthermore, the queueing mechanism needs to be modified to make it 'aware' of loops and to block it on the loop, interrupting the flow of instructions following on.

Another architectural system that is much more efficient for loops, and at the same time maintains the same prerogatives as queues in exploiting the property of linearity, while eliminating the drawbacks due to discontinuity, is the **instruction cache**.

As will be seen in Section 9.6, this may be considered as the equivalent of a chainable multibuffer system, so as to hold loops that are linear in intervals within broad limits.

9.5 Instruction queues

Instruction queues are architectural systems that improve the performance of a processor by reducing communication time in fetching instructions from memory. The extraction of instructions is superimposed on the process of executing the previous instructions.

In systems organized as pipelines, the mechanism for superimposing extraction of the current instruction on to the processing of the previous ones can be applied to each single stage, so that instruction queues can be arranged between the different stages of processing, as shown in Figure 9.5. This reduces waits in the pipeline due to different instantaneous speeds between the various stages.

This principle is adopted, for instance, in the Intel 80386 processor, which is provided with two queues, one for the instructions fetched from memory and one for those already decoded.

However, in its most common form, the queue is interposed between the memory and the processor, and these respectively perform on it operations of **insertion** and **extraction** of (parts of) instructions. Furthermore, the processor takes care of **emptying** the queue when it encounters a branch, or, more generally, any interruption of the sequential flow of instructions to be executed.

Finally, an element can be inserted into the queue provided the queue is not full, whereas extraction requires that the queue is not empty.

The fundamental models for queues to be found in computing systems are:

● the FIFO queue
● the circular queue
● the 'parallel-in serial-out' queue

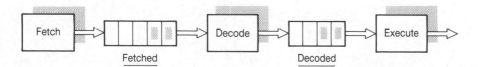
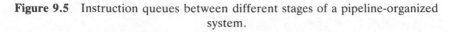

Figure 9.5 Instruction queues between different stages of a pipeline-organized system.

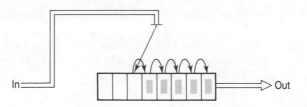

Figure 9.6   A FIFO queue together with its internal data movement.

9.5.1   The FIFO queue

In the FIFO (First In First Out) queue, the instructions are always extracted from the front, while the instructions entering it make use of an 'input instruction pointer', that contains the address of the first free location. After a location is read, any other full locations are shifted towards the front (Figure 9.6).

A system of this kind is used by the Intel 8086.

9.5.2   The circular queue

The circular queue is functionally equivalent to the simple FIFO queue, but the circular addressing it is equipped with avoids the costly operations of shifting information internally each time something is extracted.

This advantage is obtained by using two pointers, one containing the address of the element to be extracted and the other the address of the element to be inserted (Figure 9.7). Both insertion and extraction involve an increment 'modulus queue-size' of the corresponding pointers.

The procedures for managing a circular queue ensure that one location is left empty: this precaution serves to distinguish a full queue from an empty queue. Otherwise, they would both be characterized by the fact that the contents of the two pointers would be equal.

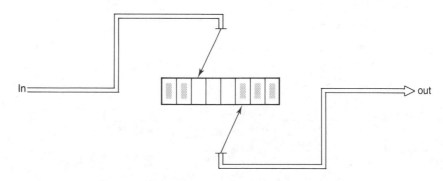

Figure 9.7   A circular queue.

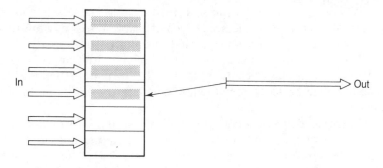

In

Out

Figure 9.8 A queue will parallel input and serial output.

9.5.3 The parallel-in serial-out queue

The parallel-in serial-out queue is represented in Figure 9.8.

It is most useful when the computing system is equipped with memories, capable of providing more than one word at a single reading. Figure 9.8 shows that only one pointer is needed for instruction output.

Some of the functions of this queue need to be re-interpreted in the following way:

- 'insertion' operations load all the queue locations at the same time;
- the 'full' condition should be understood as: 'the queue is not completely empty'. Insertion can only take place if all the locations are empty.

9.6 Cache memory

Cache memory is a fast buffer placed between main memory and the processor. In the memory hierarchy of a computing system, cache memory (on chip or on board) can be considered as intermediate between the internal registers of the processor and the main memory.

The registers, the fastest memory of the system, can contain the information most often used by the program in a segment of code, but by no means all the information that a program needs during its execution.

Moreover, the allocation of data to registers is mostly carried out *statically* by the assembly-language programmer or the compiler. One striking exception is the Am29000 processor, whose general registers can be allocated at run time (see Section 10.3.1).

In contrast, cache memories can make adjustments *dynamically*, during execution of a program, so as to contain the information that it most needs.

When a memory location is read by the processor, it is also transferred into the cache memory (cached away) so that any future access to the same information can be carried out much more rapidly.

The target aimed for is to have a memory that approximates the speed of the processor, containing stored information that has a high probability of being accessed in the immediate future and for as long a time as possible.

There needs to be a high probability that the information required by the processor will be found in cache memory, and this calls for appropriate **replacement policies** (see Section 9.6.4). The cache memory will normally be full, and each time a new item of information needs to be used, space will have to be created for it in cache memory. The information to be sacrificed will be that which has the least probability of being utilized in the immediate future. As we shall see, there exists a number of replacement algorithms, corresponding to different prediction models, and requiring different support in cache memory.

The allocation unit in cache memories is normally larger than the allocation unit in main memory. Owing to the properties of linearity and (spatial) locality, it is presumed that in the near future not only the current location may be referenced again, but also those next to or near to it. The cache memory allocation unit is known as a **block** or **line**.

But what type of information does the processor access, and for what types and in what way should the cache buffering mechanism be used?

Fundamentally, while executing a process, the processor utilizes instructions, data and the information needed for the logical–physical translation of addresses (namely, memory area descriptors).

Each type of information has its own characteristics, and this suggests specializing the cache mechanism so as to maximize efficiency for each type.

For example, the locality manifested by segment or page descriptors is simple temporal locality, whereas data exhibits both temporal and spatial locality; instructions are very often carried out in sequence.

At this point, it is worth enumerating the types of cache commonly found in computing systems.

9.6.1 Cache memories for data, instructions and memory area descriptors

Caches that store the instructions most recently used by the processing system are frequently found, even among microprocessors.

Another common type is the **branch target cache** (BTC) that stores the target instructions (and those following) of a number of branches recently carried out by the processor.

Each time a branch occurs, the system interrogates the BTC to verify whether the target is present in it, in which case a memory fetch will be avoided.

Clearly, there is no point storing the instructions that precede targets in the cache, as these will definitely not be executed when the corresponding branches occur.

There exist alternatives to the BTC, such as the **branch history table** and the **decode history table**, which will be analysed in Section 9.7.1. These are used in pipeline-organized systems as a basis for predicting the behaviour of a branch before it is decoded and executed respectively.

In any case, caches designed to contain instructions are functionally less complicated than those for data: the fact that instructions cannot be modified guarantees that no discrepancy can be created between the information in the cache and that in main memory.

Caches designed for data, on the other hand, need to deal with situations of inconsistency, caused by modifications made to the data in the cache.

Each time a cache block is removed to make room for another, it has to be copied back into main memory if it has been modified during its stay in the cache (the technique is known as 'copy-back').

The problems of inconsistency are more complicated in systems with more than one processor (or in a single processor system equipped with independent I/O channels) which can access a common main memory. It can happen that one processor accesses data in memory that has been altered in the cache of another processor and not yet copied back into memory.

The solutions to the problem are either to copy back cache data into main memory as soon as it has been modified (write-through), or alternatively to provide the system with a mechanism for checking data inconsistency by interrogating all the caches in the system as well as main memory (bus-watch).

It is evident that the first technique allows the cache only half its potential efficiency: memory accesses are avoided only for reading operations. Moreover, if there are processors operating on distinct caches, it may happen that one of them accesses inconsistent data from its own cache, because this data has been updated by another processor in main memory alone.

Caches for data or instructions consist of several blocks of several words; each word can be addressed individually by means of a **displacement** made up of the lower order bits of the address (Figure 9.9).

When an object is inserted into the cache, however, the whole block to which it belongs is stored in the cache.

If, on the other hand, the cache is destined to contain information for the memory management unit (MMU), it is called a **translation lookaside buffer** (TLB); each line contains a single descriptor of a memory area (segment or page), useful for the process of translating addresses.

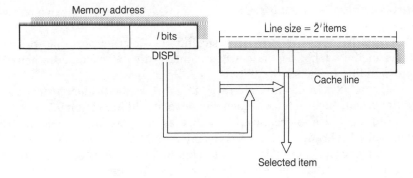

Figure 9.9 Selection of an item in the cache line.

A sufficiently powerful cache is capable of storing the descriptors of the most frequently utilized areas moment by moment. When a process emits a logical address, it is highly probable that the descriptor needed to translate it into a physical address is present in the TLB, and so the MMU can avoid consulting the descriptor tables in main memory.

Caches of this kind are now commonly found in microprocessors of recent design, as well as minicomputers and mainframes. They effectively avoid continuous memory accesses for translating addresses, which would considerably reduce the performance of the system (if each translation required a memory access, the average time for information in main memory would double).

9.6.2 Cache memory models and their operation

As was seen earlier, the DISPL field of the address is used to select an item in the addressed cache line (Figure 9.9).

Because cache memory has a much smaller number of lines than the quantity that can be stored in main memory, it is not possible to address cache memory lines using all the remaining address bits. According to the number of lines that the cache possesses, a subset of such bits will be used of a suitable size for addressing it (the LINE field in Figure 9.10). In this way, there remain a certain number of unused address bits that create a situation of mapping several main memory location blocks on to the same cache memory line. To be precise, with the conventions used in Figure 9.10, 2^t blocks of main memory correspond, as an address, to the same line of cache memory of each of the 2^k lines.

To recognize which of the 2^t main memory blocks has been loaded on to the corresponding line, it is necessary to add to the line a field containing the remaining address bits (TAG field, Figure 9.11).

A diagram of the architectural system described is given in Figure 9.12. It goes under the name of **direct mapping**. The line field of the

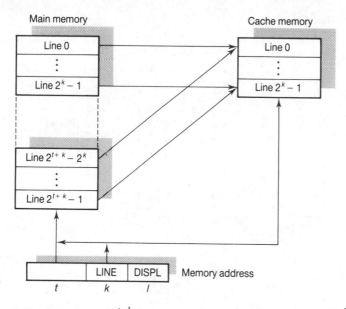

Figure 9.10 Mapping of 2^{t-k} lines resident in main memory, on to 2^k cache lines using the field LINE.

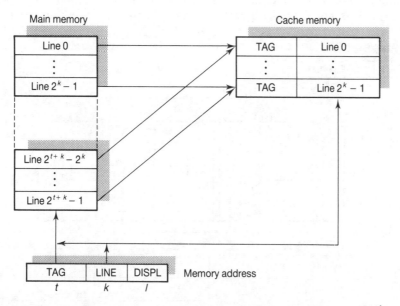

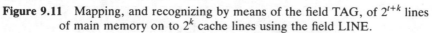

Figure 9.11 Mapping, and recognizing by means of the field TAG, of 2^{t+k} lines of main memory on to 2^k cache lines using the field LINE.

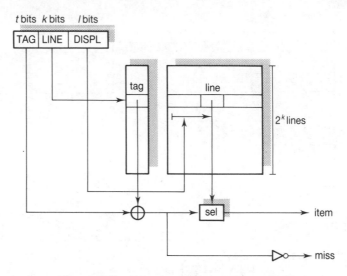

Figure 9.12   Direct mapping cache memory.

address is used as an index to read the tag and the corresponding line at the same time. The tag is then compared with the TAG field of the address and, if the result is positive (*hit*), the selection of the data item located in the line that has been read is enabled, at the displacement indicated in the DISPL field. If the result of the comparison is negative, a *miss* signal is emitted, indicating that the main memory block containing the location requested is not present in cache memory, and therefore the process of

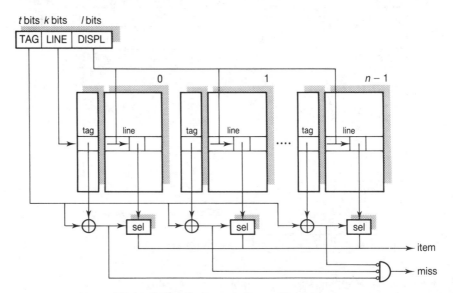

Figure 9.13   Set-associative cache memory.

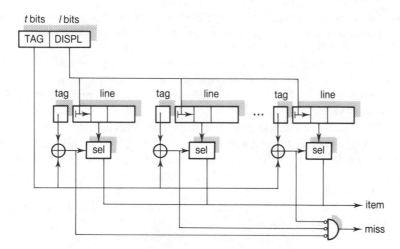

Figure 9.14   Fully associative cache memory.

accessing it in main memory and loading it into cache has to begin. The ways in which a miss is handled in cache will be examined later.

Considering that a tag field for each line is added to the data field, the former can be exploited to introduce a certain degree of **associativity** into the cache memory. Reiterating the scheme in Figure 9.12 as in Figure 9.13, we find that a number of cache memory lines, selected at the same time by the LINE field, can be made to correspond to the same group of 2^t blocks of main memory. In this way, the probability of a miss diminishes.

The set of lines selected by the LINE field effectively constitutes an associative memory, whose tags can be compared at the same time, as in Figure 9.13, with the TAG field of the address. From these comparisons, a single data item will be extracted if it resides in cache memory, otherwise a miss will be generated, if all the comparisons give a negative result. This type of cache memory is known as **set-associative**.

In the address, the LINE field controls direct mapping. On the other hand, a single field containing the TAG, without the LINE field, presupposes the use of associativity alone (Figure 9.14), resulting in cache memories of the type generally known as **fully associative**.

In conclusion, independently of the information they contain (their semantics), cache memories can be classified from a functional and structural point of view into three models:

- **Direct mapping cache memory**: each line of memory can be mapped on to a single cache block.

- **Fully associative cache memory**: each line of memory can be mapped on to any cache block.

- **Set-associative cache memory**: each line of memory can be mapped on to any line belonging to a subset of all the cache lines.

Before the cache can be operated on, it needs to be initialized. The technique generally adopted consists of associating one or more validity bits to each block of the cache, to indicate whether or not the content of the block is valid.

In reality, some systems (such as the instruction caches of the Motorola MC68020) have a single bit for each block, while others (for example the BTC of the Am29000 and the cache of the Z80000) contain a larger number, one for each item of the block. In the last case, some of the items in a block may be valid, while others are not.

In both sets of circumstances, initialization consists in resetting all the validity bits in the cache.

9.6.3 Analysis of cache memory parameters

The parameters of a cache memory, in the most general case of set-associativity (see Figure 9.13), are:

- line length, 2^l
- number of lines for each set, n
- number of sets, 2^k

Each line consists of a linear buffer of contiguous locations, the size of which is influenced by a number of factors.

First of all, effort is made to keep the line length of a size sufficient to hold meaningful groups of contiguous locations, such as: sequences of instructions between two branches, data structures, or activation records. It is important, however, to limit the line length so as to avoid phenomena of internal fragmentation, which arise when the clusters of information are shorter than a line. When this happens, costly memory space is wasted on holding information with a low frequency of use.

Moreover, communication band-width is also wasted, since useless data is transmitted.

Two extreme cases, from this point of view, are scalar data and arrays. The former, if it possesses high temporal locality, engages an entire cache line. The smaller the line is, the less fragmentation is caused by single scalar variables.

Arrays, on the other hand, would benefit from having large line lengths, which could hold, for example, entire rows or columns. Yet these can be accommodated on a number of lines of consecutive sets.

As mentioned earlier, the structure of caches is ideal for containing loops. If a loop is short enough, it will fit into a single line, otherwise it will have to occupy a number of lines.

The important thing is that a sequence between two branches manages to fit into a line: in this way only the critical sections of the loops are loaded into the cache.

The capacity of the cache is subdivided between the three parameters discussed earlier. Technological limitations impose a certain maximum capacity, and so the parameters *l*, *k* and *n* can be varied, within certain limits, so that the capacity:

$$2^l \times 2^k \times n$$

does not exceed the established value.

An increase in *l*, the line length, reduces the number of misses up to a certain point, corresponding to the size of structures of significant information; but beyond this limit, it gives rise to an increase in misses. This is because, to keep the capacity of the cache constant, an increase of 2^l involves a reduction in the number of lines ($2^k \times n$) that is, the number of blocks of main memory that can be buffered at the same time.

The mechanism of associativity gives complete freedom of allocation, whereas direct mapping has the disadvantage that the location of each block in cache memory is rigidly fixed. In the latter case, even if the cache is nearly empty, a block that collides with another already present in the cache cannot be put somewhere else, but has to take the place of the one that was there before. The **hit ratio** of the cache diminishes accordingly.

Apart from being rather costly, associativity is efficient only for low values of *n*. It is very important for cache memory to provide the data item, if it is present, within one processor pipeline cycle, and this can no longer be achieved when there are more than 8 or 16 lines. For these motives, caches are usually of the set-associative type.

The choice of the parameters of a cache memory is made on the basis of technological restrictions (for example, whether the cache is on the same chip as the processor or on another chip), and also architectural considerations, such as those discussed. According to the type of data it is designed to buffer (mixed data and instructions, data alone, instructions alone, branch target instructions, page or segment descriptors), an optimal combination of cache parameters is identified, so that both the structural and the dynamic characteristics are taken into account.

Cache memories are typical architectural systems introduced into a processor's flow of data or instructions with the aim of eliminating the bottlenecks generated by using the same architectural system – the main memory – in various points in the instruction cycle (Section 9.3, Figures 9.3, 9.4). The general characteristic of such systems, already emphasized in Section 9.3, is not being exact replicas of the main system, which would be costly and not very efficient, but rather being systems 'in tune' with the type of function or data required at the particular point of the instruction cycle where they are inserted. In this way, they not only lighten the load of the main system (in this case, the memory), but they are 'more efficient most of the time', that is, so long as the dynamic properties they are based on are adhered to.

In particular, memory architectural systems, like caches, are of limited size so as to have a flow rate equal to the execution speed of the processor. Yet this implies that not all the information that the processor may possibly refer to can be present in them at the same time. This is how the expression 'being more efficient most of the time' takes on the meaning, in this case, of 'containing useful information most of the time'. In other words, the buffered data has to evolve in such a way that the processor is presented with information it is presumed to need moment by moment. To do this, it is not enough that the cache's parameters are of the right size, but the cache also needs to be equipped with a mechanism for renewing its data appropriately.

Of the two possible loading methods, demand fetching and prefetching, caches generally make use of the former. That is to say, they only face the problem of updating the contents when they encounter a request for data that is not present, and so generate a miss. The alternative, preloading the cache with data that the architectural system believes will be referred to in the immediate future, in place of lines of low or zero activity, is not generally adopted due to the heavy demands on communication. Cache memories cannot exploit dead time, as happens in main memory management when anticipatory buffering techniques are used for sequential files or working set prefetching in paging.

Cache-reload transients are generated at each change of process in the system. As soon as control is given to a new process, there is a high number of misses, and part of the lines belonging to the previous process are replaced by lines relating to the new process.

Subsequently, the number of misses reduces until control is handed over to another process or restored to the previous process. Since no resort can be made to prefetching mechanisms, only an appropriate sizing of the cache parameters – particularly the associativity dimension – can reduce the number of misses in the initial reloading phase.

After the transient need to create the working environment for the new process, the number of misses can be kept at low levels only if a suitable line replacement policy is adopted.

9.6.4 Replacement policies

The moment a miss is generated, a new cache line needs to be loaded. If the cache is of the direct mapping type, this line will be loaded directly in the position pointed to by the LINE field of the address. Since there is only place for a single line, it will automatically substitute the line which may already be present.

If, on the other hand, the cache is of the associative kind (fully or set-associative), the new line can go into one of the *n* positions of the set selected by the LINE field, or of the whole memory if fully associative. It will go into the first free position if not all the lines of the set are occupied, otherwise a decision needs to be made as to which line to discard to make room for the new line.

This is precisely the task of a replacement policy: to identify the line that has least probability of being used. Since the future cannot be foreseen, such a policy is based on the supposition that:

(1)   the line that has just been referenced has a high probability of being used again;

(2)   the past may be a good basis for estimating future references.

Point (1) reflects the property of temporal locality that may well be present (spatial locality and linearity are inherent in using a line and not a single main memory location as the allocation unit).

Naturally, temporal locality should be checked, and this can only be done heuristically, by seeing if the conditions are created for keeping the line already loaded or whether it has revealed itself to be a 'dead' line and so one to be discarded. We shall see that the cost of maintaining dead lines is high, but it cannot be avoided, since there is no *a priori* knowledge of data with temporal locality, apart from that possibly provided by the programmer and solved by static assignment systems (for example, registers). In any case, it is assumed that any line that has just been loaded has a high probability of being re-used in the immediate future.

As regards point (2), use is made of a particular property of programs that is nearly always valid, namely that they manifest stability in their behaviour. Only on this basis can the future be predicted from a knowledge of the past.

Two important predictive models are used by replacement policies. The first consists in seeing *the future as the inverse of the past*: this leads to the presumption that, of the lines present in the cache, the one used least recently in the past is the one that will be used furthest in the future, and should therefore be discarded. The other model presupposes that *the utilization frequency of lines remains stable*, so that the line to be discarded is the one least frequently used.

Corresponding to these principles, two substitution policies have emerged: the **LRU (Least-Recently Used)** policy and the **LFU (Least-Frequently Used)** policy. Both algorithms need to gather usage data about the individual lines, and this data needs to be added to the tag and line information.

Since the LRU algorithm is most often used, let us examine in detail an architectural system that embodies it. As has been seen, the problem to be solved with this algorithm is how to introduce a mechanism to make it aware of which of a set of lines is the one least recently used. If the cache is

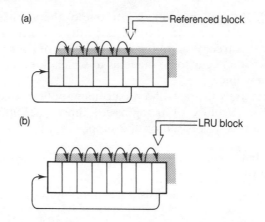

Figure 9.15 The shift operations that take place in a queue to carry out the LRU policy: (a) a block found successfully (hit); (b) failure to find a block (miss).

of the fully associative type, we need to know which is the least recently used of *all* the lines that make up the cache. If, however, the cache is set-associative, we only need to find the least recently used line among those in the set selected by the LINE field of the address.

The primary problem of the LRU algorithm is to register the order of references to the blocks in the associative set. One possibility is to attach a suitably modified queue to each set, of equal size to the cardinality of the set.

The position of the last block referenced in a set is always introduced into the first location of the queue.

In the case of a hit (Figure 9.15a), the block pointer just referenced is present in the queue in a certain position indicating its past distance. It is moved into the first position, while those of the blocks with less past distance (nearer the front) get moved back.

For a miss (Figure 9.15b), the pointer of the least recently used block, which is in the final position, must be selected. It is inserted at the front to indicate that the corresponding block is the last one to be referenced, and all the others are shifted towards the end of the queue.

With this technique, at each moment the contents of the head location is the pointer to the most recently used block, while the contents of the last location is the number of the least recently used block.

With a set-associative cache memory of 'set-number' sets, there are 'set-number' queues, each handled in the same fashion.

The above-mentioned modification of the queue requires that:

- an element must be allowed to exit from any position in the queue;
- the shift must stop at that element;
- the element that exits must re-enter at the head position.

As was stated earlier, the predictions that the replacement algorithms are based on do not always come true, and so so-called *dead* lines are generated. For instance, in the LRU algorithm, if access is sequential for a long period of time, each line, as soon as it is loaded into cache, becomes a dead line. It will not be referenced again, and, to get rid of it, it will be necessary to wait while its position number migrates towards the tail until it occupies the last position. Hence, not only is a cache line filled with useless information, but also, because of the way the LRU algorithm works, it will continue to be occupied for a very long time.

The LRU algorithm is unbalanced, since it takes no account at all of the most recent references in making its substitutions.

It excessively penalizes the references most distant in time, even when they might well be repeated. In other words, a line may be subject to a lot of activity in a short period of time, or distributed over a longer period, and even in the second case it would be worth keeping it in the cache. When a line is discarded and, after a while, reloaded, it has a greater 'value' than a line that has no history, and so might be preferable to the latter if circumstances arose where a further substitution were needed. An architectural system that implemented this kind of policy would take into account the most recent lines too.

An LRU algorithm boosted with systems of this kind can improve the hit ratio at modest cost, since it applies criteria based on dynamic properties instead of principles of 'brute force', such as simply increasing the size of the cache.

9.7 Techniques for reducing dependency waits in instruction pipelining

Some methods for reducing waits in the presence of data and control dependencies are now introduced using a simple scheme of pipeline with only three stages: fetch, decode and execute (Figure 9.16). In addition, reference is made to architectures of the RISC type (see Chapter 10), on which there is a large set of general registers and the instructions operate on the registers alone. Yet the techniques for accelerating the passage of the instructions through the pipeline, that will be described in this section, are generally applicable also to more complex pipelines.

In the pipeline in Figure 9.16, the instructions being decoded and those being executed can both need to access the processor's register file at the same time. At first sight, it seems that the problem can be solved by equipping the registers with more access ports.

But what happens if the instruction in the decode phase requires a register that has to be updated by the instruction to be found in the execute phase?

Figure 9.16   A three-stage pipeline and the operations carried out by each stage. Fetch – extraction of an instruction; Decode – decoding of an instruction, reading the contents of the operands from the registers; Execute – execution of the operation and storing the result in a register.

This constitutes a **data dependence** between instructions, because the instruction in the execute phase produces data required by the instruction that follows, which is to be found in the decode phase.

The instruction being decoded has to wait for the one being executed to be completed, or, alternatively, connections need to be made between the stages, so that the data produced in the execute stage can immediately be transferred to the decode stage, before being stored in the registers (the technique is known as **data-forwarding**).

In any case, the workings of the system are made more complicated by the presence of further connections between the stages for transmitting data or synchronization signals.

Another situation that departs from normal functioning is **control dependence** between instructions. This consists in explicit deviance from the sequential instruction processing flow, produced by jump, call and return instructions and by interrupts.

When a jump instruction is interpreted, the instructions in the following addresses are not executed. Rather, the target instruction of the jump must be read and interpreted.

But if, in the pipeline in Figure 9.16, a conditional branch is executed, the next instruction to carry out is only known after the evaluation of the branch condition. This operation is completed in the execute phase, when the decode phase already contains the instruction that follows and the fetch phase the one after that.

It therefore follows that, if the branch condition is verified, the pipeline needs to be cleared of the instructions that have been pointlessly processed. An alternative is to carry out the instruction in decode phase anyway; this technique, called **delayed branch**, has the advantage of better performance, as long as the compiler is able to postpone useful instructions to all branches, other than simple 'no-operation' instructions.

Some architectures decide to execute both branches and then select one on the basis of the condition evaluation result.

Another possibility is to use a cache memory called the **branch history table** (BHT) to associate the address of the target instruction to each branch instruction (Figure 9.17).

At each instruction fetch, in the pipeline in Figure 9.16, if the instruction's address is present in the 'branch address' field of the BHT

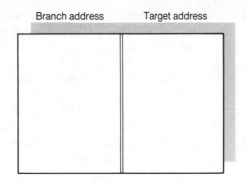

Figure 9.17   Structure of a branch history table.

(and so a branch is being handled), then the next instruction to be extracted is the one whose address is contained in the 'target address' of the same entry. Otherwise, the instruction in the next address will be extracted.

When a branch reaches the execute phase, the BHT is updated with the branch address and that of the actual next instruction, which depends on the evaluation of the branch condition.

Thus, the technique consists in predicting that a branch will behave in the same way as the last time it was executed.

The BHT system can be modified so as to be interrogated only when a branch instruction occurs, when the latter is in decode phase. Such a system is known as a **decode history table** (DHT).

In this case, the table keeps the address of the branch in the 'branch address' field and the target instruction in the 'target instruction' (Figure 9.18), rather than the target address, which is already known when a branch is in decode phase.

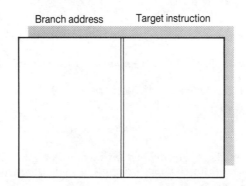

Figure 9.18   Structure of a decode history table.

If the branch address is found in the table, the next instruction to be carried out is taken from the table itself ('target instruction'). Otherwise, the instruction already in fetch phase is executed.

In this case too, the table is updated in execute phase, after the branch condition has been evaluated, and so the target instruction is known.

Another problem with pipeline architectures is what is known as an **imprecise interrupt**. If instructions are given the chance of changing sequence within the pipeline, inconsistencies can arise on returning from servicing an interrupt. For this reason, many architectures require the fixed program flow to be followed strictly.

In any case, more status information needs to be maintained for the program counter. For instance, if the delayed branch technique is adopted, both the instruction address in the execute stage and that in the decode stage need to be stored. In the case of a delayed branch, if the instruction after the branch is in the execute stage, the instruction address being decoded cannot be deduced from the one being executed, since the two instructions are not contiguous in memory.

Further reading

Dynamic properties of programs

Katevenis M.G.H. (1984). *Reduced Instruction Set Computer Architectures for VLSI*, pp. 9–41. Cambridge, MA: MIT Press

Instruction prefetching, branch target cache, branch history table

Advanced Micro Devices (1987). *Am29000 Streamlined Instruction Processor User's Manual*.
Anderson D. W., Sparacio F. J. and Tomasulo F. M. (1967). The IBM System/360 Model 91, *IBM Journal*, **11**, 8–24
Siewiorek D. P., Bell C. G. and Newell A. (1982). *Computer Structures: Principles and Examples*, pp. 227–34. McGraw-Hill

Cache memory

Kohonen T. (1987). *Content-Addressable Memories*, 2nd edn, pp. 247–56. Berlin: Springer-Verlag
Siewiorek D. P., Bell C. G. and Newell A. (1982). *Computer Structures: Principles and Examples*, pp. 227–34. McGraw-Hill
Stone H. S. (1967). *High-Performance Computer Architecture*, pp. 29–69. Reading MA: Addison-Wesley

Instruction pipelining

Advanced Micro Devices (1987). *Am29000 Streamlined Instruction Processor User's Manual*.
Katevenis M. G. H. (1984). *Reduced Instruction Set Computer Architectures for VLSI*, pp. 42–70. Cambridge MA: MIT Press
Stone H. S. (1967). *High-Performance Computer Architecture*, pp. 102–76. Reading MA: Addison-Wesley

EXERCISES

Problem 9.A Describe formally the memory–queue and processor–queue interactions in a processing system equipped with an instruction queue.

The queue, logically placed between processor and memory, has to be managed in order to have the following operations:

- *Insert*: process of inputting a new instruction (or part of instruction).
- *Extract*: process of outputting a new instruction (or part of instruction).
- *Empty*: process of emptying the queue.
- *Is-full*: check that the queue is full.
- *Is-empty*: check that the queue is empty.

The operation of these checks and processes depends on the functional characteristics of the queue. Develop simulation procedures for these operations in each of the three models presented (FIFO queue, circular queue and parallel-in serial-out queue).

9.1 Define a representation of the FIFO queue by means of the data structures of a high-level language. Leave undefined the queue size and the type of each location, in such a way that the representation is easily adaptable to specifying a real architectural system. On the basis of this representation, develop simulation procedures for:

- *Empty*: the emptying of the queue.
- *Insert*: the insertion of an object.
- *Extract*: the extraction of an object.
- *Is-full, Is-empty*: the check predicates on the queue state.

Underline the shift operations to which the data is subjected in the queue, during the extraction operation.

9.2 As for Exercise 9.1, describe formally a representation of the circular queue and the operation of processes and checks to which it is subjected. Observe that the extraction procedure is much more efficient and simpler than the equivalent procedure of the FIFO queue, because it avoids data transfer inside the queue.

As regards inserting, on the contrary, there are no considerable improvements in the circular queue, which in addition needs an increment (module queue-size) mechanism, not required in FIFO queue.

9.3 Define a representation of the parallel-in serial-out queue, and the operation of all the processes to which it is subject (Insert, Extract, Empty) and its state checks (Is-full, Is-empty). Observe that inserting gives a value to all the locations simultaneously, hence it can occur only if all the locations are empty.

Problem 9.B The set-associative cache memory combines some properties of the direct mapping and of the fully associative caches. In it, a part of the address serves for the selection of a set and another has to be compared to the 'tag' of all the blocks in the selected set.

The set-associative memory is therefore constituted by a number of sets, each of which is equivalent to a fully associative memory and is selectable in a direct manner.

From a structural point of view, the set-associative cache can be considered a bidimensional array: the rows represent the sets, while the columns number the blocks in each set.

Give a general representation of the set-associative memory, leaving undefined the set number and the block number per set. Particular values of these parameters will describe the fully associative and the direct mapping caches.

Develop the procedures for the fundamental operations on a cache:

- *Lookup*: the search for an item in the cache, to read it.
- *Update*: the updating of the contents of an item, that is, its writing.
- *Replace*: the substitution of a block in the cache, using the LRU policy.

9.4 Work out a general specification of a cache, taking into account that:

- the address is composed of three components (tag, line, displ), which are reduced to only two (tag, displ) for the fully associative;
- the length of the fields 'line' and 'displ' affects the set number and the line dimension respectively;
- each block also contains a tag field of the same length as that of the tag field in the address;
- the cache memory is definable as a bidimensional array (set-associative cache) which collapses into one-dimensional arrays in the case of direct mapping or fully associative.

9.5 Define the supports for the LRU policy, by using queues associated with the sets of the cache memory, each queue containing the pointers to the blocks of each set in the order in which they are accessed.

Define the initialization procedure and the updating of the queues in occurrence of a hit and a miss.

9.6 Describe formally the management of the cache, that is, the procedures Lookup, Update, and Replace, as defined in Problem 9.B.

Both Lookup and Update search (associatively through the field 'tag') for a block containing the item requested, inside the set accessed by means of direct mapping through the field 'line'.

In the case of 'hit', Lookup and Update have to call the procedure that updates the queue associated with the set for the LRU policy (Exercise 9.5).

In the case of 'miss', the procedure Replace has to be activated. This procedure must select the least recently used block in the set by using the LRU queue, copy back its line in main memory, and insert the tag and line including the item that generated the miss in place of the old block. Also in this case the LRU queue must be updated. For the sake of simplicity, do not consider copying back in the main memory.

Problem 9.C Describe, by means of a set of procedures, the operation of the pipeline shown in Figure 9.16, leaving out data dependencies and with the simplifying hypotheses that:

- the instructions, all of the same length, have only one operand and one result, both located in the registers;
- access to memory is allowed only to branch instructions;
- delayed branch is used.

The phases of the pipeline communicate with each other by means of connection data which is 'shared' by the simulation procedures. In particular, the fetch phase reads an instruction by means of the PC and deposits it in the IP. The latter is read by the decode phase which extracts the opcode, the instruction operand (from the register file), the register number in which the result will be stored, and the target address in the case of branch instructions.

All this data is used by the execute phase, which carries out the operation specified by the opcode and stores the result obtained in a register. In the case of branch, the target address is deposited in the PC.

Implement mutual exclusion of shared variables of procedures, by means of waiting loops on suitable semaphores on the part of the procedures themselves.

10 Concurrency Implementation

10.1 CISC and RISC architectures
10.2 Concurrency implementation in CISCs
10.3 Concurrency implementation in RISCs

10.4 General models for VLSI microprocessors
Further reading
Exercises

Until recently, the concepts of concurrency in von Neumann architectures and the architectural systems that derive from them were the prerogative of large-scale mini- and mainframe systems.

However, they have now come to form part of the design of cheaper and less complex architectures, such as microprocessors. This has become possible thanks to the very large scale integration (VLSI) of electronic components that technology allows today. The equivalent of several hundreds or thousands of components of some years ago can find room in one single chip at comparable costs.

It is easy to convince ourselves that computing powers, which in the recent past characterized supercomputers, have been gradually incorporated inside microprocessors, to the extent that these constitute nowadays the heart of many powerful systems and workstations.

In its migration from the external circuitry towards the single chip processor (or a system with few chips), concurrency has had to face up to new architectural issues influenced by implementation.

What to leave outside and what to bring into the chip is a major architectural problem created by implementation constraints, considering that the chip area is a finite resource, and so it has to be carefully managed.

The chip boundary introduces a further discontinuity, both in the time of transmission and in the capacity of the architectural systems that can be realized. In addition, the chip area can be used to enlarge the width of the buses connecting the architectural systems, if the latter are put inside the chip.

In any case, everything that is added into the architecture inside the chip subtracts resources from other architectural systems. So, designing by taking into account integration possibilities adds new variables and new constraints with respect to the situation in which concurrency was essentially external to the processor chip. We have passed from managing a virtually infinite resource to a finite, although qualitatively higher, resource.

The intention of this chapter is to complete the presentation of the concurrency concepts in such a way as to complement the previous chapter, by analysing some microprocessors which implement them.

In reality, there are two overall classes of conventional architecture, which interpret concurrency and exploit the integration possibilities in two different ways. These are commonly known as RISC and CISC architectures.

Moving on from this classification, the chapter describes the difference between the two types of systems. Examples are then presented of processors of each type, emphasizing those subsystems (queues, caches, pipelines) that are suited for introducing concurrency.

10.1   CISC and RISC architectures

CISC (Complex Instruction Set Computer) machines tend to incorporate in their architecture, instructions and mechanisms that are both highly complex from a computational point of view and also require a large amount of CPU time, such as composite addressing methods, string operations, instructions for procedure call.

These satisfy the computational needs of high-level language compilers and of operating systems by grouping sequences of operations frequently performed by such programs into single instructions.

For instance, provision is made for those addressing methods that are most useful for accessing data in block-structured programming languages (Chapter 4), or for manipulating operating system tables.

On the other hand, **RISC** (Reduced Instruction Set Computer) architectures have an instruction set made up only of simple instructions, operating mostly on registers and allowing memory access only through *load* and *store* instructions.

They tend to make best use of the internal resources of the processor; a rich set of registers, instruction queues, cache memory for instructions and/or data, but above all a pipelining organization that keeps all these resources occupied.

The design principle is therefore to increase instruction-processing efficiency on the part of the processor.

In CISC architectures, supporting complex instructions requires the use of a microprogrammed control unit, which is itself sometimes highly complex and occupies a large portion of the chip area.

Though it succeeds in its aim of speeding up the execution of such instructions, this unit may, on the other hand, considerably slow down simpler instructions, which are the ones that occur more frequently while a program is running. Thus RISC-type architectures are more oriented towards supporting instructions of this kind, which can be speeded up using a much simpler control unit.

Consequently, even though RISC architectures may at first sight seem 'reduced' in terms of computing power too, better performance is often obtained from them than from highly complex and expensive systems.

The pipeline inside a RISC system plays a predominant part in achieving such results. In fact, all the instructions are made comparable in terms of processing time, in such a manner that a careful definition of the pipeline phases might ensure that all the phases proceed in parallel for all the instructions.

This same kind of full pipeline utilization is not always achievable in CISC architectures, where one encounters complex instructions that use up all the phases of a longer pipeline (a multiple memory access even exercises the memory system a number of times), as well as simple instructions which do not make any use at all of some of the stages.

It follows that, in the presence of complex instructions, all the instructions in the pipeline slow down, while, in the presence of simple instructions, some stages are not exercised at all.

10.2   Concurrency implementation in CISCs

The class of CISC architectures is very crowded, because they represent a form of natural evolution of computers. Indeed, the continuous growth of integration density in electronic components has been seen more often as an opportunity to render more and more powerful the functionalities already existing in the previous architectures, rather than to apply new design methodologies.

The last and most impressive result of the evolution is constituted by the 32-bit microprocessors. In this category, the **Intel 80386** is analysed,

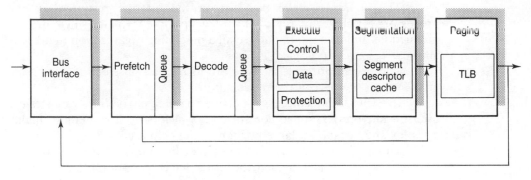

Figure 10.1 Pipeline of the Intel 80386.

since it is very widespread and popular. It is one of the Intel '86 family and succeeds the earlier 8- and 16-bit members.

Regarding the features that concern concurrency, it is worth examining the nature of its **pipeline processing**. In the block diagram of the Intel 80386 (Figure 10.1), eight pipelined logical units are present:

● the bus interface unit

● the prefetch unit

● the instruction decode unit

● the control unit, the data unit and the protection test unit, that collectively form the execution unit

● the segmentation unit

● the paging unit

In this pipeline, in addition to the sequential links, there is a direct connection between the prefetch unit and the paging unit, because the addresses generated by the former are linear addresses and so have to be translated into physical addresses before reading instructions through the bus interface unit.

Between the stages of the pipeline are located two instruction queues: one contains the instructions that have already been decoded, while the other holds those extracted from memory, waiting to be interpreted.

The queue for the decoded instructions is of particular interest: it is a queue of three very wide words, each of which contains a completely decoded instruction, with fields such as: microprogram execute phase start addresses, operand references, operand types and opcodes. All this information is therefore ready for use by the execution unit.

Moreover, address translating, which requires two processing

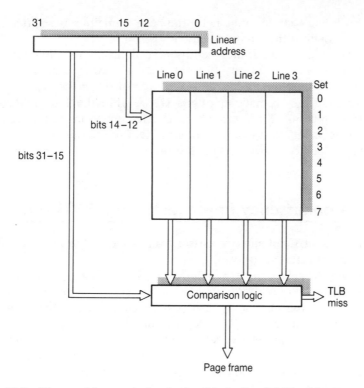

Figure 10.2   The on-chip translation look-aside buffer (TLB) of the Intel 80386.

phases for the logical address and no less than three memory accesses for each translation, is effectively accelerated by the use of two caches for memory area descriptors.

The first supports segmentation and is a small buffer memory of six segment descriptor registers, one for each segment register. Each time a new segment is selected by loading a selector into a segment register, the descriptor is extracted from the descriptor tables in main memory and loaded into the corresponding segment descriptor register.

The other cache is a translation look-aside buffer (TLB) utilized in the paging subsystem (Figure 10.2). It is of the set-associative type, having eight sets of four blocks each. It is interrogated before accessing the table structure in main memory. If the required information is present in the TLB (hit), and this is claimed to be true on average in 98% of cases, it is passed to the paging mechanism without the need for accessing memory. If it is not found (miss), the search for the page frame continues in the two-level table structure in main memory.

Once found, the descriptor is inserted in the TLB in the event that further references might be made to it; one of the old descriptors in the TLB may have to make room for it, according to the LRU policy.

Each line contains a tag field, the page frame number and a further field which defines the validity of the entry.

From Figure 10.2 it may be observed that only the high part of the address, consisting of 20 bits (bits 31–12), is used in searching for the descriptor, as the other 12 bits constitute the offset in the page.

The 'tag' field is made up of bits 31–15, while the 'line' field consists of the three bits 14–12, utilized for direct selecting of one of the eight sets. The 'displacement' field (for selecting an item in a block) does not exist, since each block contains a single descriptor.

10.3   Concurrency implementation in RISCs

The Am29000, a 32-bit microprocessor from AMD, interprets the concepts of RISC architectures very well.

From the programmer's point of view, the first relevant feature is the presence of no less than 192 general registers. These are subdivided into 64 global registers and 128 local registers. The global ones are addressed in the usual way, by a register number, whereas the local ones are accessible through relative addressing by means of an internal register called the stack pointer (Figure 10.3). Finally, all the registers can be accessed indirectly using dedicated registers that function as pointers to the general registers.

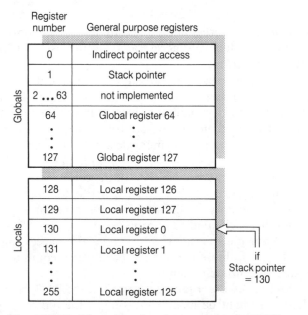

Figure 10.3   The general registers of the Am29000.

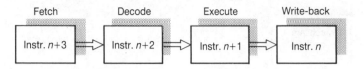

Figure 10.4 The instruction pipeline of the Am29000.

Most of the instructions have three operands, stored in the general registers, as in the case of all RISCs. The only instructions that make reference to memory are *load* and *store* for data and *branch* for instructions.

The Am29000 also has a memory management unit on the same chip as the processor. This translates 32-bit logical addresses into physical addresses, also of 32 bits. The translation is carried out using a TLB with 64 descriptors, containing the most recently used translations.

The Am29000 is organized so as to implement a 4-phase pipeline. The phases are fetch, decode, execute and write-back (Figure 10.4).

During the **fetch** phase, which manages the instruction fetch unit, a new instruction is extracted and passed to the decode phase.

During the **decode** phase, the execution unit decodes the selected instruction and fetches the required operands from the register file. The logical addresses of the branch, load, and store instructions are also calculated.

The **execute** phase takes care of executing the operation specified in the instruction. The logical address of branches, loads, and stores are translated into physical addresses by the MMU.

The results are stored in the registers during the **write-back** phase. In the case of branch, load, and store instructions, the physical address resulting from the translation is transmitted to the memory.

The pipeline organization ensures that the Am29000 can execute instructions at the rate of one instruction per clock cycle.

However, this requires the instructions to be read from memory and supplied to the pipeline at a rate at least equal to the rate they go through it.

Among the techniques adopted to reach this goal, one is to separate data accesses from instruction accesses, making use of three separate buses (data, instructions, addresses). Although the address bus has to serve both data and instructions, because of the linear property of programs it is sufficient to use the address for instructions only at the beginning of the straight-line sequences, thus leaving free the address bus for access data most of the time. This technique is known as **burst mode accesses** and is useful also for accessing data at sequential addresses, for example components of structures such as arrays and vectors.

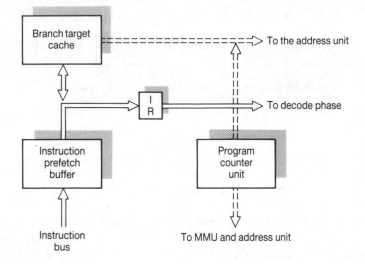

Figure 10.5 Organization and data flow of the instruction fetch unit in the Am29000. (Continuous lines indicate instruction flow; broken lines indicate address flow.)

But the unit that is fundamentally responsible for feeding the pipeline is the instruction fetch unit (Figure 10.5).

Its most notable feature is the co-presence of a circular queue for prefetching instructions, called **instruction prefetch buffer** (IPB), and of a **branch target cache** (BTC) containing the first target instructions of a certain number of recently executed branches.

The BTC is a set-associative cache memory, with 16 sets of two blocks each. Each block contains four locations: the first is for the target instruction of a branch, and the rest are for the instructions that follow on from the target (up to a maximum of three). The policy adopted for replacing the blocks is random choice.

The fetch unit makes suitable use of its own subunits according to the circumstances.

In the simplest case, the processor requests instructions in sequential addresses. The IPB system is capable of fetching them in advance, to supply them to the processor when required (Memory → IPB → IR).

Complications arise if there is an interruption of the sequential instruction flow, caused by branch, call, and return instructions, and by interrupts. In this case, the queue is flushed to make room for a new sequence of instructions. Moreover, the look-up process in the BTC is activated to verify if the instruction requested by the processor is contained in a cache block.

If the look-up succeeds, then it is the cache that supplies the target instruction and those following to the IR register for the decoding phase (BTC → IR).

Moreover, if the branch sequence is longer than four instructions, that is, all the entries in the block are 'valid', the fetch unit can meanwhile begin the fetch of the further ensuing instructions from the memory into the queue (Memory→IPB).

So, when the processor has executed all the instructions in the selected cache block, it will be able to continue with the instructions already inserted into the queue, without waiting for them to be read from memory.

On the other hand, if the look-up process fails, that is, the BTC does not contain the requested instruction, it needs to be read from the memory (Memory→IPB→IR).

During the transfer to IR for decoding, the instructions are also inserted into a BTC block, in order to be ready for a possible re-use by the same 'target sequence' (IPB→BTC).

Therefore, as can be gathered from the description, there is a considerable interaction between IPB and BTC, which together permit notably low average instruction fetch times.

10.3.1 The register file as a stack cache for activation records

The design of the RISCs, as well as of the CISCs, has been heavily influenced by the block-structured languages like C and Pascal. In these languages, as is known, the program variables and the compiler's temporary data are allocated on a structure called the run-time stack or execution stack.

Each time a procedure is called, its **activation record** is allocated on this stack. We have also spoken of dynamic measurements of program execution, which have shown that local scalar variables are the type most often referred to during execution, and moreover the depth of the stack remains more or less constant for long periods of execution time.

It follows that, if a certain number of locations near the top of the stack, where the local data of the last procedures to be executed are to be found, were stored in a cache, one could obtain a notable reduction in the number of memory references.

RISC architectures often use their register file to implement precisely a cache of this type (stack cache).

This is coherent with the fact that all the instructions in RISCs operate on data stored in registers. Moreover, the reduced 'dynamicity' of the execution stack ensures that data transfers between registers and memory are infrequent.

This is the support provided by RISCs to procedure execution and call. The technique may be considered as an alternative to the one commonly found in CISCs and examined in Chapter 4, of providing addressing methods 'suited' to the data access needs, particularly during procedure execution.

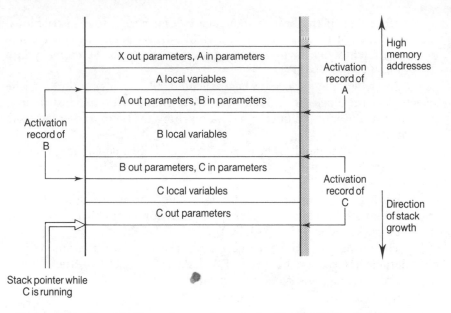

Stack pointer while
C is running

Figure 10.6 Organization of a run-time stack extending towards low memory addresses. Note the partial overlapping of the activation records.

The CISC technique incorporates sequences of a number of frequently executed operations, often involving several memory accesses, into single instructions, thus reducing the number of instructions in a program. Their efforts are then directed towards speeding up the process of interpreting the resulting 'complex' instructions.

The RISC approach, on the other hand, tries to avoid completely memory access operations, which are costly, providing for data to be processed in the registers as often as possible, and hence in a distinctly shorter time.

However, to be used as a stack cache, a register file has to be endowed with a suitable further support. This is the case, for example, of the local register file in the Am29000, where relative addressing with respect to the content of the stack pointer (SP), with which it is equipped, allows the type of access usually required by the allocation policy of the activation records in the execution stack (Chapter 4). The SP register contains the base address of the activation record in the register file, while the instruction contains the position of the data item to be accessed in that activation record.

So as to ensure that the registers contain only frequently used data, it is a good idea to use two run-time stacks, one for data structures and less-used scalars, and the other for the more often used scalars. Only the latter will be partially 'mapped' in the stack cache.

A run-time stack for scalars, extending towards decreasing memory addresses, is represented in Figure 10.6.

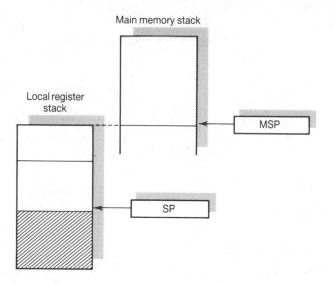

Figure 10.7 Run-time stack with stack cache. (Hatched area, not used.)

Here, one can recognize the technique commonly used of partially *overlapping* the activation records for the purpose of parameter passing. The 'out' parameters of a calling procedure are 'in' parameters for the callee and so one single area is sufficient for them.

Figure 10.7 shows a stack cache implementation which uses the local register file of the Am29000.

Generally, part of the run-time stack is in main memory, while its upper portion is allocated to the local registers. The address of the boundary is kept in one of the general registers which, in this context, is called the MSP (memory stack pointer) register.

Each time a new activation record has to be allocated, the number of locations required is subtracted from the SP, which points to the top of the run-time stack in the local registers.

If there are enough free registers to contain the activation record, these will be used in the way described with the SP containing the base address, and the instructions in the program containing the displacement of the data items in the activation record. When the procedure terminates, and before returning to the 'calling' routine, it de-allocates its own activation record from the stack cache, incrementing the SP appropriately.

However, it can occur that the activation record of a called procedure requires more registers than are free, causing what is called a **stack cache overflow**. This situation is recognizable by a wrap-around of the SP after subtraction (the local register file is managed as a circular buffer).

Part of the new activation record overlaps some of the registers on which were allocated other activation records (Figure 10.8).

The stack cache overflow is resolved by saving (in the main memory

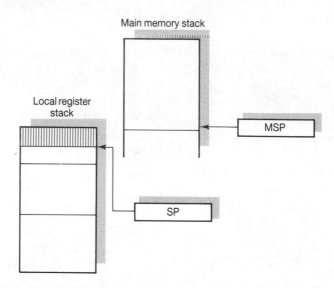

Figure 10.8 Stack cache overflow. (Hatched area, overlapped.)

stack) the previous contents of this overlap area, which is delimited by the MSP and SP.

After this operation, the MSP will assume the value of the SP, and the SP will be updated to point to the last register in the file, as the entire file now contains valid data for the run-time stack (Figure 10.9).

The opposite can arise at the return to a calling routine whose activation record has been partially or totally transferred from registers to

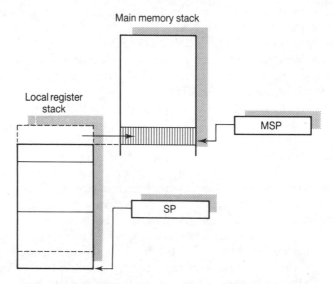

Figure 10.9 Stack cache overflow resolved. (Hatched area, saved.)

main memory. This is referred to as a *stack cache underflow*, and brings about the restoring of the registers belonging to the activation record.

Other implementations of stack caches in RISCs using general registers have the additional constraint that the register file areas to be allocated to the activation records must be of fixed size. They have been referred to with the more popular name of **register windows** and consist of sets of registers whose number is generally a power of two.

Both the fixed-size windows and the power of two features render implementation considerably simpler. Consequently, the access to an item is faster than in the more general case of single-register resolution stack cache, because there is no need to carry out any addition of displacements to a base register.

However, this mechanism suffers from the problems of any allocation policy which is based on units of fixed size: the high internal fragmentation or, alternatively, the inability to contain activation records in their entirety most of the time. In the first case, precious resources, such as registers and memory-registers communication bandwidth are wasted. In the second, variables with high locality risk being held in main memory rather than in registers.

10.4   General models for VLSI microprocessors

The ever-increasing integration densities offered by VLSI technology, which in recent years has generated the two classes of architectures and design methodologies examined here, is now being exploited to consolidate both of them. Indeed, the added potential of the latest technological advancements is being used to eliminate the residual 'weaknesses' of CISCs and RISCs, these weaknesses being due more to limitation in chip area and integration density, than in their overall architectural conception.

An interesting factor which is emerging from this tendency is the establishment of a well-defined model for integrating the several concurrent modules into the single chip processor. In the same manner, the partitioning of functions in a chip set also follows a sort of general rule.

The traits of these design methodologies are often common to new CISC and RISC architectures, bringing about what can be considered a general model of microprocessor implementation.

This model was originated by the **Clipper** by Fairchild, which is an example of 32-bit RISC architecture with suitable 'extensions', and is nowadays adopted, with further original contributions, by the state-of-art microprocessors that have been recently introduced or are being announced at the time of publishing this book (1990).

The Clipper can be considered as an *extended RISC*, since it has an instruction set that represents a compromise between the RISC and the CISC approaches.

As in RISC architectures, the arithmetic and logic instructions operate on the registers, while the only instructions allowed for memory access are loads, stores, branches, and those used for stack manipulation. Thirty-two 32-bit registers are provided, of which 16 are reserved exclusively for the operating system.

In common with CISC architectures, the Clipper has a rich set of addressing methods, which simplify access to different data structures, including strings and the stack.

One feature that is worth mentioning is the presence of a floating-point unit on the same chip as the CPU. This performs division and multiplication operations between integers in a truly rapid manner, as well as arithmetic operations on reals in floating-point format, in single and double precision.

The processor can be interfaced with two chips, called **CAMMU**s (cache-MMU), one for instructions and the other for data.

Each CAMMU contains a cache for the instructions (or data) recently referred to, a TLB for the the most recent address translations, and a complete memory management system, whose job it is to transform a 32-bit virtual address into a physical one, also 32 bits long.

Several possibilities of coupling cache with virtual memory management exist (Exercises 10.5–10.7), but the idea of implementing both of them into one single chip and the use of two of these chips, one for instructions and another for data, is one of the features introduced by the Clipper that were then adopted by the majority of the successive CISCs and RISCs.

Some of the most recently announced products, such as the RISC **Intel 80860** and the CISC **Motorola MC68040**, incorporate these CAMMUs or similar components into the processor chip itself, thanks to their greater integration scale.

Complete concurrency between the two CAMMUs is guaranteed by two separate buses, one for the instructions and another for data (Figure 10.10).

The use of two buses more than doubles the bus bandwidth for concurrent accesses, because the need for bus arbitration does not exist in this case.

Yet, the high performance of the processor, in terms of instructions executed in a given time, is obtained because of the careful definition of the instruction set and the internal organization, which uses a sophisticated pipeline (Figure 10.11).

In the execute phase of the pipeline, the instructions are interpreted either by an 'integer execution unit' or a 'floating-point unit', depending on the type of operands. Each unit is equipped with its own ALU and its own set of registers.

Most of the latest microprocessors are endowed with both these units, made independent from each other since each has its own set of

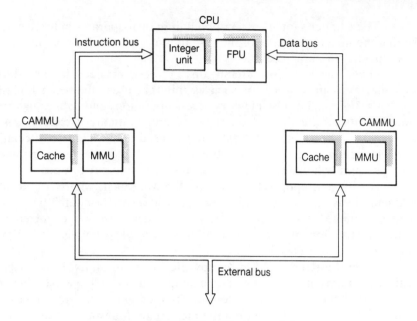

Figure 10.10 The Clipper model.

registers. The RISC **Motorola MC88000** is a very interesting example of microprocessor which introduces the more general **special function unit** (SFU) concept. Each SFU has its register file physically incorporated in it, and can be removed from the processor without any consequence for the other units.

All the SFUs communicate with each other through the internal buses and are addressed by a 3-bit field in the instructions. At present, only two SFUs are implemented inside the MC88000: the integer unit, which is treated as an SFU although it is not intended as such, and the floating-point unit.

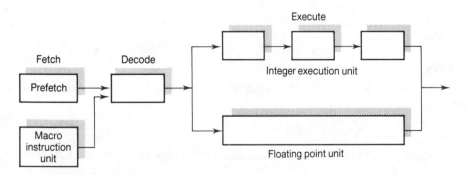

Figure 10.11 The instruction pipeline of the Clipper.

The Clipper's integer execution unit in turn operates in three stages, so that the final appearance of the system is as a pipeline containing within it a pipeline 'in miniature'.

Given the load/store architecture, there is no need for an address pipeline, even in a processor such as this that uses complex addressing methods. Indeed, because memory access operations and data transformation operations are defined on separate and mutually exclusive sets of instructions, the integer execution unit is used as an address calculation unit when a load or a store instruction is encountered, and as an arithmetic and logic unit when any other type of instruction is performed.

A different approach is used by the MC88000, where a dedicated add unit always calculates 'addresses', at each instruction fetch, in parallel with decoding. At the next stage, if the instruction is recognized as a branch instruction, the calculated address is used, otherwise it is simply rejected.

Several instructions can occupy the execution units, in accordance with their internal pipelining. For example, in the Clipper, taking into account that the integer execution unit is subdivided in three stages and that there is also a floating-point unit, up to four instructions can be executed in parallel.

Many instructions are interpreted by hard-wired logic and not with microprograms, and this accelerates their execution.

The most complex operations (string manipulations, operating system support) are, however, implemented by means of a unit (the **macro instruction unit** in Figure 10.11), which executes sequences of simpler hard-wired instructions.

The simple instructions and the macro instruction unit together give the Clipper many of the advantages of both CISC and RISC architectures.

Further reading

RISC architectures

Katavenis M. G. H. (1985). *Reduced Instruction Set Computer Architectures for VLSI*. Cambridge, MA: MIT Press

The Intel 80386

El-Ayat K. A. and Agarwal R. K. (1985). The Intel 80386 — architecture and implementation. *IEEE Micro*, Dec.

The Am29000

Advanced Micro Devices (1987). *Am29000 — Streamlined Instruction Processor, User's Manual*. Sunnyvale, CA

The Fairchild Clipper

Fairchild (1987). *Clipper 32 Bit Microprocessor: User's Manual.* Prentice Hall

Coupling cache with virtual memory

Stone H. S. (1987). *High Performance Computer Architecture*, pp. 165–8. Reading, MA: Addison-Wesley

EXERCISES

10.1 Using the description of a generic cache memory (Problem 9.B), define formally the TLB in the processor Intel 80386, and the instruction cache of the Motorola MC68020 which is of the direct mapping type with 64 entries.

10.2 The instruction queue of the Am29000 (IPB) is of the circular type and contains four locations of 32 bits. The technique with which it is managed is, however, somewhat different from that described in Section 9.5.2 of leaving a location empty. Indeed, each cache location in the IPB contains, in addition to an instruction field, a control field related to the state of the location, which can assume four different values:

- *Available*: free of receiving a new instruction.
- *Allocated*: selected to receive an instruction which has not yet been read.
- *Valid*: contains a valid instruction.
- *Error*: contains an instruction which has reported an error during reading.

Taking into account these considerations, define formally the IPB queue and its manipulation procedures, which make use of the state indicators.

10.3 Express the instruction flow in the fetch unit of the Am29000 (see Figure 10.5), by means of a high-level language procedure. Make use of the management processes of the circular queue and of the BTC, without however necessarily developing them.

10.4 Write the code for the management of the stack cache in the Am29000, using an assembly-like language. Take into account that the Am29000 uses the delayed branch technique. Do not consider the management techniques for the 'stack cache overflow' and 'stack cache underflow'.

10.5 When a cache is used in a system adopting virtual memory, the choice of tags (virtual or real) to be stored in the cache lines influences the cache performance. Compare the use of virtual and real tags in the cache lines, taking into account that the processor produces virtual addresses, while main memory needs physical addresses when a cache miss is generated.

10.6 Complete the analysis of Exercise 10.5, by considering also I/O processors, which produce physical addresses. Each time they read or write data in main memory, they have to invalidate the corresponding line in the cache, if there is one.

Consider also the **synonyms** problem. This consists in having more than one virtual address for the same memory location, as can happen if the latter is shared by several processes. Is the scheme of virtual tags reliable in this case?

10.7 Using real tags in a system with cache coupled with virtual memory, which activities in the processes of virtual-to-real address translation and cache operations are parallelizable? Take into account that cache operation includes two sequential phases: row selection and tag comparison.

11 Parallel Architectures

11.1 Control, data flow and
     dependency graphs
11.2 Serial computation
11.3 Instruction and data pipelining
11.4 Array processors
11.5 Systolic arrays
11.6 Multiprocessors

11.7 Multicomputers
11.8 Interconnection structures
11.9 Data flow and demand-driven
     architectures
     Further reading
     Exercises

The problems that computers are asked to solve often inherently contain elements of parallelism, which are obscured by the computer architecture. The von Neumann model is sequential and as such obliges us to sequentialize all the parts contained within a problem. One of the fundamental constructs of this model's architectures and languages is the **do loop**, which has the task of transforming *vector* processing, an eminently parallel operation, into *scalar* processing, performed serially in time.

The potential parallelism present in a problem may be of different types, according to how we define the computation 'grain' on which to develop the parallelism.

For example, let us consider operations more elementary than machine instructions. In this case, the 'problem' becomes the single instruction and the parallelism is introduced into the phases it is made up of. These phases constitute the computation granularity examined in Chapters 9 and 10 on concurrency in processing systems. At this level, the parallelism is independent of the particular problem to be solved since it is aimed at the way in which the architecture interprets a generic machine language instruction.

Proceeding to break down the problem into larger computations, we inevitably come up against the nature of the problems themselves and move away from the original von Neumann idea of the 'general purpose' computer. It will therefore be seen that, although parallel architectures may be considered in most cases as aggregates of von Neumann architectures, they end up establishing a variety of computation models that differ from each other.

A notable exception consists of those architectures that distinctly abandon the serial von Neumann model, in an attempt to adapt themselves more closely to the general nature of the problems. Such 'non von Neumann' architectures restore, in particular, the parallelism inherent in problems into their basic computational paradigm.

It is important, before going on to examine the computational models of the different types of parallel architectures, to investigate the nature of parallelism itself. In particular we need to ask: when might there be parallelism to be exploited, and how to proceed in order to incorporate such parallelism into the architectures.

First of all, the problems need to be subdivisible into computations that are independent as far as possible. The size of a computation, or 'grain', is determined by the quantity of communication needed between the different computations, which must be reduced to a minimum.

Computation grains correspond, in parallel architectures, to stages if a pipeline structure of sequential phases over time predominates; or to nodes if a network of computing elements capable of operating independently is present.

Having satisfied the condition that the problem, be it a single instruction or an execution phase or a program or the entire job, can be broken down into computations with little need to communicate, such parallelism needs to be exploited in reality. To this end, there needs to be a flow of data or instructions for that problem capable of feeding the architecture's set of stages or nodes continuously and for as long as possible.

The von Neumann computing model on one hand, and vector processing on the other, are typical cases in which there exist *streams* of instructions and of data respectively. But even at the program and job level, parallelism in the use of resources is ensured if there exists a continuous flow of processing requests.

In any case, whatever level the parallelism is realized on, both of these elements need to be borne in mind: the 'grain' of the computation and the characteristics of the 'stream' that feeds the architecture.

11.1 Control, data flow and dependency graphs

A program is a set of instructions waiting to be executed. Each instruction specifies what it has to do and on what data. The result of each instruction is the production of new data which, generally speaking, will serve another instruction or other instructions in logical (and temporal) succession to the previous one. In this case, it is said that there is a **dependency** relationship between the two. Any computation model has to respect such ordering.

Dependency relationships establish a necessary condition, but have nothing to say as to how to put the instructions in sequence. In other words, a computational model needs to define the **control mechanism** that makes it possible to pass from one (or more than one) instruction to another (or other) instruction(s).

Another important mechanism concerns **data storage**. In fact, it may be considered that data flows directly from a 'producer' instruction to a 'consumer' instruction. In this case, the memory has to be local to the instructions. The alternative model consists in a shared memory that the instructions can make reference to.

The first data mechanism implies a duplication of the data into several copies, if there is more than one target instruction. With shared memory, a single copy suffices. Shared memory constitutes a means of communication between the instructions.

In the von Neumann model, shared memory consists both of main memory and the registers of the processor. In a model of this kind, the concept of **state**, through which each instruction communicates with the ones that follow, becomes fundamental. Interest shifts from producing and consuming data, which ought to be the exclusive functions of an instruction, to the generation of state changes.

The introduction of a third element – shared memory – between the instructions being executed, gives rise to new functions which are not required by the problem that needs to be solved. Moreover, this type of communication does not comprise dependency relationships. There is no mechanism in it which constrains the programmer to perform accesses in order. On the other hand, a communication channel can be assimilated to a memory in which the order of accesses is determined: first the instruction that produces the data puts it on to the channel, and then the dependent instruction consumes it.

Any problem to be solved can be expressed by means of a direct graph whose nodes represent the instructions to be executed and the arcs the dependency relations. The nodes process the data input to them and produce results for the nodes that follow them on the graph.

Corresponding to the graph representing the problem, there exists another graph – the **control graph** – which expresses not dependency relations but the way in which control flows through the nodes. Such a graph depends on the physical characteristics of the machine, that is, the number of processors and the topology of the network, in cases where a number of processors are present. The nodes of the control graph correspond to possible processors which may be assigned when the corresponding instructions are ready for execution.

In the case of the von Neumann model, in which a single processor exists, only one node at a time can be enabled. Moreover, there will no longer be any resemblance between the graph of the problem and the control graph. The former is typically a two-dimensional structure, whereas the latter is linear in nature. The spatial parallelism inherent in the problem has to be forced into a temporal sequence, to adapt it to the von Neumann machine. And, to do all this, new states, required not by the problem but by the particular computation model, have to be introduced.

Every type of architecture refers to a particular model of computation. The architectures that allow control graphs to be drawn closest to the graph of the problem are the most efficient for that type of problem.

Let us now move on to define the different architectures, using control graphs to describe their models of computation.

11.2 Serial computation

In the serial computation model, or von Neumann model, a single node at a time is active, since only one processor exists.

The instructions are of a scalar type, that is, they operate on scalar data (or 'single' data, according to the terminology coined by Flynn: SISD = Single Instruction stream/Single Data stream). Any vector instructions have to be solved by means of sequences – at the same level or on underlying levels – of scalar instructions.

The control mechanism can activate single instructions one after another. Since more than one instruction may follow an instruction in the problem graph, some kind of **selection** mechanism is needed to choose between the possible instructions to be activated. Since all of them are in the same conditions, the choice is left to the programmer, who fixes the flow in the program.

Hence the processor, by advancing the program counter, will follow the order established in the program itself.

It is said that the sequential von Neumann model is of the **imperative** type, since the order of execution of the instructions is fixed by the programmer and not by the dependency relationships between the data. Naturally, it is up to the programmer to respect such relationships, but these are in no way made explicit to the system.

Since the instruction being executed has no way of communicating except with the one immediately following, though it may well need to communicate with many instructions, a shared memory needs to be used. This will be updated by the current instruction and read by the other instructions that depend on it, the moment it is their turn to receive control.

Furthermore, a primary role in the sequential model is played by the concept of loop, which permits a vector operation to be transformed into a scalar operation repeated over time. It is a characteristic of the sequential model to exchange the spatial dimension of *set* for the temporal dimension of *sequence*.

Hardly any problem has a direct correspondence with the control graph established by the von Neumann computational model. Yet on the other hand, this model constitutes the most basic model that can be imagined. It makes no hypotheses about the way the problem graph is structured, and adapts to every kind of computable problem. Nevertheless, this high degree of versatility is balanced by a high level of inefficiency.

It will be seen that architectures that introduce parallelism always make some hypothesis about the structure of the problem. In fact, many kinds of parallel architecture exist, while there is only one sequential architecture.

The aim of creating a parallel architecture that is truly general purpose, just as the sequential von Neumann architecture is, has not yet been achieved. This does not mean that the current parallel architectures are simply special purpose. They solve certain types of problem optimally and other types less efficiently: the von Neumann architecture solves them all in the same way.

Overcoming this stage of development might involve providing the architecture with a number of parallel mechanisms, so that it is capable of adapting itself to the various types of problem graph.

11.3 Instruction and data pipelining

If a high degree of repetitiveness exists in the problem graph, as is the case in processing of instruction or data streams, it is possible to organize the architecture like an assembly line. Typically, an assembly line is serial when referring to a single piece being worked on, but operates in parallel over a number of pieces to be found in the successive stages of operation. The overall result, as a rule, can be equivalent to that of an architecture n times faster, if n pieces is the capacity of the pipeline, that is, if n is the number of units placed in sequence in the assembly line.

The control flow is rigidly sequential, just like in the von Neumann model. The difference consists in the fact that not one but n processors can operate at the same time.

Another way of perceiving the matching between the problem graph and the pipeline architecture graph is its transformation into n sequential control graphs superimposed and shifted by one unit each.

Generally a pipeline architecture is not conceived on the level of problem graph. It is used on two possible levels:

- *Instruction level*. In this case the pipeline is made up of the successive stages which are carried out for interpreting an instruction: of fetching, decoding, address calculation, operand fetching, execution and result restoring. The pipeline is filled from the instruction stream.

- *Level of vector operations*. In this case the pipeline is filled by the stream of vector elements, while the units result from breaking down the execution phase of the operation into suboperations. For instance, the floating-point add operation could make use of pipelined units for comparing exponents, aligning, mantissae addition and result normalization.

11.3.1 Pipelined vector processors

In a serial computer, the four suboperations that make up floating-point addition must be completed on the first pair of elements before the next pair can be taken in consideration. In a four-stage pipelined system, however, in which each stage is specialized to carry out one of the four suboperations, each pair of elements can enter the first stage as soon as the preceding pair passes on to the second stage (Figure 11.1).

In general, if α is the number of suboperations and γ the time required to conclude each of them (supposing this to be equal for all), then the time taken to carry out an operation on vectors of a length n in a serial computer is:

$$\alpha\gamma n$$

In a system organized as a pipeline, this time is reduced to:

$$\alpha\gamma + (n-1)\gamma$$

where $\alpha\gamma$ is the time needed to obtain the first result, identical to that required in the scalar case, while $(n-1)\gamma$ is the overall time to produce the other $n-1$ results, notably lower than that needed for a scalar computer.

That is to say that while a serial computer produces a result every $\alpha\gamma$ time units, a pipeline of this kind produces a result every γ time units, once it is fully operative.

A supercomputer which uses such techniques extensively to carry out arithmetic and logic operations on vectors is the **CRAY X-MP**, a 2- or 4-processor extension of the CRAY 1.

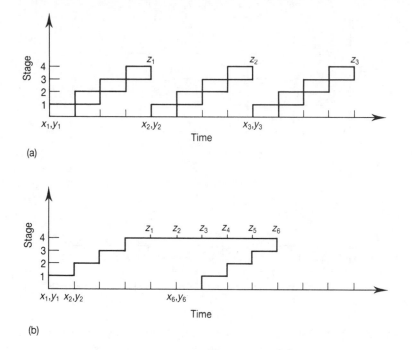

Figure 11.1 Vector addition in floating point: $Z = X + Y$. The addition of two elements is broken down into four stages: (1) comparison of the exponents; (2) aligning; (3) addition of the mantissae; and (4) normalization. In a serial computer (a), the four suboperations that compose the floating–point addition must be completed on the first pair of elements (x_1, y_1), before the next pair (x_2, y_2) can be taken into consideration. In a four-stage pipelined system, on the other hand, in which each stage is specialized to complete one of the four suboperations, each pair of elements (x_2, y_2), (x_3, y_3), . . ., can enter the first stage as soon as the previous pairs (x_1, y_1), (x_2, y_2), . . ., pass on to the second stage.

Each CPU in the system is equipped with eight floating-point vector registers, each of 64 elements. The floating-point processing units are composed of separate units for addition, multiplication and division; they are all pipelined and can be fed with the data contained in the vector registers.

The presence of multiple functional vector units, dedicated to specific tasks, is further exploited to increase the degree of parallelism in the system by means of two interesting architectural characteristics: chaining and overlapping.

Chaining, based on the same principle as pipelining, allows two functional units to be pipelined so that each result produced by the first can be inserted into the second without passing through the vector registers.

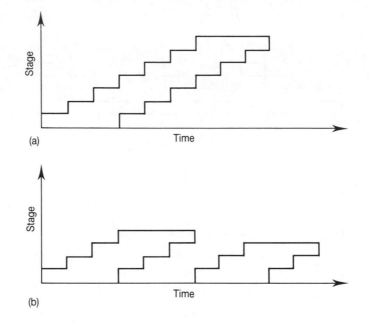

Figure 11.2 (a) Chaining of $Z = X + Y$ and $A = Z \times B$. (b) Execution without chaining.

The effect obtained is that of an extended pipeline, with a number of stages equivalent to the sum of the stages in each of the chained units.

This characteristic is useful when sequences of vector instructions need to be executed, using partial results. For example, executing the sequence:

$$Z = X + Y$$
$$A = Z \times B$$

can be accelerated considerably by chaining the multiplication and addition units (Figure 11.2). As soon as the time required to fill the pipeline with the first elements of X and Y has passed, the first result to be stored in Z is generated. But, as Z is the first operand of the next instruction (which requires use of the multiplier), the result of the first pipeline is also supplied directly to the multiplier, thus creating a 'multifunction' pipeline.

The overall time passes from:

$$t = t_1 + t_2 = \alpha_1\gamma + (n-1)\gamma + \alpha_2\gamma + (n-1)\gamma = (\alpha_1 + \alpha_2)\gamma + 2(n-1)\gamma$$

without chaining, to:

$$t_c = (\alpha_1 + \alpha_2)\gamma + (n-1)\gamma$$

with chaining.

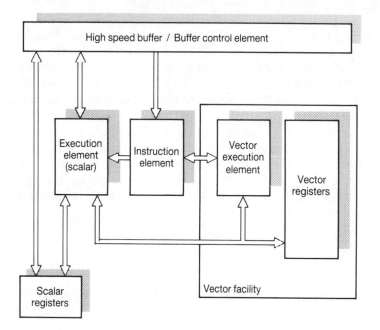

Figure 11.3 General scheme of a CPU of the IBM 3090 with vector capacity.

Overlapping, on the other hand, though it also exploits the presence of multiple vector processing units, can be activated in different circumstances, namely when there exist vector operations that are different and independent from each other. For instance, the two operations:

$$Z = X + Y$$
$$A = B \times C$$

can be performed in parallel.

In both cases, greater parallelism has been obtained on the basis of a greater opportunity for breaking down the problem into independent subproblems.

Also the **IBM 3090** is equipped with vector capacities, performed by pipelined arithmetic units. In contrast with the CRAY X-MP, the IBM Vector Facility is designed as an optional characteristic that can be added to a general-purpose processor of the System 370.

Unlike the CRAY, therefore, the vector registers of such units are not connected directly to the memory bus, but are interfaced with the scalar execution unit of the system (Figure 11.3).

The Vector Facility provides a pipelined arithmetic unit for each central processor in a 3090 system, and therefore achieves a considerable improvement in performance for many scientific applications in which most of the CPU time is taken up with arithmetic operations on vectors.

The Vector Facility has 16 vector registers with 32-bit elements. One pair of registers can be used to contain 64-bit elements. Two formats of floating-point numbers are used: 32-bit and 64-bit. Also the integers in a vector may be of two different lengths, using the registers singly or in pairs.

Apart from the vector registers, the Vector Facility has other registers: the Vector-Mask register, the Vector-Status register and the Vector-Activity count.

The first of these allows selective processing to be carried out on vectors, that is, only on some elements of the vector registers.

The Vector-Status register contains certain control fields, among which is the number of elements in the vector registers to be processed.

The Vector-Activity count keeps trace of the time employed in the execution of vector instructions.

11.4 Array processors

These architectures are the equivalent of the von Neumann model, applied to **vector** or **array** rather than scalar operations. Control is rigidly sequential, as in the von Neumann model.

In the control graph, the nodes represent array operations and the arcs convey arrays. To the node activated by the control are assigned n processing elements (typically ALU), which operate in parallel on n elements of an array. In the terminology introduced by Flynn, these architectures are known as the type SIMD (Single Instruction stream/Multiple Data stream).

The control graph of an array processor is equivalent to n identical and independent control graphs, each corresponding to the sequential model, which perform the same scalar instruction on different elements or groups of elements of one or two arrays. By this interpretation, the n nodes that carry out the same instruction are reached by the control at the same time. For each serial graph, a single node at a time is active.

There are no dependency relationships between the data in the array. Generally the result of a processing element is a function of data belonging to its local memory and/or to that of its neighbours or other predetermined processing elements. For this reason, a suitable interconnection needs to be provided between the processing elements of the array processor.

The processing elements that form part of the array are all identical, and, as stated earlier, they carry out the same instruction extracted by a single control unit. The only departure from this rule consists in the possibility to make execution of the instruction conditional, so as to allow subsets of the array to be processed.

For each processing element, the data model allows for sufficient local memory to contain one element of the array(s) in the successive stages of its processing. That is, it eliminates frequent data fetch and store operations, so costly in large-scale information structures.

It should be noted that, from this point of view, the array processor is the *dual* of data pipelining, where it is not data but rather instruction execution stages that are preloaded.

In one case, parallelism is achieved with respect to the data structure; in the other, with respect to the computational structure. Correspondingly, the computing time depends, in the case of array processors, only on the computational depth of the algorithm and not on the number of elements, whereas in pipeline architectures it depends in linear fashion on the number of elements and not on the computational depth.

11.4.1 The scalar product

One example of the potential of array processors to carry out parallel operations is the case of the scalar product. This is a fundamental operation in numerous scientific calculations, where it is performed very frequently.

Let us consider the following scalar product:

$$c = \sum_{i=0}^{n-1} a_i b_i$$

To perform this computation, a scalar computer needs to perform the products $a_0 b_0$, $a_1 b_1$, . . ., $a_{n-1} b_{n-1}$ in sequence, and then add them together. Such products are independent from each other, yet nevertheless they are performed in sequence in a scalar machine. Even the addition of the products obtained is carried out serially by accumulation, namely as a sequence of (dyadic) additions between the products $a_k b_k$ and partial sums:

$$\sum_{i=0}^{k-1} a_i b_i \quad (k = 1, 2, \ldots, n-1)$$

The execution time is therefore proportional to $n + (n-1)$, since n products and $n-1$ sums are needed.

If we examine the problem graph of the scalar product obtained by the method of **cascaded partial additions** (Kronsjö, 1985), also known as **cyclic reduction**, (Figure 11.4), we realize that there exists a very high degree of inherent parallelism, which could be usefully exploited with the use of a suitable parallel architecture.

Not only are the operations required (multiplications, additions) typical of the nodes in an array processor, but also one may detect a certain

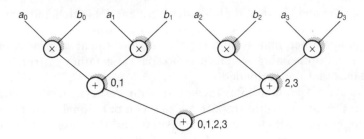

Figure 11.4 Problem graph of the scalar product using the method of cascaded partial additions, or cyclic reduction.

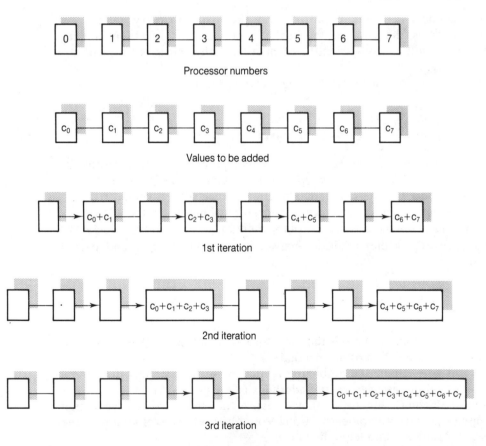

Figure 11.5 Scalar product of two 8-element vectors with an 8-node linear array processor.

repetitiveness within the problem graph, which could be translated into regular structures, linear or bidimensional, like those of an array processor.

If a linear scheme of an array processor with n interconnected nodes (Figure 11.5) is employed, the n pairs $(a_i b_i)$ can be distributed among the n nodes in order to perform the products in parallel. After the multiplication, it is necessary to proceed to the first step of reduction, adding together the products obtained pairwise in the even position places to the products obtained in the places that are contiguous (in odd positions). To do this, the processing nodes need to be provided with a further operation: that of **routing**, which consists of directing data towards nodes it is connected to. Routing is essentially a shift of data rightwards (or leftwards), which may be made conditional. In our case, it is useful that each *even* node transmits its result to the *odd* node to its right so that the latter can bring about its addition to its product. It is evidently not desirable that odd nodes should do the same towards even nodes, so the routing operation should be disabled on odd nodes.

The results obtained in the odd positions are to be shifted in their turn (by two positions, since we are now at the second step of reduction) and added in pairs. Then further reductions are carried out, clearly $\log_2 n$ in number, until the total sum is obtained in the final node.

The overall time taken is drastically reduced as compared with scalar treatment. It is of the order of $\log_2 n$ steps, where each step also includes routing operations.

However, there are numerous ways of connecting the processing cells of an array processor. The scalar product itself may be performed

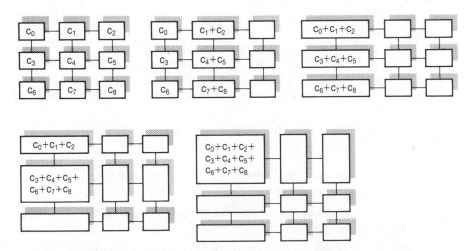

Figure 11.6 Scalar product of two vectors of nine elements using an array processor of $3 \times 3 = 9$ cells.

using various techniques, using one- and multi-dimensional configurations of cells.

For example, a two-dimensional matrix may be used, made up of $\sqrt{n}$ rows and $\sqrt{n}$ columns (Quinn,1987). Also in this case, the n pairs to be multiplied are distributed on the n nodes of the array. Once the n products have been obtained in parallel, the sum of all the elements of each row is performed, at the same time for each row. This can be performed iteratively by adding the last column (to the right) to the penultimate one, then the result obtained on the penultimate on to the next, and so on, until the sum of all the elements of each row in column 0 is obtained (Figure 11.6). At this point, applying the same method to column 0, the total sum in the element in position (0,0) is obtained.

It is easy to calculate the order of execution time using this latter type of topology. Since the rows and the columns are made up of $\sqrt{n}$ processing elements, a time of the order of $\sqrt{n}$ steps will be employed. Moreover, unlike the previous case, the routing operations are always carried out between directly connected elements.

11.5 Systolic arrays

Unlike array processors, which respect the structure of data, systolic arrays, like pipeline architectures, realize the structure of the algorithms directly.

They are made up of arrays (linear or two-dimensional) of identical processing elements, which are mesh-connected. Thus each cell communicates only with its own neighbours. Communication with the outside is the concern of the boundary cells (only two in the case of linear systolic arrays, all those on the edge for two-dimensional arrays).

The computation model is like a pipeline, though it may be multiple or extend in a number of directions. Note that an essential constraint that differentiates systolic arrays from pipeline systems is that the cells must all be identical.

It is possible to depart from the 'pure-systolic' scheme described here, by means of:

(1)   global communication (of the 'broadcast' type, with the same data item being transmitted to all the processing elements);

(2)   gathering the output data from all the cells (fan-in) and not just from the boundary cells;

(3)   the possibility of sending an instruction (a single instruction at a time as in array processors) to all the processing elements. In this case, the cell is a programmable systolic element.

Points (1) and (2) add the opportunity for multiprocessing to that of pipelining.

Point (3), though it does not abandon the hardware-oriented scheme of systolic processors, allows for greater adaptability to more classes of problems.

Typically, since the cells of a systolic processor are all the same (or are all programmed to perform the same function), the type of problems best adapted to this architecture are recursive algorithms. The result is obtained by ensuring that each cell utilizes the output of the preceding cell for at least one of its inputs. In turn, the previous cell has performed the same function on the output of the cell before. Hence the result is constructed recursively through the various cells and obtained from the last one.

In the same way as in pipelining, the systolic array is used on a data stream for the simultaneous processing of a number of sequential, but **recursive**, graphs, out of phase one from another by one or more units.

A further consequence of recursiveness is that the superimposition can be performed not only on separate graphs, but also on the same graph. In this way, the size of the array has no influence on that of the problem graph, since the latter can be reiterated by returning over the same elements a number of times.

Hence, the computational model is a recursive graph partly or totally 'unrolled', superimposed on other identical graph shifted by one or more units.

11.5.1 The pattern-matching problem

One particular kind of computation, in which systolic arrays are exploited diffusely, is solving the 'pattern matching' problem (Kung, 1982).

This consists in determining the positions of all the occurrences of a sample string in a given text. For instance, if the text is represented by 'WXAYWXBY' and the sample used is 'WX*Y', where the symbol '*' stands for 'any letter', the result can be represented by the Boolean string '10001', in which each 1 indicates the initial position of an occurrence of the sample in the text.

More formally, the problem can be expressed in the following way. Given the text

$$(s_1, s_2, \ldots, s_n)$$

and the sample string

$$(p_1, p_2, \ldots, p_m)$$

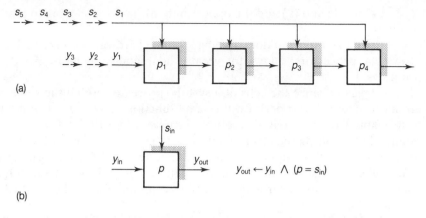

(a)

(b)

Figure 11.7 Semisystolic array for the pattern matching problem:
(a) configuration of the systolic array; (b) base cell and transfer function.

calculate the Boolean string

$$(y_1, y_2, \ldots, y_{n-m+1})$$

in which

$$y_k = 1 \text{ if and only if } (s_k \ldots, s_{k+m-1}) = (p_1, \ldots, p_m)$$

that is

$$y_k = (p_1 = s_k) \wedge (p_2 = s_{k+1}) \wedge \ldots \wedge (p_m = s_{k+m-1})$$

One of the possible solutions consists in utilizing a systolic array with as many cells as there are characters in the sample string, so as to preload the sample string into the array.

The partial results y_k, initially set as equal to 1, move systolically rightwards from cell to cell and the characters of the text s_i are transmitted globally (broadcast) to all the cells, one for each cycle.

Figure 11.7 shows the configuration of the systolic array and the function performed by each cell.

Figure 11.8 traces the working of the system to obtain the final result.

Such a system is an example of a **semisystolic** array, since the global transmission of data is adopted.

There exist alternative solution schemes, of a pure systolic kind.

For example, $n - m + 1$ cells can be used, destined this time to contain the y_k. Such variables, initially set as equal to 1, reside in the cells

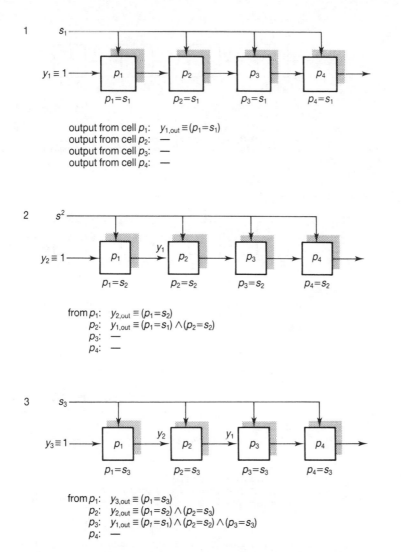

Figure 11.8 The succession of the time cycles needed to perform pattern matching of a string of four characters with a text eight characters long, according to the method shown in Figure 11.7. The pattern is preloaded into the array, while the characters of the text are transmitted globally to the various cells, so as to allow all the characters of the sample to be compared in parallel with the corresponding character in the text. The result is built up by sending a string of '1s' systolically in input to the leftmost cell. The first result is obtained at the fourth cycle from the rightmost cell. Note that index *i*, characterizing y_i, refers to the position of such bits in the result string, and not to the cell number.

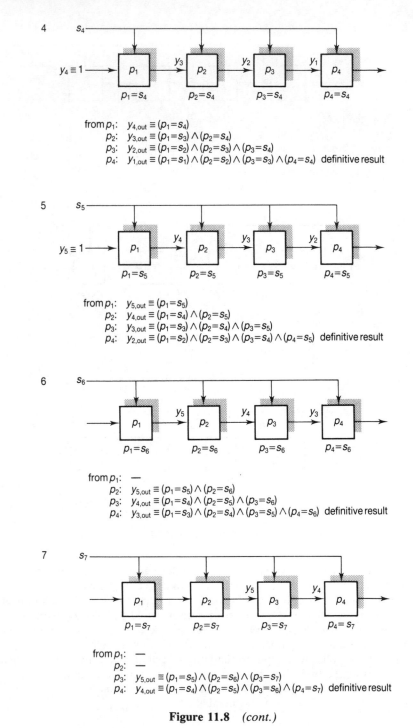

4   s_4

$y_4 \equiv 1 \longrightarrow$ p_1 $\xrightarrow{y_3}$ p_2 $\xrightarrow{y_2}$ p_3 $\xrightarrow{y_1}$ p_4 $\longrightarrow$

$p_1 = s_4$ $p_2 = s_4$ $p_3 = s_4$ $p_4 = s_4$

from p_1: $y_{4,out} \equiv (p_1 = s_4)$
p_2: $y_{3,out} \equiv (p_1 = s_3) \wedge (p_2 = s_4)$
p_3: $y_{2,out} \equiv (p_1 = s_2) \wedge (p_2 = s_3) \wedge (p_3 = s_4)$
p_4: $y_{1,out} \equiv (p_1 = s_1) \wedge (p_2 = s_2) \wedge (p_3 = s_3) \wedge (p_4 = s_4)$ definitive result

5   s_5

$y_5 \equiv 1 \longrightarrow$ p_1 $\xrightarrow{y_4}$ p_2 $\xrightarrow{y_3}$ p_3 $\xrightarrow{y_2}$ p_4 $\longrightarrow$

$p_1 = s_5$ $p_2 = s_5$ $p_3 = s_5$ $p_4 = s_5$

from p_1: $y_{5,out} \equiv (p_1 = s_5)$
p_2: $y_{4,out} \equiv (p_1 = s_4) \wedge (p_2 = s_5)$
p_3: $y_{3,out} \equiv (p_1 = s_3) \wedge (p_2 = s_4) \wedge (p_3 = s_5)$
p_4: $y_{2,out} \equiv (p_1 = s_2) \wedge (p_2 = s_3) \wedge (p_3 = s_4) \wedge (p_4 = s_5)$ definitive result

6   s_6

$\longrightarrow$ p_1 $\xrightarrow{y_5}$ p_2 $\xrightarrow{y_4}$ p_3 $\xrightarrow{y_3}$ p_4 $\longrightarrow$

$p_1 = s_6$ $p_2 = s_6$ $p_3 = s_6$ $p_4 = s_6$

from p_1:   —
p_2: $y_{5,out} \equiv (p_1 = s_5) \wedge (p_2 = s_6)$
p_3: $y_{4,out} \equiv (p_1 = s_4) \wedge (p_2 = s_5) \wedge (p_3 = s_6)$
p_4: $y_{3,out} \equiv (p_1 = s_3) \wedge (p_2 = s_4) \wedge (p_3 = s_5) \wedge (p_4 = s_6)$ definitive result

7   s_7

$\longrightarrow$ p_1 $\longrightarrow$ p_2 $\xrightarrow{y_5}$ p_3 $\xrightarrow{y_4}$ p_4 $\longrightarrow$

$p_1 = s_7$ $p_2 = s_7$ $p_3 = s_7$ $p_4 = s_7$

from p_1:   —
p_2:   —
p_3: $y_{5,out} \equiv (p_1 = s_5) \wedge (p_2 = s_6) \wedge (p_3 = s_7)$
p_4: $y_{4,out} \equiv (p_1 = s_4) \wedge (p_2 = s_5) \wedge (p_3 = s_6) \wedge (p_4 = s_7)$ definitive result

Figure 11.8   *(cont.)*

8

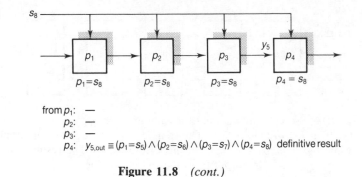

from p_1: —
p_2: —
p_3: —
p_4: $y_{5,\text{out}} \equiv (p_1=s_5) \wedge (p_2=s_6) \wedge (p_3=s_7) \wedge (p_4=s_8)$ definitive result

Figure 11.8 *(cont.)*

throughout the calculation, changing their value according to the law of transition:

$$y_{\text{final}} \leftarrow y_{\text{init}} \wedge (p_{\text{in}} = s_{\text{in}})$$

The characters of the sample and those of the text move systolically in opposite directions (Figure 11.9). When an s_i meets a p_j in a cell, a comparison is made between the two, and the value of y_k resident there is updated in consequence. The subsequent s_i (and p_j) are separated from each other by two time cycles, to ensure that all the s_i meet all the p_j.

This latter scheme has been used to design a chip to solve the 'pattern matching' problem, by virtue of its simplicity and regularity, and therefore its modular expandability. These characteristics, which belong more generally to all systolic arrays, permit several such components to be assembled together so as to obtain systems with a greater number of cells (Figure 11.10).

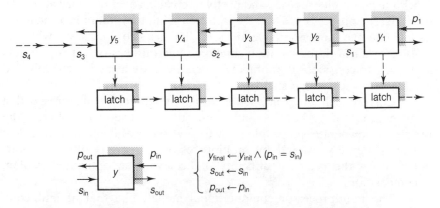

Figure 11.9 Characters of the sample and text move systolically in opposite directions.

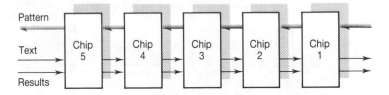

Figure 11.10   Serial combination of a number of chips, each corresponding to the systolic array in Figure 11.9. The sample string feeds the chip input to the right, while the text string is input to the leftmost chip. The results are obtained in output from the rightmost chip.

11.6   Multiprocessors

If, apart from performing execution functions, the single nodes of the architecture are also provided with control, then the nodes take on the role of processors and the architecture becomes known as multiprocessor.

The presence of control in each node of the architecture involves radical changes with respect to the parallel architectures examined so far.

First of all, the single processing elements proceed in an **asynchronous** way. In the previous cases, on the other hand, centralized control imposed the constraint that every unit operated synchronously with the others. Without a doubt, losing the restriction of synchronism allows us to have more general computational models. On the other hand, synchronization mechanisms such as queues or semaphores need to be adopted, if the processors in a multiprocessor system are to cooperate effectively in solving the same problem.

The second difference is partly linked to the overhead involved in synchronization mechanisms and partly to conflicts over memory access by the different processors. To keep both to a minimum, there is a tendency to increase the computation grain size. This is also consistent with the 'natural' grains offered by the technology: microprocessors. It is pointless and costly to consider other objects, when these are available cheaply and produced to such a high standard.

Current technology allows the design of parallel architectures with a large number of processors, but even so it is essential to break the problems down into subproblems with few reciprocal interactions. The greater generality offered by multiprocessor systems is often counterbalanced by the practical difficulty of achieving an optimum problem decomposition.

The multiprocessor computational model, like that of multicomputers, is referred to in Flynn's classification as MIMD (Multiple Instruction stream/Multiple Data stream). This definition emphasizes the autonomy with which the processors operate on their data flows.

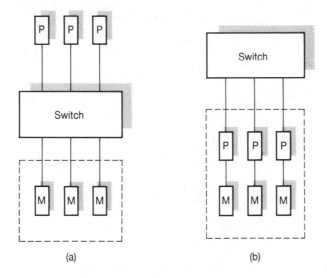

Figure 11.11 Multiprocessor systems: (a) tightly coupled system, and (b) loosely coupled system.

Remaining with multiprocessors, note that these systems can be seen as systems in which the computational component is distributed in different elements, all similar to each other. That is to say, the computing power of the whole systems is obtained by replicating a large number of systems of inferior computing power, operating in parallel.

In an architecture with distributed processing, one may wonder how the other two components, memory and processor-memory communication, are reconfigured.

As regards memory, this too is commonly implemented by replicating different modules of lower capacity, accessible in parallel. These modules can all be grouped together, in which case they constitute a **shared** memory for the set of processors (**tightly coupled** systems).

Alternatively, the modules can also be distributed among the processing elements as memories **local** to these (**loosely coupled** systems). However, in this case too there needs to be some mechanism that makes them still appear as a shared memory for all the processors. That is, we talk about local access if the module a processor refers to is local to it, and about remote access if instead it is local to another processor.

In both cases of coupling, the communication structure, or **switching** unit, must permit the linking of any of the processors P with any of the memories M. In the first case, the switch will put the processor in communication with the desired memory. In the second case, it will put it in communication with the processor that has that memory locally (Figure 11.11).

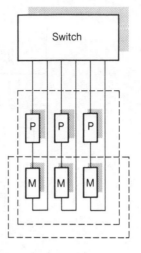

Figure 11.12 'Hybrid' multiprocessor systems, with memories with two ports.

There exists a third possibility, that of adopting local memories with two ports. One of the ports links it to its own processor, while the other connects it to the switch. In this way, each processor can communicate with its own local memory and, through the switch, directly with the memory local to other processors (Figure 11.12).

To sum up, the characteristics of a multiprocessor system are that they have:

● distributed processing

● concentrated communication

● shared memory, obtained by means of a set of concentrated modules, or else distributed among the processors.

11.6.1 The switching unit

It can be clearly seen that a large part of the efficiency of multiprocessor systems depends on the switch, which often tends to be the most complex part of such systems.

One way of implementing a switching unit, which is the simplest that can be imagined, is the complete **crossbar** network, in which each pair of nodes can be directly connected. The unit is a two-dimensional network, made up of switches, that connects the nodes set in the rows with those set in the columns.

The complexity of this type of unit is clearly of the order of N^2 (if N is the number of nodes) and it is therefore of high cost; it is principally used in systems with a small number of nodes.

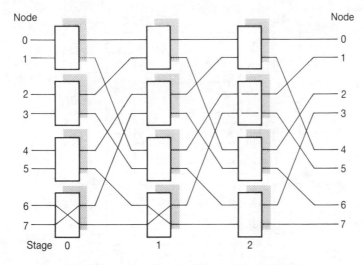

Figure 11.13   Omega network with eight input and eight output nodes.

A valid alternative to crossbar switches are **multistage connections**. These allow connection paths between any two nodes through a number of switches greater than 1. Each of these switches is itself a low-capacity crossbar switch. If N nodes need to be connected to each other (or with other nodes) using crossbar switches $M \times M$ ($M < N$), a network of $\log_M N$ stages is employed, in which each stage has N/M crossbar switches (Figures 11.13 and 11.14).

Such networks, known as **reconfigurable**, allow a number of processors to be connected to each other (in loosely coupled systems) or to a set of memory modules (in tightly coupled systems). The advantage as compared with crossbar networks lies in the reduction of the total number of switches, obtained at a cost of lengthening the communication paths.

Two multistage connections which are fairly commonly found in present-day multiprocessor systems are the Omega network and the Butterfly switch.

The **Omega network** uses crossbar switches with two input and two output lines. In line with what was stated in general about multistage networks, it is composed of $\log_2 N$ stages, each of $N/2$ switches of the 2×2 type, where N is the number of nodes to be connected.

Figure 11.13 shows an Omega network with eight input and eight output nodes. The communication path between two nodes is brought into being by programming the switches. The signal transmitted has to pass through as many switches as there are stages, hence with a delay proportional to $\log_2 N$.

The **Butterfly switch** is used in the BBN Butterfly Parallel Processor. It is very similar to the Omega network, except that it uses switches with

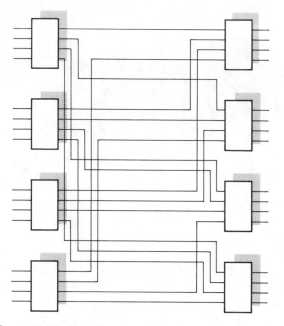

Figure 11.14 Switch connections for a 16-node Butterfly.

four input and four output lines, as against the two input and two output lines of the Omega network.

The advantage consists in reducing the number of stages ($\log_4 N$) and the number of switches for each stage ($N/4$). The reduced number of obviously reduces the transmission times, but on the other hand increases the average wait times for a free path, due to the greater probability that there are simultaneous requests for the same switch. Figure 11.14 shows how a Butterfly switch is used to connect together 16 input lines with 16 output lines.

The **Butterfly system** is made up of three principal components: the processor nodes, the Butterfly switch, and the I/O hardware.

Each processor node (Figure 11.15) consists of: a Motorola MC68020 CPU, a floating-point co-processor, 1 or 4 Mbytes of local memory, memory management hardware, a processor node controller (PNC) co-processor, an I/O bus and a Butterfly switch interface.

The processor node controller determines whether a reference in memory is local or remote, and sends and receives messages through the switch. To the programmer, the memory appears as a single large shared memory, in which remote references are only slightly slower than local ones (about 6 μs as against 2 μs). The PNC makes use of the memory management hardware for translating virtual addresses into physical addresses, carries out communication through the Butterfly switch, and

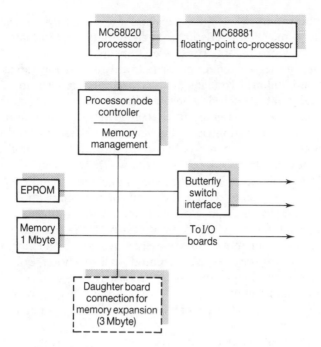

Figure 11.15 Block diagram of a Butterfly.

implements the operations needed for parallel processing, such as queue handling, semaphore interrogation and process scheduling.

The system's Butterfly switch guarantees that at least one path exists between each pair of processors. Yet, as we have already observed, cases of conflict are possible between two messages for the same output port of the switch, and these are resolved by delaying one of the messages for a brief period. By adding further switch nodes, an extra path for each pair of processor nodes can be defined. This is especially useful in large configurations, in order to improve reliability in case of some switch component breakdown. The alternative path also reduces conflict in the switch.

11.7 Multicomputers

Multicomputers adhere to a model in which each of the three components – processing, memory and communication – is distributed. One thing that can be recognized in a multicomputer is a network **topology**, rather than a switching unit separated from the processors and memory.

Hence the topology becomes the most distinctive characteristic of a multicomputer network, and represents the structure of the problem graph. The same characteristic, though in more accentuated form, is present in array processors. These are connected in structures that reflect the structure of the problem graph as faithfully as possible, so as to reduce delays to a minimum, by means of their multiple connections. Multicomputers reveal greater generality because the nodes perform more complex tasks, that is, they are assigned to **coarser grains** of computation.

Data communication times between the nodes of a multicomputer network are greater than for either array processors or multiprocessor systems. They lie between the latter and those required in local or geographical networks. Correspondingly, problems need to be broken down in such a way as to reduce the need for communication as much as possible, by increasing the size of the computation grain.

The technique by which communication takes place is not through registers or shared memory, but by means of **message passing**. That is to say, one or more processes are executed on each node, communicating with each other through **channels**. If the processes are in the same node, the channel is implemented by means of a memory word. If the processes are on different nodes, the channel is implemented by means of a direct point-to-point connection.

Communication between processes may or may not be synchronized. If it is, both processes need to be ready for communication to take place. A process that is ready to communicate a message has to wait for the other process to be ready too. If, on the other hand, an asynchronous type of message passing schema is adopted, the nodes also need to have a data buffering capacity.

Given the greater generality of multicomputer architectures with respect to array processors, the problem of communication between nodes presents itself in a completely different way. In fact, in array processors, the typical communication operation is routing, in which all the nodes transmit in parallel to the nodes directly connected to them. Certain nodes may possibly be excluded from the routing, but the case never arises that a single node must transmit data to one other single node (whatever it may be).

In multicomputer networks, on the other hand, any node must be given the opportunity to transmit data to any other node. There should not be any preferential or more efficient routes, if the multicomputer is to be truly general purpose. However, any network topology, unless it is a complete connection network, necessarily imposes that certain communications will be more efficient than others.

Complete connection is no longer feasible as soon as the number of nodes exceeds a few units. In fact, for n nodes, complete connection implies that each node should have $n-1$ link interfaces, while there exist physical limits to the number of links that each node can support (about ten links). Thus, it is necessary to adopt interconnection schemes that simulate complete connection, albeit with reduced performance. A number of interconnection networks are presented in Section 11.8, together with suitable evaluation criteria.

11.7.1 Multicomputer building blocks

The internal structure of the nodes of a multicomputer network assumes considerable importance. Indeed, since the nodes incorporate all three functions, of processing, memory and communication, they constitute the only building blocks needed to build up the network.

A node in a multicomputer network can be built up on the basis of commercial microprocessors, adding memory and communication components. The whole thing can also be integrated in a chip to reduce the number of parts in the network. The **modularity** of such systems is very high, since they are made up of a repetitive model, in which each node consists of the same component, or a small number of components if, for instance, one wishes to add extra local memory or further processing power, such as a graphic co-processor.

One building block that has been designed specifically to be used as a node in multicomputer networks is the **transputer** from Inmos. It is a highly efficient 32-bit microcomputer, with RISC characteristics, equipped with a 2 kbyte on-chip fast memory, with possibility of extension using external (local) memory up to 4 Gbytes. Yet the thing that marks it as a building block for multicomputers is the presence of four **link interfaces** (Figure 11.16), which allows it to be connected to another four transputers. In this way, multicomputers networks can conveniently be built, with different types of topology. The most powerful models include a floating-point unit.

In contrast to RISC architectures, the number of registers is very limited and they are all dedicated. On the other hand, the presence of fast memory (50 ns) on the chip replaces the RISC's needs for a large number of general registers. Moreover, the small number of registers together with the reduced and uniform set of instructions, simplify the data path and so favour efficiency, by the sound principles of RISC architecture.

The registers on the transputer are six in number (Figure 11.17):

- three registers A, B and C, which form a simple but efficient evaluation stack for arithmetic and logic operations;
- a pointer to an area of memory where local variables are held (workspace pointer);
- a pointer to the next instruction in the program area;
- an operand register, used to *form* the operands of the instruction, as will be explained in the following.

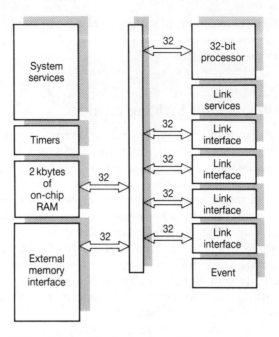

Figure 11.16 Block diagram of the transputer.

Arithmetic and logic instructions make reference to the stack, and therefore have zero addresses. The only instructions that make reference to memory are *load*, *store*, *jump*, and *call*.

The instruction format is very simple and regular (Figure 11.18). The instructions are all 1 byte long, divided into two fields of 4 bit each. The highest order half-byte represents the function, while the second half-byte (data) is destined for the operand. The latter represents a data item or reference to a data item as a displacement with respect to the workspace pointer, in the instructions which need explicit reference to an operand like

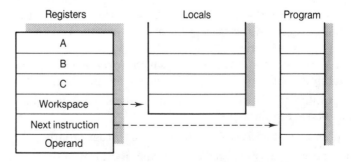

Figure 11.17 The registers of the transputer.

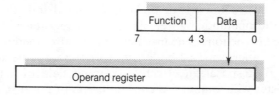

Figure 11.18 Instruction format of the transputer.

the above-mentioned operations of load and store. Otherwise, for the zero-operand instructions, the operand field constitutes an expansion of the code. In fact, a single function code is dedicated to all of these: *opr* (operate).

The operand field, whether it is used as a data item or reference to a data item or as an expansion of the code, may turn out to be too short, as it is only 4 bits long. In many cases this is sufficient, since small constants are used very frequently, just like the local variables closest to the location addressed by the workspace pointer.

However, if constants of greater length or greater displacement are needed, or instructions whose code expansion will not fit into 4 bits, a particular instruction, the *pfix* (prefix) can be used. This instruction serves to build an operand longer than 4 bits into the operand register.

	Mnemonic	Function code	Memory code
(a)	ldc #3	#4	#43
	ldc #35 *is coded as*		
	pfix #3	#2	#23
	ldc #5	#4	#45
	ldc #987 *is coded as*		
	pfix #9	#2	#29
	pfix #8	#2	#28
	ldc #7	#4	#47
(b)	add (op. code #5) *is coded as*		#F5
	opr add	#F	#F5
	ladd (op. code #16) *is coded as*		#21F6
	pfix #1	#2	#21
	opr #6	#F	#F6

Figure 11.19 Use of the instruction 'pfix' to extend the data field. (a) Load constants of different lengths; (b) opcodes of different length.

All the instructions load the operand field into the lowest order positions of the operand register, so that this register will be utilized in executing the instructions. The instruction pfix, after loading the data field into the register, performs a 4-bit left shift. In this way, the next instruction will have at its disposal an effective operand field of 8 bits, since the operand register will contain the concatenation of the first 4 bits with the current ones. Constants, displacements and function codes of even greater length can be constructed in the same way, simply by using a series of pfix instructions. Some examples are shown in Figure 11.19.

The mechanism described allows only the bits that each instruction needs to be utilized and, at the same time, creates instructions all of the same length, with internal fields of constant size and hence not involving complex decoding. Without a doubt, this constitutes a valid alternative to the usual techniques of code expansion.

11.7.2 Channel implementation

As stated earlier, communication between processes takes place through a logical structure defined as a **channel**. Transputers follow Hoare's CSP (Communicating Sequential Processes) model, and adopt **occam** (which is modelled on CSP) as their lowest level programming langue.

In occam, each instruction or set of instructions to be executed sequentially is known as a process. A number of processes can proceed in parallel in an asynchronous manner. The way in which two processes are synchronized and enter into communication is by one issuing an output instruction and the other an input instruction on the same channel.

In fact, communication in occam is synchronized in nature; namely, the first of the two processes that arrives at its I/O instruction has to wait (that is, it is momentarily descheduled) until the other one also reaches its I/O instruction.

An input instruction assumes the following form:

channel_name? variable

while an output instruction is of the type:

channel_name! expression

Physically, a channel is implemented in a transputer in one of two possible ways. In processes that execute on the same transputer, the channel is implemented by a single word in memory, whereas if the processes are on different transputers, the channel is implemented by **links**.

In any case, a process that needs to perform an I/O operation loads on to the stack the following: a pointer to the message, the address of the channel and the number of bytes to be transmitted (Figure 11.20). In the

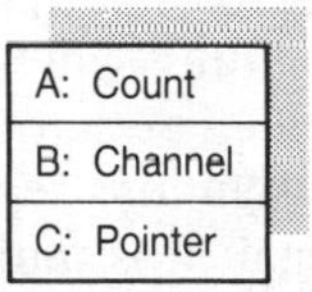

A: Count
B: Channel
C: Pointer

Figure 11.20 A process that has to execute an I/O instruction loads on to the stack a pointer to the message, the address of the channel and the number of bytes to be transmitted.

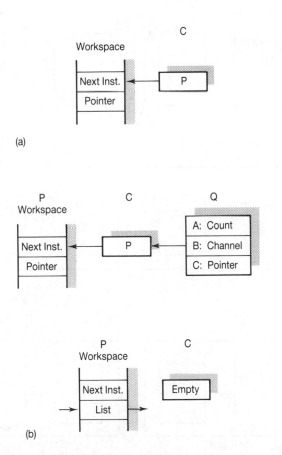

(a)

(b)

Figure 11.21 The channel, implemented by means of a memory location, at the moment when the first process reaches its I/O statement; (b) the channel, implemented by means of a memory location, at the moment when the second process arrives.

two cases mentioned above, of internal communication and external communication, the channel address will be that of the memory location in which the channel is implemented or that of the link interface respectively. Let us now examine the two solutions separately.

If the channel is internal, it is initialized to a special **empty** value before being used. It will subsequently take on the identity of the first of the two processes to refer to it, that is, it will be updated with a pointer to the workspace of that process.

Furthermore, the pointer to the message is stored in the workspace

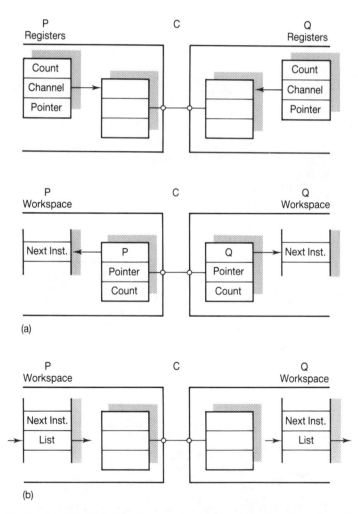

(a)

(b)

Figure 11.22 (a) Channels implemented by means of a link interface. P and Q are the communicating processes, and C is the channel; (b) the two processes have been put in the scheduling lists.

of the process (Figure 11.21a). The process is then descheduled while waiting for the second process to reach its communication statement. When this happens (Figure 11.21b), the message is copied, the first process is added to the scheduling list and the channel returns to the empty value.

In the case of external communication to another transputer, a link interface is used to free the processor from the task of transferring the message and descheduling the process. The link interface has three registers for:

- the pointer to the workspace of the communicating process
- the pointer to the message
- the number of bytes of the message

These three registers are initialized when a process executes a communication statement, using the values stored in the evaluation stack. Next, the process is descheduled. This occurs for both of the communication processes, independently of their order of arrival. When both link interfaces have obtained the information needed, they will carry out the communication and bring the two processes into the scheduling lists. (See Figure 11.22).

11.8 Interconnection structures

Whatever the nature of the nodes in a network, be they switches in a switching unit of a multiprocessor, or processing elements of an array processor, or building blocks in a multicomputer network, they are all interconnected according to a specific topology. One very important element in studying parallel architectures is to analyse and evaluate the different interconnection structures.

Let p be the number of nodes in a network. In order to identify them, we may use an integer from 0 to $p-1$, or else two integers i and j that go from 0 to $\sqrt{p}-1$, if the nodes are arranged in a two-dimensional matrix. An adequate representation is important if we wish to express the connections between the nodes and the data paths in the network by means of formal relations.

Certain networks are based on a number of nodes that is a power of 2. It is proposed to extend this restriction to all networks, as in this way it is possible to express the node connection relations more simply and systematically.

Suppose, therefore, that the number of nodes is:

$$p = 2^k$$

The integer that identifies a node may be expressed using binary representation:

$$i = i_{k-1} i_{k-2} \cdots i_0$$

If there are two integers, as in a square matrix, we will have:

$$i = i_{k/2-1} i_{k/2-2} \cdots i_0$$
$$j = j_{k/2-1} j_{k/2-2} \cdots j_0$$

The most immediate transformation is to add 1 to i, to express the connection between two numerically contiguous nodes. In addition, such a transformation needs to take account of the nodes around the edge. If these are connected cyclically or **wrap-around**, the transformation assumes the form:

$$i \to (i+1) \bmod p$$

and, in the two-dimensional case:

$$i \to (i+1) \bmod \sqrt{p}, \text{ for connections along the columns}$$

and

$$j \to (j+1) \bmod \sqrt{p}, \text{ for connections along the rows}$$

Two further transformations are of particular interest in expressing connection relations between the nodes. The first refers to the changing of a single bit:

$$i \to i^{(b)} = i_{k-1} i_{k-2} \cdots i_{b+1} \bar{i}_b i_{b-1} \cdots i_0$$

indicating that $i^{(b)}$ is the number obtained from i complementing the bit in position b.

Another transformation concerns the node number obtainable by left or right rotation of the binary string representing node i:

$$i \to i_{k-2} \cdots i_1 i_0 i_{k-1}$$
$$i \to i_0 i_{k-1} i_{k-2} \cdots i_1$$

Finally, the nodes can be coded using binary strings of non-constant length and the nodes connected to them can be obtained by eliminating or adding a bit in the lowest order position:

$$i \to i_{k-1} i_{k-2} \cdots i_1$$
$$i \to i_{k-1} i_{k-2} \cdots i_1 i_0 0$$
$$i \to i_{k-1} i_{k-2} \cdots i_1 i_0 1$$

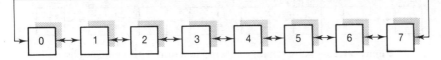

Figure 11.23 Linear cyclic-shift interconnection with eight nodes.

Having defined the most usual transformations on numbers representing the nodes in a network, let us now look at a number of networks and the interconnection relations that apply to them.

The **linear cyclic-shift interconnection** or **ring** (Figure 11.23) is regulated by a bidirectional interconnection relationship of the type:

$$i \leftrightarrow (i+1) \bmod p$$

The **bidimensional cyclic-shift interconnection** or **mesh** (Figure 11.24) satisfies the following bidirectional interconnection relationships:

$$(i,j) \overset{\nearrow (i,(j+1) \bmod 2^{k/2})}{\underset{\searrow ((i+1) \bmod 2^{k/2},j)}{}}$$

in the case of **wrap-around** connection.

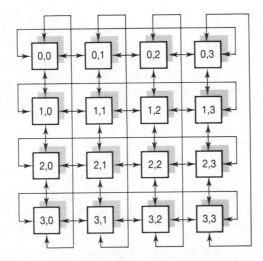

Figure 11.24 Bidimensional wrap-around cyclic-shift interconnection with 16 nodes.

Figure 11.25 An exchange interconnection with eight nodes.

Exchange connection (Figure 11.25) is regulated by the bidirectional relationship:

$$i \leftrightarrow i^{(0)}$$

Shuffle (Figure 11.26) and **unshuffle** connections (Figure 11.27) have the following unidirectional relationships respectively:

$$i \rightarrow i_{k-2} \ldots i_1 i_0 i_{k-1}$$

and

$$i \rightarrow i_0 i_{k-1} i_{k-2} \ldots i_1$$

All three of these connections, though interesting for certain kinds of problem, suffer from the fact that not all the nodes are connected. By joining the three types of interconnections together, a network known as

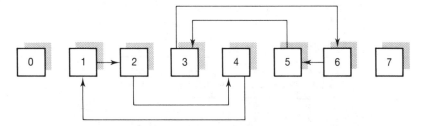
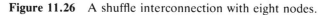

Figure 11.26 A shuffle interconnection with eight nodes.

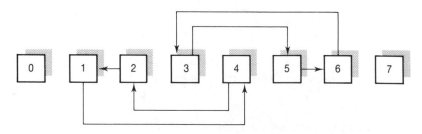

Figure 11.27 An unshuffle interconnection with eight nodes.

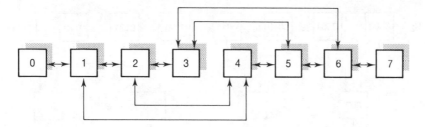

Figure 11.28 A perfect shuffle interconnection with eight nodes.

a **perfect shuffle** is obtained with all the nodes that are connected (Figure 11.28). Such networks have interesting properties that derive from the shuffle-type interconnections they are made up of.

Among these, it is worth mentioning the so-called **necklaces**: closed paths along which messages return to the start node after k steps, due to the particular interconnection relationship (Figure 11.29). The disjoint sets of nodes that were mentioned earlier are made up of such necklaces.

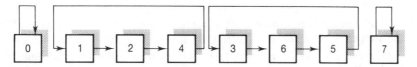

Figure 11.29 Necklaces of a shuffle connection with eight nodes.

A network of the **cube** or **hypercube** type (Figure 11.30) has each node connected to all those nodes that have a Hamming distance equal to 1, that is, they have binary configurations that differ by a single bit:

$i \leftrightarrow i^{(b)}$ with $0 \leq b \leq k-1$

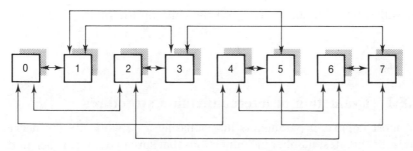

Figure 11.30 A binary 3-cube interconnection.

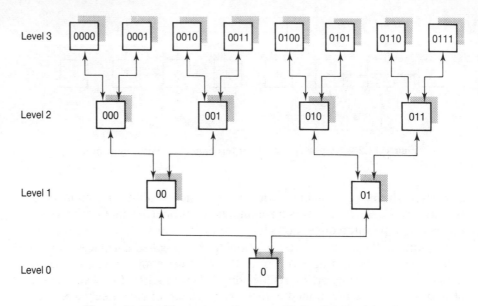

Figure 11.31 Binary tree diagram with $\log_2 8 + 1 = 4$ levels.

The **binary tree** connection scheme (Figure 11.31) is characterized by the fact that each node is connected bidirectionally to a *parent* and to two *children*. The root has no parent, while the leaves have no children. Following the coding given in the figure, the interconnection relations are given by the deletion of the lowest order bit for the connection towards the parent:

$$i \leftrightarrow i_{k-1} i_{k-2} \ldots i_1$$

and by the concatenation in the lowest order position of a bit 0 for connection with the child on the left:

$$i \leftrightarrow i_{k-1} i_{k-2} \ldots i_1 i_0 0$$

and with a bit 1 for connection with the child on the right:

$$i \leftrightarrow i_{k-1} i_{k-2} \ldots i_1 i_0 1$$

11.8.1 Evaluation of interconnection structures

The most important parameters in evaluating a network are the **degree**, that is, the greatest number of connections that spread out from each node, and the **diameter**, defined as the minimum distance between the two furthest nodes. The distance is measured in the number of nodes that a message has to cross to reach the destination node.

The ideal case, the completely connected network, has maximum degree and minimum diameter (equal to 1). A high degree signifies a lot of parallelism in the communication. A low diameter stands for short delays in the communication.

As we have already observed, a high degree is costly and, beyond a certain limit, impractical. Because of this, as always, help is sought from the temporal dimension, by making the message cross more nodes in the network.

All networks have been designed to keep the two variables, degree and diameter, to a minimum.

For instance, problems that involve a high probability of communication with a small number of predefined nodes are solved efficiently by linear cyclic shift or two-dimensional networks, in which the degree is 2 and 4 respectively.

Hierarchical networks, such as binary trees, also have a low degree, of only three connections, and a diameter lower than the previous types.

In the linear cyclic shift, the diameter is equal to $p/2 = 2^{k-1}$, in the two-dimensional type it is equal to $\sqrt{p} = 2^{k/2}$, while in the binary tree it is $2(k-1)$.

In the binary tree, this means that the diameter is commensurate with the number of levels, which is in a logarithmic relationship with the number of nodes.

The degree of the perfect shuffle is 3, and the connections are between nodes considered 'near' for many classes of problem.

To reach a high degree of parallelism for each class of problems, and not only for those with a high communication frequency between nodes close together, we need to resort to structures with greater degree, such as hypercubes. In this type of network, the degree is equal to the diameter, and both are equal to k. Hence, not only is the diameter in logarithmic relation with the number of processors, but there also exists a parallelism of k in the communication. This is reflected in the ability to nearly always find a free pathway between two nodes. In a tree, on the other hand, many communications take place through the same nodes, such as the root, and therefore they cannot be performed at the same time.

Another parameter used for evaluating a network is its capacity for **incremental growth**. This varies widely from one type to another. It ranges from the possibility for unitary increments in the case of linear cyclical networks, through increments by a whole row or column ($\sqrt{p}$ nodes) in two-dimensional mesh networks, up to a doubling of all the nodes in the case of hypercube networks.

Though the need to double the entire structure each time the size of the network has to be increased may seem a rather unattractive feature, on the other hand it favours modularity. For instance, eight transputers,

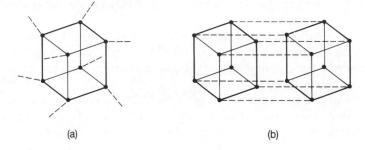

(a)   (b)

Figure 11.32 Eight transputers, connected in a binary cube of dimension 3, each use three of their links to construct the network. Since each transputer remains with one unused link, by joining two such cubes by means of the links left free, a dimension 4 hypercube is obtained.

connected in a binary cube of dimension 3, each use three of their links to construct the network (Figure 11.32). Commercially available boards, that can be used in a 'host' such as a PC, exist with this configuration. Since each transputer remains with one unused link, by joining two such cubes by means of the links left free, a dimension 4 hypercube is obtained. Boards are provided that make it easy to perform such further connections.

To build hypercubes of a dimension greater than 4, it would be necessary to make use of nodes with a greater number of links. One solution offered by **Floating Point System**, with its **FPS T** Series, is to use transputers as nodes, that is still using four-link components, but connecting a 1-to-4 multiplexer to each link, so that the number of links goes up from 4 to 16 (Figure 11.33). The result is a hypercube structure with up to 14 dimensions (two of the links are used for system functions). Yet, at the same time, it is equivalent to a reconfigurable network, due to the need to program the four multiplexers of each transputer each time two nodes have to communicate.

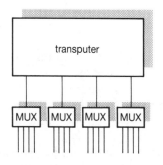

Figure 11.33 System adopted by Floating Point System to increase the links from 4 to 16 in its FPS T series.

11.9   Data flow and demand-driven architectures

These architectures are definitely far removed from the von Neumann model.

Data flow architectures faithfully reflect the graph of the problem. An instruction is executed if the dependency relations for it are satisfied, that is, when the data it needs to process is ready. Thus the parallelism is incorporated implicitly, without either the programmer or the compiler having to seek out possible sources of parallelism.

The data is passed directly along the arcs of the graph from one instruction to another. If a number of instructions need the same data item, a number of copies will need to be made, as there is no such thing as shared memory. This can become a problem when dealing with large data structures. On the other hand, this mechanism eliminates the risk of side effects, which derive from the fact that any instruction can access and modify a variable expressed as a shared memory location.

As stated before, an instruction can be executed if its input data has been produced and, naturally, if there is a processor free to execute it. In data flow terminology, data items with the identification of the destination instruction are known as **tokens**, while an instruction that can proceed to be executed is said to be able to be **fired**. Tokens are absorbed by a fired instruction to produce a result on its output arc (Figure 11.34).

Because data flow architectures follow the graph of the problem faithfully, it is possible to take steps relating to parallelism by examining this graph directly. Specifically, **maximum parallelism** is given by the maximum number of nodes of each level; the **bottlenecks** are the levels with the lowest number of nodes; the **critical branch** is the longest branch to be found on the graph. These measurements are important also to determine the sizing in terms of processors that the architecture needs to have. In this, one needs to take account not only of achieving a high degree of parallelism, but also the average utilization of the processors is high.

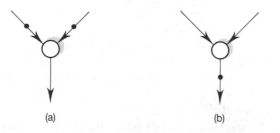

(a)   (b)

Figure 11.34   Data items with the identification of the destination instruction are known as tokens and are represented by a black dot on the arrows (a). When all the tokens are present on the input arcs, they are absorbed by the instruction, which is then 'fired' to produce a result on its output arc (b).

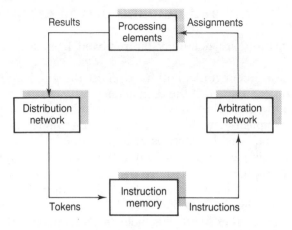

Figure 11.35 A data flow architecture.

The component parts of a data flow architecture (Figure 11.35) are: a memory containing the program instructions, a set of processing elements which can be assigned to the instructions ready to be executed, an arbitration network to decide such assignments, and a distribution network for the tokens produced by the processing elements to reach the instructions they are directed to.

This architecture, though simple in theory, suffers from communication problems, which inevitably arise when there is a large number of instructions and tokens to be distributed. For this reason, the two networks, for processing element arbitration and token distribution, must be designed very carefully and so represent a considerable element in the architecture.

To relieve the task of the two communication networks, it is possible to go down the road of increasing the size of the computation grain, so as to reduce the number of elements. In this case, the nodes no longer refer to individual instructions, but to more complex computations.

One criticism levelled against data flow architectures is that, due to the way the conditions for enabling instructions to be executed are examined, there is a risk of wasting a great deal of processing power. Indeed, entire branches that come out of if–then–else instructions and do not need to be executed, are performed in data flow architectures if the data is ready. For the same reason, a program may not even terminate after it has produced its result.

These disadvantages derive from the fact that control passes to an instruction when its data is ready, and this is right, but no account is taken of whether its result is needed or not.

Reduction or **demand-driven** architectures, on the other hand, insist that an instruction can be declared ready to be executed only if both of these conditions are satisfied.

Whereas in data flow the processing of an arithmetic expression follows the usual order of beginning with the innermost subexpressions and proceeding outwards (the 'innermost' rule), demand-driven architectures go about it in exactly the opposite way. That is to say, the string is examined from the outside inwards (the 'outermost' rule), with the aim of progressively identifying which instructions need to be executed to obtain the required result. Thus, the entire formula is initially considered; this in turn calls for the nested subexpressions to be taken into account, and so on, until the numeric values are reached. At this point, the direction is inverted and processing proceeds outwards, progressively producing the values that go to obtain the final result (an **inward–outward** procedure).

The term 'reduction' takes account of the transformations that the original formula undergoes, through ever more reduced intermediate formulae, until the final result is obtained.

By way of conclusion, we are now in a position to compare the three execution models: control flow, data flow and reduction.

In all three models there exists an instruction **selection** phase. In the control flow or von Neumann model, even if parallel, the instruction is selected by means of the value of the program counter. In contrast, the selection rule is of the 'innermost' type for data flow architectures and 'outermost' for reduction architectures.

Once the instruction is selected, the von Neumann model supposes that the instruction automatically satisfies the requirements for execution. In the other two models, on the other hand, the instruction is **examined** to see if it has all its input data (data flow) and also if its result is required by another instruction (demand driven).

The flow of control is separated from the flow of data in von Neumann architectures, while in the other two types they coincide completely.

The **parallelism specification** is **explicit**, that is, up to the programmer or compiler, in control flow architectures, but **implicit** in the other two types. This is the most important feature of this kind of architecture, since it allows parallelism to be exploited to best advantage. On the other hand, a fraction of the work may be lost in data flow since all the instructions that have data ready are executed, and not just those required by each particular execution of the program. Reduction architectures have been designed to overcome this inefficiency, yet nevertheless they have to perform extra work in going through the string twice, once 'inward' and again 'outward'. This extra work, though not enormous, is always present, unlike that carried out unproductively in data flow architectures.

Nowadays, there exists a large number of data flow and demand-driven architectures in research laboratories all over the world. Although it is still too early for them to provide results comparable with those derived from the enormous body of knowledge concerning von Neumann architectures, the principles they are based on are highly persuasive and contribute to the conviction that other, completely different, computational paradigms can in the future take the place of the von Neumann model.

Further reading

Guo-Jie Li and Wah B. W. (1985). The design of optimal systolic arrays. *IEEE Trans. on Computers*, Jan., 66–77
Hockney R. W. and Jesshope C. R. (1988). *Parallel Computers: Architecture, Programming and Algorithms* 2nd edn. Bristol, UK: Adam Hilger
INMOS Limited (1988). *Transputer Reference Manual*. Englewood Cliffs, NJ: Prentice-Hall
Kronsjö L. (1985). *Computational Complexity of Sequential and Parallel Algorithms*. John Wiley
Kung H. T. (1982). Why systolic architectures? *IEEE Computer*, Jan., 37–46
Quinn M. J. (1987). *Designing Efficient Algorithms for Parallel Computers*. New York: McGraw Hill

EXERCISES

11.1 The **speed-up** of a parallel algorithm is defined as the time taken in a serial execution divided by the time taken on a parallel architecture.

Calculate the speed-up of a vector floating-point addition between two vectors of 64 elements each, on a vector processor with a floating-point add pipeline unit six stages long.

11.2 Compute the speed-up in executing the following computation:

$A \times B + C$

with **chaining** and without chaining, on a vector processor with two pipeline functional units, one for floating-point multiply and the other for add, which are seven stages and six stages long respectively. Let us suppose that A, B and C, are three vectors each of 64 elements.

11.3 Try to identify dependency relationships within the following FORTRAN DO loops:

```
(1)      DO 1 I=1,N
         A(I)=B(I)+C(I)
         D(I)=A(I)+E(I)
      1 CONTINUE
```

```
(2)      DO 2 I=2,N
         A(I)=A(I-1)+B(I)
       2 CONTINUE
(3)      DO 3 I=2,N
         A(I)=B(I-1)+C(I)
         B(I)=D(I)+E(I)
       3 CONTINUE
(4)      C(0)=0
         DO 4 I=1,N
         A(I)=D(I)/E(I)
         B(I)=A(I)*F(I)
         C(I)=B(I)+C(I-1)
       4 CONTINUE
```

Take into account that a dependency relationship can be present *inside* the single iterations or *between* different iterations. In the last case they are called **recurrence** relationships and involve different values of the indexes in the same statement.

Which of the following: (a) overlapping, (b) chaining, (c) multitasking, are applicable or not applicable to each of the (1) to (4) DO loops?

11.4 The **complexity** of a (parallel) algorithm is the order of magnitude of the time needed to carry out the algorithm, that is, the time span from when the first processor initiates the algorithm execution until the last processor terminates it. Often the computational complexity which involves the contribution of arithmetic operations alone is reported.

The **cost** of a (parallel) algorithm is defined as the computational complexity multiplied by the number of processors. Calculate the total execution time, the computational complexity and the cost for the scalar product in each of the three cases analysed in the text: serial computation, linear cyclic-shift interconnection and two-dimensional cyclic-shift interconnection.

11.5 Work out the problem of scalar product using a cube-connected interconnection scheme. The products to be added are distributed in the 16 nodes of a four-dimensional hypercube:

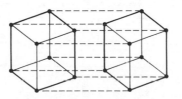

The algorithm consists of adding the elements contained in the vertexes of one of the two hypercubes of dimension $d - 1$ into the vertexes of the other hypercube.

Then, apply the same operation to the two hypercubes of dimension $d - 2$, in which the sums have been obtained, and proceed iteratively until the scalar product is obtained in the last node.

Calculate the total time, the complexity, and the cost.

11.6 Try to devise a tree parallel architecture for the scalar product problem, and calculate its total time, complexity and cost.

Compare the different interconnection schemes analysed in Exercises 11.4, 11.5 and 11.6. Which variable(s) would you select for this comparison?

11.7 In the following project, used for the problem of pattern matching, a semisystolic array with *fan-in* is employed:

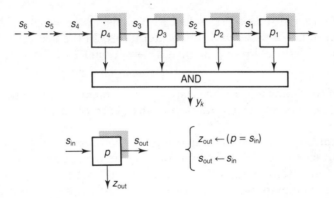

The same conventions as those in the semisystolic solution given in Section 11.5.1 are used. In the present project, however, the characters of the text are not broadcasted but are transmitted systolically throughout the cells.

At which cycle is y_1 ready?

11.8 In the following semisystolic scheme:

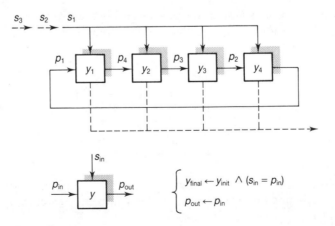

the partial results are stored into the cells, as well as the final results which will be extracted using a bus after m cycles y_1, $m+1$ cycles y_2, and so on. All the y_k have to be initialized to '1'.

The peculiarity of this scheme is its circularity, which makes it possible to have fewer cells than the number of results.

How many cells are needed?

It is necessary, in this scheme, to associate a 'tag' bit to the pattern p_1. Why?

11.9   Some applications admit similar computational models. For example, the **convolution** problem is formulated in the following manner. Given a numeric m-uple (weight sequence)

$$(w_1, w_2, \ldots, w_m)$$

and the input sequence

$$(x_1, x_2, \ldots, x_n)$$

calculate the resultant sequence

$$(y_1, y_2, \ldots, y_{n-m+1})$$

defined by:

$$y_k = w_1 x_k + w_2 x_{k+1} + \ldots + w_m x_{k+m-1}$$

This procedure is frequently used as intermediate computation in the matrix operations, in Fourier transforms, and in numerous other numeric applications.

Is it possible to reduce the convolution problem to that of pattern matching? How?

11.10   The communication path between two nodes in an Omega network is obtained in the following manner. The bits of equal position in the binary representation of the two node numbers that have to communicate are summed up, then divided by two, then the remainder is taken. If it is 0, all the switches in the corresponding stage will be programmed with a direct link, otherwise they will be programmed with crossed links:

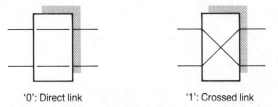

'0': Direct link   '1': Crossed link

In Figure 11.13, nodes 6 and 5 are connected. Apply the rule described above in this case.

Solutions to Selected Problems and Exercises

2.1

'0' and '1'.
From $(a_{n-1}\ldots a_1 a_0 a_{-1} a_{-2}\ldots)_x = (a_{n-1}\ldots a_1 a_0 a_{-1} a_{-2}\ldots)_y$, it follows that

$$a_{n-1}X^{n-1}+\ldots+a_1 X+a_0+a_{-1}X^{-1}+a_{-2}X^{-2}+\ldots$$
$$=a_{n-1}Y^{n-1}+\ldots+a_1 Y+a_0+a_{-1}Y^{-1}+a_{-2}Y^{-2}+\ldots$$

If $X \neq Y$, this equality can be satisfied only if $a_i = 0$ for each $i \neq 0$, and for all values that a_0 assumes in the numbering system which has the smallest base.

2.2

The condition of even or odd of a binary integer is determined only by its lowest order figure. Indeed, all the other figures give a contribution of 2 or higher powers of 2 which are all even.

2.3

$100_2 = 0 \times 2^0 + 0 \times 2^1 + 1 \times 2^2 = 4$
$100_8 = 0 \times 8^0 + 0 \times 8^1 + 1 \times 8^2 = 64$
$100_{10} = 0 \times 10^0 + 0 \times 10^1 + 1 \times 10^2 = 100$
$100_{16} = 0 \times 16^0 + 0 \times 16^1 + 1 \times 16^2 = 256$

2.4

$2 \times 4^2 + 1 \times 4^1 + 3 \times 4^0 = 39_{10}$

2.5

(a) $X^1 + 3X^0 = X + 3 = 7$

(b) $7Y^1 + 0 \times Y^0 = 7Y = 56$

(c) $Z^2 + A \times Z^1 + 0 \times Z^0 = Z^2 + 10Z = 416$

From these, we have:
$X = 4,\ Y = 8,\ Z = 16$

359

2.6 ———

(a) $11_{10} = 23_4$, $27_{10} = 123_4$

(b) $120_{10} = 1111000_2$, $27_{10} = 11011_2$, $0.8125_{10} = 0.1101_2$, $0.122_{10} = 0.0001111_2$,
      $43.75_{10} = 101011.11_2$

(c) $39_{10} = 47_8$, $27_{10} = 33_8$

2.7 ———

+	1	10	11	100
1	10	11	100	101
10	11	100	101	110
11	100	101	110	111
100	101	110	111	1000

×	1	10	11	100
1	1	10	11	100
10	10	100	110	1000
11	11	110	1001	1100
100	100	1000	1100	10000

2.8 ———

10. Indeed, the following equation has to be satisfied:

$$X = a_{n-1}X^{n-1} + \ldots + a_1X + a_0$$

and it can only be so when $a_1 = 1$ and all the other $a_i = 0$.

2.9 ———

(a)   0.1

(b)   0.010101 . . .

The fact of being periodic is a characteristic which depends on the particular positional system.

2.10 ———

$0.9 = 0.11100110011 \ldots$

2.11 ———

Each time a borrow is used in the difference between two BCD figures, it is necessary to

subtract '6' from the corresponding figure of the result.
For example:

```
00100011 −    (23)
00001000      (8)
00011011 −
    0110      (6)
00010101
```

2.12

(a)
```
0010 1001 0101 +    (295)
0011 0111 1000      (378)
0110 0000 1101

0110 0000 1101 +
     0110 0110      (66)
0110 0111 0011 =    (673)
```

(b)
```
0010 0100 −    (24)
0001 1000      (18)
0000 1100

0000 1100 −
     0110      (6)
0000 0110 =    (6)
```

(c)
```
0110 0100 0010 −    (642)
0011 0101 0100      (354)
0010 1110 1110

0010 1110 1110 −
     0110 0110      (66)
0010 1000 1000      (288)
```

2.13

The parity bits will be:

$$P1 = 1, P2 = 0, P4 = 1, P8 = 1$$

and the Hamming code:

1	0	0	1	0	0	0	1	1	0	1
1	2	3	4	5	6	7	8	9	10	11

An error in position 6 of the original code means an error in position 11 of the corresponding Hamming code. Calculating again the parity bits, we have:

$$P1' = 0, P2' = 1, P4' = 1, P8' = 0$$

Comparing bitwise the parity bits, we have:

$$EX\_OR(P1,P1') = 1 \quad \text{position 1}$$
$$EX\_OR(P2,P2') = 1 \quad \text{position 2}$$
$$EX\_OR(P4,P4') = 0$$
$$EX\_OR(P8,P8') = 1 \quad \text{position 8}$$

and then an error will be signalled in the position $(8 + 2 + 1) = 11$.

2.A

Type
```
  Bit = 0..1;
  Half_byte = array [0..3] of Bit;
  Byte = array [0..7] of Bit;
```

Const
```
  Word_max_bit = . . .;
```

Type
```
  Word = array [0..Word_max_bit] of Bit;
  Longword = array [0..1] of Word;
  Quadword = array [0..3] of Word;
```

2.B

Const
```
  Addr_max_val = . . .;
    (* max value of address field *)
  Mem_max_addr = . . .;
    (* max address of memory *)
```

Type
```
  Elem_type = . . .;
  Address = 0..Addr_max_val;
  Mem_range = 0..Mem_max_addr;
```

Var
```
  memory : array [Mem_range] of Elem_type;
```

Type
```
  Mem_error = (Out_of_range, No_error);
```

Procedure Mem_read (addr : Address; **Var** elem : Elem_type;
                        Var error : Mem_error);
```
  Begin
    if addr in [0..Mem_max_addr]
      then begin
              elem := memory [addr];
              error := No_error
           end
      else error := Out_of_range
  End;
```

```
Procedure Mem_write (addr : Address; elem : Elem_type;
                        Var error : Mem_error);
   Begin
     if addr in [0..Mem_max_addr]
       then begin
               memory [addr] := elem;
               error := No_error
           end
       else error := Out_of_range
   End;
```

2.C

```
Const
   Reg_max_number = . . .;

Type
   Reg_type = . . .;
   Reg_range = 0..Reg_max_number;

Var
   register_set : array [Reg_range] of Reg_type;

Procedure Reg_read (number : Reg_range; Var elem : Reg_type);
   Begin
     elem := register_set [number]
   End;

Procedure Reg_write (number : Reg_range;
                        elem : Reg_type);
   Begin
     register_set [number] := elem
   End;
```

2.D

```
Const
   Stack_dim = . . .;

Type
   Stack_element = . . .;
   Stack_error = (Stack_full, Stack_empty, No_Stack_error);

Var
   stack : array [1..Stack_dim] of Stack_element;
   Stack_pointer : 1..Stack_dim +1;

Procedure Init_stack;
   Begin
     stack_pointer := stack_dim +1;
   End;
```

```
Procedure Push (elem : Stack_element; Var error : Stack_error);
  Begin
    if stack_pointer > 1
      then
        begin
          stack_pointer := stack_pointer −1;
          stack [stack_pointer] := elem;
          error := No_stack_error
        end
    else error := Stack_full
  End;

Procedure Pop (Var elem : Stack_element;
               Var error : Stack_error);
  Begin
    if stack_pointer < Stack_dim +1
      then
        begin
          elem := stack [stack_pointer];
          stack_pointer := stack_pointer +1;
          error := No_stack_error
        end
    else error := Stack_empty
  End;
```

3.A ───

```
Type
  Effective_address = . . .;   (* array of Bit *)
  Displ_type = Effective_address;

Var
  Program_counter : Effective_address;
```

3.1 ───

```
Procedure Address_add (addr : Effective_address;
                       displ : Displ_type;
                       Var result_addr : Effective_address);
Var
  sum : 0..3; j : 0..Word_max_bit; carry : Bit;
  Begin
    carry := 0;
    for j := Word_max_bit downto 0 do
      begin
        sum := addr[j] + displ[j] + carry;
        result_addr[j] := sum mod 2;
        carry := sum div 2
      end
  End;
```

Procedure Address_sub (addr : Effective_address;
                               displ : Displ_type;
                               Var result_addr : Effective_address);

Var
  sum : 0..3; j : 0..Word_max_bit; carry : Bit;
  Begin
    for j := 0 **to** Word_max_bit **do**
      displ[j] := (displ[j] + 1) **mod** 2;   (* 1'complement *)
    carry := 1;
    for j := Word_max_bit **downto** 0 **do**
      begin
        sum := addr[j] + displ[j] + carry;
        result_addr[j] := sum **mod** 2;
        carry := sum **div** 2
      end
  End;

3.2

Procedure Register_indirect_Addressing
  (reg_numb : Reg_range; **Var** out_addr : Effective_address);
  Begin
    Reg_read (reg_numb, out_addr)
  End;

3.3

Procedure Indirect_Addressing (in_addr : Effective_address;
                               Var out_addr : Effective_address;
                               Var error : Mem_error);
  Var
    physical_addr : Address;
  Begin
    Addr_translate (in_addr, physical_addr);
    Mem_read (physical_addr, out_addr, error)
  End;

3.4

Procedure Relative_Addressing (displacement : Displ_type;
                               Var out_addr : Effective_address);
  Begin
    Address_add (Program_counter, displacement, out_addr)
  End;

Procedure Base_Addressing (reg_numb : Reg_range;
                             displacement : Displ_type;
                             Var out_addr : Effective_address);
  Var
    reg_addr : Effective_address;

```
Begin
  Reg_read (reg_numb, reg_addr);
  Address_add (reg_addr, displacement, out_addr)
End;
```

3.5 ───

```
Procedure Indexed_addressing (reg_numb : Reg_range;
                              in_addr : Effective_address;
                              Var out_addr : Effective_address);
  Var
    displacement : Displ_type;
  Begin
    Reg_read (reg_numb, displacement);
    Address_add (in_addr, displacement, out_addr)
  End;
```

3.6 ───

```
Procedure Autodecrement_Addressing (reg_numb : Reg_range;
                                    length : Displ_type;
                                    Var out_addr : Effective_address);
  Var
    reg_addr : Effective_address;
  Begin
    Reg_read (reg_numb, reg_addr);
    sub (reg_addr, length, out_addr);
    Reg_write (reg_numb, out_addr)
  End;

Procedure Autoincrement_Addressing (reg_numb : Reg_range;
                                    length : Displ_type;
                                    Var out_addr : Effective_address);
  Var
    reg_addr : Effective_address;
  Begin
    Reg_read (reg_numb, reg_addr);
    out_addr := reg_addr;
    Add (reg_addr, length, reg_addr);
    Reg_write (reg_numb, reg_addr)
  End;
```

3.7 ───

In the instruction: the address 1299.
In the index register: the displacement 8.
If the start address changes, one has to modify the address in the instruction.

3.8 ───

In the instruction: 299, that is, the relative address of the vector with respect to the start address of the area.

In the index register: the displacement 8 of the element.
In the base register: the start address of the data area: 1000.
The advantages are that (1) in the instruction there is only the displacement, that is, less bits; (2) the start address of the area is dynamically modifiable, that is, it can be allocated at run time by the compiler.

4.1

Pointer of E area: address = 630, contents = 691;
pointer of B area: address = 629, contents = 801;
pointer of Main area: address = 628, contents = 1001

4.2

Base + displacement;
(Local frame pointer) = 631; displacement = −6

4.5

Ry ← ((Local frame pointer) − 2)
Rx ← ((Ry) − 100)

4.6

Base + displacement indirect + displacement:

$$Rx \leftarrow ((Local\ frame\ pointer) - 2) - 100)$$

4.7

(a)   Using base + displacement:

Ry ← ((Local frame pointer) − 100)
Rx ← ((Ry));

(b)   using base + displacement indirect:

Rx ← ((Local frame pointer) − 100)

4.8

(a)   Base + displacement:

Rz ← ((Local frame pointer) − 20)
Ry ← ((Rz))
Rx ← ((Ry))

(b)   Base + displacement indirect:

Ry ← ((Local frame pointer) − 20))
Rx ← ((Ry))

(c)   Base + displacement indirect + displacement indirect:

Rx ← (((((Local frame pointer) − 20) + 0))

4.11 _____

The displacement of R.b is: −25 − 1 = −26.
The displacement of R.d is: −25 − 1 − 2 − 12 = −40.
When the instruction R.a := R.c (10) is encountered, the compiler uses the addressing methods base + displacement with index in the following manner:

Ri ← (−10)
Rx ← ((Local frame pointer) − 28 + (Ri) shl0)
     (* −28 is the displacement of R.c *)
(Local frame pointer) − 25 ← (Rx)

5.1 _____

Type
  Transf_error = Mem_error;

Procedure Load (mem_address : Address; reg_numb : Reg_range;
                Var error : Transf_error);
  Var item : Elem_type;
  Begin
    Mem_read (mem_address, item, error);
    if error = No_error
      then Reg_write (reg_numb, item)
  End;

Procedure Store (reg_numb : Reg_range; mem_address : Address;
                Var error : Transf_error);
  Var
    item : Elem_type;
  Begin
    Reg_read (reg_numb, item);
    Mem_write (mem_address, item, error)
  End;

5.2 _____

Type
  Loc_type = (Memory_location, Register_location);

Procedure Move (source_type : Loc_type; source_addr : Address;
                dest_type : Loc_type; dest_addr : Address;
                Var error : Transf_error);
  Var
    read_error, write_error : Transf_error;
    item : Elem_type;

```
Begin
    read_error := No_error; write_error := No_error;
    if source_type = Memory_location
        then Mem_read (source_addr, Item, read_error)
        else Reg_read (source_addr, item);
if read_error = No_error
    then
        begin
            if dest_type = Memory_location
                then Mem_write (dest_addr, item, write_error)
                else Reg_write (dest_addr, item)
        end;
    if (read_error = No_error) and (write_error = No_error)
        then error := No_error
        else error := Out_of_range
End;
```

5.5 _____

```
Var
    processor_status_word : record
                                sign,
                                zero,
                                overflow,
                                carry : Bit
                            end;
```

5.6 _____

```
Procedure Set_flags (elem : Word; carry, ov_carry : Bit);
    Var
        zero : boolean;
        j : 0..Word_max_bit;
    Begin
        Processor_status_word.carry := carry;
        Processor_status_word.sign := elem[0];
        if carry <> ov_carry
            then Processor_status_word.overflow := 1
            else Processor_status_word.overflow := 0;
        zero := true;
        for j := 0 to Word_max_bit do
            zero := zero and (elem[j] = 0);
        if zero   (* All the bits are null *)
            then Processor_status_word.zero := 1
            else Processor_status_word.zero := 0
    End;
```

5.7 _____

```
Type
    Binary_integer = Word;
```

```
Procedure Inc (Var elem : Binary_integer);
  Var
    carry, ov_carry : Bit;
    sum : 0..2;
    j : -1..Word_max_bit;
  Begin
    carry := 1;
    j := Word_max_bit;
    ov_carry := 0;
    repeat
      if j = 0 then ov_carry := carry;
      (* carry on the most significant figure *)
      sum := elem[j] + carry;
      elem[j] := sum mod 2;
      carry := sum div 2;
      j := j - 1
    until (j < 0) or (carry = 0);
    Set_flags (elem, carry, ov_carry)
  End;
```

5.9

```
Procedure Add (elem1, elem2 : Binary_integer;
               Var result : Binary_integer);
  Var carry, ov_carry : Bit;
      sum : 0..3;
      j : 0..Word_max_bit;
  Begin
    carry := 0;
    for j := Word_max_bit downto 1 do
      begin
        sum := elem1[j] + elem2[j] + carry;
        result[j] := sum mod 2;
        carry := sum div 2
      end;
    ov_carry := carry;   (* carry on the most significant figure *)
    sum := elem1[0] + elem2[0] + carry;
    result[0] := sum mod 2;
    carry := sum div 2;
    Set_flags(result, carry, ov_carry)
  End;
```

5.10

```
Procedure Adc (elem1, elem2 : Binary_integer;
               Var result : Binary_integer);
  Var carry, ov_carry : Bit;
      sum : 0..3; j : 0..Word_max_bit;
```

```
Begin
  carry := Processor_status_word.carry;
  for j := Word_max_bit downto 1 do
    begin
      sum := elem1[j] + elem2[j] + carry;
      result[j] := sum mod 2;
      carry := sum div 2
    end;
  ov_carry := carry;   (* carry on the most significant figure *)
  sum := elem1[0] + elem2[0] + carry;
  result[0] := sum mod 2;
  carry := sum div 2;
  Set_flags(result, carry, ov_carry)
End;
```

5.14

```
Procedure Mul (elem1, elem2 : Binary_integer;
                Var result_low, result_high : Binary_integer);
  Var carry : Bit;
      j : 0..Word_max_bit;
  Begin
    for j := 0 to Word_max_bit do
      begin result_low[j] := 0; result_high[j] := 0 end;
    for j := 0 to Word_max_bit do
      begin
        Shr_(elem2)   (* shift to right *);   carry := 0;
        if Processor_status_word.carry = 1
          then
            begin Add(elem1,result_high,result_high);
                  carry := Processor_status_word.carry
            end;
        Shr_(result_high);
        result_high[0] := carry;
        carry := Processor_status_word.carry;
        Shr_(result_low);
        result_low[0] := carry
      end
  End;
```

5.15

Type Floating_point = Longword;   (* with word of 16 bits *)

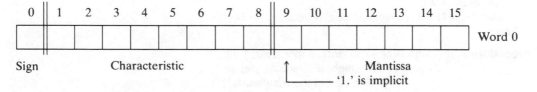

0	1	2	3	4	5	6	7	8	9	10	11	12	13	14	15

Word 1

Mantissa

5.16 _____

```
Procedure Extract_float (elem : Floating_point; Var sign : Bit;
                         Var exponent, elem_high : Byte);
   Var excess : Byte; i : 0..7;
   Begin
      excess[0] := 0;
      for i := 1 to 7 do excess[i] := 1;   (* excess = 127 *)
      sign := elem[0][0];
      for i := 0 to 7 do exponent[i] := elem[0][i+1];
      Sub_byte (exponent, excess, exponent);
      elem_high[0] := 1;   (* '1.' is implicit *)
      for i := 1 to 7 do elem_high[i] := elem[0][i+8]
   End;

Procedure Insert_float (Var elem : Floating_point; sign : Bit;
                        exponent, elem_high : Byte; elem_low : Word);
   Var excess : Byte; i : 0..7;
   Begin
      excess[0] := 0;
      for i := 1 to 7 do excess[i] := 1;   (* excess = 127 *)
      elem[0][0] := sign;
      Add_byte (exponent, excess, exponent);
      for i := 0 to 7 do elem[0][i+1] := exponent[i];
      for i := 1 to 7 do elem[0][i+8] := elem_high[i];
      elem[1] := elem_low
   End;

Procedure Shr_float (Var elem_high : Byte; Var elem_low : Word);
   Begin
      Shr_(elem_low);
      Shr_byte(elem_high);
      elem_low[0] := Processor_status_word.carry
   End;

Procedure Shl_float (Var elem_high : Byte; Var elem_low : Word);
   Begin
      Shl_byte(elem_high);
      Shl_(elem_low);
      elem_high[7] := Processor_status_word.carry
   End;

Procedure Float_align (Var exponent1, exponent2 : Byte;
                       Var el1_high, el2_high : Byte;
                          (* high part of the mantissae *)
                       Var el1_low, el2_low : Word);
                          (* low part of the mantissae *)
```

```
Begin
  Cmp_byte (exponent1, exponent2);
  if Processor_status_word.sign = 1 (* exp1 < exp2 *)
    then while Processor_status_word.zero <> 1 do
          begin
            Inc_byte (exponent1);
            Shr_float (el1_high, el1_low);
            (* shift to right of the whole mantissa *)
            Cmp_byte (exponent1, exponent2)
          end
    else while Processor_status_word.zero <> 1 do
          begin
            Inc_byte (exponent2);
            Shr_float (el2_high, el2_low);
            Cmp_byte (exponent1, exponent2)
          end
End;
```

5.17

```
Procedure Float_add (sign1, sign2 : Bit;
                     exponent1, exponent2 : Byte;
                     el1_high, el2_high : Byte;
                     el1_low, el2_low : Word;
                     Var result_sign : Bit;
                     Var result_exp : Byte;
                     Var result_high : Byte;
                     Var result_low : Word);
  Var zero : 0..2;
  Begin
    Float_align (exponent1, exponent2, el1_high, el2_high,
                 el1_low, el2_low);
    if sign1 = sign2
      then begin
              result_exp := exponent1; result_sign := sign1;
              Add (el1_low, el2_low, result_low);
              Adc_byte(el1_high, el2_high, result_high);
              if Processor_status_word.carry = 1
                then begin (* normalization of the result *)
                        Inc_byte (result_exp);
                        Shr_float (result_high, result_low);
                        result_high[0] := 1
                     end
           end
      else begin (* signs are different *)
              result_exp := exponent1;
              result_sign := sign1;
              Sub (el1_low, el2_low, result_low);
              zero := Processor_status_word.zero
              Subc_byte (el1_high, el2_high, result_high);
              zero := zero + Processor_status_word.zero;
```

```
            if Processor_status_word.carry = 0
                (* negative result *)
            then begin
                    Neg (result_low);
                    Neg_byte (result_high);
                    result_sign := (result_sign + 1) mod 2
                        (* complements sign *)
                end;
            if (Processor_status_word.sign = 0)
                and (zero < 2)    (* result <> 0 *)
                then repeat (* result normalization *)
                        Dec_byte (result_exp);
                        Shl_float (result_high, result_low);
                        Tst_byte (result_high)
                            (* compares with 0 *)
                    until Processor_status_word.sign = 1
        end
    End;
```

5.20 ──

Type
```
    Packed_digit = Half_byte;
    Packed_number = Word;
```

5.21 ──

```
Procedure Pack_BCD_adc (elem1, elem2 : Packed_number;
                            Var result: Packed_number);
    Var
        Six_number, digit1, digit2,
        result_digit : Packed_digit;
        i, j : 0..3;
        greater_than_nine : boolean;
    Begin
        Six_number[0] := 0; Six_number[1] := 1;
        Six_number[2] := 1; Six_number[3] := 0;
        for j := 3 downto 0 do
          begin
            for i := 0 to 3 do begin
                            digit1[i] := elem1[i+4*j];
                            digit2[i] := elem2[i+4*j]
                        end;
            Half_byte_adc (digit1, digit2, result_digit);
            greater_than_nine := (result_digit[0] = 1) and
            ((result_digit[1]=1) or (result_digit[2]=1));
            if (processor_status_word.carry=1)
                or greater_than_nine
```

```
        then begin
                Half_byte_add (result_digit, Six_number,
                                result_digit);
                processor_status_word.carry := 1
                    (* carry for the next figure *)
              end;
       for i := 0 to 3 do result[i+j*4] := result_digit[i]
    end
  End;
```

5.22 _____

```
Procedure Pack_BCD_sub (elem1, elem2 : Packed_number;
                              Var result : Packed_number);
  Var
    Nine_number, digit2 : Packed_digit;
    i, j : 0..3;
  Begin
    Nine_number[0] := 1; Nine_number[1] := 0;
    Nine_number[2] := 0; Nine_number[3] := 1;
    for j := 3 downto 0 do
      begin
        for i := 0 to 3 do digit2[i] := elem2[i+4*j];
        Half_byte_sub (Nine_number, digit2, digit2);
            (* 9' complement of every figure *)
        for i := 0 to 3 do elem2[i+4*j] := digit2[i]
      end;
    processor_status_word.carry := 1;
    (* to obtain 10' complement of elem2 *)
    Pack_BCD_adc (elem1, elem2, result)
  End;

Procedure Pack_BCD_add (elem1, elem2 : Packed_number;
                             Var result : Packed_number);
  Begin
    processor_status_word.carry := 0;
    Pack_BCD_adc (elem1, elem2, result)
  End;
```

5.23 _____

```
Type
  Bit_range = 0..Word_max_bit;

Procedure Set_bit (bit_number: Bit_range; addr: Address;
                    Var error : Mem_error);
  Var
    destination : Word;
  Begin
    Mem_read (addr, destination, error);
```

```
    if error = No_error
      then
        begin
          destination [bit_number] := 1;
          Mem_write (addr, destination, error)
        end
  End;
```

6.1 ——

```
EXECUTE: <instruction>;
          <evaluate condition>;
          If condition = False
            Then Jump_to EXECUTE;
```

6.2 ——

(a)   Translation with the loop termination check at the beginning of the loop:

```
   BEGIN:  <evaluate condition>;
           If condition = False Then Jump_to END;
           <instruction>;
           Jump_to BEGIN;
     END:  . . .
```

(b)   Translation with the loop termination check at the end of the loop:

```
            Jump_to CHECK;
  EXECUTE:  <instruction>;
    CHECK:  <evaluate condition>;
            If condition = True Then Jump_to EXECUTE;
```

In both cases, the compiler generates the same number of instructions. If this number is N, and K is the number of instructins for the evaluation of condition and the conditional jump, we can calculate the number of instructions carried out as a function of the times M that the loop is executed:

(a) $M \times N + K$

(b) $1 + M \times (N - 1) + K$

6.4 ——

```
              K := 1;
              Repeat
                If variable = CONST[K]
                  Then Jump_to ADDRESS[K];
                K := K+1;
              Until K > n;
              Jump_to ADDRESS[n+1]
              (* if there is not ELSE branch, Jump_to END *)
```

```
ADDRESS[1]:      <instruction 1>;
                 Jump_to END;
ADDRESS[2]:      <instruction 2>;
                 Jump_to END;
                      .
                      .
                      .
ADDRESS[n]:      <instruction n>;
                 Jump_to END;
ADDRESS[n+1]:    <instruction n+1>;
           END:  . . .
```

6.6

```
Procedure Test (src: Address; Var error: Mem_error);
  Var
    item, zero, dummy_result: Word;
    j : 0..Word_max_bit;
  Begin
    for j := 0 to Word_max_bit do zero[j] := 0;
    Mem_read (src, item, error);
    if error = No_error
      then Sub (item, zero, dummy_result)
  End;
```

6.7

```
Procedure Branch_if_carry (displ : Displ_type);
  Var
    addr : Effective_address;
  Begin
    if Processor_status_word.carry = 1
      then
        begin
          Relative_Addressing (displ, addr);
          Program_counter := addr
        end
  End;
```

7.1

(a)   Each opcode is constituted of 4 bits: $x1$, $x2$, $x3$, $x4$.

In order to optimize the decoding path, it is useful to test first the bit which carries the greatest information quantity and then the others in decreasing order of information quantity.

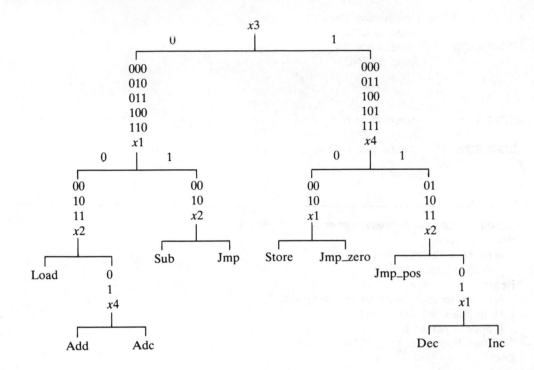

(b) Using the Huffman coding, the following codes are obtained:

INC	000
ADD	001
ADC	010
SUB	011
LOAD	100
STORE	101
JMP_ZERO	1100
JMP	1101
DEC	1110
JMP_POS	1111

The decoding tree becomes:

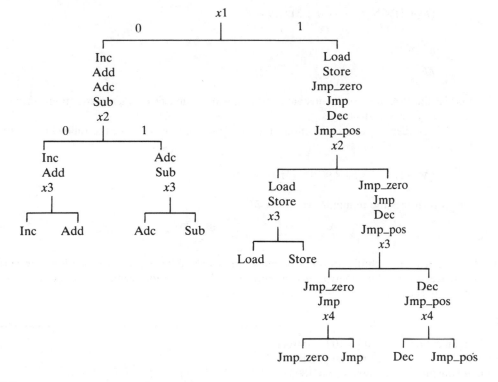

7.3

The 'execute' phases of the instructions:

Store	Reg_number, Target_addr
Jmp_if_zero	Target_addr

are realized by the following microprograms:

Store:	MAR := Target_addr(IR); MBR := Register_set[Reg_number(IR)]; WR
	WR; GOTO Fetch
Jmp_if_zero:	IF Processor_status_word.zero = 0 THEN GOTO Fetch
	PC := Target_addr(IR); GOTO Fetch

7.6

(a) Let M be the mean number of microinstructions in sequence that do not effect microjumps, this implies that on average after M microinstructins there is one of jump. If in a microprogram there are N microinstructions which effect microjumps, there will be:

$(M + 1) \times N$ 50-bit microinstructions, if residual control is not used;

$(M + 3) \times N$ 40-bit microinstructions, if residual control is used

From:

$$(M + 1) \times N \times 50 > (M + 3) \times N \times 40$$

it follows:

$$M > 7$$

that is, the technique is inconvenient if the linear sequences of microinstructions have less than 7 microinstructions.

In order to have a reduction of 10% of memory occupation, the following has to be valid:

$$(M + 1) \times N \times 50 \times 9/10 > (M + 3) \times N \times 40$$

which furnishes the minimum value for M:

$$M > 15$$

(b) If one does not exploit with other functions the two microinstructions which load the field sequencer for residual control, it is more conve..'ent to use the technique of explicit jumps, because in this case one microinstruction suffices.

7.7

Initial organization:	$1800 \times 100 = 180\,000$ bits
Coded fields:	$1800 \times 60 = 108\,000$ bits
Residual control:	$(1800 \times 55 + 1800/9 \times 55) = 110\,000$ bits
Nanomemory:	$[\log_2 300] \times 1800 + 300 \times 100 = 46\,200$ bits

8.1

```
Type Segment_descriptor = record
                    base_address:
                        array [0..15] of Bit;
                    length:
                        array [0..7] of Bit;
                    ref, chg, dirw, dma, exc,
                    cpu, sys, rd: Bit
                  end;
Var
  descriptors_table: array [0..63] of Segment_descriptor;
  virtual_address: record
                    segment_number: 0..63;
                    offset: array [0..15] of Bit
                  end;
Procedure Offset_comparator (Var trap: Boolean);
  Var
    j := −1..7;
    length: array [0..7] of Bit;
```

```
Begin
  length := descriptors_table
           [virtual_address.segment_number].length;
  trap := false;
  j := 7;
  repeat
    if length [j] > virtual_address.offset[j + 8]
      then j := 0
      else
      trap := (length[j] < virtual_address.offset [j + 8]);
      j := j - 1
    until trap or (j < 0)
End;
```

Type
  Base, Offset, Result = **array** [0..15] **of** Bit;
Var
  physical_address: **array** [0..23] **of** Bit;

Procedure Addr_add (base_address: Base;
                   offset_address: Offset;
                   Var result_address: Result);
  Begin . . . End;
Procedure Address_translate;
  Var
    j: 0..23;
    base_address: Base;
    offset_address: Offset;
    result_address: Result;
  Begin
    base_address := descriptors_table
                  [virtual_address.segment_number].base_address;
    for j := 15 **downto** 8 **do**
      offset_address[j] := 0;
    for j := 7 **downto** 0 **do**
      offset_address[j] := virtual_address.offset[j + 8];
    Addr_add (base_address, offset_address, result_address);
    for j := 23 **downto** 8 **do**
      physical_address[j] := result_address[j - 8];
    for j := 7 **downto** 0 **do**
      physical_address[j] := virtual_address.offset[j]
  End;

8.5

Let t be the access time in main memory, $t_c = t/10$ the access time in cache memory, and n the number of levels. If the hit ratio is 98%, then we have the following times:

(a)   not hierarchical system:
     $t \times 2\% + t_c \times 98\% = (0.02 + 0.098)t = 0.118 \times t$

(b)   *n*-level hierarchical system:
$$n \times t \times 2\% + t_c \times 98\% = (0.02 \times n + 0.098)t$$

8.7

Type
  Access_type = (read, write);
Var
  pte: **record**
        valid: Bit;
        protection: **array** [0..3] **of** Bit;
        page_frame_number: **array** [0..20] **of** Bit
      end;
  virtual_address: **record**
                     virtual_page_number:
                       array [0..22] **of** Bit;
                     offset: **array** [0..8] **of** Bit
                   end;
  physical_address: **array** [0..29] **of** Bit;
  processor_status_word: **record**
                           . . .
                           current_mode: **array** [0..1] **of** Bit;
                           . . .
                         end;

Procedure Translate_and_verify_process_rights
  (intended_access: Access_type;
   Var page_fault, protection_fault: Boolean);
  Var
    decimal_prot: 0..15;
    dec_curr_mode: 0..3;
    j: 0..20;
  Begin
      page_fault := false;
      protection_fault := false;
      decimal_prot := decode_pte (pte.protection);
      dec_curr_mode :=
        decode_psw(processor_status_word.current_mode);
      case decimal_prot **of**
        0: protection_fault := true;
        1:
        2: protection_fault := dec_curr_mode > 0;
        3: protection_fault := (dec_curr_mode > 0) or
                               (intended_access≠read);
        4: protection_fault := false;
        . . .
      end;
      if not protection_fault
        then

```
    begin
      page_fault := (pte.valid = 0);
      if not page_fault
        then
          begin
            for j := 20 downto 0 do
              physical_address[j + 9] := pte.page_frame_number[j];
            for j := 8 downto 0 do
              physical_address[j] := virtual_address.offset[j];
          end
    end
End;
```

9.4

```
Const
  Addr_tag_length = . . .;
  Addr_line_length = . . .;
  Addr_displ_length = . . .;
  Address_length = . . .; (* Addr_tag_length +
                              Addr_line_length +
                              Addr_displ_length *)
  Set_number = . . .; (* 2^Addr_line_length: number of sets *)
  Block_number_per_set = . . .; (* number of blocks in one set *)
  Line_dim = . . .; (* 2^Addr_displ_length: dim.of every block *)
Type
  Cache_element = . . .;
  Memory_line = array [1..Line_dim] of Cache_element;
  Tag_type = array [1..Addr_tag_length] of Bit;
  Cache_block = record
                    tag: Tag_type;
                    line: Memory_line
                  end;
Var
  Cache_memory: array [1..Set_number, 1..Block_number_per_set]
                       of Cache_block;
  Addr_register: array [1..Address_length] of Bit;
```

9.5

```
Type
  Set_range = 1..Set_number;
  Block_range = 1..Block_number_per_set;
  LRU_queue = array [Block_range] of Block_range;
Var
  LRU_queue_set: array [Set_range] of LRU_queue;

Procedure LRU_initialize;
  Var
    set_select: Set_range;
    block_select: Block_range;
```

```
Begin
  for set_select := 1 to Set_number do
    for block_select := 1 to Block_number_per_set do
    LRU_queue_set [set_select][block_select] := block_select
    (* in position "block_select" there is the value "block_select" *)
End;
Procedure LRU_update (set_select: Set_range;
                      block_select: Block_range);
  Var
    position: 0..Block_number_per_set;
  Begin
    position := 0;
      repeat
        position := position + 1
      until LRU_queue_set [set_select][position] = block_select;
      (* find the position of the pointer to the referenced block *)
      while position > 1 do
        begin
          LRU_queue_set [set_select][position] := LRU_queue_set [set_select][position − 1];
          position := position − 1
        end;
      (* movement of the pointers to the blocks most recently used *)
      LRU_queue_set [set_select][1] := block_select
      (* insert the pointer to the referenced block in the first position of the queue *)
  End;
Procedure LRU_block_select (set_select: Set_range;
                            Var block_select: Block_range);
  Begin
    block_select := LRU_queue_set [set_select][Block_number_per_set];
    (* selection of the block in the last position *)
    LRU_update (set_select, block_select)
    (* update the queue *)
  End;
```

9.6

```
Procedure Lookup (Var miss: Boolean;
                  Var item: Cache_element);
  Var
    tag_field: Tag_type;
      set_selection: 1..Set_number;
    block_selection: 1..Block_number_per_set + 1;
      item_selection: 1..Line_dim;
  Begin
    Extract_tag_field (Addr_register, tag_field);
    set_selection := Decode (Addr_register, Addr_tag_length + 1,
                             Addr_line_length);
                    (* decode the bits of the line field *)
```

```
        item_selection := Decode (Addr_register, Addr_tag_length +
                                   Addr_line_length + 1,
                                   Addr_displ_length);
                        (* decode the bits of the displ field *)
     block_selection := 1; miss := true;
     repeat
        if Equal_tags (Cache_memory[set_selection, block_selection].tag, tag_field)
          then
             begin
                miss := false;
                item := Cache_memory [set_selection, block_selection]
                                   .line[item_selection]
             end
          else block_selection := block_selection + 1
     until (not miss) or (block_selection > Block_number_per_set);
     if not miss    (* if there is an hit *)
        then LRU_update (set_selection, block_selection)
   End;
Procedure Update (Var miss: Boolean; item: Cache_element);
   Var
     tag_field: Tag_type;
     set_selection: 1..Set_number;
     block_selection: 1..Block_number_per_set + 1;
     item_selection: 1..Line_dim;
   Begin
     Extract_tag_field (Addr_register, tag_field);
     set_selection := Decode (Addr_register, Addr_tag_length + 1,
                              Addr_line_length);
                       (* decode the bits of the line field *)
     item_selection := Decode (Addr_register, Addr_tag_length +
                               Addr_line_length + 1, Addr_displ_length);
                       (* decode the bits of the displ field *)
     block_selection := 1; miss := true;
       repeat
          if Equal_tags (Cache_memory [set_selection,
                                       block_selection].tag,tag_field)
            then
               begin
                  miss := false;
                  Cache_memory [set_selection, block_selection]
                                .line [item_selection] := item
               end
          else block_selection := block_selection + 1
       until (not miss) or
             (block_selection > Block_number_per_set);
       if not miss (* if there is an hit *)
          then LRU_update (set_selection, block_selection)
   End;
```

```
Procedure Replace (line_to_insert: Memory_line);
  Var
    tag_field: Tag_type;
    set_selection: 1..Set_number;
    block_selection: 1..Block_number_per_set;
    line_to_replace: Memory_line;
  Begin
    Extract_tag_field (Addr_register, tag_field);
    set_selection := Decode (Addr_register, Addr_tag_length + 1,
                             Addr_line_length);
    LRU_block_select (set_selection, block_selection);
      line_to_replace := Cache_memory [set_selection,
                                       block_selection].line;
      (* this line must be copied back in main memory if there is inconsistency *)
    with Cache_memory [set_selection, block_selection] do
      begin
        tag := tag_field;
        line := line_to_insert
      end
  End;
```

9.C _____

```
Var
  Instruction_register, Program_counter: Reg_type;
  Op_code: Byte;   (* the opcode requires one byte *)
    Result_reg_number: 0..Reg_max_number;
    Operand: Word;
    Target_addr: Address;
    Target_addr: Address;

Procedure Fetch;
  Begin
    repeat
      if Instruction_register_is_empty then
      begin
        Extract_new_instruction;
        Insert_into_Instruction_register;
        Update (Program_counter)
      end
    until false   (* endless loop *)
  End;
Procedure Decode;
  Var
    code: Byte;
    operand_addr, result_addr: 0..Reg_max_number;
  Begin
    repeat
      if Instruction_register_is_full then
        begin
        Extract_from_Instruction_register (code, operand_addr, result_addr);
```

```
          while not Op_code_is_empty do
          Op_code := code;
          if Is_branch (Op_code)
            then Compute (Target_addr)
            else
              begin
                Operand := Register_file [operand_addr];
                Result_reg_number := result_addr
              end
        end
    until false
  End;
Procedure Execute;
  Begin
    repeat
      if Op_code_is_full then
        begin
          if Is_branch (Op_code)
          then Program_counter := Target_addr
          else Register_file [Result_reg_number] := ALU(Op_code)
        end
    until false (* endless loop *)
  End;
```

10.3

```
Var
    program_counter: Register;
    fetch_state : (Buffer, Cache, Cache_store);
      (* it indicates the 3 alternative paths in Fig. 10.9 *)
    instr_numb : Integer;
      (* instruction counter in every BTC block *)

Procedure Non_sequential_fetch; Forward;

Procedure Fetch;
  Var valid : Boolean;
  Begin
    case fetch_state of
      Buffer, Cache_store:
        begin
          IPB_extract (valid);
            if not valid
              then Non_sequential_fetch
              else begin
                      if fetch_state = Cache_store
                        then begin
                                BTC_update (instr_numb);
                                if instr_numb > BTC_entry_instr_number
                                (* if the block is full *)
```

```
                              then fetch_state := Buffer
                              (* the next instruction will be fetched from IPB *)
                          end
                  end
          end;
      Cache:
        begin
          BTC_fetch (instr_numb, valid);
          if not valid
            then Non_sequential_fetch
            else if instr_numb > BTC_entry_instr_number
              (* all the instructions in the block have been read *)
                  then fetch_state := Buffer
                      (* the next instructions from IPB *)
        end
    end;
End; (* Fetch *)

Procedure Non_sequential_fetch;
  Var found : boolean;
  Begin
    IPB_Invalidate;
      (* All the instructions in IPB are invalid *)
    MMU_translate (program_counter);
      (* the contents of PC are translated in the corresponding physical address *)
    BTC_lookup (found);
      (* finds the target in the BTC *)
    if found then    (* if the target is in the BTC *)
              begin
                if BTC_all_valid then
                (* if all the instructions in the block are valid *)
                  IPB_fetch_ahead;
                  (* the following may be fetched from IPB *)
                instr_numb := 0;
                fetch_state := Cache;
                Fetch
              end
            else    (* if the target is not in the BTC *)
              begin
                IPB_prefetch;
                  (* the instructions are read from memory in IPB *)
                BTC_replace;
                  (* a block in BTC is selected to contain the new target *)
                instr_numb := 0;
                  (* instructions counter to insert in the block of the BTC *)
                fetch_state := Cache_store;
                  (* the instructions read from IPB must be inserted in BTC *)
                Fetch
              end
    End;
```

10.5

If virtual tags are used, the tag in the address produced by the processor (which is a virtual address) is compared directly with the tags in the cache lines, without the need for any translation. Only when a cache miss is generated, has the virtual address produced by the processor to be translated into a physical one in order to fetch a new line from main memory.

The alternative of using real tags is more inefficient because translation is required at each cache cycle, while it is no longer performed at the cache misses.

10.6

(a) The I/O processors produce addresses (which are real addresses) for reading or writing data in main memory.

For reasons of consistency they must invalidate the corresponding line in the cache, if there is one. If the mechanism of virtual tags is used, the real address produced by I/O processors has to be subjected to a translation (inverse) process before being sent to the cache for invalidation.

(b) If the processor sends one of these (synonyms) virtual addresses, and the cache stores the corresponding memory location with another of its virtual tags, an improper miss signal will be generated.

10.7

Substantial efficiency improvements, while using real tags, can be reached taking into account that generally the translation process and the row selection in the cache use different fields of the virtual address. So, row selection can be anticipated and carried out parallel to translation.

If the latter lasts less than the former, as happens each time there is a hit in the TLB, most of the time the translation phase becomes transparent to the cache.

11.1

Indicating by T_1 the time with serial execution, T_2 the time with parallel execution, $\alpha = 6$, the number of stages, $\gamma = $ the duration of each stage, and $n = 64$ the length of the vectors, we have:

$$T_1 = \alpha \, \gamma \, n = 6 \times 64 \times \gamma = 384 \, \gamma$$
$$T_2 = \alpha \, \gamma + (n - 1) \, \gamma = 6\gamma + 63\gamma = 69\gamma$$

and the speed up $= T_1/T_2 = 384/69 = 5.56$

11.2

$A \times B + C$ is obtainable as the following sequence:

$$Z = A \times B \quad (1)$$
$$Y = Z + C \quad (2)$$

With chaining, the results of (1) are passed directly to (2) as they are produced (the structure is similar to a unique pipeline). The speed up using chaining is given by:

$$
\begin{aligned}
\text{speed up} &= T_1/T_2 \\
&= (\alpha_1\gamma + (n-1)\,\gamma + \alpha_2\gamma + (n-1)\,\gamma)/((\alpha_1 + \alpha_2)\,\gamma + (n-1)\,\gamma) \\
&= (7 + 63 + 6 + 63)/(7 + 6 + 63) = 139/76 = 1.8
\end{aligned}
$$

11.3

(1) Dependency relation between $A(I)$ and $D(I)$.
No recurrence relation.
The chaining is applicable to pass the partial results of $A(I)$ to $D(I)$.
Loop iterations can be carried out in parallel by multiple processors.
(2) Recurrence relation between $A(I)$ and $A(I-1)$, calculated in the preceding iteration.
(3) Recurrence between $A(I)$ and $B(I-1)$.
Overlapping is applicable because there is no data to pass from $A(I)$ to $B(I)$ in the same iteration.
(4) Dependence relation between $A(I)$ and $B(I)$.
Dependence relation between $B(I)$ and $C(I)$.
Recurrence relation between $C(I)$ and $C(I-1)$.
Chaining is applicable between $A(I)$ and $B(I)$ and between $B(I)$ and $C(I)$.

11.4

(a)   In a scalar computer (with one processor) the time necessary to carry out the scalar product of two vectors of n elements each is proportional to $n + (n-1)$. Indeed n products and $n-1$ additions are needed, all carried out sequentially.

(b)   Linear cyclic-shift interconnection.

Given:

t_p = the time necessary to carry out the product between two data items;
t_r = the time necessary to carry out the shift between two processing elements;
t_s = the time necessary to carry out the sum of two data items.

we have:

$$
\begin{aligned}
t_{tot} &= t_p + \sum_{i=1}^{\log_2 n}(t_s + 2^{i-1}\,t_r) \\
&= t_p + \log_2 n \times t_s + \sum_{i=1}^{\log_2 n} 2^{i-1}\,t_r \\
&= t_p + \log_2 n \times t_s + (n-1)\,t_r
\end{aligned}
$$

Indeed the number of products and sums carried out sequentially is equal respectively to 1 and $\log_2 n$; the routing operations at iteration i are 2^{i-1}, with $1 < i < \log_2 n$, for a total of $(n-1)$ routings.

The complexity of the algorithm will be $\log_2 n$, the cost $= n\log_2 n$, where n is the number of processors.

(c′)   Array of processing elements formed by $\log_2 n + 1$ rows and n columns.
       The products and sums are 1 and $\log_2 n$ respectively; the number of routing operations at iteration i $(1 < i < \log_2 n)$ is:

2^{i-1} for right shifts
1 for down shifts

for a total of $(n - 1) + \log_2 n$ routing operations. So the complexity is $\log_2 n$.
The total time is:

$$t_{tot} = t_p + \sum_{i=1}^{\log_2 n} [t_s + (2^{i-1} + 1) \times t_r]$$
$$= t_p + \log_2 n \times t_s + \left(\sum_{i=1}^{\log_2 n} 2^{i-1} + 1 \right) \times t_r$$
$$= t_p + \log_2 n + (n - 1 + \log_2 n)\, t_r$$

The cost is $n\,(\log_2 n)^2$, where $n\,\log_2 n$ is the number of processors. The number of shift operations is high, so a considerable part of the execution time of the algorithm will be taken up in data transfers from one node to another.

(c″)   Array of processing elements formed by $\sqrt{n}$ rows and $\sqrt{n}$ columns. A total of $2\sqrt{n} - 2$ iterations are needed, of which $\sqrt{n} - 1$ are to sum up in parallel the elements of the $(i + 1)$th column with the elements of the ith column, with i varying from $\sqrt{n} - 1$ to 1. The other $\sqrt{n} - 1$ iterations serve to sum up the elements of the first column in the element of position (1,1). The complexity of the algorithm is $\sqrt{n}$. The number of shift operations is equal to the number of sums carried out.
       The total time is:

$$t_{tot} = t_p + (2\sqrt{n} - 2) \times t_s + (2\sqrt{n} - 2) \times t_r$$

and the cost:

$$\text{cost} = n\sqrt{n}$$

11.5

The number of iterations is $\log_2 n$, each one requiring the same time, so the complexity of the algorithm is $\log_2 n$. The sums are carried out between nodes directly connected with one another, so the routing operations are also $\log_2 n$.
       The total time is:

$$t_{tot} = t_p + \log_2 n \times t_s + \log_2 n \times t_r$$

The cost:

$$\text{cost} = n\,\log_2 n$$

11.6

(a)   Let n be the number of leaves containing the n products $c_i = a_i b_i$. Taking into account that the root has level 0 and the leaves have the highest level equal to $\log_2 n - 1$, the complexity of this algorithm is $\log_2 n$ with total time:

$$\text{The total time} = t_p + \log_2 n \times t_s + \log_2 n \times t_r$$
$$\text{and the cost} = (2n - 1)\log_2 n;$$

(b) In the evaluation of the interconnection schemes we can take into account the parameters:

  - number of processors
  - complexity of the algorithm implemented
  - the number of sum and routing operations
  - the cost

It is not necessary to consider the time needed to carry out the n products, since they can be calculated in parallel in each of the interconnection schemes.

11.7

At every cycle the characters of the text move systolically one cell to the right; in all of the cells comparison is carried out simultaneously; their results are fanned-in in a single device which executes their logical AND, and transmits a definitive result y_k.

y_1 will be ready after m cycles.

11.8

(a) The possibility of using the cells for the calculation of several y_k allows a more efficient use and the reduction of their number to m (number of the characters of the pattern string) rather than $n - m + 1$ (number of y_k). This is advantageous when $n \gg m$, ($n =$ number of characters of the text).

(b) In order to indicate the completion of the calculation of y_1, determine the output and initialize the cell to 1.

11.9

If we substitute multiplications with comparison operations and additions with boolean ANDs, the convolution problem becomes that of pattern matching.

Computer Index

Advanced Micro Devices
  Am29000   165, 273, 280, 298–305

BBN Butterfly Parallel Processor   333–5

Cray
  X–MP   316–9

Digital Equipment Corporation
  PDP–8   77–80
  PDP–11   135
  VAX   63, 73, 85, 87–90, 113, 136, 137,
    151, 152, 153, 165, 166, 174, 175–8, 181,
    247–52

Fairchild
  Clipper   305–8

Floating Point Systems
  FPS T series   350

IBM
  3090   319–20
  370   73, 81–2, 137, 241
  4341   186
  3084   188

Inmos
  transputer   337–43, 349–50

Intel
  8086   64, 147, 150, 152, 165, 168–9, 174,
    179, 256, 257, 272
  80386   113, 242–6, 248–52, 271, 296–8
  80860   306

Motorola
  MC68000   64, 87, 121, 125, 147, 166,
    168–9, 174, 175, 179, 190, 229, 255, 257
  MC68020   113, 280
  MC68040   306
  MC88000   307, 308

National Semiconductor
  NS32032   113

Rockwell
  6502   76, 84, 127

Zilog
  Z80   74, 121
  Z8000   44, 147, 149, 152, 166, 168–9, 174,
    175, 179, 235–7, 255, 257, 280
  Z80000   113

Index

access attributes 231
access matrix 246–7
accumulator 43
activation record 97, 301–5
address
  absolute 49, 74–6
  auto-decrement 85
  auto-increment 85–6
  base register 81, 101–13
  direct 49, 74–6
  immediate 73
  implicit 70–3
  index-register 83–4
  indirect 76–81
  register 74
  register indirect 74
  relative 81
address calculation unit 147, 212, 213
address processing 146–8
address space 192
address translation 230–46
Advanced Micro Devices Am29000 165, 273,
  280, 298–305
alphabet 22, 31
  external 31
  internal 31
arbitration of the bus 191
architecture
  definition 6–9
  general registers 43–4
  memory–memory 44
argument pointer 176
arithmetic and logic unit 211–13

arithmetic instructions 125–42
arithmetic shift 133
array processors 320–4
ASCII 33, 34
assemblers 7
associative memory 240

BBN Butterfly Parallel Processor 333–5
BCD 34–6
Boolean vector processing 142–5
Butterfly switch 333–4
binary codes 24–9, 31–4
binary integers 124–34
binary tree connection 348
bit manipulation 142–6
bottleneck in von Neumann computer 15
branch history table 286–7
branch instructions 163
branch target cache 274
broadcast 324
buffer memory 16
burst mode access 299
bus 15, 186, 189–96
  arbitration 191
  errors 227
  lock 256
  master 189
  read–modify–write cycle 256–7
bus-watch technique 275
busy-waiting 224

cache memory 16, 273–85
  analysis of parameters 280–2

consistency 275
copy-back 275
dead lines 285
direct mapping 276–9
fully associative 279
models 276–80
reload transient 282
replacement policies 282–5
set-associative 279
write-through 275
call gates 250–2
call instruction 175–8
CAMMU 306–7
capabilities 246
carry 125
cascaded partial additions 321–4
chaining of vector instructions 317–18
channels 336, 340–3
character codes 31–4
characteristic 134
checkerboard effect 231
CISC architectures 294–8
closure property 126
comparison instructions 164–6
compilation 7, 10
compile time 11
computational models
    control mechanism 313
    data flow 351–4
    data storage mechanism 313
    demand driven 352–4
    dependency relations 313
    examination mechanism 353
    selection mechanism 314, 353
    von Neumann 12–17, 314–15
computer architecture 8, 59–60
condition codes 166–70
condition flags 127, 164
conditional jumps 166–70
consistency of caches 275
control dependence 263, 286
control graphs 313
control unit 290–11
copy-back technique 275
coroutine instruction 180–1
Cray X-MP 316–19
critical regions 254
crossbar networks 332
cube connection 347

cyclic reduction 321–4
cyclic-shift interconnection
    bidimensional 345
    linear 345

daisy-chain 191, 225–6
data dependence 263, 286, 313
data flow architectures 351–4
data flow graphs 313
data path 21
    internal 41
data transfer instructions 120–2
data-forwarding technique 286
decimal adjustment 35–6, 140–2
decimal integers 140–2
decode history table 287–8
decoding tree 207
degree of a network 348–50
delayed branch 286
demand-driven architectures 352–4
dependence
    control 263, 286
    data 263, 286, 313
dependency graphs 313
descriptor table 232, 235, 239
    global 246
    local 246
diameter of a network 348–50
display 99–100
Digital Equipment Corporation
    PDP-8 77–80
    PDP-11 135
    VAX 63, 73, 85, 87–90, 113, 136, 137,
        151, 152, 153, 165, 166, 174, 175–8, 181,
        247–52
DMA 187
dyadic instructions 61

EBCDIC 32, 34
effective address 87
error correction codes 37–40
error detection codes 36–37
exceptions 219–30
    multiple 226
    priority 222, 224–6
    processing sequence 229–30
    vectors 228–9
excess 134
exchange connection 346

execute phase   13, 198
expanding opcodes   64–6
explicit reference   46–7
extension specifier   87

Fairchild Clipper   305–8
faults   226–7
fetch phase   13, 198–201
FIFO queue   272
fifth generation architectures   12
firing rule   351
Floating Point Systems FPS T series   350
floating-point addition   138–9
floating-point formats
   IBM 370   137
   IEEE   135–6
   VAX   136–7
floating-point multiplication   139
floating-point numbers   134–9
formal description   17–19
fragmentation
   external   234
   internal   234, 305
frame pointer   176
frequency-dependent opcodes   66–8

global data   96, 102
global frame pointer   97
grain size of parallelism   311–12, 330, 335–6, 352

Hamming codes   37–40
Hamming distance   36
hardware level   8
hardwired control   213–14
hierarchical systems   1–9
horizontal microinstructions   203
Huffman code   66–8
hypercube connection   347

IBM
   3090   319–20
   370   73, 81–2, 137, 241
   4341   186
   3084   188
implicit reference   46–7
imprecise interrupt   288
index registers   83–4
Inmos transputer   337–43, 349–50

input–output instructions   122
instruction
   bandwidth   267
   cycle   196–8
   decoding   207–9
   format   60–4
   latency   267
   pipeline   267
   queues   270, 271–3
   variable length   62–3
Intel
   8086   64, 147, 150, 152, 165, 168–9, 174, 179, 256, 257, 272
   80386   113, 242–6, 248–52, 271, 296–8
   80860   306
interconnection structures   186–96, 343–50
   degree   348–50
   diameter   348–50
   incremental growth   349–50
interpretation   5, 10
interpreter of instructions   185, 202
interrupts   223–6
   imprecise   288
   maskable   223
   non-maskable   223
   selective inhibition   224
   see also exceptions

jump instructions   163
jump table   208
jump-to-subroutine instructions   170

levels of a computing system   2–9
lexical level   98–100
LFU (Least Frequently Used) policy   283
linearity of references   265
link interfaces   337, 343
local data   96, 101
local frame pointer   97
local scalars   101
local vectors   107
locality
   principle   81, 231, 265
   spatial   265
   temporal   265
lock of the bus   256–7
logical address   230
logical instructions   142–3
loop control instructions   178–80

loosely coupled systems 331
LRU (Least Recently Used) policy 283–5

macro instruction unit 308
mantissa 134
mapping
    function 231–2
    hierarchical 241–6
mapping memory 209
master 189
memory
    associative 240
    cache 16, 273–85
    local 14
    main 14
    mass 14
    random access 46
memory management unit 234
memory-mapped I/O 122, 193–5
mesh connection 345
message passing 336
microinstruction
    coding techniques 204–7
    format 202–3
microprogramming level 8, 199–214
mode and register addressing 86–90
monadic instructions 61
monophase control 214
Motorola
    MC68000 64, 87, 121, 125, 147, 166,
        168–9, 174, 175, 179, 190, 229, 255, 257
    MC68020 113, 280
    MC68040 306
    MC88000 307, 308
multicomputers 335–43
multiple precision arithmetic 125–6
multiprocessors 330–5
multistage interconnection network 333
mutual exclusion 254

n-state device 22
nanostore 204–6
National Semiconductor NS32032 113
non-local data 102
non-local vectors 108
non-von Neumann architectures 12
normalized exponential notation 134

numbering systems
    binary 25–9
    conversion rules 29–31
    hexadecimal 31
    octal 30–1
    positional 27–31

occam 340
offset 232
Omega network 333
one's complement representation 128–30
opcode
    variable length 64–8
    frequency-dependent 66–8
operand specifier 87
operating system 7
orthogonality 63–4
overflow 127, 132, 137

packed BCD 34–5
page fault 239
paging 232, 237–8
parallelism specification
    explicit 353
    implicit 353
parity check 37
pattern-matching problem 325–30
perfect shuffle connection 347
physical address 230
physical information structures 40–5
pipelined model of computation 266–9
pipelined vector processors 316–20
    chaining 317–18
    overlapping 319
polling 223, 229
polyphase control 214
position independent code 81–3
prefetching 17, 271–2
privilege states 222
privileges 246
    instruction execution 222
    memory access 222
procedure calls 175–8
process state diagram 253
processing states 220–1
properties of programs
    dynamic 11, 264–6
    static 11, 264

protection   232, 246–52
  access matrix   246–7
  call gates   250–1
  conforming code   251–2
  hierarchical domains   247
  minimum necessary privilege   250
  privilege levels   247
  rings   248

queue model
  circular   272
  FIFO   272
  parallel-in serial-out   273

read–modify–write cycle   256–7
real machine   2
real numbers   134–9
reconfigurable networks   333
reduction architectures   352–4
redundancy   25
re-entrant programs   78–9
register windows   305
registers   13, 42–4
  dedicated   47
  general   43, 47–8
relative numbers   127–34
reliability   23–4
relocation, dynamic   81, 231
reset   227–8
residual control   207
return instructions   173–5
ring interconnection   345
RISC architectures   214, 294–5, 298–305
  extended   305–7
Rockwell 6502   76, 84, 127
root congestion in tree networks   349
rotation instructions   122–4
routing operation   323
run time   11
run-time stack   97, 301–5

scalar product problem   321–4
segmentation   232–7
sequencer   203
service routines   220
shared memory   331
shift instructions   122–4
shuffle connection   346

sign propagation   130, 134
signed magnitude representation   128–30, 138
slave   189
special function unit   307
stack   46, 71–2
stack cache   301–5
stack frame   176
states of processing   13
static scope   98
status word   127
steering bit   206
string processing   148–53
supercomputers   316–20
supervisor state   222
switching unit   331–5
system architecture   6
system call   226
system state   222
systolic arrays   324–30
  broadcast   324
  fan-in   324
  pure-systolic   324
  programmable   324
  semisystolic   326

TLB (translation look-aside buffer)   242, 275–6
tagged architectures   63–4
test-and-set instruction   254–7
tightly coupled systems   331
trace state   227
translation   5
transputer   337–43
traps   226
two's complement representation   128–34
two-port RAM   211

unconditional jumps   166–7
unpacked BCD   34–5
unshuffle connection   346
user state   222

variable
  global   96, 102
  local   101, 107
  non-local   102, 108
vertical microinstructions   203
vertical migration   150

virtual machine   2
virtual memory   230, 238–41
visibility   96
  nested   97
von Neumann computer model   12–17

word, definition   41–2
write-through technique   275

Zilog
  Z80   74, 121
  Z8000   44, 147, 149, 152, 166, 168–9, 174,
    175, 179, 235–7, 255, 257, 280
  Z80000   113